TEACHER'S ANNOTATED EDITION

MOSAIK 1

German Language and Culture

VISTA®
HIGHER LEARNING

Boston, Massachusetts

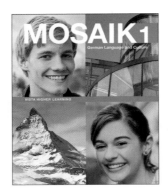

Publisher: José A. Blanco

President: Janet Dracksdorf

Vice President, Editorial Director: Amy Baron

Managing Editor: Elvira Ortiz

Senior National Language Consultant: Norah Lulich Jones

Editorial Development: Judith Bach, Deborah Coffey, Aliza B. Krefetz, Thomas Kroy, Katie Van Adzin

Project Management: Maria Rosa Alcaraz, Cécile Engeln, Sharon Inglis

Technology Editorial: Darío González, Egle Gutiérrez, Paola Ríos Schaaf

Design and Production Director: Marta Kimball

Senior Creative Designer, Print & Web/Interactive: Susan Prentiss

Production Manager: Oscar Díez

Design and Production Team: Liliana Bobadilla, María Eugenia Castaño, Michelle Groper, Mauricio Henao, Jhoany Jiménez, Fabián Darío Montoya, Erik Restrepo, Sónia Teixeira, Andrés Vanegas, Nick Ventullo

Student Edition ISBN-13: 978-1-61857-183-0
Teacher's Annotated Edition (TAE) ISBN-13: 978-1-61857-186-1
Library of Congress Card Number: 2013930654

1 2 3 4 5 6 7 8 9 WC 17 16 15 14 13

TEACHER'S ANNOTATED EDITION

Table of Contents

KONTEXT	FOTOROMAN	KULTUR	STRUKTUREN	WEITER GEHT'S

Your source for integrated text-technology resources

Powerful tools that you can customize for your personal course management, along with the integrated content students need to improve—and enjoy—learning.

Focused uniquely on world language, with robust features that speak to you and your students' needs. How do we know? Feedback from our 20,000 language teachers and 1 million students.

Simplified experience so you can navigate the site easily, have flexible options, and quickly sort a wealth of information.

- **Stop Student Frustration:** Make it a cinch for students to track due dates, save work, and get access to all available Supersite resources.

- **Set-Up Ease:** Customize your class(es), create your own grading categories, plus copy previous settings to save time.

- **All-in-One Gradebook:** Save time with multi-level viewing, easy grade adjustment, and options to add outside grades for a true, cumulative grade.

- **Grading Options:** Choose to grade student-by-student, question-by-question, or spot check. Plus, use in-line editing and voice comments for targeted feedback.

- **Accessible Student Data:** Share information one-on-one with convenient views, and produce class reports in the formats that best fit you and your department.

Teaching and learning all in one place

Supersite Integrated text-technology resources with multiple levels of access.

For you

- A gradebook to manage classes, view rosters, set assignments, and manage grades

- A communication center for announcements and notifications

- Teacher resources, including answer keys, videoscripts, audioscripts, info gap activities, and worksheets

- Online assessments, plus the complete Testing Program in Rich Text Format (RTF)

- MP3 files of the complete Lab and Testing Audio Programs

- Grammar presentation slides

- Lesson plan RTFs

- Pre-made syllabi

- Complete access to the Student Supersite

- Voiceboards for oral assignments, group discussions, homework, projects, and explanation of complex material

- Online tools to support communication and collaboration

- vText—the online, interactive student edition

For your students

- Textbook activities with auto-grading and instant feedback

- Additional auto-graded activities for extra practice

- Streaming video with teacher-controlled subtitles and translations

- Internet search activities

- Recorded readings

- Textbook and Lab audio MP3s

- Auto-graded tests and exams

- Chat activities for conversational skill-building and oral practice

- Pronunciation practice

- WebSAM, the online Workbook and Video/Lab Manual that includes:
  - Audio record-submit activities
  - Auto-grading for select activities

- vText—the online, interactive student edition

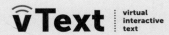

virtual interactive text

Integrated with the Supersite, the **Mosaik vText** provides teachers and students with an online interactive textbook that has links to textbook activities, audio, video, and more. Lighten backpacks! The Supersite and vText are iPad® friendly.

CHAPTER OPENERS

outline the content and features of each chapter.

Familie und Freunde

KAPITEL 3

LEKTION 3A	LEKTION 3B	WEITER GEHT'S
Kontext Seite 96–99 • Sabine Schmidts Familie • Final consonants	**Kontext** Seite 116–119 • Wie sind sie? • Consonant clusters	Seite 136–142 **Panorama: Die Vereinigten Staaten und Kanada** **Lesen:** Read an article about pets. **Hören:** Listen to a conversation between two friends. **Schreiben:** Write a letter to a friend. **Kapitel 3 Wortschatz**
Fotoroman Seite 100–101 • Ein Abend mit der Familie	**Fotoroman** Seite 120–121 • Unsere Mitbewohner	
Kultur Seite 102–103 • Eine deutsche Familie	**Kultur** Seite 122–123 • Auf unsere Freunde!	
Strukturen Seite 104–115 • **3A.1** Possessive adjectives • **3A.2** Descriptive adjectives and adjective agreement • **3A.3 Gern** and **nicht gern** • Wiederholung • Zapping	**Strukturen** Seite 124–135 • **3B.1** Modals • **3B.2** Prepositions with the accusative • **3B.3** The imperative • Wiederholung	

Chapter opener photos highlight scenes from the **Fotoroman** that illustrate the chapter theme. They are snapshots of the characters that students will come to know throughout the program.

Content lists break down each chapter into its two lessons and one **Weiter geht's** section, giving you an at-a-glance summary of the vocabulary, grammar, cultural topics, and language skills covered in the chapter.

Supersite

Supersite resources are available for every section of each chapter at **vhlcentral.com.** Icons show you which textbook activities are also available online, and where additional practice activities are available. The description next to the (S) icon indicates what additional resources are available for each section: videos, audio recordings, readings, presentations, and more!

Supersite features vary by access level. Visit **vistahigherlearning.com** to explore which Supersite level is right for you.

KONTEXT

presents and practices vocabulary in meaningful contexts.

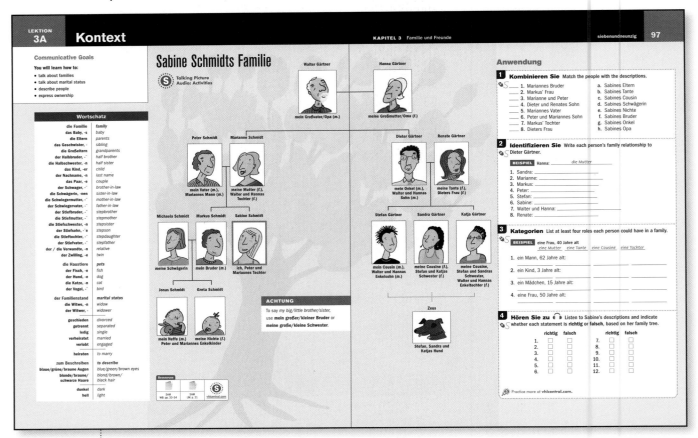

Communicative goals highlight the real-life tasks you will be able to carry out in German by the end of each lesson.

Illustrations introduce high-frequency vocabulary through expansive, full-color images.

Wortschatz sidebars call out important theme-related vocabulary in easy-to-reference German-English lists.

Ressourcen boxes let you know what print and technology ancillaries reinforce and expand on every section of every lesson.

Achtung boxes give you additional information about how and when to use certain vocabulary words or grammar structures.

Kontext always contains one audio activity that accompanies either the **Anwendung** or the **Kommunikation** practice activities. **Anwendung** follows a pedagogical sequence that starts with simpler, shorter, discrete recognition activities and builds toward longer, more complex production activities.

Supersite

- Audio recordings of all vocabulary items
- Audio for **Kontext** listening activity
- Talking Picture activity
- Textbook activities
- Additional online-only practice activities

Supersite features vary by access level. Visit **vistahigherlearning.com** to explore which Supersite level is right for you.

KONTEXT

practices vocabulary using communication activities.

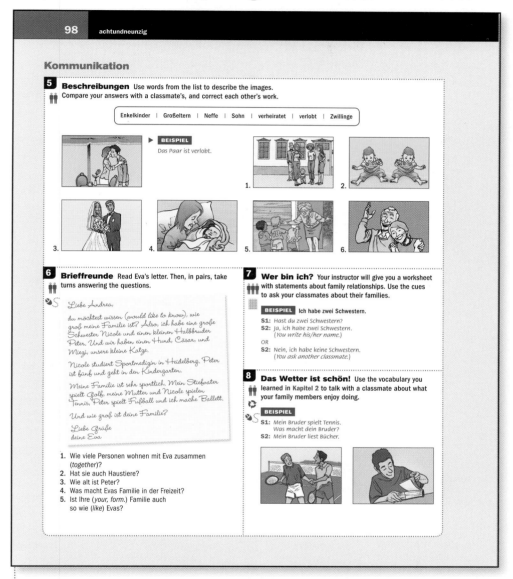

Kommunikation

5 **Beschreibungen** Use words from the list to describe the images. Compare your answers with a classmate's, and correct each other's work.

Enkelkinder | Großeltern | Neffe | Sohn | verheiratet | verlobt | Zwillinge

▶ **BEISPIEL**
Das Paar ist verlobt.

1. 2. 3. 4. 5. 6.

6 **Brieffreunde** Read Eva's letter. Then, in pairs, take turns answering the questions.

Liebe Andrea,

du möchtest wissen (would like to know), wie groß meine Familie ist? Also, ich habe eine große Schwester Nicole und einen kleinen Halbbruder Peter. Und wir haben einen Hund, Cäsar, und Miezi, unsere kleine Katze.

Nicole studiert Sportmedizin in Heidelberg. Peter ist fünf und geht in den Kindergarten.

Meine Familie ist sehr sportlich. Mein Stiefvater spielt Golf, meine Mutter und Nicole spielen Tennis, Peter spielt Fußball und ich mache Ballett.

Und wie groß ist deine Familie?

Liebe Grüße
deine Eva

1. Wie viele Personen wohnen mit Eva zusammen (together)?
2. Hat sie auch Haustiere?
3. Wie alt ist Peter?
4. Was macht Evas Familie in der Freizeit?
5. Ist Ihre (your, form.) Familie auch so wie (like) Evas?

7 **Wer bin ich?** Your instructor will give you a worksheet with statements about family relationships. Use the cues to ask your classmates about their families.

BEISPIEL Ich habe zwei Schwestern.

S1: Hast du zwei Schwestern?
S2: Ja, ich habe zwei Schwestern.
(You write his/her name.)
OR
S2: Nein, ich habe keine Schwestern.
(You ask another classmate.)

8 **Das Wetter ist schön!** Use the vocabulary you learned in **Kapitel 2** to talk with a classmate about what your family members enjoy doing.

BEISPIEL
S1: Mein Bruder spielt Tennis.
Was macht dein Bruder?
S2: Mein Bruder liest Bücher.

Kommunikation activities make use of discourse-level prompts, allowing you to use the vocabulary creatively in interactions with a partner, a small group, or the entire class.

Icons provide on-the-spot visual cues for pair, small group, language recycling, listening-based, and worksheet-based or information gap activities.

For a legend explaining the icons used in the student text, see page xii.

Supersite

- Virtual Chat activities for recording and submitting a simulated conversation online.
- Work with a partner online to record and submit an activity with the Partner Chat feature.

Supersite features vary by access level. Visit **vistahigherlearning.com** to explore which Supersite level is right for you.

AUSSPRACHE UND RECHTSCHREIBUNG

presents the rules of German pronunciation and spelling.

Explanations of German pronunciation and spelling are presented clearly, with abundant model words and phrases. The red highlighting feature focuses your attention on the target structure.

Practice pronunciation and spelling at the word- and sentence-levels. The final activity features illustrated sayings and proverbs that present the target structures in an entertaining cultural context.

The headset icon at the top of the page indicates that the explanation and activities are recorded for convenient use in or outside of class.

Supersite

- Audio recording of the **Aussprache und Rechtschreibung** presentation
- Record-and-compare activities

FOTOROMAN

tells the story of a group of students living in Berlin.

Fotoroman is a versatile episodic video that can be assigned as homework, presented in class, or used as review. To learn more about using the **Fotoroman** video, turn to page T27.

Conversations reinforce vocabulary from **Kontext**. They also preview structures from the upcoming **Strukturen** section in context.

Personen features the cast of recurring **Fotoroman** characters, including students: George, Sabite, Meline, and Hans.

Nützliche Ausdrücke calls out the most important words and expressions from the **Fotoroman** episode that have not been formally presented. This vocabulary is not tested. The blue numbers refer to the grammar structures presented in the lesson.

Übungen activities include comprehension questions, a communicative task, and a research-based task.

Supersite

- Streaming video with teacher-controlled captioning for all 8 episodes of the **Fotoroman**
- End-of-video **Zusammenfassung** section where key vocabulary and grammar from the episode are re-inforced
- (S) students work with a partner online to record and submit an activity

Supersite features vary by access level. Visit **vistahigherlearning.com** to explore which Supersite level is right for you.

KULTUR

explores cultural themes introduced in KONTEXT.

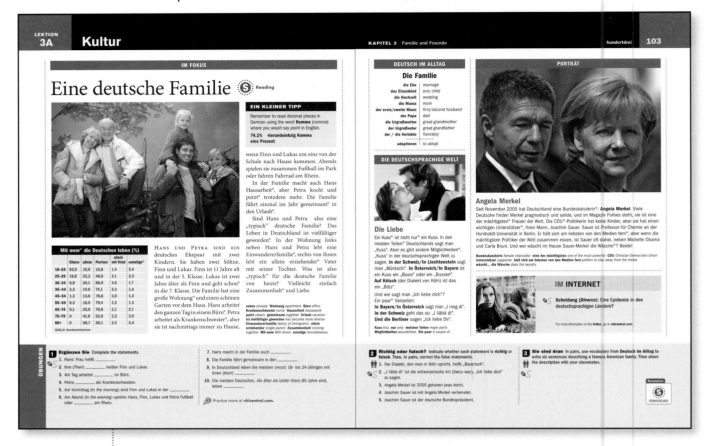

Im Fokus presents an in-depth reading about the lesson's cultural theme. Full-color photos bring to life important aspects of the topic, while charts support the main text with statistics and additional information.

Ein kleiner Tipp boxes provide helpful tips for reading and understanding German.

Porträt spotlights notable people, places, events, and products from the German-speaking world. This article is thematically linked to the lesson.

Deutsch im Alltag presents additional vocabulary related to the lesson theme, showcasing words and phrases used in everyday spoken German. This vocabulary is not tested.

Die deutschsprachige Welt focuses on the people, places, dialects, and traditions in regions where German is spoken. This short article is thematically linked to the lesson.

Im Internet boxes, with provocative questions and photos, direct you to the **MOSAIK** Supersite where you can continue to learn about the topics in **Kultur**.

Supersite

- **Kultur** reading
- **Im Internet** research activity expands on the lesson theme
- Reading-based activity

Supersite features vary by access level. Visit **vistahigherlearning.com** to explore which Supersite level is right for you.

STRUKTUREN

presents German grammar in a graphic-intensive format.

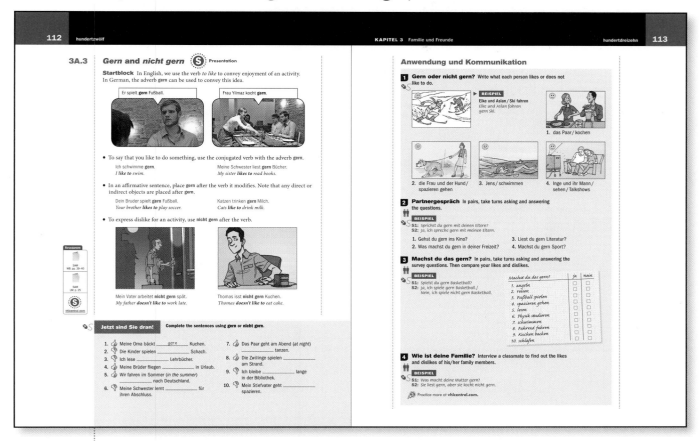

Format includes one to two pages of explanation for each grammar point, followed by one to two pages of activities. Two to three grammar points are featured in each lesson.

Startblock eases you into each grammar explanation, with definitions of grammatical terms and reminders about grammar concepts with which you are already familiar.

Photos from the **Fotoroman** consistently integrate the lesson's video episode with the grammar explanations.

Querverweis boxes call out information covered in earlier lessons or provide cross-references to related topics you will see in future chapters.

Achtung boxes clarify potential sources of confusion and provide supplementary information.

Jetzt sind Sie dran! is your first opportunity to practice the new grammar point.

Anwendung offers a wide range of guided activities that combine lesson vocabulary and previously learned material with the new grammar point.

Kommunikation activities provide opportunities for self-expression using the lesson grammar and vocabulary. These activities feature interaction with a partner, in small groups, or with the whole class.

⟨S⟩upersite

- Grammar presentations
- Textbook activities
- Additional online-only practice activities
- Chat activities for conversational skill-building and oral practice

Supersite features vary by access level. Visit **vistahigherlearning.com** to explore which Supersite level is right for you.

WIEDERHOLUNG

pulls the lesson together.

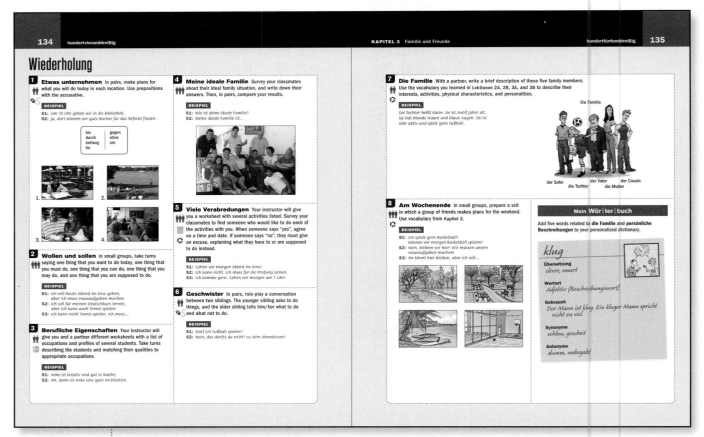

Wiederholung activities integrate the lesson's grammar points and vocabulary with previously learned vocabulary and structures, providing consistent, built-in review as you progress through the text.

Pair and group icons indicate communicative activities such as role play, games, personal questions, interviews, and surveys.

Information gap activities, identified by interlocking puzzle pieces, engage you and a partner in problem-solving situations.

Recycling icons call out the activities in which you will practice the lesson's grammar and vocabulary along with previously learned material.

Mein Wörterbuch in the B lesson of each chapter offers the opportunity to increase your vocabulary and contextualize new words.

Supersite

- Virtual Chat activities for recording and submitting a simulated conversation online.
- Work with a partner online to record and submit an activity with the Partner Chat feature.

Supersite features vary by access level. Visit **vistahigherlearning.com** to explore which Supersite level is right for you.

ZAPPING

features TV commercials and public service announcements.

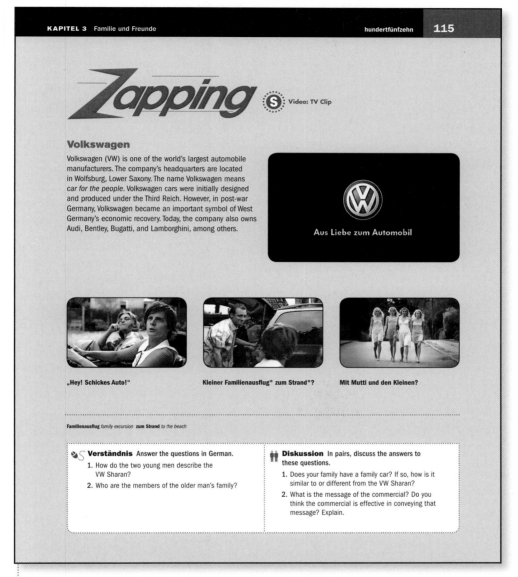

Zapping

(S) Video: TV Clip

Volkswagen

Volkswagen (VW) is one of the world's largest automobile manufacturers. The company's headquarters are located in Wolfsburg, Lower Saxony. The name Volkswagen means *car for the people*. Volkswagen cars were initially designed and produced under the Third Reich. However, in post-war Germany, Volkswagen became an important symbol of West Germany's economic recovery. Today, the company also owns Audi, Bentley, Bugatti, and Lamborghini, among others.

Aus Liebe zum Automobil

„Hey! Schickes Auto!"

Kleiner Familienausflug° zum Strand°?

Mit Mutti und den Kleinen?

Familienausflug *family excursion* zum Strand *to the beach*

Verständnis Answer the questions in German.
1. How do the two young men describe the VW Sharan?
2. Who are the members of the older man's family?

Diskussion In pairs, discuss the answers to these questions.
1. Does your family have a family car? If so, how is it similar to or different from the VW Sharan?
2. What is the message of the commercial? Do you think the commercial is effective in conveying that message? Explain.

Zapping presents authentic TV commercials and public service announcements from the German-speaking world.

Summary provides context for each video clip.

Photos and captions provide key information to facilitate comprehension.

Post-viewing activities check comprehension and encourage you to explore the broader themes presented in each film.

Supersite

- Streaming video of the TV clips with teacher-controlled subtitle options
- Textbook activity

WEITER GEHT'S

Panorama presents geographical, historical, and cultural information about the German-speaking world.

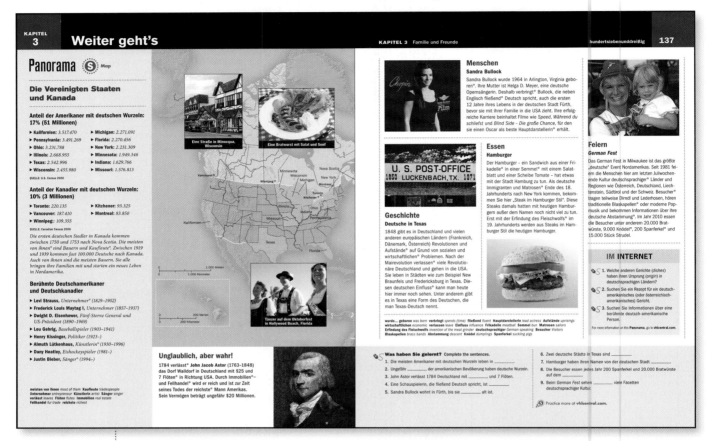

Panorama offers interesting facts about the featured city, region, or country.

Maps point out major geographical features and situate the featured region in the context of its immediate surroundings.

Readings explore different aspects of the featured region's culture, such as history, landmarks, fine art, literature, and insight into everyday life.

Unglaublich aber wahr! highlights an intriguing fact about the featured place, person, or thing.

Comprehension questions check your understanding of key ideas.

ⓢupersite

- Map with statistics and cultural notes
- **Im Internet** research activity
- Textbook activity
- Partner Chat activities

WEITER GEHT'S

Lesen provides practice for reading skills in the context of the chapter's theme.

Vor dem Lesen presents useful strategies and activities to help you improve your reading abilities.

Readings are tied to the chapter theme. The selections recycle vocabulary and grammar you have learned.

Nach dem Lesen consists of post-reading activities that check your comprehension.

Supersite

- Audio-sync reading that highlights text as it is being read
- Textbook reading-based activities
- Work with a partner online to record and submit an activity with the Partner Chat feature

Supersite features vary by access level. Visit **vistahigherlearning.com** to explore which Supersite level is right for you.

WEITER GEHT'S

Hören and **Schreiben** provide support for listening and writing skills in the context of the chapter's theme.

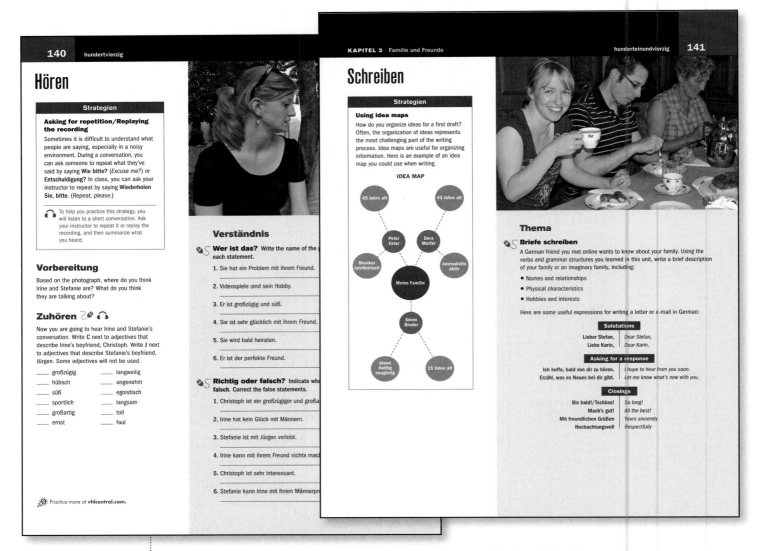

Hören

Strategien

Asking for repetition/Replaying the recording

Sometimes it is difficult to understand what people are saying, especially in a noisy environment. During a conversation, you can ask someone to repeat what they've said by saying **Wie bitte?** (*Excuse me?*) or **Entschuldigung?** In class, you can ask your instructor to repeat by saying **Wiederholen Sie, bitte.** (*Repeat, please.*)

To help you practice this strategy, you will listen to a short conversation. Ask your instructor to repeat it or replay the recording, and then summarize what you heard.

Vorbereitung

Based on the photograph, where do you think Irine and Stefanie are? What do you think they are talking about?

Zuhören

Now you are going to hear Irine and Stefanie's conversation. Write **C** next to adjectives that describe Irine's boyfriend, Christoph. Write **J** next to adjectives that describe Stefanie's boyfriend, Jürgen. Some adjectives will not be used.

_____ großzügig   _____ langweilig
_____ hübsch   _____ angenehm
_____ süß   _____ egoistisch
_____ sportlich   _____ langsam
_____ großartig   _____ toll
_____ ernst   _____ faul

Practice more at **vhlcentral.com.**

Verständnis

Wer ist das? Write the name of the ___ each statement.

1. Sie hat ein Problem mit ihrem Freund.

2. Videospiele sind sein Hobby.

3. Er ist großzügig und süß.

4. Sie ist sehr glücklich mit ihrem Freund.

5. Sie wird bald heiraten.

6. Er ist der perfekte Freund.

Richtig oder falsch? Indicate whe ___ falsch. Correct the false statements.

1. Christoph ist ein großzügiger und groß___

2. Irine hat kein Glück mit Männern.

3. Stefanie ist mit Jürgen verlobt.

4. Irine kann mit ihrem Freund nichts mac___

5. Christoph ist sehr interessant.

6. Stefanie kann Irine mit ihrem Männerpr___

Schreiben

Strategien

Using idea maps

How do you organize ideas for a first draft? Often, the organization of ideas represents the most challenging part of the writing process. Idea maps are useful for organizing information. Here is an example of an idea map you could use when writing.

IDEA MAP

- 45 Jahre alt
- 43 Jahre alt
- Peter Vater
- Dora Mutter
- Musiker intellektuell
- Journalistin aktiv
- Meine Familie
- Sören Bruder
- blond fleißig neugierig
- 15 Jahre alt

Thema

Briefe schreiben

A German friend you met online wants to know about your family. Using the verbs and grammar structures you learned in this unit, write a brief description of your family or an imaginary family, including:

- Names and relationships
- Physical characteristics
- Hobbies and interests

Here are some useful expressions for writing a letter or e-mail in German:

Salutations	
Lieber Stefan,	*Dear Stefan,*
Liebe Karin,	*Dear Karin,*

Asking for a response	
Ich hoffe, bald von dir zu hören.	*I hope to hear from you soon.*
Erzähl, was es Neues bei dir gibt.	*Let me know what's new with you.*

Closings	
Bis bald!/Tschüss!	*So long!*
Mach's gut!	*All the best!*
Mit freundlichen Grüßen	*Yours sincerely*
Hochachtungsvoll	*Respectfully*

Hören uses a recorded conversation or narration to develop your listening skills in German.

Strategien and **Vorbereitung** prepare you to listen to the audio recording.

Zuhören guides you through the recorded segment, and **Verständnis** checks your understanding of what you've heard.

Strategien provides useful preparation for the writing task presented in **Thema**.

Thema presents a writing topic and includes suggestions for approaching it. It also provides words and phrases that may be useful in writing about the topic.

Supersite

- Audio for **Hören** activities
- Partner Chat activities
- Textbook activities and additional online-only practice activity
- Submit your writing assignment online using the composition engine.

Supersite features vary by access level. Visit **vistahigherlearning.com** to explore which Supersite level is right for you.

WORTSCHATZ

summarizes the chapter's active vocabulary.

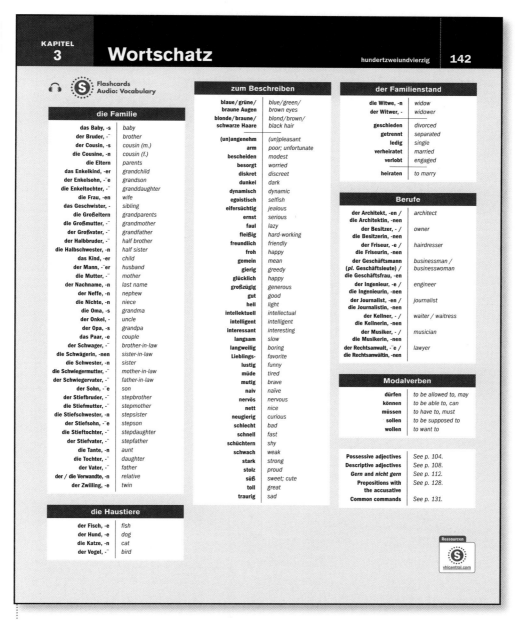

🎧 Ⓢ Flashcards
Audio: Vocabulary

die Familie

das Baby, -s	baby
der Bruder, -¨	brother
der Cousin, -s	cousin (m.)
die Cousine, -n	cousin (f.)
die Eltern	parents
das Enkelkind, -er	grandchild
der Enkelsohn, -¨e	grandson
die Enkeltochter, -¨	granddaughter
die Frau, -en	wife
das Geschwister, -	sibling
die Großeltern	grandparents
die Großmutter, -¨	grandmother
der Großvater, -¨	grandfather
der Halbbruder, -¨	half brother
die Halbschwester, -n	half sister
das Kind, -er	child
der Mann, -¨er	husband
die Mutter, -¨	mother
der Nachname, -n	last name
der Neffe, -n	nephew
die Nichte, -n	niece
die Oma, -s	grandma
der Onkel, -	uncle
der Opa, -s	grandpa
das Paar, -e	couple
der Schwager, -¨	brother-in-law
die Schwägerin, -nen	sister-in-law
die Schwester, -n	sister
die Schwiegermutter, -¨	mother-in-law
der Schwiegervater, -¨	father-in-law
der Sohn, -¨e	son
der Stiefbruder, -¨	stepbrother
die Stiefmutter, -¨	stepmother
die Stiefschwester, -n	stepsister
der Stiefsohn, -¨e	stepson
die Stieftochter, -¨	stepdaughter
der Stiefvater, -¨	stepfather
die Tante, -n	aunt
die Tochter, -¨	daughter
der Vater, -¨	father
der / die Verwandte, -n	relative
der Zwilling, -e	twin

die Haustiere

der Fisch, -e	fish
der Hund, -e	dog
die Katze, -n	cat
der Vogel, -¨	bird

zum Beschreiben

blaue/grüne/ braune Augen	blue/green/ brown eyes
blonde/braune/ schwarze Haare	blond/brown/ black hair
(un)angenehm	(un)pleasant
arm	poor; unfortunate
bescheiden	modest
besorgt	worried
diskret	discreet
dunkel	dark
dynamisch	dynamic
egoistisch	selfish
eifersüchtig	jealous
ernst	serious
faul	lazy
fleißig	hard-working
freundlich	friendly
froh	happy
gemein	mean
gierig	greedy
glücklich	happy
großzügig	generous
gut	good
hell	light
intellektuell	intellectual
intelligent	intelligent
interessant	interesting
langsam	slow
langweilig	boring
Lieblings-	favorite
lustig	funny
müde	tired
mutig	brave
naiv	naïve
nervös	nervous
nett	nice
neugierig	curious
schlecht	bad
schnell	fast
schüchtern	shy
schwach	weak
stark	strong
stolz	proud
süß	sweet; cute
toll	great
traurig	sad

der Familienstand

die Witwe, -n	widow
der Witwer, -	widower
geschieden	divorced
getrennt	separated
ledig	single
verheiratet	married
verlobt	engaged
heiraten	to marry

Berufe

der Architekt, -en / die Architektin, -nen	architect
der Besitzer, - / die Besitzerin, -nen	owner
der Friseur, -e / die Friseurin, -nen	hairdresser
der Geschäftsmann (pl. Geschäftsleute) / die Geschäftsfrau, -en	businessman / businesswoman
der Ingenieur, -e / die Ingenieurin, -nen	engineer
der Journalist, -en / die Journalistin, -nen	journalist
der Kellner, - / die Kellnerin, -nen	waiter / waitress
der Musiker, - / die Musikerin, -nen	musician
der Rechtsanwalt, -¨e / die Rechtsanwältin, -nen	lawyer

Modalverben

dürfen	to be allowed to, may
können	to be able to, can
müssen	to have to, must
sollen	to be supposed to
wollen	to want to

Possessive adjectives	See p. 104.
Descriptive adjectives	See p. 108.
Gern and *nicht gern*	See p. 112.
Prepositions with the accusative	See p. 128.
Common commands	See p. 131.

Ressourcen
Ⓢ
vhlcentral.com

Wortschatz presents the chapter's active vocabulary in logical groupings, including notation of plural forms.

Ⓢupersite

- Audio recordings of all vocabulary items
- Vocabulary flashcards with audio

MOSAIK and the *Standards for Foreign Language Learning*

Since 1982, when the *ACTFL Proficiency Guidelines* were first published, that seminal document and its subsequent revisions have influenced the teaching of modern languages in the United States. **MOSAIK** was written with the concerns and philosophy of the *ACTFL Proficiency Guidelines* in mind, incorporating a proficiency-oriented approach from its planning stages.

MOSAIK's pedagogy was also informed from its inception by the *Standards for Foreign Language Learning in the 21st Century.* First published in 1996 under the auspices of the National Standards in Foreign Language Education Project, the Standards are organized into five goal areas, often called the Five Cs: Communication, Cultures, Connections, Comparisons, and Communities.

Since **MOSAIK** takes a communicative approach to the teaching and learning of German, the Communication goal is central to the student text. For example, the diverse formats used in the **Kommunikation** and **Wiederholung** activities in each lesson—pair work, small group work, class circulation, information gap, task-based, and so forth— engage students in communicative exchanges, providing and obtaining information, and expressing feelings, emotions, and ideas.

The **Schreiben** section focuses on developing students' communication skills in writing. The Cultures goal is most overtly evident in the **Fotoroman** and **Kultur** sections, as well as in the **Panorama** feature in the **Weiter geht's** section at the end of each chapter. Students can also acquire information and recognize distinctive cultural viewpoints in the literary texts of the **Lesen** sections. **MOSAIK** also weaves culture into virtually every page, exposing students to the multiple facets of practices, products, and perspectives of the German-speaking world. In keeping with the Connections goal, students can connect with other disciplines such as communications, business, geography, history, fine arts, science, and math in the **Zapping** and **Panorama** features. Moreover, **Im Internet** boxes in **Kultur** and **Panorama** support the Connections and Communities goals as students work through those sections and complete the related activities on the **MOSAIK** Supersite. As for the Comparisons goal, it is reflected in **Aussprache und Rechtschreibung** and the **Strukturen** sections.

Special Standards icons appear on the student text pages of your Teacher's Annotated Edition to call out sections that have a particularly strong relationship with the Standards. These are a few examples of how **MOSAIK** was written with the Standards firmly in mind, but you will find many more as you work with the student textbook and its ancillaries.

Six Steps in Using the MOSAIK Instructional Design

Step 1: Context

Begin each lesson by asking students to provide *from their own experience words*, concepts, categories, and opinions related to the theme. Spend quality time evoking words, images, ideas, phrases, and sentences; group and classify concepts. You are giving students the "hook" for their learning, focusing them on their most interesting topic—themselves—and encouraging them to invest personally in their learning.

Step 2: Vocabulary

Now turn to the vocabulary section, inviting students to experience it as a new linguistic *code* to express what they *already know and experience* in the context of the lesson theme. Vocabulary concepts are presented in context, carefully organized, and frequently reviewed to reinforce student understanding. Involve students in brainstorming, classifying and grouping words and thoughts, and personalizing phrases and sentences. In this way, you will help students see German as a new tool for self-expression.

Step 3: Media

Once students see that German is a tool for expressing their own ideas, bridge their experiences to those of German speakers through the **Fotoroman** section. The **Fotoroman** Video Program storyline presents and reviews vocabulary and structure in accurate cultural contexts for effective training in both comprehension and personal communication.

Step 4: Culture

Now bring students into the experience of culture as seen *from the perspective* of those living in it. Here we share German-speaking cultures' unique geography, history, products, perspectives, and practices. Through **Kultur** readings and internet activities students experience and reflect on cultural experiences beyond their own.

Step 5: Structure

We began with students' experiences, focusing on bridging their lives and language to the target cultures. Through context, media, and culture, students have incorporated both previously-learned and new grammatical structures into their personalized communication. Now a formal presentation of relevant grammar demonstrates that grammar is a tool for clearer and more effective communication. Clear presentations and invitations to compare German to English build confidence, fluency, and accuracy.

Step 6: Skill Synthesis and Communication

Pulling all their learning together, students now integrate context, personal experience, communication tools, and cultural products, perspectives, and practices. Through extended reading, writing, listening, speaking, and cultural exploration in scaffolded progression, students apply all their skills for a rich, personalized experience of German.

Differentiation

Knowing how to appeal to learners of different abilities and learning styles will allow you to foster a positive teaching environment and motivate all your students. Here are some strategies for creating inclusive learning environments. Extension and expansion activities are also suggested.

Learners with Special Needs

Learners with special needs include students with attention priority disorders or learning disabilities, slower-paced learners, at-risk learners, and English language learners. Some inclusion strategies that work well with such students are:

Clear Structure By teaching concepts in a predictable order, you can help students organize their learning. Encourage students to keep outlines of materials they read, classify words into categories such as colors, or follow pre–writing steps.

Frequent Review and Repetition Preview material to be taught and review material covered at the end of each lesson. Pair proficient learners with less proficient ones to practice and reinforce concepts. Help students retain concepts through continuous practice and review.

Multi-sensory Input and Output Use visual, auditory, and kinesthetic tasks to add interest and motivation, and to achieve long-term retention. For example, vary input with the use of audio recordings, video, guided visualization, rhymes, and mnemonics.

Additional Time Consider how physical limitations may affect participation in special projects or daily routines. Provide additional time and recommended accommodations.

Different Learning Styles

Visual Learners learn best by seeing, so engage them in activities and projects that are visually creative. Encourage them to write down information and to think in pictures as a long-term retention strategy. Reinforce their learning through visual displays such as diagrams, videos, and handouts.

Auditory Learners best retain information by listening. Engage them in discussions, debates, and role-playing. Reinforce their learning by playing audio versions of texts or reading aloud passages and stories. Encourage them to pay attention to voice, tone, and pitch to infer meaning.

Kinesthetic Learners learn best through moving, touching, and doing hands-on activities. Involve such students in skits and dramatizations; to infer or convey meaning, have them observe or model gestures such as those used for greeting someone or getting someone's attention.

Advanced Learners

Advanced Learners have the potential to learn language concepts and complete assignments at an accelerated pace. They may benefit from assignments that are more challenging than the ones given to their peers. The key to differentiating for advanced learners is adding a degree of rigor to a given task. Examples include sharing perspectives on texts they have read with the class, retelling detailed stories, preparing analyses of texts, or adding to discussions. Here are some other strategies for engaging advanced learners:

Timed Answers Have students answer questions within a specified time limit.

Persuading Adapt activities so students have to write or present their points of view in order to persuade an audience. Pair or group advanced learners to form debating teams.

Best Practices

The creators of **MOSAIK** understand that there are many different approaches to successful language teaching and that no one method works perfectly for all teachers or all learners. These strategies and tips may be applied to any language-teaching method.

Maintain the Target Language
As much as possible, create an immersion environment by using German to *teach* German. Encourage the exclusive use of the target language in your classroom, employing visual aids, mnemonics, circumlocution, or gestures to complement what you say. Encourage students to perceive meaning directly through careful listening and observation, and by using cognates and familiar structures and patterns to deduce meaning.

Cultivate Critical Thinking
Prompt students to reflect, observe, reason, and form judgments in German. Engaging students in activities that require them to compare, contrast, predict, criticize, and estimate will help them to internalize the language structures they have learned.

Encourage Use of Circumlocution
Prompt students to discover various ways of expressing ideas and of overcoming potential blocks to communication through the use of circumlocution and paraphrasing.

Assessment

As you use the **MOSAIK** program, you can employ a variety of assessments to evaluate progress. The program provides comprehensive, discrete answer assessments, as well as more communicative assessments that elicit open-ended, personalized responses.

Diagnostic Testing
The **Wiederholung** section in each lesson provides you with an informal opportunity to assess students' readiness for the listening, reading, and writing activities in the **Weiter geht's** section. If some students need additional practice or instruction in a particular area, you can identify this before students move on.

Writing Assessment
At the end of each chapter, the **Weiter geht's** section includes a **Schreiben** page that introduces a writing strategy, which students apply as they complete the writing activity. These activities include suggestions that will focus students' attention on what is important for attaining clarity in written communication.

Testing Program
The **MOSAIK** Testing Program offers two Quizzes for each **Lektion**.
A **Test** is available for each chapter, and a **Cumulative Exam** for chapters 1-4 is provided. The tests are available on the Supersite so that you can customize them by adding, eliminating, or moving items according to your classroom and student needs.

Portfolio Assessment

Portfolios can provide further valuable evidence of your students' learning. They are useful tools for evaluating students' progress in German and also suggest to students how they are likely to be assessed in the real world. Since portfolio activities often comprise classroom tasks that you would assign as part of a lesson or as homework, you should think of the planning, selecting, recording, and interpreting of information about individual performance as a way of blending assessment with instruction.

You may find it helpful to refer to portfolio contents, such as drafts, essays, and samples of presentations when writing student reports and conveying the status of a student's progress to his or her parents.

Ask students regularly to consider which pieces of their own work they would like to share with family and friends, and help them develop criteria for selecting representative samples of essays, stories, poems, recordings of plays or interviews, mock documentaries, and so on. Prompt students to choose a variety of media in their activities wherever possible to demonstrate development in all four language skills. Encourage them to seek peer and parental input as they generate and refine criteria to help them organize and reflect on their own work.

Strategies for Differentiating Assessment

Here are some strategies for modifying tests and other forms of assessment according to your students' needs and your own purposes for administering the assessment.

Adjust Questions Direct complex or higher-level questions to students who are equipped to answer them adequately and modify questions for students with greater needs. Always ask questions that elicit thinking, but keep in mind the students' abilities.

Provide Tiered Assignments Assign tasks of varying complexity depending on individual student needs.

Promote Flexible Grouping Encourage movement among groups of students so that all learners are appropriately challenged. Group students according to interest, oral proficiency levels, or learning styles.

Adjust Pacing Pace the sequence and speed of assessments to suit your students' learning needs. Time advanced learners to challenge them and allow slower-paced learners more time to complete tasks or answer questions.

Performance Assessment

As we move toward increasing students' use of German within real-life contexts, our assessment strategies need to expand in focus too. Students need to demonstrate what they can *do* with German, so we want to employ assessments that come as close as possible to the way German is used in authentic settings. *Performance assessments* provide meaningful contexts in which to measure authentic communication. They begin with a goal, a real-life task that makes sense to students and engages their interest. To complete the task, students progress through the three modes of communication: they

read, view, and listen for information (interpretive mode); they talk and write with classmates and others on what they have experienced (interpersonal mode); and they share formally what they have learned (presentational mode).

Within the **MOSAIK** activity sequence, you will find several opportunities for performance assessment. Consider using the Voiceboard tool or Partner Chat activities as the culmination of an oral communication sequence. The **Schreiben** assignment in the **Weiter geht's** section has students apply the chapter context to a real-life task.

General Suggestions for Using the MOSAIK *Fotoroman* Video Episodes

The **Fotoroman** section in each lesson and the **Fotoroman** video were created as interlocking pieces. All photos in **Fotoroman** are actual video stills from the corresponding video episode, while the printed conversations are abbreviated versions of the dramatic segment. Both the **Fotoroman** conversations and their expanded video versions represent comprehensible input at the discourse level; they were purposely written to use language from the corresponding lesson's **Kontext** and **Strukturen** sections. Thus, they recycle known language, preview grammar points students will study later in the lesson, and, in keeping with Krashen's concept of "i + 1," contain some amount of unknown language.

Because the **Fotoroman** textbook sections and the dramatic episodes of the **Fotoroman** video are so closely connected, you may use them in many different ways. For instance, you can use **Fotoroman** as a preview, presenting it before showing the video episode. You can also show the video episode first and follow up with **Fotoroman**. You can even use **Fotoroman** as a stand-alone, video-independent section.

Depending on your teaching preferences and campus facilities, you might decide to show all video episodes in class or to assign them solely for viewing outside the classroom. You could begin by showing the first one or two episodes in class to familiarize yourself and students with the characters, storyline, style, and **Summary** sections. After that, you could work in class only with **Fotoroman** and have students view the remaining video episodes outside of class. No matter which approach you choose, students have ample materials to support viewing the video independently and processing it in a meaningful way. For each video episode, there are activities in the **Fotoroman** section of the corresponding textbook lesson, as well as additional activities in the **MOSAIK** Video Manual section of the *Student Activities Manual.*

You might also want to use the **Fotoroman** video in class when working with the **Strukturen** sections. You could play the parts of the dramatic episode that correspond to the video stills in the grammar explanations or show selected scenes and ask students to identify certain grammar points.

You could also focus on the **Zusammenfassung** sections that appear at the end of each episode to summarize the key language functions and grammar points used. In class, you could play the parts of the **Zusammenfassung** section that exemplify individual grammar points as you progress through each **Strukturen** section. You could also wait until you complete a **Strukturen** section and review it and the lesson's **Kontext** section by showing the corresponding **Summary** section in its entirety.

On the **MOSAIK** Supersite, teachers can control what, if any, subtitles students can see. They are available in German or in English, and in transcript format.

When showing the **Fotoroman** video segments in your classes, you might want to implement a process approach. You could start with an activity that prepares students for the video segment, implementing the vocabulary they learned in the **Kontext** section. This could be followed by an activity that students do while you play parts of, or the entire, video segment. The final activity, done in the same class period or in the next one as warm-up, could recap what students saw and heard and move beyond the video segment's topic. The following suggestions for using the **Fotoroman** video segments in class are in addition to those on the individual pages of the Teacher's Annotated Edition, and they can be carried out as described or expanded upon in any number of ways.

Before viewing

- Ask students to guess what the segment might be about based on what they've learned in **Kontext** or by asking them to look at the video stills.

- Have pairs make a list of the lesson vocabulary they expect to hear in the video.

- Read a list of true-false or multiple-choice questions about the video to the class, and have students use what they know about the characters to guess the answers. Have them confirm their guesses after watching the segment.

While viewing

- Show the video segment with the audio turned off and ask students to use lesson vocabulary and previously learned structures to describe what they see. Have them confirm their guesses by showing the segment again with the audio on.

- Have students refer to the list of words they brainstormed before viewing the video and put a check in front of any words they actually hear or see in the segment.

- First, have students simply watch the video. Then, show it again and ask students to take notes on what they see and hear. Finally, have them compare their notes in pairs or groups for confirmation.

- Print the episode's videoscript from the Supersite and white out words and expressions related to the lesson theme. Distribute the scripts for pairs or groups to complete as cloze paragraphs.

- Show the video segment before moving on to **Kontext** to jump-start the lesson's vocabulary, grammar, and cultural focus. Have students tell you what vocabulary and grammar they recognize from previous lessons.

After viewing

- Have students say what aspects of the information presented in the corresponding textbook lesson are included in the video segment.

- Ask groups to write a brief summary of the content of the video segment. Have them exchange papers with another group for peer review.

- Have students pick one new aspect of the corresponding textbook lesson's cultural theme that they learned about from watching the video segment. Then ask them to research more about that topic and write a list or paragraph to expand on it.

About Zapping TV Clips and Short Films

A TV clip or a short film from the German-speaking world appears in the first **Lektion** of each **Kapitel**. The purpose of this feature is to expose students to the language and culture contained in authentic media pieces. The following list of the television commercials and short films is organized by **Kapitel** and **Lektion**.

MOSAIK 1

Kapitel 1 *Deutsche Bahn* (29 seconds)

Kapitel 2 *TU Berlin* (1 minute, 15 seconds)

Kapitel 3 *Volkswagen* (41 seconds)

Kapitel 4 *Yello Strom* (39 seconds)

MOSAIK 2

Kapitel 1 *Shopping in München*
        (2 minutes, 55 seconds)

Kapitel 2 *Hausarbeit* (1 minute, 13 seconds)

Kapitel 3 *Urlaub im Grünen Binnenland*
        (3 minutes, 41 seconds)

Kapitel 4 *Mercedes mit Allradantrieb*
        (45 seconds)

MOSAIK 3

Kapitel 1 *Du bist Deutschland*
        (2 minutes, 3 seconds)

Kapitel 2 *Fanny* (13 minutes, 45 seconds)

Kapitel 3 *Die Berliner Mauer* (15 minutes)

Kapitel 4 *Kursdorf* (15 minutes, 7 seconds)

Learning to Use Your Teacher's Annotated Edition

MOSAIK offers you a comprehensive, thoroughly developed Teacher's Annotated Edition (TAE). It features student text pages overprinted with answers to all activities with discrete responses. Each page also contains annotations for a few selected activities that were written to complement and support varied teaching styles, to extend the already rich contents of the student textbook, and to save you time in class preparation and course management.

Because the **MOSAIK** TAE is different from teacher's editions available with other German programs, this section is designed as a quick orientation to the principal types of teacher annotations it contains. As you familiarize yourself with them, it is important to know that the annotations are suggestions only. Any German question, sentence, model, or simulated teacher-student exchange is not meant to be prescriptive or limiting. You are encouraged to view these suggested "scripts" as flexible points of departure that will help you achieve your instructional goals.

For the Chapter Opening Page

- **Suggestion** A discussion topic idea, based on the Chapter Opener photo

For the Lessons

- **Suggestion** Teaching suggestions for working with on-page materials, carrying out specific activities, and presenting new vocabulary or grammar

- **Expansion** Expansions and variations on activities

- **Vorbereitung** Suggestions for talking about the **Fotoroman** pages before students have watched the video or studied the pages

- **Nützliche Ausdrücke** A list of expressions taken from the **Fotoroman** that students may need to study before watching the episode

---

Please check the **MOSAIK** Supersite at **vhlcentral.com** for additional teaching support.

Teacher Ancillaries

- **Workbook/Video Manual/Lab Manual Answer Key**

- **MOSAIK Teacher's DVD**
  This DVD contains the complete **MOSAIK Fotoroman** episodes with German and English subtitles.

- **Digital Image Bank**
  The Digital Image Bank consists of maps of German-speaking regions and the textbook's **Kontext** illustrations. It is available on the Supersite only.

- **Sample Lesson Plans**
  The **MOSAIK** Sample Lesson Plans offer two different kinds of lesson plans: Language/Structure-Based Lesson Plans and Culture/Context-Based Lesson Plans. Both cover the core materials, but while the Language/Structure-Based Lesson Plans focus on vocabulary and grammar, the Culture/Context-Based Lesson Plans emphasize the cultural elements in each chapter. The Sample Lesson Plans are available only on the Supersite.

- **Testing Program**
  The Testing Program contains quizzes for every lesson, tests for every chapter, mid-term exams, and final exams. There is a quiz for each of the text's 8 lessons, in two versions ("A" and "B"), for a total of 16 quizzes.

  There are 4 chapter-level tests (one for each chapter), plus one cumulative exam covering all of **MOSAIK 1**. The Testing Program includes the answer key to all quizzes, tests, and exams, and printed audioscripts for listening comprehension sections on tests and exams. They are available as customizable RTF files on the Supersite.

- **Testing Program MP3 files**
  These audio files provide the recordings of the Testing Program's listening sections, and they are available on CD or on the Supersite.

- **MOSAIK Supersite**
  In addition to full access to the Student Supersite, the password-protected Teacher Supersite offers a robust course management system that allows you to assign and track student progress.

The Vista Higher Learning Story
Your Specialized Foreign Language Publisher

Independent, specialized, and privately owned, Vista Higher Learning was founded in 2000 with one mission: to raise the teaching and learning of world languages to a higher level. This mission is based on the following beliefs:

- It is essential to prepare students for a world in which learning another language is a necessity, not a luxury.
- Language learning should be fun and rewarding, and all students should have the tools they need to achieve success.
- Students who experience success learning a language will be more likely to continue their language studies both inside and outside the classroom.

With this in mind, we decided to take a fresh look at all aspects of language instructional materials. Because we are specialized, we dedicate 100 percent of our resources to this goal and base every decision on how well it supports language learning.

That is where you come in. Since our founding, we have relied on the invaluable feedback of language teachers and students nationwide. This partnership has proved to be the cornerstone of our success, allowing us to constantly improve our programs to meet your instructional needs.

The result? Programs that make language learning exciting, relevant, and effective through:

- unprecedented access to resources
- a wide variety of contemporary, authentic materials
- the integration of text, technology, and media
- a bold and engaging textbook design

By focusing on our singular passion, we let you focus on yours.

The Vista Higher Learning Team

VISTA®
HIGHER LEARNING

500 Boylston Street, Suite 620, Boston, MA 02116-3736 TOLL-FREE: 800-618-7375
TELEPHONE: 617-426-4910 FAX: 617-426-5209 www.vistahigherlearning.com

MOSAIK 1

German Language and Culture

VISTA®
HIGHER LEARNING

Boston, Massachusetts

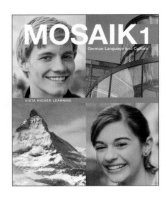

Publisher: José A. Blanco

President: Janet Dracksdorf

Vice President, Editorial Director: Amy Baron

Managing Editor: Elvira Ortiz

Senior National Language Consultant: Norah Lulich Jones

Editorial Development: Judith Bach, Deborah Coffey, Aliza B. Krefetz, Thomas Kroy, Katie Van Adzin

Project Management: Maria Rosa Alcaraz, Cécile Engeln, Sharon Inglis

Technology Editorial: Darío González, Egle Gutiérrez, Paola Ríos Schaaf

Design and Production Director: Marta Kimball

Senior Creative Designer, Print & Web/Interactive: Susan Prentiss

Production Manager: Oscar Díez

Design and Production Team: Liliana Bobadilla, María Eugenia Castaño, Michelle Groper, Mauricio Henao, Jhoany Jiménez, Fabián Darío Montoya, Erik Restrepo, Sónia Teixeira, Andrés Vanegas, Nick Ventullo

Student Edition ISBN-13: 978-1-61857-183-0
Teacher's Annotated Edition (TAE) ISBN-13: 978-1-61857-186-1
Library of Congress Card Number: 2013930654

1 2 3 4 5 6 7 8 9 WC 17 16 15 14 13

MOSAIK 1

German Language and Culture

Table of Contents

Kultur

Strukturen

Weiter geht's

Kontext

Fotoroman

Kultur

Strukturen

Weiter geht's

THE *FOTOROMAN* EPISODES

Fully integrated with your textbook, the **MOSAIK Fotoroman** contains 8 dramatic episodes—one for each lesson of the text. The episodes relate the adventures of four students who are studying in Berlin.

The **Fotoroman** dialogues in the printed textbook lesson are an abbreviated version of the dramatic episode featured in the video. Therefore, each **Fotoroman** section can be used as preparation before you view the corresponding video episode, as post-viewing reinforcement, or as a stand-alone section.

As you watch the video, you will see the characters interact using the vocabulary and grammar you are studying. Their conversations incorporate new vocabulary and grammar with previously taught language. At the conclusion of each episode, the **Zusammenfassung** segment summarizes the key language functions and grammar points used in the episode.

THE CAST

Learn more about each of the characters you'll meet in **MOSAIK Fotoroman**:

George
is from Milwaukee, Wisconsin. He is studying Architecture.

Hans
is from Straubing, in Bavaria. He studies Political Science and History.

Meline
is from Vienna. She is studying Business.

Sabite
is from Berlin. She studies Art.

ANCILLARIES

- **Student Activities Manual (SAM)**

  The Student Activities Manual consists of three sections: the Workbook, the Video Manual, and the Lab Manual. The Workbook activities provide additional practice of the vocabulary and grammar for each textbook lesson. The Video Manual section includes activities for the **MOSAIK Fotoroman**, and the Lab Manual activities focus on building your listening comprehension, speaking, and pronunciation skills in German.

- **Lab Program MP3s**

  The Lab Program MP3 files, which are available on CD or online, contain the recordings needed to complete the activities in the Lab Manual.

- **Textbook MP3s**

  The Textbook MP3 files contain the recordings needed to complete the listening activities in **Kontext**, **Aussprache und Rechtschreibung**, **Hören**, and **Wortschatz** sections. The files are available on the **MOSAIK** Supersite or on CD.

- **FOTOROMAN DVD**

  The **Fotoroman** DVD, available for purchase, comes with optional German and English subtitles for every episode. All episodes are also available on the **MOSAIK** Supersite.

- **WebSAM**

  Completely integrated with the **MOSAIK** Supersite, the **WebSAM** provides access to the online Workbook, Video Manual, and Lab Manual activities with instant feedback and grading. The complete audio program is online and features record-submit functionality for select activities.

- **MOSAIK Supersite**

  The Supersite (**vhlcentral.com**) gives you access to a wide variety of interactive activities for each section of every lesson of the student text, including: auto-graded activities for extra practice with vocabulary, grammar, video, and cultural content; reference tools; the **Zapping** TV commercials and short films; the **Fotoroman** episodic videos; the Textbook MP3 files, the Lab Program MP3 files, and more.

Each section of your textbook comes with activities on the **MOSAIK** Supersite, many of which are auto-graded with immediate feedback. Plus, the Supersite is iPad®-friendly, so it can be accessed on the go! Visit **vhlcentral.com** to explore the wealth of exciting resources.

KONTEXT
- Talking Picture for **Kontext** illustration followed by audio activities
- Additional activities for extra practice
- **Aussprache und Rechtschreibung** presentation followed by record-compare activities
- Textbook activities
- Partner Chat and Virtual Chat activities for conversational skill-building and oral practice

FOTOROMAN
- Streaming video for all 8 episodes of the **Fotoroman** with teacher-controlled options for subtitles
- Textbook activities
- **Zusammenfassung** section where key vocabulary and grammar from the episode are called-out
- Partner Chat activities

KULTUR
- Culture reading
- Internet search activity
- Textbook activities
- Partner Chat activities

STRUKTUREN
- Grammar presentations
- Virtual Chat and Partner Chat activities for conversational skill-building and oral practice
- **Zapping** streaming video of TV clip
- Textbook activities
- Additional activity for extra practice
- **Wiederholung** Partner Chat and Virtual Chat activities

WEITER GEHT'S

Panorama
- Map with statistics and cultural notes
- Textbook activity
- Internet search activity

Lesen
- Audio-sync reading
- Partner Chat activities
- Textbook activities

Hören
- Textbook activities
- Additional activities for extra practice
- Partner Chat activities

Schreiben
- Submit your writing assignment online

WORTSCHATZ
- Audio recordings of all vocabulary items
- Vocabulary flashcards with audio

Plus! Also found on the Supersite:

- All textbook and lab audio MP3 files
- Communication center for teacher notifications and feedback
- A single gradebook for all Supersite activities
- WebSAM online Workbook/Video Manual and Lab Manual
- **v̂Text** online, interactive student edition with access to Supersite activities, audio, and video

INTEGRATED TECHNOLOGY

 virtual interactive text

This interactive text includes the complete Student Edition and integrated Supersite resources that can be accessed from any computer.

- Access all textbook activities with a mouse icon, audio, and video right from the vText—now you have a single platform for completing assignments and accessing resources

- Submit work online and have it flow directly into your teacher's gradebook

- Take notes or highlight important information right on the vText page

- Quickly search table of contents or browse by page number

- Print vocabulary and grammar pages for use as study guides

- Access on the go—now iPad® friendly

ICONS AND *RESSOURCEN* BOXES

Icons

These icons in **MOSAIK** alert you to the type of activity or section involved.

Icons legend			
🎧	Listening activity/section	Ⓢ	Content found on the Supersite: audio, video, and presentations
	Activity on the Supersite		Information Gap activity
👥	Pair activity	▦	Worksheet activity
👥👥	Group activity	♻	Recycling activity

- The Information Gap activities and Worksheet activities require handouts that your teacher will give you.

- The listening icon indicates that audio is available. You will see it in the **Kontext**, **Aussprache und Rechtschreibung**, **Hören**, and **Wortschatz** sections.

- The Supersite icon appears on pages for which there is online content, such as audio, video, or presentations.

- The recycling icon tells you that you will need to use vocabulary and/or grammar learned in previous lessons.

Ressourcen Boxes

Ressourcen boxes let you know exactly which print and technology ancillaries you can use to reinforce and expand on every section of each lesson in your textbook. They include page numbers, when applicable.

Ressourcen boxes legend			
SAM WB: pp. 29–30	Workbook	**SAM** VM: pp. 5–6	Video Manual
SAM LM: p. 17	Lab Manual	Ⓢ	MOSAIK Supersite vhlcentral.com

ACKNOWLEDGMENTS

On behalf of its authors and editors, Vista Higher Learning expresses its sincere appreciation to the teachers nationwide who reviewed materials from **MOSAIK**. Their input and suggestions were vitally helpful in forming and shaping the program in its final, published form.

We also extend a special thank you to the contributing writers of **MOSAIK** whose hard work was central to the publication.

REVIEWERS

Andreas Aebi
California Institute of Technology

Inge Baird
Anderson University

Julia Baker
Tennessee Technological University

John Beatty
Brooklyn College

Dr. E. Berroth
Southwestern University

Iris Bork-Goldfield
Wesleyan University

Cordula Brown
Seattle University

Anita Campitelli
University of North Carolina at Greensboro

Gisela Chappelle
College of the Redwoods

Siegfried Christoph
University of Wisconsin—Parkside

Albrecht Classen
University of Arizona

Richard DCamp
University of Wisconsin Oshkosh

Sandra Dillon
Idaho State University

Dr. David L. Dysart
Stetson University

Prof. Beate T. Engel-Doyle
Franciscan University of Steubenville

Angela Ferguson
Samford University

Sonja Fritzsche
Illinois Wesleyan University

Margarete Froelicher-Grundmann
Armstrong Atlantic University

Marion Gehlker
Yale University

Mary M. Gell
University of Michigan

Kathie Godfrey
Portland State University

Andrea Golato
University of Illinois at Urbana-Champaign

Beatrice Haase-Dubuis
Missouri Southern State University

Brenda Hansen
Bob Jones University

George E. Harding
Francis Mairon University

James W. Harrison
Southern Utah University

Deborah Horzen
University of Central Florida

Cornelius G. House
Purdue University Calumet

James Jones
Central Michigan University

Christa Keister
Lafayette College

Eric Klaus
Hobart and William Smith Colleges

Dr. Seth Knox
Adrian College

Kathy Krause
University of Missouri—Kansas City

Doreen Krueger
Concordia University Wisconsin

Dr. Ute S. Lahaie
Gardner-Webb University

Stephen Della Lana
College of Charleston

Uta Larkey
Goucher College

Thomas Leek
University of Wisconsin—Stevens Point

Dr. William Lehman
Western Carolina University

Enno Lohmeyer
Case Western Reserve University

Barbara Merten-Brugger
University of Wisconsin

Jean-François Mondon
Minot State University

Dr. David E. Nagle
Oklahoma Baptist University

Vince Redder
Dakota Wesleyan University

Sunka Simon
Swarthmore College

Regina Smith
Grand Valley State University

Jane Sokolosky
Brown University

Maria Grazia Spina
University of Central Florida

Luke Springman
Bloomsburg University of Pennsylvania

Tim Straubel
Western Kentucky University

Dr. Amy Kepple Strawser
Otterbein University

Martin Sulzer-Reichel
University of Richmond

Theodore N. Thomas
Milligan College

Kevin Walton
Fort Lewis College

Carl Wiltse
Southern Methodist University

Lidia Zhigunova
Tulane University

Gesa Zinn
University of Minnesota—Duluth

Suggestion Ask students what the people in the photo are doing and what they might be saying to each other. Ask if students know any German greetings.

Communicative Goals

You will learn how to:

- greet people and say good-bye
- make introductions
- use polite expressions

Wie geht's?

(S) Talking Picture
Audio: Activities

Wortschatz

Begrüßung und Abschied	hellos and good-byes
Guten Morgen.	Good morning.
Guten Abend.	Good evening.
Gute Nacht.	Good night.
Bis dann.	See you later.
Bis gleich.	See you soon.
Bis morgen.	See you tomorrow.
Auf Wiedersehen.	Good-bye.
Schönen Tag noch!	Have a nice day!
Prima.	Great.
So lala.	So-so.
(Nicht) schlecht.	(Not) bad.
Mir geht's nicht (so) gut.	I'm not (so) well.

Höflichkeiten	polite expressions
Gern geschehen.	My pleasure.
Entschuldigung.	Excuse me.
Entschuldigen Sie.	Excuse me. (form.)
Es tut mir leid.	I'm sorry.

sich vorstellen	introducing oneself
Wie heißen Sie?	What is your name? (form.)
Schön dich/Sie kennen zu lernen.	Nice to meet you. (inf./form.)

Personen	people
die Frau	woman
der Freund / die Freundin	friend (m./f.)
der Junge	boy
das Mädchen	girl
der Mann	man

Herr	Mr.
Frau	Mrs.; Ms.

wo?	where?
hier	here
da/dort	there

Suggestion Point out that **Morgen** with a capital *M* means *morning*, as in **Guten Morgen**, while **morgen** with a lowercase *m* means *tomorrow*, as in **bis morgen**.

Suggestion Point out that Frau is used to address a woman regardless of her marital status.

Suggestion Explain that German speakers often end a phone conversation with **Auf Wiederhören** (*Until we hear each other again*) instead of **Auf Wiedersehen** (*Until we see each other again*).

MICHAEL Guten Tag, Herr Brenner, wie geht es Ihnen?
HERR BRENNER Hallo, Michael! Es geht mir ziemlich gut. Und dir?
MICHAEL Mir auch, danke.

Suggestion Point out that **Gut(en)** means *good* and **Tag** means *day*. Tell students that this greeting can be used from morning to afternoon.

PAUL Vielen Dank!
JOHANNES Bitte!

MARIA Bis später, Lukas!
LUKAS Tschüss, Maria. Bis bald!

Suggestion Explain to students the differences between **Bis bald, Bis gleich, Bis dann**, and **Bis später**.

CHRISTOPH Guten Tag, Herr Arnold. Das ist Christina Schöller.
HERR ARNOLD Guten Tag, Frau Schöller!
CHRISTINA Freut mich.

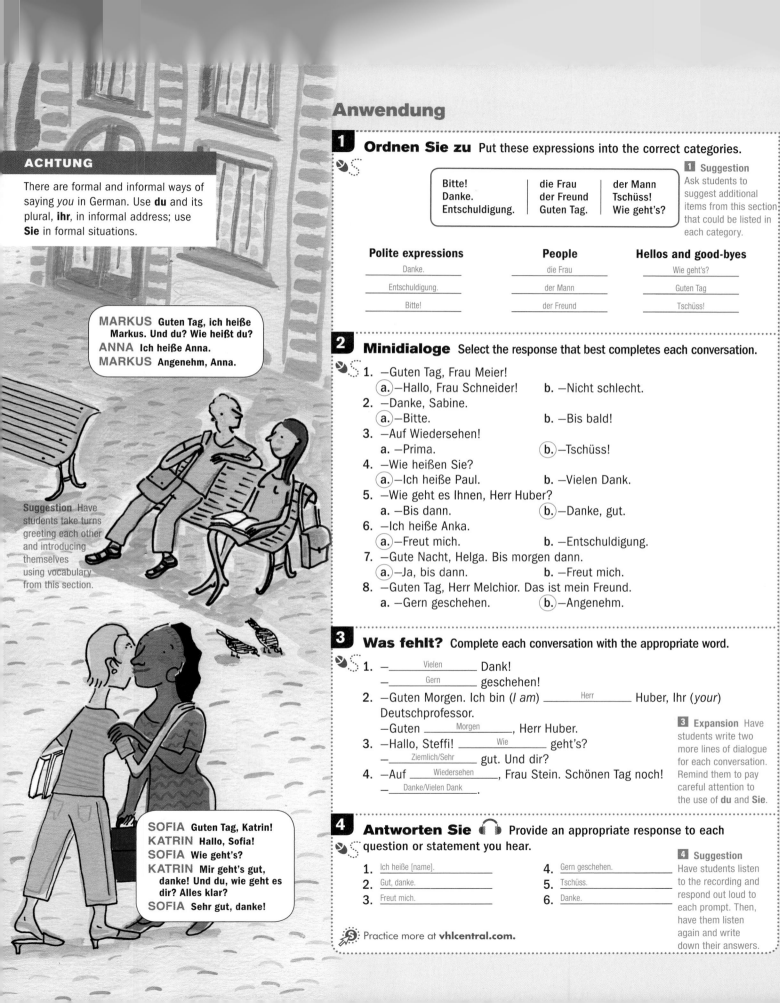

MARKUS Guten Tag, ich heiße Markus. Und du? Wie heißt du?
ANNA Ich heiße Anna.
MARKUS Angenehm, Anna.

Suggestion Have students take turns greeting each other and introducing themselves using vocabulary from this section.

SOFIA Guten Tag, Katrin!
KATRIN Hallo, Sofia!
SOFIA Wie geht's?
KATRIN Mir geht's gut, danke! Und du, wie geht es dir? Alles klar?
SOFIA Sehr gut, danke!

Anwendung

1 Ordnen Sie zu Put these expressions into the correct categories.

Bitte!	die Frau	der Mann
Danke.	der Freund	Tschüss!
Entschuldigung.	Guten Tag.	Wie geht's?

1 Suggestion Ask students to suggest additional items from this section that could be listed in each category.

Polite expressions	People	Hellos and good-byes
Danke.	die Frau	Wie geht's?
Entschuldigung.	der Mann	Guten Tag
Bitte!	der Freund	Tschüss!

2 Minidialoge Select the response that best completes each conversation.

1. —Guten Tag, Frau Meier!
   a. —Hallo, Frau Schneider!   b. —Nicht schlecht.
2. —Danke, Sabine.
   a. —Bitte.   b. —Bis bald!
3. —Auf Wiedersehen!
   a. —Prima.   **b.** —Tschüss!
4. —Wie heißen Sie?
   a. —Ich heiße Paul.   b. —Vielen Dank.
5. —Wie geht es Ihnen, Herr Huber?
   a. —Bis dann.   **b.** —Danke, gut.
6. —Ich heiße Anka.
   a. —Freut mich.   b. —Entschuldigung.
7. —Gute Nacht, Helga. Bis morgen dann.
   a. —Ja, bis dann.   b. —Freut mich.
8. —Guten Tag, Herr Melchior. Das ist mein Freund.
   a. —Gern geschehen.   **b.** —Angenehm.

3 Was fehlt? Complete each conversation with the appropriate word.

1. —_____Vielen_____ Dank!
   —_____Gern_____ geschehen!
2. —Guten Morgen. Ich bin (*I am*) _____Herr_____ Huber, Ihr (*your*) Deutschprofessor.
   —Guten _____Morgen_____, Herr Huber.
3. —Hallo, Steffi! _____Wie_____ geht's?
   —_____Ziemlich/Sehr_____ gut. Und dir?
4. —Auf _____Wiedersehen_____, Frau Stein. Schönen Tag noch!
   —_____Danke/Vielen Dank_____.

3 Expansion Have students write two more lines of dialogue for each conversation. Remind them to pay careful attention to the use of **du** and **Sie**.

4 Antworten Sie 🎧 Provide an appropriate response to each question or statement you hear.

1. Ich heiße [name].
2. Gut, danke.
3. Freut mich.
4. Gern geschehen.
5. Tschüss.
6. Danke.

4 Suggestion Have students listen to the recording and respond out loud to each prompt. Then, have them listen again and write down their answers.

S Practice more at **vhlcentral.com**.

Kommunikation

5 Kurze Gespräche
Listen to the conversations and decide whether each conversation is **förmlich** (*formal*) or **vertraut** (*informal*). Then, with a partner, discuss how you made your decisions.

	förmlich	vertraut
1.	☐	☑
2.	☑	☐
3.	☐	☑
4.	☐	☑
5.	☑	☐
6.	☐	☑

5 Suggestion Before playing the audio recording, ask students to brainstorm ways of indicating formal and informal speech, such as the use of titles and last names versus first names.

6 Begrüßungen
In small groups, look at the illustrations, then act out a short dialogue in which the people greet each other, ask each other's names, and ask each other how they are. Pay attention to the use of **du** and **Sie**. Answers will vary.

1. Professor Fink

2. Frau Sperber

3. Anja

4. Franz

6 Suggestion Have students act out their conversations in front of the class.

7 Stellen Sie sich vor
Your instructor will give you and a partner worksheets with descriptions of five people. Use the information from your worksheet to introduce yourself and talk about how you are. Role-play each of the five people on your worksheet. Answers will vary.

BEISPIEL

S1: *Hallo, ich heiße Martin. Und du?*
S2: *Hallo, ich heiße Sandra. Wie geht's?*
S1: *Ziemlich gut. Und dir?*

8 Sich kennen lernen
In groups of three, introduce yourself and ask your partners how they are. Then introduce your partners to the members of another group. Answers will vary.

BEISPIEL

S1: *Hallo, ich heiße Sina. Und wie heißt du?*
S2: *Ich heiße Katja. Hallo, Sina.*
S1: *Und wie geht's dir?*
S2: *Prima, danke. Und du? Wie geht's dir?*
S1: *Ziemlich gut. Katja, das hier ist Thomas.*
S3: *Hallo, Katja. Schön dich kennen zu lernen.*

Aussprache und Rechtschreibung

🎧 The German alphabet

The German alphabet is made up of the same 26 letters as the English alphabet. Although the alphabet is the same, many of the letters (**Buchstaben**) are pronounced differently.

Suggestion Pronounce the words **Buchstabe** and **Beispiel** for students and ask them what they think these words mean.

Buchstabe		Beispiel	Buchstabe		Beispiel	Buchstabe		Beispiel
a	(ah)	Abend	i	(ih)	Idee	r	(err)	Regen
b	(beh)	Butter	j	(yot)	ja	s	(ess)	singen
c	(tseh)	Celsius,	k	(kah)	Katze	t	(teh)	tanzen
		Café	l	(ell)	lesen	u	(ooh)	Universität
d	(deh)	danke	m	(emm)	Mutter	v	(fau)	Vogel, Vase
e	(eh)	Elefant	n	(enn)	Nase	w	(veh)	Wasser
f	(eff)	finden	o	(oh)	Oper	x	(iks)	Xylophon
g	(geh)	gut	p	(peh)	Papier	y	(üpsilon)	Yacht, Typ
h	(hah)	hallo	q	(koo)	Quatsch	z	(tset)	Zelt

Suggestion Tell students that the letter **v** is pronounced like an English *v* in words of foreign origin. Ex.: **Vanille, Viktor, Vatikan, Venedig.**

The symbol **ß** (**Eszett** or **scharfes S**) is used instead of a double **s** in certain words. **Eszett** is never used at the beginning of a word. It is capitalized as **SS**.

ß (Eszett, scharfes S)   **Straße** (*street*)

Suggestion Tell students about the German spelling reform (**Rechtschreibreform**) of 1996, and the controversies it generated.

An **Umlaut** (¨) can be added to the vowels **a**, **o**, and **u**, changing their pronunciation.

a	Apfel	ä	(a-Umlaut)	Äpfel
o	Ofen	ö	(o-Umlaut)	Öfen
u	Mutter	ü	(u-Umlaut)	Mütter

In German, all nouns are capitalized, no matter where they appear in a sentence. When spelling aloud, say **großes a** for *capital a*, or **kleines a** for *lowercase a*. To ask how a word is spelled, say: **Wie schreibt man das?** (lit. *How does one write this?*)

---

1 **Sprechen Sie nach** Practice saying the German alphabet and sample words aloud.

2 **Buchstabieren Sie** Spell these words aloud in German.

1. hallo
2. Morgen
3. studieren
4. Explosion
5. typisch
6. Universität
7. Bäcker
8. Straße
9. Juwelen
10. Frühling
11. tanzen
12. Querflöte

2 Expansion Ask students to identify cognates among the sample words. Tell students the meanings of any unfamiliar words.

3 **Sprichwörter** Practice reading these sayings aloud.

Wer A sagt, muss auch B sagen.[1]

Übung macht den Meister.[2]

[1] You have to finish what you've started. (lit. *Whoever says A must also say B*.)

[2] Practice makes perfect.

Ressourcen

SAM: LM: p. 2

vhlcentral.com

Willkommen in Berlin!

 Video: Fotoroman

Meline und George kommen nach Berlin. Hier treffen sie Sabite und Hans.
Ist es eine freundliche Begrüßung (*friendly welcome*)?

Vorbereitung Before showing the video, have students preview the images and text on the page and guess what this episode will be about. Encourage them to focus on overall comprehension of the video, and not to worry if they don't understand every word.

1

MELINE (*am Telefon*) Lukas... ah, Kreuzberg, okay. Lukas...

SABITE Hallo?
GEORGE Hallo. Ich bin George. Wie heißt du?
SABITE Ich heiße Sabite. Nett dich kennen zu lernen.
GEORGE Nett dich kennen zu lernen, Sabite.

SABITE Alles in Ordnung?
GEORGE Hier sind die Schlüssel. Danke, vielen Dank.
SABITE Gern geschehen. Keine Ursache. Bis später.

GEORGE *Talk to you later.*
Auf Wiederhören.

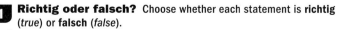

5

HANS Entschuldigung. Was für ein Chaos! Hier ist die Bürste... und der Lippenstift. Und hier ist das Handy.
MELINE (*am Telefon*) Tschüss, Lukas.

HANS Ich heiße Hans. Schönen Tag!

6

ÜBUNGEN

1 **Richtig oder falsch?** Choose whether each statement is **richtig** (*true*) or **falsch** (*false*).

1. Sabite hilft (*helps*) Hans. Falsch.
2. Meline ist am Flughafen (*airport*). Falsch.
3. George hat (*has*) die Schlüssel. Richtig.
4. Meline telefoniert mit (*calls*) Lukas. Richtig.
5. George trifft (*meets*) Sabite. Richtig.

6. Hans geht es ganz okay. Falsch.
7. Meline geht nach (*is going to*) Kreuzberg. Richtig.
8. Meline hat eine Bürste, einen Lippenstift und ein Handy. Richtig.
9. Sabite geht es gut. Richtig.
10. Hans sagt: „Willkommen in München." Falsch.

7

MELINE Ich bin's, Meline.
SABITE Meline, hallo. Nett dich kennen zu lernen.
MELINE Freut mich. Wie geht es dir?
SABITE Mir geht es gut.

8

SABITE Oh, das ist George. Hallo, George. Das ist Meline. Meline, George.
GEORGE Hallo.
MELINE Nett dich kennen zu lernen.
GEORGE Freut mich.

9

HANS George?
GEORGE Ja!
HANS Hallo! Ich bin Hans. Willkommen in Deutschland. Nett dich kennen zu lernen. Wie geht's?
GEORGE Ganz okay.

10

GEORGE Das ist Sabite.
SABITE Hallo.
HANS Hi.

Nützliche Ausdrücke

- **Wie heißt du?**
  What's your name?
- **Nett dich kennen zu lernen.**
  Nice to meet you.
- **Ist jemand da?**
  Anyone there?
- **Gern geschehen.**
  My pleasure.
- **Keine Ursache.**
  Don't mention it.
- **Auf Wiederhören.**
  Talk to you later.
- **Entschuldigung.**
  Excuse me.
- **Was für ein Chaos!**
  What a mess!
- **der Lippenstift**
  lipstick
- **das Handy**
  cell phone
- **Freut mich.**
  It's a pleasure.
- **Willkommen in Deutschland.**
  Welcome to Germany.

1A.1
- **Hier ist die Bürste.**
  Here's the brush.

1A.2
- **Hier sind die Schlüssel.**
  Here are the keys.

1A.3
- **Ich bin George.**
  I'm George.

Suggestion Tell students that they will learn more about the grammar structures previewed in each episode in the lesson's **Strukturen** section.

---

2 **Zum Besprechen** In groups of three, imagine that you are exchange students meeting for the first time. Greet each other, give your names, and be sure to include an appropriate goodbye. Be prepared to present your conversation to the class. Answers will vary.

3 **Vertiefung** Germany's tallest structure is the television tower (**Fernsehturm**) in Berlin. Use the Internet to find its nicknames in German. Answers include: Alex, Telespargel, St. Walter

3 **Expansion** Ask students to find out what the "Pope's Revenge" (**Rache des Papstes**) is. **Answer:** The reflection of the sun on the dome of the **Fernsehturm**, forming a giant cross.

Ressourcen		
SAM VM: p. 1	DVD Folge 1	vhlcentral.com

Hallo, Deutschland!  Reading

SAYING "HELLO" CAN BE A COMPLEX social interaction. Should you shake hands? Kiss cheeks? Keep your distance? The answers depend on where you are, who you are, and who you're talking to.

In general, Germans shake hands more than Americans do, and eye contact is an important feature of this gesture. If you've just been introduced to someone, shake hands, look them in the eye, and say **Freut mich**. In a business setting, a handshake is more or less obligatory, but friends may or may not shake hands when greeting. As in North America, friends in Germany, Austria, and Switzerland can often be seen greeting each other

with a hug or a kiss on the cheek.

Greetings vary depending on time of day, level of formality, and region. In formal situations, you can say **Guten Morgen** in the morning, **Guten Tag** from morning to late afternoon, and **Guten Abend** in the evening. In Bavaria or Austria, you are likely to hear **Grüß Gott°** at any time of day. **Hallo**, **Tag**, and **Grüß dich°** are all common informal greetings. In Bavaria, use **Servus°** to say hello or good-bye to friends.

Deciding between informal and polite forms of address requires some judgment. In general, use the familiar forms **du** and **ihr** with children, teenagers, family members, and fellow

EIN KLEINER TIPP

As a rough guideline, use **Guten Morgen** until 10 a.m., **Guten Tag** until 6 p.m., and **Guten Abend** after 6 p.m.

students. Use the polite form **Sie** with anyone else until they invite you to call them **du**. Always use **Sie** with people with whom you are not on a first-name basis. Address men as **Herr** and women as **Frau**, regardless of their marital status.

Grüß Gott *Hello. (lit. Greet God)* **Grüß dich** *Hello. (lit. Greet you (inf.))* **Servus** *Hello; Good-bye (inf.)*

1 **Richtig oder falsch?** Indicate whether each statement is **richtig** (*true*) or **falsch** (*false*). Then, in pairs, correct any false statements.

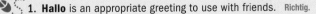

1. **Hallo** is an appropriate greeting to use with friends. Richtig.
2. When meeting someone new, shake hands and say **Freut mich**. Richtig.
3. You should always use **Sie** with other students.
   Falsch. You should use **du** with other students.
4. You should shake hands to greet business partners. Richtig.
5. German friends often greet each other with a hug. Richtig.

6. **Guten Abend** is an appropriate way to greet your boss in the morning.
   Falsch. **Guten Morgen** is an appropriate greeting in the morning.
7. You are more likely to hear **Grüß Gott** in Austria than in Berlin. Richtig.
8. **Du** is used to address adults you don't know.
   Falsch. **Du** is used with friends and family, not with strangers.
9. It is appropriate to address children with **du**. Richtig.
10. When you are not sure whether to use **Sie** or **du**, you should follow the lead of the other person. Richtig.

 Practice more at **vhlcentral.com**.

DEUTSCH IM ALLTAG

Was geht ab?

Geht's dir gut?	Are you all right? (inf.)
Und dir?	And you? (inf.)
Geht es Ihnen gut?	Are you all right? (form.)
Und Ihnen?	And you? (form.)
So weit, so gut.	So far, so good.
Spitze!	Great!
Schön dich zu sehen.	Nice to see you. (inf.)
Schön Sie zu sehen.	Nice to see you. (form.)
Herzlich willkommen.	Welcome.
Was geht ab?	What's up?

DIE DEUTSCHSPRACHIGE WELT

Auf Wiedersehen, Goodbye

One characteristic feature of the German language is its wealth of regional differences. Many dialects have their own greetings, from **Moin Moin** along the North Sea Coast to Switzerland's **Grüezi mitenand**. But how do German speakers say good-bye?

- **Auf Wiedersehen** and **tschüss** are the most standard good-byes.
- The formal Swiss counterpart is **Uf Widerluege.**
- The informal **Mach's gut** is similar in meaning to *Take care.*
- In Baden-Württemberg and the Saarland, **Ade** is common.
- In Austria, **Pfiati** is often used among friends.

PORTRÄT

Das Brandenburger Tor°

On December 22, 1989, thousands cheered as West German Chancellor Helmut Kohl walked through the Brandenburg Gate to shake hands with East German Prime Minister Hans Modrow. It was the first time since the construction of the **Berliner Mauer°** in 1961 that East and West Germans had been permitted to pass through the gate.

Built in 1791, the **Brandenburger Tor** was one of fourteen toll gates that encircled the city. Over the next two centuries, the **Tor** withstood an invasion by Napoleon's soldiers, falling bombs in World War II, and the Cold War partition of East and West Germany. Today, the **Tor** is one of Berlin's most popular attractions, a symbol of German unity, and a monument to Berlin's tumultuous past.

Tor *Gate* **Berliner Mauer** *Berlin Wall*

IM INTERNET

Fashionably late isn't always fashionable. How do German and American manners differ when it comes to punctuality, greetings, and formality?

For more information on this **Kultur**, go to **vhlcentral.com**.

2 Was haben Sie gelernt? Answer the questions.

1. How would you say good-bye to a friend or fellow student in a German-speaking country? List three options.
   Sample answers: Tschüss, Ade, Pfiati, Mach's gut.
2. What did Germans celebrate at the Brandenburg Gate in 1989?
   They celebrated the opening of the border crossing and the fall of the Berlin Wall.
3. Name some historical events that occurred near the Brandenburg Gate.
   Sample answers: The invasion of Berlin by Napoleon, WWII, the building of the Wall, the fall of the Wall.
4. What does the Brandenburg Gate now symbolize?
   It symbolizes German unity.

3 Sie sind dran In pairs, practice meeting and greeting people in these situations. Answers will vary.

1. It's 10 a.m. and you run into your German professor at the grocery store. What do you say?
2. Now you're purchasing your groceries. How do you say "hello" and "good-bye" to the cashier?
3. Just as you're leaving the store, you run into an old friend. Say "hi" and ask how your friend is doing.

Ressourcen

vhlcentral.com

Gender, articles, and nouns  Presentation

Startblock Like English nouns, German nouns can be either singular or plural and may be preceded by a definite or indefinite article. Unlike English nouns, all German nouns have a gender. German nouns are always capitalized, regardless of where they appear in a sentence.

> Was für **ein Chaos**!

> Hier ist **die Bürste**. Hier ist **das Handy**.

Suggestion Point out that nouns taught in this text are listed with their corresponding singular definite articles. Encourage students to memorize the article along with each noun, in order to remember its gender.

Gender

- All German nouns have a gender: masculine, feminine, or neuter. While most nouns referring to males are masculine and most nouns referring to females are feminine, the gender of nouns representing objects and ideas need to be memorized.

MASCULINE	FEMININE	NEUTER
der **Mann**	die **Frau**	das **Buch**
*the **man***	*the **woman***	*the **book***
der **Junge**	die **Blume**	das **Mädchen**
*the **boy***	*the **flower***	*the **girl***

ACHTUNG

Other feminine noun endings include **-ei**, **-heit**, **-schaft**, **-ung**, and **-tät**.

Nouns ending with **-chen** are always neuter.

- Nouns ending with -**in** that refer to people are always feminine.

die Freund**in**	die Student**in**
*the (**female**) friend*	*the (**female**) student*
die Professor**in**	die Klassenkamerad**in**
*the (**female**) professor*	*the (**female**) classmate*

Definite and indefinite articles

- The definite article, equivalent to *the* in English, precedes a noun and indicates its gender. The masculine article is **der**, the feminine article is **die**, and the neuter article is **das**.

Suggestion Give students examples of nouns with these feminine endings. Ex: **die Bäckerei, die Freiheit, die Freundschaft, die Wohnung, die Universität**.

MASCULINE	FEMININE	NEUTER
der **Tisch**	die **Tür**	das **Fenster**
the table	*the door*	*the window*

QUERVERWEIS

You will learn more about forming plurals in **1A.2**.

- The definite article **die** is used with all plural nouns, regardless of gender.

	SINGULAR	PLURAL	
MASCULINE	der Tisch	die Tische	*the tables*
FEMININE	die Tür	die Türen	*the doors*
NEUTER	das Fenster	die Fenster	*the windows*

- The indefinite article **ein(e)** corresponds to *a* or *an* in English. It precedes the noun and matches its gender. Note that both masculine and neuter nouns take the form **ein**, while feminine nouns take **eine**.

MASCULINE	FEMININE	NEUTER
ein Tisch	**eine** Tür	**ein** Fenster
a table	*a door*	*a window*
ein Mann	**eine** Frau	**ein** Mädchen
a man	*a woman*	*a girl*

- There is no plural form of the indefinite article.

Er ist **ein Mann**.
*He is **a man**.* ▶ Sie sind **Männer**.
*They are **men**.*

Compound nouns

- Compound words are very common in German. As in English, two or more simple nouns can be combined to form a compound noun.

die Nacht		das Hemd		**das Nachthemd**
night	+	*shirt*	=	*nightshirt*

Hier ist **der Lippenstift**.

- The gender and number of a compound noun is determined by the last noun in the compound.

das Haus		**die** Aufgabe		**die Hausaufgabe**
house	+	*assignment*	=	*homework*

die Nacht		**der** Tisch		**der Nachttisch**
night	+	*table*	=	*night table*

Expansion Give students additional examples of nouns that can combine to form compounds. Have them figure out the appropriate articles for the compound forms. Ex.: **das Land** (*the country*) **+ die Karte** (*the map*) **= die Landkarte** (*the (country) map*); **der Arm** (*the arm*) **+ das Band** (*the strap*) **+ die Uhr** (*the clock*) **= die Armbanduhr** (*the watch*).

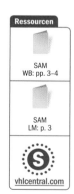

Ressourcen

SAM
WB: pp. 3–4

SAM
LM: p. 3

S

vhlcentral.com

Jetzt sind Sie dran! Tell students that all the nouns listed are singular.

Jetzt sind Sie dran! Indicate whether each noun is **männlich** (*masculine*), **weiblich** (*feminine*), or **sächlich** (*neuter*).

1. der Mann _____männlich_____
2. die Freundin _____weiblich_____
3. der Junge _____männlich_____
4. das Hemd _____sächlich_____
5. die Tür _____weiblich_____
6. ein Freund _____männlich_____

7. eine Frau _____weiblich_____
8. ein Mädchen _____sächlich_____
9. ein Tisch _____männlich_____
10. eine Nacht _____weiblich_____
11. die Aufgabe _____weiblich_____
12. ein Buch _____sächlich_____

Anwendung

1 **Was fehlt?** Write the appropriate article.

der, die, das	ein, eine
1. ___das___ Fenster	5. ___eine___ Frau
2. ___der___ Tisch	6. ___eine___ Tür
3. ___der___ Student	7. ___ein___ Mann
4. ___die___ Nacht	8. ___ein___ Mädchen

2 **Ergänzen Sie** Write each noun in the appropriate column. Include the definite and indefinite article.

Buch	Haus
Frau	Hemd
Freund	Junge
Freundin	Studentin

masculine	feminine	neuter
der Mann; ein Mann	die Frau; eine Frau	das Buch; ein Buch
der Freund; ein Freund	die Freundin; eine Freundin	das Haus; ein Haus
der Junge; ein Junge	die Studentin; eine Studentin	das Hemd; ein Hemd

3 **Bilden Sie Wörter** Write the appropriate definite article.

◀ **BEISPIEL**

das Haus + die Aufgabe =
die Hausaufgabe

1. die Kinder + der Garten
= ___der___ Kindergarten

2. der Schlaf (*sleep*) +
das Zimmer (*room*) =
___das___ Schlafzimmer

3. das Telefon +
die Nummer =
___die___ Telefonnummer

4. der Computer +
das Spiel (*game*) =
___das___ Computerspiel

Kommunikation

4 **Was ist das?** In pairs, take turns identifying each person or object. Provide both the definite and indefinite articles.

▶ **BEISPIEL**
S1: *der Junge*
S2: *ein Junge*

1. das Buch, ein Buch

2. die Frau, eine Frau

3. der Mann, ein Mann

4. die Tür, eine Tür

5. das Fenster, ein Fenster

6. das Mädchen, ein Mädchen

5 **Mehr Wörter** In pairs, take turns creating compound nouns using words from the list. Write down each compound noun with the appropriate article. Sample answers are provided.

BEISPIEL

S1: *der Brief (letter) / das Papier*
S2: *das Briefpapier*

der Handschuh, der Apfelbaum, der Eisbär, der Schlüsselring, der Käsekuchen, die Kartoffelsuppe, das Videospiel, das Haustier

A	B
der Apfel (*apple*)	der Bär (*bear*)
das Eis (*ice*)	der Baum (*tree*)
die Hand	der Kuchen (*cake*)
das Haus	der Ring
die Kartoffel (*potato*)	der Schuh (*shoe*)
der Käse (*cheese*)	das Spiel (*game*)
der Schlüssel (*key*)	die Suppe
das Video	das Tier (*animal*)

6 **Rate was ich zeichne** In small groups, take turns drawing pictures of nouns you've learned so far, for your partners to guess. The person who guesses correctly is the next to draw. Don't forget the article! Answers will vary.

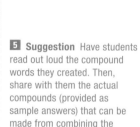

Plurals  Presentation

Startblock Plurals in German follow several patterns. These patterns can help you remember the plural form of each noun you learn.

- In German dictionaries and vocabulary lists, singular nouns are listed along with a notation that indicates how to form the plural. There are five main patterns for forming plural nouns.

notation	singular	plural
-	das Fenster ⟶	die Fenster
-¨	die Mutter (*mother*) ⟶	die Mütter
-e	der Freund ⟶	die Freunde
-¨e	der Stuhl (*chair*) ⟶	die Stühle
-er	das Kind (*child*) ⟶	die Kinder
-¨er	der Mann ⟶	die Männer
-n	der Junge ⟶	die Jungen
-en	die Frau ⟶	die Frauen
-nen	die Freundin ⟶	die Freundinnen
-s	der Park ⟶	die Parks

ACHTUNG

The best way of knowing a noun's plural form is to memorize it when you learn the singular form. Being familiar with the patterns of plural formation can help you learn them.

Suggestion Point out that irregular plural forms exist in English as well as German. Ask students to brainstorm examples. Ex.: *child, children*; *mouse, mice*; *woman, women*; *deer, deer*.

ACHTUNG

Two important exceptions to this pattern are **die Mütter**, plural of **Mutter**, and **die Töchter** (*daughters*), plural of **Tochter**.

Ressourcen

SAM
WB: pp. 5–6

SAM
LM: p. 4

vhlcentral.com

- Most masculine and neuter nouns form the plural by adding -e or -er. Plurals with the -er ending always add an **Umlaut** when the vowel in the singular form is **a**, **o**, or **u**.

  der Tag (*day*) ⟶ die Tage   das Buch ⟶ die Bücher

- If the singular form of a noun ends in -el, -en, or -er, there is no additional plural ending, but an **Umlaut** is added to the stem vowel **a**, **o**, or **u**.

  der Apfel (*apple*) ⟶ die Äpfel   das Zimmer (*room*) ⟶ die Zimmer

- For feminine nouns ending with -in, add -nen to form the plural.

  die Freundin ⟶ die Freundinnen   die Studentin ⟶ die Studentinnen

- For other feminine nouns, add -n if the singular form ends in -e, -el, or -er. Add -en if it does not. Note that feminine nouns with regular plural endings never add an **Umlaut**.

  die Blume (*flower*) ⟶ die Blumen   die Frau ⟶ die Frauen

- The -s ending is added to most words borrowed from other languages and to nouns ending with vowels other than **e**.

  die DVD ⟶ die DVDs   das Auto ⟶ die Autos

 Jetzt sind Sie dran!   Give the plural form of each singular noun and vice versa.

Singular

1. das Café ___die Cafés___
2. die Bürste (*brush*) ___die Bürsten___
3. der Vater (*father*) ___die Väter___
4. die Frage (*question*) ___die Fragen___

Plural

5. die Wochentage (*weekdays*) ___der Wochentag___
6. die Universitäten ___die Universität___
7. die Äpfel ___der Apfel___
8. die Studenten (*m.*) ___der Student___

Anwendung und Kommunikation

1 **Schreiben Sie** Write the plural form.

1. das Buch ___die Bücher___
2. der Mann ___die Männer___
3. der Tag ___die Tage___
4. die Blume ___die Blumen___
5. die Mutter ___die Mütter___

6. das Auto ___die Autos___
7. der Junge ___die Jungen___
8. die Tür ___die Türen___
9. das Kind ___die Kinder___
10. der Park ___die Parks___

2 **Die Plurale** Complete each sentence with the plural form of the appropriate word.

BEISPIEL Holiday Inn und Marriott sind ___Hotels___.

Apfel	Computer	Hotel
Auto	Freund	Künstler (*artist*)
Blume	Freundin	Tag

1. BMW und Volkswagen sind ___Autos___.
2. Rosen und Tulpen (*tulips*) sind ___Blumen___.
3. Dell, HP und Acer sind ___Computer___.
4. Granny Smith und Macintosh sind ___Äpfel___.
5. Eine Woche (*week*) hat sieben (*seven*) ___Tage___.
6. Anna, Monika und Emma sind ___Freundinnen___.
7. Leonardo da Vinci und Paul Klee sind ___Künstler___.
8. Lukas und Felix sind ___Freunde___.

3 **Was ist das?** In pairs, take turns identifying each object, place, or person. Give both singular and plural forms. Sample answers are provided.

▶ **BEISPIEL**

S1: *die Blume*
S2: *die Blumen*

1. das Mädchen, die Mädchen/ das Kind, die Kinder

2. der Park, die Parks

3. der Junge, die Jungen/ das Kind, die Kinder

4. das Auto, die Autos

5. das Fenster, die Fenster

6. die Tür, die Türen

3 **Expansion** Write nouns from this lesson's vocabulary on the back of note cards and distribute them to students. Have each student make a drawing of their noun on the opposite side of the card. Then have them take turns identifying each other's drawings and giving the plural form of each noun.

1A.3

Subject pronouns, *sein*, and the nominative case

S Presentation

QUERVERWEIS

German speakers often use the third-person singular pronoun **man** where English speakers would say *one* or *you*.

Students will learn more about the use of **man** in **Vol. 2, 3B.3**.

Suggestion Tell students that **ich** is capitalized only when it begins a sentence, unlike the pronoun *I* in English. Remind them that the formal **Sie** is always capitalized.

Subject pronouns

- In German, as in English, any noun can be replaced with an equivalent pronoun. A subject pronoun replaces a noun that functions as the subject of a sentence.

Maria ist nett. **Sie** ist nett. **Der Junge** ist groß. **Er** ist groß.
Maria is nice. *She is nice.* *The boy is tall.* *He is tall.*

subject pronouns				
		singular		**plural**
1ˢᵗ person		ich *I*		wir *we*
2ⁿᵈ person		du *you* (inf.) Sie *you* (form.)		ihr *you* (inf.) Sie *you* (form.)
3ʳᵈ person		er *he/it* sie *she/it* es *it*		sie *they*

- The gender of a noun determines the gender of the pronoun that replaces it. German uses **er** for all masculine nouns, **sie** for all feminine nouns, and **es** for all neuter nouns.

Der Tisch ist klein. ▶ **Er** ist klein. **Das Buch** ist neu. ▶ **Es** ist neu.
The table is small. *It's small.* *The book is new.* *It's new.*

Suggestion Give students additional examples using **sie** and **Sie** and have them figure out which meaning is intended, based on context.

- The pronoun **Sie/sie** can mean *you*, *she*, *it*, or *they*, depending on context. Write **Sie** with a capital **S** to mean *you* in a formal context, and **sie** with a lowercase **s** to mean *she*, *it*, or *they*.

Sie ist Professorin und **sie** sind Studenten. Woher kommen **Sie**?
*She is a professor, and **they** are students.* *Where are **you** from?*

The verb *sein*

- **Sein** (*To be*) is an irregular verb: its conjugation does not follow a predictable pattern.

Suggestion Explain to students that the conjugation of a verb is the set of verb forms corresponding to the different possible subjects.

sein (*to be*)			
singular		**plural**	
ich **bin**	*I am*	wir **sind**	*we are*
du **bist**	*you are* (inf.)	ihr **seid**	*you are* (inf.)
Sie **sind**	*you are* (form.)	Sie **sind**	*you are* (form.)
er/sie/es **ist**	*he/she/it is*	sie **sind**	*they are*

Ich bin Amerikaner.
I'm American.

Sie ist Deutsche.
She's German.

Wir sind Freunde.
We are friends.

The nominative case

- German has four *cases* that indicate the function of each noun in a sentence. The case of a noun determines the form of the definite or indefinite article that precedes the noun, the form of any adjectives that modify the noun, and the form of the pronoun that can replace the noun.

German cases		
Nominativ	**Der** Professor ist alt.	*The professor is old.*
Akkusativ	Ich verstehe **den** Professor.	*I understand the professor.*
Dativ	Der Assistent zeigt **dem** Professor den neuen Computer.	*The assistant is showing the professor the new computer.*
Genitiv	Das ist der Assistent **des** Professor**s**.	*This is the professor's assistant.*

- The grammatical subject of a sentence is always in the nominative case (**der Nominativ**). Subject pronouns are, by definition, nominative pronouns. The nominative case is also used for nouns that follow a form of **sein**, **werden** (*to become*), or **bleiben** (*to stay, to remain*).

Das ist **eine gute Idee**.
*That's **a good idea**.*

Wir bleiben **Freunde**.
*We're still **friends**.*

- The definite and indefinite articles you learned in **1A.1** are the forms used with nouns in the nominative case.

nominative articles				
	masculine	**feminine**	**neuter**	**plural**
definite	der Junge	die Frau	das Mädchen	die Jungen
indefinite	ein Junge	eine Frau	ein Mädchen	– Jungen

Suggestion Point out that the conjugated form of **sein** is the same for **wir**, **Sie**, and **sie** (*pl.*). Tell students that all verbs have the same conjugated form for these three subjects.

Suggestion Point out that **Amerikaner** and **Deutsche** are nouns, even though they are translated as adjectives in this context. Tell students that the feminine form of **Amerikaner** is **Amerikanerin**, and the masculine form of **Deutsche** is **Deutscher**.

QUERVERWEIS

You will learn more about cases in **1B.1**, **3B.2**, **4B.1**, and **4B.2**.

Suggestions

- Tell students that dictionaries and vocabulary lists always give nouns in their nominative form.
- Tell students that the set of forms that change depending on the number, case, and gender of a word are called declensions (**die Deklination, -en**).

Students will learn more about cases in **Vol. 2, 4B.1**.

Ressourcen

SAM WB: pp. 7–8

SAM LM: p. 5

S

vhlcentral.com

Jetzt sind Sie dran!	For each noun, write the correct subject pronoun. For each pronoun, write the appropriate form of **sein**.

1. der Apfel ___er___
2. das Haus ___es___
3. die Jungen ___sie___
4. die Hausaufgabe ___sie___
5. Brigitte und ich ___wir___
6. die Studentin und du ___ihr___
7. wir ___sind___
8. ihr ___seid___
9. du ___bist___
10. Sie ___sind___
11. ich ___bin___
12. er ___ist___

Anwendung

2 **Expansion** Have students transform the subjects of items 1, 4, 6, and 8 into subject pronouns.

1 Wählen Sie Select the appropriate subject pronoun.

1. (**Ihr** / Wir) seid in Deutschland.
2. (**Er** / Ich) ist ein Freund.
3. (Du / **Sie**) sind sehr sympathisch!
4. (**Ihr** / Ich) seid Amerikaner.

5. (**Wir** / Ich) sind jung.
6. (**Ich** / Du) bin Studentin.
7. (Es / **Du**) bist zu Hause.
8. (Ihr / **Sie**) ist intelligent.

2 Was fehlt? Write the correct form of sein.

1. Mein Vater (*My father*) und meine Mutter __sind__ hier.
2. Ich __bin__ Student.
3. Herr Professor, Sie __sind__ Experte.
4. Petra und ich __sind__ zu Hause (*at home*).
5. Du __bist__ Lehrer (*teacher*).
6. Das Buch __ist__ sehr interessant.
7. Ihr __seid__ Schüler.
8. Das Fenster und die Tür __sind__ offen (*open*).

3 Ergänzen Sie Write the pronoun and the appropriate form of sein.

▶ **BEISPIEL**

__Sie sind__ im (*at the*) **Restaurant.**

1. __Sie sind__ Freundinnen.

2. __Er ist__ Deutschprofessor.

3. Mia, Tim und ich, __wir sind__ Studenten.

4. Sara, __du bist__ allein (*alone*).

5. __Sie ist__ müde (*tired*).

6. Jan und du, __ihr seid__ Freunde.

4 Bilden Sie Sätze Write complete sentences using sein. Then, replace the subjects with subject pronouns, where possible.

BEISPIEL Samuel / Professor

Samuel ist Professor. Er ist Professor.

1. Alfred und ich / sympathisch
Alfred und ich sind sympathisch. Wir sind sympathisch.
2. du / romantisch
Du bist romantisch.
3. es / ein gutes (*good*) Buch
Es ist ein gutes Buch.
4. Michael und du / in Deutschland
Michael und du seid in Deutschland. Ihr seid in Deutschland.

5. Danielle und Donna / aus Los Angeles
Danielle und Donna sind aus Los Angeles. Sie sind aus Los Angeles.
6. ich / Amerikaner
Ich bin Amerikaner.
7. Sie / unfair, Frau Henke / !
Sie sind unfair, Frau Henke!
8. das Haus / gigantisch
Das Haus ist gigantisch. Es ist gigantisch.

Kommunikation

5 **Beschreiben Sie** In pairs, take turns asking and answering questions about the illustrations. Answers will vary.

WERKZEUG

Place the verb first when asking a yes-or-no question.

Ist/sind das...?
Ja/Nein, das ist/sind...
Bist du...?
Ja/Nein, ich bin...

▶ **BEISPIEL**

S1: *Sind das Studentinnen?*
S2: *Ja, das sind Studentinnen.*

 1.

 2.

 3.

 4.

 5.

6.

6 **Fragen** In pairs, ask and answer questions using the prompts. Answers will vary.

BEISPIEL

S1: *Bist du romantisch?*
S2: *Ja, ich bin romantisch.*

A	B
ich	gut
du	in Deutschland
der Film	intelligent
wir	romantisch
Inge und du	Studenten
Sebastian und Katie	tolerant

7 **Freut mich!** In groups of three, role-play these situations. Each person should say something about him-/herself using a form of **sein**.

7 **Expansion** Have group members introduce themselves to the rest of the class.

1. You are meeting your classmates for the first time. Introduce yourself and ask how each person is doing.

2. You and your friend are invited to a birthday party. Exchange greetings and introduce yourselves to other guests.

Wiederholung

4 **Expansions**
- Repeat this activity using the cards students created for **Memory-Spiel**.
- Divide the class into teams and play Pictionary using the lesson vocabulary.

1 **Memory-Spiel** With a partner, create a set of cards to play Memory, featuring ten nouns you learned in this lesson. For each noun you draw, create a matching card showing the word with the definite article. Shuffle the cards and place them face down. Take turns matching pictures and words. Answers will vary.

2 **Freut mich!** In pairs, practice introducing yourselves in formal and informal situations. Answers will vary.

3 **Galgenmännchen** In small groups, play Hangman using the vocabulary you learned in **Kontext 1A** and **Strukturen 1A.1** and **1A.2**. For nouns, include the definite article. Give your partners a hint about each word. Answers will vary.

BEISPIEL

3 **Suggestion** Tell students that letters of the alphabet are neuter.

S1: Es ist eine Person. / Es ist ein Ding (*thing*). / Es ist ein Ausdruck (*expression*).
S2: Gibt es (*Is there*) ein S?

4 **Was ist das?** In pairs, take turns identifying the objects and people.

▶ **BEISPIEL**

S1: Was ist das?
S2: Das ist ein Auto.

1. Das ist ein Buch.

2. Das ist eine Blume./Das sind Blumen.

3. Das ist ein Fenster.

4. Das sind DVDs.

5. Das ist ein Park.

6. Das sind Kinder.

5 **Bilderrätsel** Your instructor will give you and a partner two worksheets with different images and labels. Work together to form the compound words.

6 **Wie heißt du?** Your instructor will give you a worksheet. Ask your classmates to say their names and spell them for you. Don't forget to greet them, ask how they are, and say thank you! Answers will vary.

BEISPIEL

S1: Guten Morgen!
S2: Hallo!
S1: Wie geht's?
S2: Es geht mir gut.
S1: Wie heißt du?
S2: Ich heiße Nadia.
S1: Wie schreibt man das?
S2: N-A-D-I-A.
S1: Wie ist dein Nachname (*last name*)?
S2: Mueller. M-U-E-L-L-E-R.
S1: Danke!

 Zapping

 **S** **Video: TV Clip**

Suggestion After showing students the video, ask questions to facilitate comprehension. Ex: In the first scene, why do some of the people in the child's drawing have blank faces? In the second scene, why are the children happier?

Familien fahren° besser mit der Bahn

Deutsche Bahn (**DB**) is the German railway company, based in Berlin. The **Deutsche Bahn** offers a **Sparpreis** (*discount price*) for families. Children under age 15 ride free when accompanied by an adult and pay half-price fares when traveling alone. This advertisement presents the **Deutsche Bahn** as a convenient and comfortable transportation option for families, allowing parents and children to interact and enjoy themselves on the way to their destination.

Die Bahn macht mobil: www.bahn.de

Sag mal°, weißt du noch wie° die Beiden von vorne° aussehen°?

Warum fragst du mich?° Du kennst die° länger als° ich.

Jetzt mit Gratiseis° für Kinder.

---

fahren *ride* **Sag mal** *Say...* **weißt du...wie** *do you know how* **die...von vorne** *those two up front* **aussehen** *look* **Warum fragst du mich?** *Why are you asking me?* **Du kennst die** *You've known them* **länger als** *longer than* **Gratiseis** *free popsicle*

 Verständnis Circle the correct answers.

1. How much does the **DB** family package cost?
   a. 49 euro   b. 60 euro   c. 39 euro   d. 55 euro

2. What do children riding the train receive?
   a. Bücher   b. Äpfel   c. Eis   d. Blumen

 Diskussion Discuss the following questions with a partner. Answers will vary.

1. What is train service like in your country? How do you think it compares with the services offered by the **Deutsche Bahn**?

2. Does this commercial make you want to travel by train in Germany? Why or why not?

Suggestion Point out that many of these vocabulary items are compound nouns. Ask students to identify the compound nouns, then help them to figure out the meaning of the component words.

In der Schule

Talking Picture Audio: Activities

die Uhr, -en

der Rucksack, -̈e

der Bleistift, -e

das Fenster, -

der Schüler, -

das Buch, -̈er

die Schülerin, -nen

das Heft, -e

das Wörterbuch, -̈er

der Stift, -e

der Papierkorb, -̈e

das Blatt Papier, (*pl.* Blätter Papier)

Wortschatz	
im Unterricht	*in class*
der Computer, -	*computer*
das Ergebnis, -se	*result; score*
das Foto, -s	*photo*
die Frage, -n	*question*
die Hausaufgabe, -n	*homework*
die Klasse, -n	*class*
der Kuli, -s	*ball-point pen*
das Lehrbuch, -̈er	*(college/university) textbook*
die Note, -n	*grade (on an assignment)*
die Notiz, -en	*note*
das Problem, -e	*problem*
die Prüfung, -en	*test; exam*
der Radiergummi, -s	*eraser*
die Sache, -n	*thing*
das Schulbuch, -̈er	*(K–12) textbook*
die Stunde, -n	*lesson*
der Taschenrechner, -	*calculator*
der Terminkalender, -	*personal planner*
der Tisch, -e	*table; desk*
die Tür, -en	*door*
das Zeugnis, -se	*report card; grade report*
Da ist/sind...	*There is/are...*
Ist/Sind hier...?	*Is/Are there... here?*
Hier ist/sind...	*Here is/are...*
Was ist das?	*What is that?*
Orte	*places*
das Klassenzimmer, -	*classroom*
die Schule, -n	*school*
die Universität, -en	*university, college*
die Bibliothek, -en	*library*
die Mensa, Mensen	*(college/university) cafeteria*
Personen	*people*
Wer ist das?	*Who is it?*
der Klassenkamerad, -en / die Klassenkameradin, -nen	*classmate*
der Professor, -en / die Professorin, -nen	*professor*
der Student, -en / die Studentin, -nen	*(college/university) student*

Suggestion Tell students that **Schüler(in)** refers to a student in elementary school through high school, while **Student(in)** refers to a college/ university student.

ACHTUNG

Don't confuse **Da ist...** (*There is...*) with **Das ist...** (*This is...*).

Ressourcen

SAM WB: pp. 9–10

SAM LM: p. 6

S vhlcentral.com

The illustration on the left side of the page contains the following labels:

die Tafel, -n

DEUTSCHLAND
LIECHTENSTEIN
DIE SCHWEIZ ÖSTERREICH

die Karte, -n

der Lehrer, -
(die Lehrerin, -nen f.)

Schreibtisch, -e

der Stuhl, -̈e

Anwendung

1 Expansion Ask students what other words from the lesson vocabulary could be included in each group.

1 Was passt nicht? Select the word that doesn't belong.

1. der Professor / (das Problem) / die Universität / die Studentin
2. (das Fenster) / das Schulbuch / die Notizen / das Heft
3. der Stift / der Bleistift / (der Papierkorb) / der Kuli
4. die Tafel / der Schreibtisch / der Stuhl / (die Prüfung)
5. die Tür / (das Ergebnis) / der Tisch / die Uhr
6. das Problem / (der Radiergummi) / die Frage / das Ergebnis

2 Was ist das? Label each item.

2 Suggestion Have students identify items in your own classroom. Ask students: **Ist hier eine Uhr? Wo ist die Tür?**, etc.

 ► **BEISPIEL** *der Bleistift*

1. der Stift/ der Kuli
2. das Buch/das Schulbuch/das Lehrbuch/das Wörterbuch
3. der Stuhl
4. der Rucksack
5. die Uhr
6. die Tür

3 Ergänzen Sie Select the words that best complete each sentence.

1. Christa ist...
   a. der Stuhl.   (b.) die Schülerin.   c. die Stunde.
2. Wer ist das? Das ist...
   a. der Bleistift.   b. der Taschenrechner.   (c.) der Professor.
3. Wo sind die Bücher? Sie sind...
   (a.) in der Bibliothek.   b. im Ergebnis.   c. im Papierkorb.
4. Frau Meier ist...
   (a.) die Lehrerin.   b. die Schülerin.   c. die Schule.
5. Im Klassenzimmer sind...
   (a.) Tische.   b. Noten.   c. Universitäten.
6. Das Quiz und der Test sind...
   a. Hausaufgaben.   (b.) Prüfungen.   c. Ergebnisse.

4 Zuordnungen 🎧 Write each word you hear in the correct category.

Orte		Personen	
1. die Schule		5. die Freundin	
2. die Mensa		6. der Lehrer	
3. das Klassenzimmer		7. die Professorin	
4. die Universität		8. der Schüler	

4 Expansion Have students give the plural form of each word.

Kommunikation

5 Was ist das?
In pairs, take turns pointing at items and people in your classroom and asking each other to identify them. Answers will vary.

BEISPIEL

S1: *Was ist das?*
S2: *Das ist ein Bleistift. Wer ist das?*
S1: *Das ist der Professor.*

5 Expansion Repeat the activity as a class, having students ask and answer questions about items in the classroom.

6 Im Rucksack
List six items that are in your backpack. Then, work with a partner and compare lists. Answers will vary.

In meinem (*my*) Rucksack ist/sind...

1. _____
2. _____
3. _____
4. _____
5. _____
6. _____

In _____s Rucksack ist/sind...

1. _____
2. _____
3. _____
4. _____
5. _____
6. _____

WERKZEUG

To say that something belongs to someone, add an **-s** to the person's name (**Marias Heft**; **Alfreds Buch**). Add an apostrophe if the name already ends in **-s** (**Thomas' Heft**; **Markus' Buch**).

6 Expansion Bring in a bag filled with items such as pens, a planner, a calculator, and so on. Pull them out one by one and ask students: **Ist das ein Bleistift oder ein Kuli? Ist das eine Uhr oder ein Taschenrechner? Ein Schulbuch oder ein Wörterbuch?** etc.

7 Ist da...?
In pairs, take turns asking each other questions about what you see in the illustration. Answers will vary.

BEISPIEL

S1: *Ist da ein Papierkorb?*
S2: *Nein. Da ist ein Bleistift. Ist da...?*

8 Ratespiel
Play Pictionary as a class. Answers will vary.

- Take turns going to the board and drawing images representing words from the lesson vocabulary.
- The person drawing may not write any letters or numbers.
- The person who correctly identifies the drawing in German gets to go next.

Aussprache und Rechtschreibung

Audio: Presentation
Record & Compare Activities

NATIONAL STANDARDS — comparisons

🎧 The vowels *a*, *e*, *i*, *o*, and *u*

Each German vowel may be pronounced with either a long or a short sound. A vowel followed by **h** is always long. A double **oo**, **aa**, or **ee** also indicates a long vowel sound. In some words, long **i** is spelled **ie**.

Fahne	**wen**	**ihn**	**doof**	**Mut**	**diese**

A vowel followed by two or more consonant sounds is usually short.

Pfanne	**wenn**	**in**	**Sonne**	**Mutter**	**singst**

When the German letter **e** appears in the unstressed syllable at the end of a word, it is pronounced like the *e* in the English word *the*.

danke	**Schule**	**Frage**	**Klasse**	**Dinge**	**Vase**

In certain words, an **Umlaut** (¨) is added to the vowel **a**, **o**, or **u**, changing the pronunciation of the vowel.

Bank	**Bänke**	**schon**	**schön**	**Bruder**	**Brüder**

Suggestion To produce the **ü** sound, tell students to round their lips as if to pronounce the letter **o**, but then make the long **i** sound.

🔊Ⓢ **1** Sprechen Sie nach Practice saying these words aloud.

1. Kahn / kann
2. beten / Betten
3. Robe / Robbe
4. Buch / Butter
5. den / denn
6. Saat / satt
7. Rogen / Roggen
8. Sack / Säcke
9. Wort / Wörter
10. Stuhl / Stühle
11. Hefte
12. Tage

1 Expansion Tell students the meanings of any unfamiliar words.

🔊Ⓢ **2** Artikulieren Sie Practice saying these sentences aloud.

1. Der Mann kam ohne Kamm.
2. Wir essen Bienenstich und trinken Kaffee.
3. Am Sonntag und am Montag scheint die Sonne.
4. Das U-Boot ist unter Wasser.
5. Ich habe viele Freunde in der Schule.
6. Der Mantel mit den fünf Knöpfen ist schöner als die Mäntel mit einem Knopf.

🔊Ⓢ **3** Sprichwörter Practice reading these sayings aloud.

BANK

Sag mir, mit wem du gehst, und ich sage dir, wer du bist.[1]

Der frühe Vogel fängt den Wurm.[2]

[1] Tell me who your friends are, and I will tell you who you are.

[2] The early bird catches the worm.

Ressourcen

SAM LM: p. 7

Ⓢ vhlcentral.com

Oh, George! 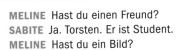 Video: *Fotoroman*

George und Hans treffen (*meet*) Meline und Sabite im Biergarten.
Melines Handy klingelt...

Vorbereitung Have students review the **Nützliche Ausdrücke** before watching the video, in order to preview the episode content.

SABITE Wer ist es?
MELINE Lukas.
SABITE Oh, dein Freund?
MELINE Ja. Nein. Ja.

MELINE Wir haben Probleme.

KELLNERIN Bitte schön?
HANS Ein Wasser, bitte.
GEORGE Einen Kaffee und ein
Stück Strudel.

MELINE Ich habe keinen Freund mehr.
SABITE Wie geht's dir?
MELINE Mir geht es sehr gut.

MELINE Hast du einen Freund?
SABITE Ja. Torsten. Er ist Student.
MELINE Hast du ein Bild?

GEORGE Sabite? Sabite, hallo.
SABITE Hallo.
HANS Hallo.
SABITE Was ist da drin?
GEORGE Lehrbücher! Wörterbuch... Hefte...
Stifte... Kalender.
HANS Hast du auch einen Computer?

ÜBUNGEN

1 **Richtig oder falsch?** Indicate whether each statement is **richtig** (*true*) or **falsch** (*false*).

1. George hat ein Wörterbuch. Richtig.
2. Sabite hat ein Bild von (*of*) Torsten. Richtig.
3. George will (*wants*) das Brandenburger Tor sehen (*to see*). Richtig.
4. Im Bauhaus-Museum gibt es viele Bücher. Falsch.
5. Meline telefoniert mit Lukas. Richtig.

6. Die Kellnerin hat einen Freund. Richtig.
7. Torsten ist Student. Richtig.
8. Hans hat einen Stadtplan. Richtig.
9. Die Kellnerin heißt Laura. Falsch.
10. George bestellt (*orders*) einen Kaffee und ein Steak. Falsch.

George

Hans

Meline

Sabite

Kellnerin

7

GEORGE Ich habe eine Idee. Hast du einen Stadtplan?
HANS Ja!
GEORGE Was muss ich sehen in Berlin? Das Brandenburger Tor!
HANS Checkpoint Charlie!

8

SABITE Potsdamer Platz!
GEORGE Marlene-Dietrich-Platz!
KELLNERIN Das Bode-Museum. Und das Jüdische Museum!

9

HANS Wie viele Kurse hast du belegt?
SABITE Ah, vier.
MELINE Bauhaus-Museum.
HANS Ja!
MELINE Im Bauhaus-Museum gibt es viele...
SABITE Stühle! Viele Stühle. Und Tische.

10

GEORGE Wie heißt sie?
SABITE Ähm, Leyna? Oh, George.
HANS Sie hat einen Freund?
GEORGE Ja.

Nützliche Ausdrücke

- **Prost!**
  Cheers!
- **Wer ist es?**
  Who is it?
- **Hast du ein Bild?**
  Do you have a picture?
- **Was ist da drin?**
  What's in there?
- **Hast du auch einen Computer?**
  Do you have a computer, too?
- **die Kellnerin**
  waitress
- **Bitte schön?**
  May I take your order?; May I help you?
- **das Wasser**
  water
- **der Kaffee**
  coffee
- **das Stück Strudel**
  a piece of strudel
- **Ich habe keinen Freund mehr.**
  I don't have a boyfriend anymore.
- **die Idee**
  idea
- **der Stadtplan**
  city map
- **Was muss ich sehen in Berlin?**
  What do I have to see in Berlin?
- **Ist alles in Ordnung?**
  Is everything alright?
- **Wie heißt sie?**
  What's her name?

1B.1
- **Wir haben Probleme.**
  We have problems.

1B.2
- **Hast du einen Stadtplan?**
  Do you have a city map?

1B.3
- **—Wie viele Kurse hast du?**
  —How many classes are you taking?
- **—Vier.**
  —Four.

---

2 **Zum Besprechen** In groups of three, role-play a scene where two of you order food at a **Biergarten**. Here are some common items to order. *Answers will vary.*

eine Cola	ein Stück Strudel
einen Kaffee	einen Tee
einen Saft (*juice*)	ein Wasser

3 **Vertiefung** The characters mention several important sites and museums in Berlin. Research these and other monuments and plan a day of sightseeing in Berlin to present to the class. Mention at least three sites that interest you and include their names in German. *Answers will vary.*

Suggestion Preview the expression **es gibt** and encourage students to list some of the things they can see at each site.

Ressourcen

| SAM VM: p. 2 | DVD Folge 2 | vhlcentral.com |

Die Schulzeit **S** Reading

Suggestion Explain that the **Abitur** is awarded based on a points system. For each course and each exam they take, students can earn a maximum of 15 points. At the completion of all courses and exams, the points are tallied, and students are awarded a final grade from 1 to 6. The minimum qualifying score for the **Abitur** is 280 points (out of 840).

ALTHOUGH THE WORD AND THE concept were invented by **Friedrich Fröbel**, a teacher in 19th-century Germany, **Kindergarten** is not a part of today's German public school system. There are many privately-run **Kindergärten**, but attendance is not universal.

Public school for German children starts at age six, with **Grundschule°**. For the first four years, all **Grundschüler** attend school together. But after age ten, students are streamed into three different kinds of schools, usually as recommended by their teacher.

The most academically rigorous option is **Gymnasium**. **Gymnasium** lasts eight years, and graduates need to pass difficult exit exams to earn their **Abitur°**. The "Abi" gives students access to competitive internships and a university education.

A more vocationally-oriented option is **Hauptschule**. Students typically finish **Hauptschule** at age 15 or 16. They may then attend **Berufsfachschule°**, where they can train for a variety of professions, from mechanics to physical therapy.

The third option is **Realschule**, which has stricter academic requirements than **Hauptschule**. After graduation, students may seek further schooling that will lead them into careers like banking, IT, or social work.

This three-track system has been in use for decades, but in recent years it has come under serious criticism. The **Abitur** is associated with higher social status, and more and more families push to have their children admitted into **Gymnasium**. **Realschule** still generally leads to solid employment opportunities, but there is now a stigma attached to **Hauptschule**, which makes the job search more difficult for its graduates.

In some states, there is a fourth option for secondary school students: the **Gesamtschule°**. These comprehensive schools have no entrance requirements. They offer college preparatory classes for students who perform well, general education classes for students with average performance, and remedial courses for those who need additional support. **Gesamtschulen** were introduced in the 1970s with the hope of eliminating inequalities associated with the three-track system, but they have been slow to take root.

Grundschule *elementary school* **Abitur** *high school diploma* **Berufsfachschule** *vocational school* **Gesamtschule** *comprehensive school*

Suggestion Tell students that the Austrian and Swiss version of the **Abitur** is called **die Matura**.

ÜBUNGEN

1 Ergänzen Sie Complete the statements.

1. _____Kindergarten_____ is not part of the German public school system.
2. _____Friedrich Fröbel_____ invented the word **Kindergarten**.
3. German elementary school is called _____Grundschule_____.
4. Children normally begin school at age _____six_____.
5. **Grundschule** lasts _____four_____ years.
6. After age ten, students are streamed into three kinds of schools: **Gymnasium**, **Hauptschule**, and _____Realschule_____.
7. **Gymnasium** graduates receive a diploma called the _____Abitur_____.
8. Students who have earned their **Abitur** can attend _____university_____.
9. After finishing _____Hauptschule_____, students may attend **Berufsfachschule**.
10. The _____Gesamtschule_____ offers an alternative to the three-track system.

 Practice more at **vhlcentral.com**.

Die Schule

der Abschluss, -ˉe	graduation
die Pause, -n	break, recess
der Schulleiter, -	(male) principal
die Schulleiterin, -nen	(female) principal
bestehen	to pass a test
durchfallen	to flunk; to fail
schwänzen	to cut class
langweilig	boring

Ein süßer° Beginn

In German-speaking countries, the first day of school is a festive occasion. Excited **Erstklässler°** are presented with **Schultüten** by their parents on the morning of their first day of school. The **Schultüte** is a decorated paper cone, filled with candies, chocolates, school supplies, and other treats. With their unopened **Tüten** in hand, the **Erstklässler** set off for **Grundschule**. **Alles Gute für den ersten Schultag!°**

süßer sweet **Erstklässler** first-graders **Alles Gute für den ersten Schultag!** Best wishes on your first day of school!

Noten in Deutschland

Deutsche Noten:	1	2	3	4	5/6
US-Äquivalente:	A/A+	A-/B+	B/B-	C/D	D-/F

Der Schultag

Die Deutschsprachige Welt Tell students that children often craft their own **Schultüten** in **Kindergarten**. Their parents then fill the **Tüten** before the first day of **Grundschule**.

The school day in Germany typically lasts from 7:30 or 8:00 in the morning until 1:00 in the afternoon, with a 15-20 minute mid-morning break, called the **Große° Pause**. Many schools do not have cafeterias, since students go home at lunch time. They then have the afternoon to do homework and participate in extracurricular activities. Students have only 6 weeks of summer vacation, but they get longer breaks during the school year, with 2 weeks off in the fall, 2 weeks for Christmas, and 2 weeks in the spring.

Große Big

EIN KLEINER TIPP

The German word for *one* is **eins**. A straight-A student is called **ein(e) Einser-Schüler(in)**.

IM INTERNET

Subjects: What subjects do students study at **Gymnasium**? What are **Pflichtfächer**? What are **Wahlfächer**?

For more information on this **Kultur**, go to vhlcentral.com.

---

2 **Richtig oder falsch?** Indicate whether each statement is **richtig** or **falsch**. Then, in pairs, correct the false statements.

1. Most German students eat lunch in their school cafeterias.
   Falsch. Many schools do not have cafeterias, since students go home at lunch time.
2. Students get a midmorning break called the **Große Pause**. **Richtig.**
3. Students get 12 weeks of vacation every summer.
   Falsch. Students have only 6 weeks of summer vacation.
4. Children in their first year of school are called **Kindergärtner**.
   Falsch. They are called **Erstklässler**.
5. The **Schultüte** is a test that elementary school students take on the first day. **Falsch.** The **Schultüte** is a cone full of treats.

3 **Die Schule: anders in Deutschland** In pairs, discuss the similarities and differences between school life in Germany or other German-speaking countries and in your country. What do you like best about each system? Why?

Suggestion Tell students that many changes to the German educational system have been proposed and/or implemented over the last decade. **Gymnasium** originally lasted nine years, but was shortened to eight, and the government is considering extending the number of years spent in elementary school and lengthening the school day.

Ressourcen

vhlcentral.com

1B.1 *Haben* and the accusative case  **Presentation**

Startblock To describe what someone or something has, use the irregular verb **haben** with the accusative case.

Haben

haben (*to have*)			
ich **habe**	*I have*	wir **haben**	*we have*
du **hast**	*you have* (inf.)	ihr **habt**	*you have* (inf.)
Sie **haben**	*you have* (form.)	Sie **haben**	*you have* (form.)
er/sie/es **hat**	*he/she/it has*	sie **haben**	*they have*

Ich **habe** ein Buch.
*I **have** a book.*

Petra **hat** eine Karte.
*Petra **has** a map.*

Wir **haben** eine Frage.
*We **have** a question.*

The accusative case

- In **1A.3**, you learned that the function of a noun in a sentence determines its case, as well as the case of any article or adjective that modifies it. A noun that functions as a direct object is in the accusative case (**der Akkusativ**).

definite articles				
	masculine	**feminine**	**neuter**	**plural**
nominative	der Stuhl	die Tür	das Fenster	die Notizen
accusative	de**n** Stuhl	die Tür	das Fenster	die Notizen

indefinite articles				
	masculine	**feminine**	**neuter**	**plural**
nominative	ein Stuhl	eine Tür	ein Fenster	– Notizen
accusative	eine**n** Stuhl	eine Tür	ein Fenster	– Notizen

Der Lehrer hat **den Stift**.
*The teacher has **the pen**.*

Sie öffnet **die Tür**.
*She's opening **the door**.*

Ich kaufe **einen Schreibtisch**.
*I'm buying **a desk**.*

Wir haben hier **ein Problem**.
*We have **a problem** here.*

 S

Jetzt sind Sie dran!	In the first column, complete the sentences using **haben**. In the second column, indicate whether each underlined phrase is in the **Nominativ (N)** or **Akkusativ (A)** case.

1. Wir _____haben_____ die Bücher.
2. Ich _____habe_____ Fotos.
3. Herr Müller _____hat_____ ein Haus.
4. Ihr _____habt_____ morgen Schule.
5. Max und Julia _____haben_____ viele Hausaufgaben.
6. Lena _____hat_____ eine Theorie.

__N__ 7. Sie ist <u>eine Schülerin</u>.
__A__ 8. David hat <u>eine Frage</u>.
__A__ 9. Ich habe <u>ein Problem</u>.
__A__ 10. Wir haben nur (*only*) <u>einen Stuhl</u>.
__N__ 11. Ihr seid <u>Studenten</u>.
__A__ 12. Ich esse (*eat*) <u>einen Apfel</u>.

Anwendung und Kommunikation

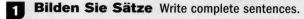

1 Bilden Sie Sätze Write complete sentences.

BEISPIEL ich / haben / ein Radiergummi

Ich habe einen Radiergummi.

1. du / haben / ein Computer   Du hast einen Computer.
2. ihr / haben / ein Taschenrechner   Ihr habt einen Taschenrechner.
3. der Lehrer / haben / ein Buch   Der Lehrer hat ein Buch.
4. wir / haben / ein Problem   Wir haben ein Problem.
5. ich / haben / eine Frage   Ich habe eine Frage.
6. das Mädchen / haben / ein Freund   Das Mädchen hat einen Freund.

2 Was haben wir? Rewrite the sentences.

BEISPIEL Das ist ein Computer. (Inge)

Inge hat einen Computer.

1. Das ist ein Rucksack. (Peter)   Peter hat einen Rucksack.
2. Das ist ein Kuli. (ich)   Ich habe einen Kuli.
3. Das ist ein Schulbuch. (ihr)   Ihr habt ein Schulbuch.
4. Das sind Fotos. (du)   Du hast Fotos.
5. Das ist ein Wörterbuch. (Erik und Nina)   Erik und Nina haben ein Wörterbuch.
6. Das ist eine Karte. (wir)   Wir haben eine Karte.

3 Was haben sie? With a partner, take turns saying what each person has.

▶ **BEISPIEL**

Patrick hat Fotos.

Patrick

1. du

Du hast Bücher.

2. die Klassenkameraden

Die Klassenkameraden/Sie haben Hefte.

3. Bettina

Bettina/Sie hat eine Uhr.

4. ich

Ich habe einen Taschenrechner.

5. du und Abdel

Du und Abdel/Ihr habt einen Rucksack.

6. wir

Wir haben einen Computer.

4 Im Klassenzimmer In groups, take turns discussing what items are in your classroom and what each of you has brought to class. Answers will vary.

BEISPIEL

S1: *Was haben wir hier?*
S2: *Wir haben Stühle und Bänke.*

S1: *Was hast du da?*
S2: *Ich habe ein Heft.*

4 Expansion Call on individual students and have them describe what they and their group members have brought to class. Ex.: **Er hat ein Heft und einen Bleistift. Ich habe auch ein Heft und sie hat einen Kuli.**

 Practice more at **vhlcentral.com**.

Word order  Presentation

Startblock By changing the order of words in a sentence, you can shift emphasis or turn a statement into a yes-or-no question.

QUERVERWEIS

You will learn how to form negative statements in **2B.3**.

Ressourcen

SAM
WB: pp. 13–14

SAM
LM: p. 9

vhlcentral.com

Statements

- In German, the verb is always the second element in a statement. The first element is often the subject, but it can also be a time expression or a prepositional phrase.

1ST	2ND	3RD
Ich	**habe**	heute Abend viele Hausaufgaben.

*I **have** a lot of homework tonight.*

	1ST	2ND	3RD
Heute Abend	**habe**	ich viele Hausaufgaben.

*Tonight I **have** a lot of homework.*

- A direct or indirect object may be placed in first position, but this is a less common phrasing, used to place emphasis on the object. When the subject is not the first element in the sentence, it immediately follows the verb.

1ST	2ND	3RD
Viele Hausaufgaben	**habe**	ich heute Abend.

*I **have** a lot of homework tonight.*

Yes-or-no questions

- To turn a statement into a yes-or-no question, move the verb to the first position. Move the subject to the second position, since it must immediately follow the verb. Use **ja** (*yes*) or **nein** (*no*) to respond to this type of question.

STATEMENT	QUESTION
Die Professorin ist nett.	**Ist die Professorin** nett?
The professor is nice.	*Is the professor nice?*
Jetzt habt ihr einen Computer.	**Habt ihr jetzt** einen Computer?
Now you have a computer.	*Do you have a computer now?*
Die Schüler haben jetzt Unterricht.	**Haben die Schüler** jetzt Unterricht?
The students have class now.	*Do the students have class now?*

Jetzt sind Sie dran! **Turn each statement into a yes-or-no question.**

1. Ich habe ein Buch.
   Habe ich ein Buch?/Hast du ein Buch? /Haben Sie ein Buch?

2. Ich bin Studentin.
   Bin ich Studentin?/Bist du Studentin?/Sind Sie Studentin?

3. Das sind Klassenkameraden.
   Sind das Klassenkameraden?

4. Der Apfel ist schlecht (*bad*).
   Ist der Apfel schlecht?

5. Wir haben viele Fotos.
   Haben wir viele Fotos?/Habt ihr viele Fotos?/Haben Sie viele Fotos?

6. Tobias und Jasmin haben Rucksäcke.
   Haben Tobias und Jasmin Rucksäcke?

7. Er hat ein Handy (*cell phone*) und einen Taschenrechner.
   Hat er ein Handy und einen Taschenrechner?

8. Ich habe ein großes (*big*) Problem.
   Habe ich ein großes Problem?/Hast du ein großes Problem? /Haben Sie ein großes Problem?

9. Das Wörterbuch ist gut.
   Ist das Wörterbuch gut?

10. Der Student hat Bücher.
    Hat der Student Bücher?

Anwendung und Kommunikation

1 **Ein paar Fragen** Write out the questions.

1 Expansion Have students pose these questions to their classmates.

BEISPIEL Maria und Michael / haben / ein Computer

Haben Maria und Michael einen Computer?

1. du / haben / ein Heft   Hast du ein Heft?

2. der Junge / haben / eine Uhr   Hat der Junge eine Uhr?

3. die Lehrerin / eine Karte / haben   Hat die Lehrerin eine Karte?

4. sein / du / Student   Bist du Student?

5. wir / Hausaufgaben / viele (*a lot*) / haben   Haben wir viele Hausaufgaben?

6. das Buch / sein / schlecht   Ist das Buch schlecht?

2 **Noch einmal** Rewrite each sentence twice, changing the order of the underlined elements.

BEISPIEL <u>Ich</u> habe <u>heute</u> (*today*) <u>eine Prüfung</u>.

Heute habe ich eine Prüfung.
Eine Prüfung habe ich heute.

1. Stefan hat <u>heute Abend</u> <u>Deutschhausaufgaben</u>.   Heute Abend hat Stefan Deutschhausaufgaben. Deutschhausaufgaben hat Stefan heute Abend.

2. <u>Wilhelm und Uta</u> haben <u>ein Haus</u> <u>in Berlin</u>.   Ein Haus haben Wilhelm und Uta in Berlin. In Berlin haben Wilhelm und Uta ein Haus.

3. <u>Eine Freundin und ich</u> gehen (*are going*) <u>morgen</u> <u>zur Bäckerei</u> (*to the bakery*).   Morgen gehen eine Freundin und ich zur Bäckerei. Zur Bäckerei gehen eine Freundin und ich morgen.

4. <u>Ich</u> bin <u>jetzt</u> (*now*) <u>in Berlin</u>.   Jetzt bin ich in Berlin. In Berlin bin ich jetzt.

3 **Wer hat was?** In pairs, take turns asking and answering questions.

BEISPIEL Professor / Problem (nein / Frage)

S1: *Hat der Professor ein Problem?*
S2: *Nein, er hat eine Frage.*

1. Frau / Blatt Papier (nein / Foto)   Hat die Frau ein Blatt Papier? Nein, sie hat ein Foto.

2. Emil und ich / Bleistifte (ja)   Haben Emil und ich Bleistifte? Ja, ihr habt Bleistifte.

3. Lehrerin / Terminkalender (ja)   Hat die Lehrerin (einen) Terminkalender? Ja, sie hat (einen) Terminkalender.

4. Schüler / Buch (nein / Heft)   Hat der Schüler/Haben die Schüler ein Buch? Nein, er hat/sie haben ein Heft.

4 **Was ist los?** In groups, take turns asking and answering yes-or-no questions about the images.   Answers will vary.

BEISPIEL

S1: *Haben die Schüler Bücher?*
S2: *Ja, sie haben Bücher.*

Numbers  Presentation

Startblock As in English, numbers in German follow patterns. Memorizing the numbers from **1** to **20** will help you learn numbers **21** and above.

Sabite hat **vier** Kurse.

George ist **21** Jahre alt.

- Every number up to one million is written as a single word. Numbers from **13** to **19** follow a pattern similar to English, adding the ending **-zehn** to each single-digit number. Numbers from **21** to **99** repeat this pattern, adding **und** plus the number in the tens place to each single-digit number: [*ones*] + **und** + [*tens*].

25 = **fünf** + **und** + zwanzig ▶ **fünfund**zwanzig

numbers 0–99

0	null	10	zehn	20	zwanzig	30	dreißig
1	eins	11	elf	21	einundzwanzig	31	einunddreißig
2	zwei	12	zwölf	22	zweiundzwanzig	40	vierzig
3	drei	13	dreizehn	23	dreiundzwanzig	45	fünfundvierzig
4	vier	14	vierzehn	24	vierundzwanzig	50	fünfzig
5	fünf	15	fünfzehn	25	fünfundzwanzig	60	sechzig
6	sechs	16	sechzehn	26	sechsundzwanzig	70	siebzig
7	sieben	17	siebzehn	27	siebenundzwanzig	80	achtzig
8	acht	18	achtzehn	28	achtundzwanzig	90	neunzig
9	neun	19	neunzehn	29	neunundzwanzig	99	neunundneunzig

- Note that the **s** in **eins** is dropped at the beginning of a compound word.

41 = eins + vierzig ▶ **ein**undvierzig   **81** = eins + achtzig ▶ **ein**undachtzig

- Likewise, **sechs** and **sieben** are shortened when they precede the letter **z**.

16 = **sech**zehn   **66** = sechsund**sech**zig
17 = **sieb**zehn   **77** = siebenund**sieb**zig

- In German, decimals are indicated by a comma (**Komma**), not a period (**Punkt**). When giving a unit of measurement (length, currency, etc.), say the unit instead of **Komma**. Note that units of currency are usually written after the number.

25,4 = fünfundzwanzig **Komma** vier   **0,5** = null **Komma** fünf
4,99 € = vier **Euro** neunundneunzig   **10,18 m** = zehn **Meter** achtzehn

numbers 100 and higher			
100	(ein)hundert	1.000	(ein)tausend
101	hunderteins	1.300	tausenddreihundert
128	hundertachtundzwanzig	5.000	fünftausend
200	zweihundert	10.000	zehntausend
300	dreihundert	50.000	fünfzigtausend
400	vierhundert	100.000	hunderttausend
500	fünfhundert	460.000	vierhundertsechzigtausend
600	sechshundert	1.000.000	eine Million
700	siebenhundert	1.050.000	eine Million fünfzigtausend
800	achthundert	7.000.000	sieben Millionen
900	neunhundert	1.000.000.000	eine Milliarde

- Note that German uses a period where English typically uses a comma to separate thousands, millions, etc.

2.320.000	1.999,99 €	5.225,00 $
2,320,000	*€1,999.99*	*$5,225.00*

- Numbers in the millions and higher are written as separate words.

2.016.000
zwei Millionen sechzehntausend

1.000.050.000
eine Milliarde fünfzigtausend

Mathematical expressions

- Use these expressions to talk about math.

mathematical expressions					
+	plus	×	mal	=	ist (gleich)
–	minus	÷	geteilt durch	%	Prozent

6 + 7 = 13 ▶ **Sechs plus sieben ist dreizehn.**
Six plus seven is thirteen.

8 – 2 = 6 ▶ **Acht minus zwei ist gleich sechs.**
Eight minus two equals six.

3 · 3 = 9 ▶ **Drei mal drei ist gleich neun.**
Three times three equals nine.

20 : 5 = 4 ▶ **Zwanzig geteilt durch fünf ist vier.**
Twenty divided by five is four.

Suggestion Have students practice reading these numbers aloud.

ACHTUNG

Note that German speakers typically use the symbol · to indicate multiplication and the symbol : to indicate division.

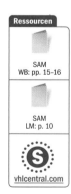

Ressourcen

SAM
WB: pp. 15–16

SAM
LM: p. 10

vhlcentral.com

Jetzt sind Sie dran! Write each number or equation in words.

1. 37
siebenunddreißig

2. 212
zweihundertzwölf

3. 49
neunundvierzig

4. 368
dreihundertachtundsechzig

5. 24
vierundzwanzig

6. 75
fünfundsiebzig

7. 1991
eintausendneunhunderteinundneunzig

8. 587
fünfhundertsiebenundachtzig

9. 16 + 15 = 31
Sechzehn plus fünfzehn ist (gleich) einunddreißig.

10. 97 – 17 = 80
Siebenundneunzig minus siebzehn ist achtzig.

11. 18 : 9 = 2
Achtzehn geteilt durch neun ist zwei.

12. 12 · 3 = 36
Zwölf mal drei ist sechsunddreißig.

Anwendung

1 Expansion Distribute blank Bingo cards and have students fill them in with numbers from 0–30 in random order. Pick numbers from a hat and call them out in German. The first student to get five numbers in a row wins.

1 Zählen Sie Fill in the missing number, then write the number in words.

BEISPIEL 0, 5, 10, _____15_____ , 20; _fünfzehn_

1. 2, 4, __6__, 8, 10; _____sechs_____
2. 0, 10, 20, ____30____, 40; _____dreißig_____
3. 670, 671, 672, 673, ____674____; _____sechshundertvierundsiebzig_____
4. 3.456, 3.457, 3.458, ___3.459___, 3.460; _____dreitausendvierhundertneunundfünfzig_____
5. 35, 40, 45, 50, ___55___; _____fünfundfünfzig_____
6. 1.899.996, 1.899.997, 1.899.998, 1.899.999, ___1.900.000___; _____eine Million neunhunderttausend_____

2 Beschreiben Sie Write how many there are of each item.

▶ **BEISPIEL**

(860) Student
Da sind achthundertsechzig Studenten.

(5.937) Buch
1. _____ Da sind fünftausendneunhundertsiebenunddreißig Bücher.

(16) Mädchen
2. _____ Da sind sechzehn Mädchen.

(217) Tisch
3. _Da sind zweihundertsiebzehn Tische._

(54) Auto
4. _Da sind vierundfünfzig Autos._

(12) Stuhl
5. _Da sind zwölf Stühle._

(4) Studentin
6. _Da sind vier Studentinnen._

3 Expansion Ask students to write out their own equations. Have them take turns reading their equations and figuring out the answers.

3 Matheprofi In pairs, take turns reading the equations out loud.

1. $67 + 4 = 71$
2. $16 + 28 = 44$
3. $91 - 6 = 85$
4. $45 - 7 = 38$
5. $24 : 4 = 6$
6. $989 : 43 = 23$
7. $58 \cdot 2 = 116$
8. $213 \cdot 3 = 639$

1. Siebenundsechzig plus vier ist (gleich) einundsiebzig.
2. Sechzehn plus achtundzwanzig ist (gleich) vierundvierzig.
3. Einundneunzig minus sechs ist (gleich) fünfundachtzig.
4. Fünfundvierzig minus sieben ist (gleich) achtunddreißig.
5. Vierundzwanzig geteilt durch vier ist (gleich) sechs.
6. Neunhundertneunundachtzig geteilt durch dreiundvierzig ist (gleich) dreiundzwanzig.
7. Achtundfünfzig mal zwei ist (gleich) (ein) hundertsechzehn.
8. Zweihundertdreizehn mal drei ist (gleich) sechshundertneununddreißig.

4 Wie viele Einwohner? In pairs, take turns reading the population of each city out loud.

BEISPIEL München: 1.330.440

München hat eine Million dreihundertdreißigtausendvierhundertvierzig Einwohner (inhabitants).

1. Berlin: 3.450.889   Berlin hat drei Millionen vierhundertfünfzigtausendachthundertneunundachtzig Einwohner.
2. Gelsenkirchen: 259.744   Gelsenkirchen hat zweihundertneunundfünfzigtausendsiebenhundertvierundvierzig Einwohner.
3. Hamburg: 1.783.975   Hamburg hat eine Million siebenhundertdreiundachtzigtausendneunhundertfünfundsiebzig Einwohner.
4. Dresden: 532.058   Dresden hat fünfhundertzweiunddreißigtausendachtundfünfzig Einwohner.
5. Stuttgart: 601.646   Stuttgart hat sechshunderteintausendsechshundertsechsundvierzig Einwohner.

Kommunikation

 5 **Wie viele?** In pairs, take inventory of these office supplies.

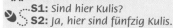 **BEISPIEL** Kuli / 50

S1: *Sind hier Kulis?*
S2: *Ja, hier sind fünfzig Kulis.*

1. Buch / 6.663 Hier sind sechstausendsechshundertdreiundsechzig Bücher.
2. Heft / 258 Hier sind zweihundertachtundfünfzig Hefte.
3. Radiergummi / 42 Hier sind zweiundvierzig Radiergummis.
4. Bleistift / 926 Hier sind neunhundertsechsundzwanzig Bleistifte.

5. Uhr / 5 Hier sind fünf Uhren.
6. Karte / 3.170 Hier sind dreitausend(ein)hundertsiebzig Karten.
7. Taschenrechner / 7.153 Hier sind siebentausend(ein)hundertdreiundfünfzig Taschenrechner.
8. Rucksack / 67 Hier sind siebenundsechzig Rucksäcke.

 6 **Wie viel kostet...?** In pairs, take turns asking about and saying the cost of each item. Answers will vary.

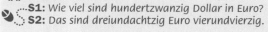 **BEISPIEL**

S1: Wie viel (*How much*) kostet ein Computer?
S2: Er kostet eintausenddreihundertvierundzwanzig Euro siebzehn.

Auto	Apfel
Haus	Blume
Tisch	Kuchen
Computer	Stuhl

 7 **Wie viel ist...?** In pairs, discuss these exchange rates.

 BEISPIEL $120 = 83,44 €

S1: *Wie viel sind hundertzwanzig Dollar in Euro?*
S2: *Das sind dreiundachtzig Euro vierundvierzig.*

1. $450 = 312,70 €
2. $573 = 452,08 CHF (Schweizer Franken)
3. 781,45 € = 86.074,17 ¥ (Yen)
4. $1.628,50 = £985,88 (Pfund Sterling)

5. 3.816 € = £3.321,67
6. 6.487,15 CHF = $8.222,89
7. $14.005,90 = 9.733,30 €
8. £251.029 = $414.884,04

8 **Ich habe mehr!** In small groups, take turns exaggerating the number of items you have at home.

BEISPIEL

S1: *Ich habe sieben Handys (cellphones).*
S2: *Ich habe dreihundertfünfundneunzig Taschenrechner!*
S3: *OK, aber (but) ich habe neuntausendvierundzwanzig Stifte!*

1.253.687

6 **Suggestion** Bring in price listings from German-language web sites and have students read the prices aloud.

7 **Answers**
1. vierhundertfünfzig Dollar/ dreihundertzwölf Euro siebzig.
2. fünfhundertdreiundsiebzig Dollar/ vierhundertzweiundfünfzig Schweizer Franken acht.
3. siebenhunderteinundachtzig Euro fünfundvierzig/sechsundachtzigtausendvierundsiebzig Yen siebzehn.
4. eintausendsechshundertachtundzwanzig Dollar fünfzig/neunhundertfünfundachtzig Pfund Sterling achtundachtzig.
5. dreitausendachthundertsechzehn Euro/dreitausenddreihunderteinundzwanzig Pfund Sterling siebenundsechzig.
6. sechstausendvierhundertsiebenundachtzig Schweizer Franken fünfzehn/achttausendzweihundertzweiundzwanzig Dollar neunundachtzig.
7. vierzehntausendfünf Dollar neunzig/neuntausendsiebenhundertdreiunddreißig Euro dreißig.
8. zweihunderteinundfünfzigtausendneunundzwanzig Pfund Sterling/vierhundertvierzehntausendachthundertvierundachtzig Dollar vier.

8 **Expansion** Ask each student to make a list of items and quantities before beginning this activity. (Ex: **7 Handys, 86 Rucksäcke, 98 Taschenrechner**....) As they do the activity, have students write down the numbers they hear and then compare with what their partner actually said.

Wiederholung

1 Fragespiel

Fragespiel In pairs, play **20 Fragen** using the lesson vocabulary. Choose a person or object in the classroom. Your partner will ask yes-or-no questions to figure out the word you've chosen. Answers will vary.

1 Suggestion Help students to select vocabulary that they can ask questions about. Circulate around the room to ensure that everyone is forming appropriate questions.

BEISPIEL

S1: Bist du eine Sache?
S2: Nein.
S1: Bist du eine Person?
S2: Ja.
S1: Hast du einen Schreibtisch?
S2: Ja.
S1: Bist du ein Lehrer?
S2: Genau (*Exactly*)!

2 Mathespaß

Mathespaß Write two numbers between 1 and 100 on separate index cards. Then, in small groups, make a pile of everyone's cards, shuffle, and take turns drawing two cards from the pile. The person who draws must create a math problem using the numbers. The first person to answer the math problem correctly draws next. Answers will vary.

2 Expansion Have the whole class play this game, as a group or in teams.

BEISPIEL

S1: (*draws 55 and 5*) Fünfundfünfzig geteilt durch fünf.
S2: Fünfundfünfzig geteilt durch fünf ist elf.

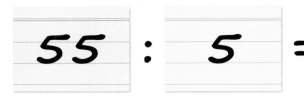

3 Ratespiel

Ratespiel In small groups, collect the items listed. One student leaves the group while the others distribute the items among themselves. The student then returns and tries to guess who has each item. Answers will vary.

3 Suggestion Remind students to pay attention to articles when using nouns in the accusative case.

BEISPIEL

S1: Hast du den Radiergummi?
S2: Nein.
S1: Hat Megan den Radiergummi?
S2: Nein, Simon hat den Radiergummi.

der Bleistift	der Radiergummi
das Buch	der Rucksack
das Heft	der Taschenrechner
der Kuli	die Uhr

4 Im Schreibwarenladen

Im Schreibwarenladen In groups of three, make a shopping list of school supplies. Then, role-play a trip to the store to buy the items you need. Present your scene to the class. Answers will vary.

BEISPIEL

S1: Guten Tag.
S2: Guten Tag. Wir brauchen (*need*) zwei Hefte und einen Bleistift, bitte.
S3: Wie viel (*How much*) kosten die Hefte?
S1: Sie kosten fünf Euro neunzig.

5 Sieben Unterschiede

Sieben Unterschiede Your instructor will give you and your partner worksheets with different pictures of a classroom. Do not look at each other's pictures. Ask and answer questions to identify seven differences (**Unterschiede**) between the two pictures. Answers will vary.

BEISPIEL

S1: Ich habe einen Computer. Hast du auch einen Computer?
S2: Nein. Ich habe einen Papierkorb. Hast du auch einen Papierkorb?
S1: Ich habe zwei Papierkörbe. Hast du fünf Schülerinnen?

6 Leiterspiel

Leiterspiel Your instructor will give you a game board. Play **Leiterspiel** (*Snakes and Ladders*) with your partners. Count the spaces aloud in German as you play.

7 **Interview** Interview as many classmates as possible to find out if these statements (Behauptung) apply to them. Write down their names.

S1: *Hallo! Hast du eine Katze?*
S2: *Ja, ich habe eine Katze./*
Nein, aber ich habe einen Hund.

Behauptung	Name
1. Ich habe eine Katze (*cat*).	Alexia
2. Ich bin 21 Jahre alt.	Markus
3. Ich habe ein Auto.	
4. Ich bin aus (*from*) New York.	
5. Ich bin im Dezember geboren (*was born*).	
6. Ich bin müde (*tired*).	
7. Ich habe ein Heft.	
8. Ich habe viele Hausaufgaben.	

8

Strategien

Throughout this text, you will be encouraged to keep a personalized dictionary, **Mein** (*My*) **Wörterbuch**. This is a place for you to record German words and expressions, together with cues that will help you remember their meanings and use them correctly. By associating words with images, examples of usage (**Gebrauch**) in context, synonyms (**Synonyme**), and antonyms (**Antonyme**), you will create entries that are relevant to you, and you will be better able to retain these new words.

Your personalized dictionary is also a convenient place to make a note of gender and plural forms. As your vocabulary expands, your personalized dictionary will become a meaningful record of your progress in learning German.

Mein Wör|ter|buch

Add five words to your personalized dictionary related to the themes **Begrüßung und Abschied** and **In der Schule**.

die Weißwandtafel, -n

Übersetzung (*translation*)
whiteboard

Wortart (*part of speech*)
ein Substantiv

Gebrauch
Der Professor schreibt an (writes on) die Weißwandtafel.

Synonyme
die Tafel, -n

Antonyme
——

Panorama 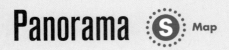 Map

Die deutschsprachige Welt°

Länder° mit Deutsch als Amtssprache°

▶ Belgien
▶ Deutschland
▶ Italien (Region: Südtirol)
▶ Liechtenstein
▶ Luxemburg
▶ Österreich
▶ die Schweiz

Bevölkerung°

▶ **Belgien:** *10,8 Millionen Einwohner° (78.000 deutsche Muttersprachler°)*
▶ **Deutschland:** *81,8 Millionen Einwohner*
▶ **Italien:** *60,6 Millionen Einwohner (336.000 deutsche Muttersprachler)*
▶ **Liechtenstein:** *36.400 Einwohner*
▶ **Luxemburg:** *500.000 Einwohner (474.000 deutsche Muttersprachler)*
▶ **Österreich:** *8,2 Millionen Einwohner*
▶ **die Schweiz:** *7,8 Millionen Einwohner (4,9 Millionen deutsche Muttersprachler)*

QUELLE: das Haus der deutschen Sprache

Hauptstädte°

▶ **Belgien:** *Brüssel*
▶ **Deutschland:** *Berlin*
▶ **Liechtenstein:** *Vaduz*
▶ **Luxemburg:** *Luxemburg*
▶ **Österreich:** *Wien*
▶ **die Schweiz:** *Bern*
▶ **Südtirol (Italien):** *Bozen*

deutschsprachige Welt *German-speaking world* **Länder** *countries*
Amtssprache *official language* **Bevölkerung** *population*
Einwohner *inhabitants* **Muttersprachler** *native speakers*
Hauptstädte *capitals* **Sprachen** *languages* **Circa** *Approximately*
leben *live* **mindestens** *at least*

Wien, Österreichs Hauptstadt

Bern, Hauptstadt der Schweiz

— Landesgrenzen
● Stadt
◎ Landeshauptstadt
✪ Hauptstadt

Unglaublich, aber wahr!

Belgien hat drei offizielle Sprachen°: Französisch, Niederländisch und Deutsch. Die deutschsprachige Region ist im Osten Belgiens. Circa° 75.000 Menschen leben° hier. Viele Belgier sprechen mindestens° zwei Sprachen.

Österreich

Die Alpen

Die Alpen sind das höchste Gebirge° in Europa. Es ist circa 1.200 Kilometer lang, und 29% der Fläche° ist in Österreich. Deshalb heißt Österreich auch die „Alpenrepublik". In Österreich leben circa 4 Millionen Menschen° in den Alpen. Das sind 50% aller Österreicher. Der höchste Berg° in Österreich ist der Großglockner. Er ist 3.798 Meter hoch.

Die Schweiz

Schokolade

Die Schweiz ist bekannt für Banken, Uhren, Messer° und natürlich° Schokolade. Die bekanntesten Schokoladenfirmen sind Lindt, Tobler, Sprüngli und Suchard. Suchard produziert Milka Schokolade. Vor allem die Schweizer essen Schokolade gern°. Pro Jahr isst° jeder Schweizer 11,7 Kilogramm Schokolade. Niemand° auf der Welt isst mehr Schokolade als° die Schweizer. In Deutschland isst man 11,4 Kilogramm Schokolade pro Person, in Österreich 7,9, und in den USA nur 5,2 Kilogramm.

Geschichte

Die Hanse Point out that the **Hanse** was the precursor to the European Union and one of the first international trade unions.

Die Hanse

Die Deutsche Hanse ist eine Union von Kaufleuten°. Sie existiert zwischen Mitte des 12. Jahrhunderts° und Mitte des 17. Jahrhunderts. Bis zu 200 Städte im nördlichen Europa sind in der Union, wie zum Beispiel Zuidersee (heutiges° Holland), Hamburg, Bremen und Lübeck (heutiges Deutschland), Stockholm (heutiges Schweden), Danzig (heutiges Polen) und Riga (heutiges Lettland). Diese Städte liegen° vor allem an der Nordsee und der Ostsee°.

Deutschland

Die Berliner Mauer°

Die Berliner Mauer
Tell students that *3,40 Meter* is read out loud as **drei Meter vierzig**.

Vom 13. August 1961 bis 9. November 1989 ist die Berliner Mauer eine Grenze° zwischen° Ost- und Westdeutschland. Die Mauer umgibt° ganz Westberlin und kreiert eine Insel°. Sie ist das Symbol des Kalten Krieges°. Die Mauer ist 167,8 Kilometer lang. Sie ist zwischen 3,40 Meter und 4,20 Meter hoch. Rund um Westberlin stehen 302 Beobachtungstürme°.

IM INTERNET

1. Machen Sie eine Liste mit den wichtigsten (*most important*) Städten in Deutschland, Österreich und der Schweiz.

2. Der 9. November 1989 ist das Ende der Berliner Mauer. Suchen Sie (*Look for*) Informationen über diesen Tag.

For more information on this **Panorama**, go to **vhlcentral.com**.

---

höchste Gebirge *highest mountain range* **Fläche** *area* **Menschen** *people* **Berg** *mountain* **Mauer** *Wall* **Grenze** *border* **zwischen** *between* **umgibt** *surrounds* **kreiert eine Insel** *creates an island* **des Kalten Krieges** *of the Cold War* **Beobachtungstürme** *watchtowers* **Messer** *knives* **natürlich** *of course* **essen... gern** *like to eat* **isst** *eats* **Niemand** *Nobody* **mehr... als** *more... than* **von Kaufleuten** *of merchants* **des 12. Jahrhunderts** *of the 12th century* **heutiges** *present-day* **liegen** *are located* **Ostsee** *Baltic Sea*
Die Berliner Mauer Tell students that the dates **13. August** and **9. November** are read out loud as **der dreizehnte August** and **der neunte November**. Explain that students will learn more about reading and writing dates in **2A.3**.

Was haben Sie gelernt? Complete the statements.

1. Belgien hat ____drei____ offizielle Sprachen.

2. Die deutschsprachige Region ist im ____Osten____ Belgiens.

3. Ein anderer (*other*) Name für Österreich ist die ___Alpenrepublik___

4. Der ___Großglockner___ ist der höchste Berg in Österreich.

5. Die Berliner Mauer existiert von 1961 bis ____1989____.

6. Die Berliner Mauer ist 167,8 ___Kilometer___ lang.

7. Die Schweizer Firma Suchard produziert ___Milka___ Schokolade.

8. Jeder ___Schweizer___ isst 11,7 Kilogramm Schokolade pro Jahr.

9. Die Hanse existiert im ___nördlichen___ Europa.

10. Bis zu ___200___ Städte sind in der Hanse.

Practice more at **vhlcentral.com**.

Lesen  **Reading: Audio**

Vor dem Lesen

Strategien

Recognizing cognates

Cognates are words in two or more languages that are similar in meaning and in spelling. Look for cognates to increase your comprehension when you read in German. However, watch out for false cognates. For example, you've already learned that in German, **Note** means *grade*, not *note*. Likewise, **bald** means *soon*, not *bald*, and **fast** means *almost*, not *fast*. Can you guess the meaning of these German words?

das Café	das Programm
der Doktor	das Restaurant
das Hotel	der Sommer
der Juli	das Telefon
das Museum	das Theater

Untersuchen Sie den Text

Look at this text. What kind of information does it present? Where do you usually find such information? Can you guess what this is?

Suchen Sie verwandte Wörter

Read the list of cognates in **Strategien** again. How many of them can you find in the reading? Do you see any additional cognates? Can you guess their English equivalents?

Raten Sie die Bedeutung

Besides using cognates and words you already know, you can also use context to guess the meaning of unfamiliar words. Find the following words in the reading and try to figure out what they mean. Compare your answers with a classmate's.

ägyptisch	Platz
Abakus	Straße

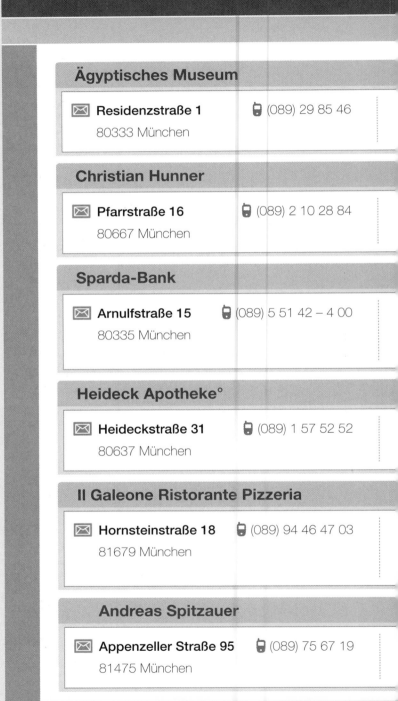

Adressbuch

Ägyptisches Museum

✉ **Residenzstraße 1**
80333 München
📱 (089) 29 85 46

Christian Hunner

✉ **Pfarrstraße 16**
80667 München
📱 (089) 2 10 28 84

Sparda-Bank

✉ **Arnulfstraße 15**
80335 München
📱 (089) 5 51 42 – 4 00

Heideck Apotheke°

✉ **Heideckstraße 31**
80637 München
📱 (089) 1 57 52 52

Il Galeone Ristorante Pizzeria

✉ **Hornsteinstraße 18**
81679 München
📱 (089) 94 46 47 03

Andreas Spitzauer

✉ **Appenzeller Straße 95**
81475 München
📱 (089) 75 67 19

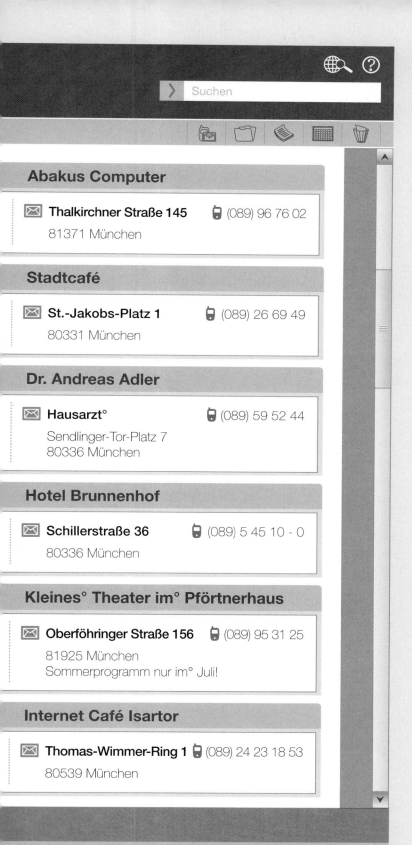

Abakus Computer

✉ **Thalkirchner Straße 145** 📱 (089) 96 76 02
81371 München

Stadtcafé

✉ **St.-Jakobs-Platz 1** 📱 (089) 26 69 49
80331 München

Dr. Andreas Adler

✉ **Hausarzt°** 📱 (089) 59 52 44
Sendlinger-Tor-Platz 7
80336 München

Hotel Brunnenhof

✉ **Schillerstraße 36** 📱 (089) 5 45 10 - 0
80336 München

Kleines° Theater im° Pförtnerhaus

✉ **Oberföhringer Straße 156** 📱 (089) 95 31 25
81925 München
Sommerprogramm nur im° Juli!

Internet Café Isartor

✉ **Thomas-Wimmer-Ring 1** 📱 (089) 24 23 18 53
80539 München

Nach dem Lesen

Wohin gehen sie? Say where each of these people should go, based on the clues.

> **BEISPIEL** Lena loves to eat pasta but hates to cook.
> *Il Galeone Ristorante Pizzeria*

1. Frau Scholz needs to reserve some hotel rooms.
   Hotel Brunnenhof

2. Christiane's computer is broken.
   Abakus Computer

3. Herr Meier thinks he has the flu.
   Dr. Adler

4. Nina would like to see some ancient Egyptian art.
   Ägyptisches Museum

5. Herr and Frau Hansel want to go somewhere for coffee or tea.
   Stadtcafé

6. Andrea is meeting some friends for Italian food.
   Il Galeone Ristorante Pizzeria

7. Frau Müller needs to buy some aspirin for her daughter.
   Heideck Apotheke

8. Thomas wants to take his girlfriend to a play.
   Kleines Theater im Pförtnerhaus

9. Herr Trüb needs to deposit his paycheck.
   Sparda-Bank

10. Sebastian's computer is broken, but he needs to send an e-mail.
    Internet Café Isartor

Unsere Einträge In pairs, select three listings from the reading and use them as models to create similar listings in German that advertise places or services in your area.

> **BEISPIEL**
>
> *Stonydale Bank*
> *Hunter Straße 206*
> *50555 Stonydale*
> *Tel. (555) 337-0665*

Apotheke *pharmacy* **Hausarzt** *family physician* **Kleines** *Small* **im** *in (the)* **nur im** *only in (the)*

Hören

Listening for words you know

You can get the gist of a conversation by listening for words and phrases you already know.

 To help you practice this strategy, listen to these statements and make a list of the words you have already learned.

_____ _____

_____ _____

Vorbereitung

Where are the people in the photograph? What are they doing? Do you think they know each other? Why or why not? What do you think they are talking about?

Zuhören

As you listen, check the words you associate with Tanja and those you associate with Rainer.

Tanja

✓ der Taschenrechner

___ der Computer

✓ das Blatt Papier

✓ zwei Bleistifte

___ die Prüfung

Rainer

___ der Radiergummi

✓ die Hausaufgaben

___ das Heft

✓ das Problem

___ die Karte

Verständnis

 Richtig oder falsch? Based on the conversation you heard, indicate whether each statement is **richtig** or **falsch**.

1. Rainer ist Deutschprofessor.
   Falsch.
   _____

2. Tanja geht es gut.
   Richtig.
   _____

3. Rainer braucht (*needs*) einen Taschenrechner.
   Richtig.
   _____

4. Tanja hat ein Problem mit den Hausaufgaben.
   Falsch.
   _____

5. Rainer hat einen Bleistift für Tanja.
   Falsch.
   _____

6. Tanja hat ein Blatt Papier für Rainer.
   Richtig.
   _____

7. Tanja hat zwei Bleistifte.
   Richtig.
   _____

8. Rainer hilft (*helps*) Tanja bei den Hausaufgaben.
   Falsch.
   _____

 Stellen Sie sich vor Introduce yourself in German to a classmate you do not know well.

- Greet your partner.
- Ask his or her name.
- Ask how he or she is doing.
- Introduce your partner to another student.
- Say good-bye.

Suggestion Students often gravitate towards other students they already know. Make sure to direct students to new partners.

Schreiben

Strategien

Writing in German

Writing can take many forms and serve many functions. You might write an e-mail to get in touch with someone, a blog entry to share your feelings or opinions, or an essay to persuade others to accept a point of view. Good writing requires time, thought, effort, and a lot of practice. Here are some tips to help you write more effectively in German.

DO

- Try to write your ideas in German.
- Decide what the purpose of your writing will be.
- Make an outline of your ideas.
- Use the grammar and vocabulary that you know.
- Use your textbook for examples of punctuation, style conventions, and expressions in German.
- Use your imagination and creativity to make your writing interesting.
- Put yourself in your reader's place to determine if your writing is interesting.

DON'T

- Translate your ideas from English to German.
- Simply repeat what is in the textbook or on a Web page.
- Use a bilingual dictionary until you have learned how to use it effectively.
- Use an online translator.

Strategien Emphasize the importance of outlining ideas in German, instead of translating from English. Encourage students to use the vocabulary and grammar they already know to complete this **Thema**.

Thema

 Machen Sie eine Liste

A group of German-speaking students will be spending a year at your school. Put together a list of people and places that might be useful or interesting to them. Your list should include:

- Your name, address, phone number(s), and e-mail address
- The names of two or three other students in your German class, their addresses, phone numbers, and e-mail addresses
- Your German instructor's name, office phone number, and e-mail address
- The names, addresses, and phone numbers of three places near your school where students like to go (a bookstore, a café or restaurant, a movie theater, etc.)

NAME: Prof. Reinhard (Deutschprofessor)
ADRESSE: Stonydale University
TELEFONNUMMER: (555) 654-3458 (Büro)
HANDY: (555) 919-0040
E-MAIL-ADRESSE: prof.reinhard@stonydale.edu
NOTIZEN: Ist aus Hamburg

NAME: Zest Coffee House
ADRESSE: 8970 McNeil Road
TELEFONNUMMER: (555) 654-0349
HANDY: —
E-MAIL-ADRESSE: info@zest.com
NOTIZEN: Hat sehr guten Kaffee und gute Musik

 **Flashcards**
Audio: Vocabulary

Begrüßung und Abschied

Hallo./Guten Tag.	Hello.
Guten Morgen.	Good morning.
Guten Abend.	Good evening.
Gute Nacht.	Good night.
Bis bald./Bis gleich.	See you soon.
Bis dann./ Bis später.	See you later.
Bis morgen.	See you tomorrow.
Auf Wiedersehen.	Good-bye.
Schönen Tag noch!	Have a nice day!
Tschüss.	Bye.
Alles klar?	Is everything OK?
Wie geht's (dir)?	How are you? (inf.)
Wie geht es Ihnen?	How are you? (form.)
Prima.	Great.
Sehr gut.	Very well.
Ziemlich gut.	Fine.
Und dir/Ihnen?	And you?
Mir auch.	Me, too.
So lala.	So-so.
(Nicht) schlecht.	(Not) bad.
Mir geht's (sehr) gut.	I'm (very) well.
Mir geht's nicht (so) gut.	I'm not (so) well.

Höflichkeiten

Danke.	Thank you.
Vielen Dank.	Thank you very much.
Bitte.	Please./ You're welcome.
Gern geschehen.	My pleasure.
Entschuldigung.	Excuse me.
Entschuldigen Sie.	Excuse me. (form.)
Es tut mir leid.	I'm sorry.

Orte

die Schule, -n	school
die Universität, -en	university, college
die Bibliothek, -en	library
die Mensa, Mensen	(college/university) cafeteria
wo?	where?
hier	here
da / dort	there
ja	yes
nein	no

im Unterricht

das Blatt Papier, (pl. Blätter Papier)	sheet of paper
der Bleistift, -e	pencil
das Buch, -̈er	book
der Computer, -	computer
das Ergebnis, -se	result; score
das Fenster, -	window
das Foto, -s	photo
die Frage, -n	question
die Hausaufgabe, -n	homework
das Heft, -e	notebook
die Karte, -n	map
die Klasse, -n	class
das Klassenzimmer, -	classroom
der Kuli, -s	ball-point pen
das Lehrbuch, -̈er	(college/university) textbook
die Note, -n	grade (on an assignment)
die Notiz, -en	note
der Papierkorb, -̈e	wastebasket
das Problem, -e	problem
die Prüfung, -en	test; exam
der Radiergummi, -s	eraser
der Rucksack, -̈e	backpack
der Schreibtisch, -e	desk
die Sache, -n	thing
das Schulbuch, -̈er	(K–12) textbook
der Stift, -e	pen
der Stuhl, -̈e	chair
die Stunde, -n	lesson
die Tafel, -n	(black)board
der Taschenrechner, -	calculator
der Terminkalender, -	personal planner
der Tisch, -e	table; desk
die Tür, -en	door
die Uhr, -en	clock
das Wörterbuch, -̈er	dictionary
das Zeugnis, -se	report card; grade report
Da ist/sind...	There is/are...
Ist/Sind hier...?	Is/Are there... here?
Hier ist/sind...	Here is/are...
Was ist das?	What is that?

sich vorstellen

Wie heißt du?	What is your name? (inf.)
Wie heißen Sie?	What is your name? (form.)
Und du/Sie?	And you? (inf./form.)
Das ist.../ Das sind...	This is.../ These are...
Ich heiße...	My name is...
Freut mich./ Angenehm.	Pleased to meet you.
Schön dich/Sie kennen zu lernen.	Nice to meet you. (inf./form.)

Personen

die Frau, -en	woman
der Freund, -e / die Freundin, -nen	friend
der Junge, -n	boy
der Klassenkamerad, -en /die Klassenkameradin, -nen	classmate
der Lehrer, - / die Lehrerin, -nen	teacher
das Mädchen, -	girl
der Mann, -̈er	man
der Professor, -en / die Professorin, -nen	professor
der Schüler, - / die Schülerin, -nen	(K–12) student
der Student, -en / die Studentin, -nen	(college/university) student
Herr	Mr.
Frau	Mrs.; Ms.
Wer ist das?	Who is it?

Subject pronouns	See p. 16.
sein	See p. 17.
Nominative articles	See p. 17.
haben	See p. 30.
Accusative articles	See p. 30.
Numbers and math expressions	See pp. 34–35.

Suggestion Ask students who the people in the photo are, where they are, and what they are doing.

Communicative Goals

You will learn how to:

- talk about classes
- ask questions
- tell time

An der Universität

Talking Picture
Audio: Activities

Suggestion Explain to students that the **Abschlusszeugnis** is a document similar to a transcript, itemizing the course credits required to obtain a degree, including grades and GPA.

die Biologie

die Architektur

Ich studiere Physik (f.) und Chemie (f.).

Was studierst du?

die Kunst

die Mathematik

die Informatik

Ressourcen

SAM WB: pp. 17–18

SAM LM: p. 11

vhlcentral.com

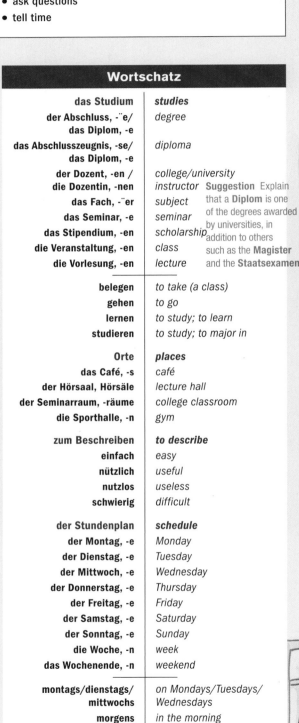

Wortschatz

das Studium	*studies*
der Abschluss, -̈e/ das Diplom, -e	*degree*
das Abschlusszeugnis, -se/ das Diplom, -e	*diploma*
der Dozent, -en / die Dozentin, -nen	*college/university instructor*
das Fach, -̈er	*subject*
das Seminar, -e	*seminar*
das Stipendium, -en	*scholarship*
die Veranstaltung, -en	*class*
die Vorlesung, -en	*lecture*
belegen	*to take (a class)*
gehen	*to go*
lernen	*to study; to learn*
studieren	*to study; to major in*
Orte	*places*
das Café, -s	*café*
der Hörsaal, Hörsäle	*lecture hall*
der Seminarraum, -räume	*college classroom*
die Sporthalle, -n	*gym*
zum Beschreiben	*to describe*
einfach	*easy*
nützlich	*useful*
nutzlos	*useless*
schwierig	*difficult*
der Stundenplan	*schedule*
der Montag, -e	*Monday*
der Dienstag, -e	*Tuesday*
der Mittwoch, -e	*Wednesday*
der Donnerstag, -e	*Thursday*
der Freitag, -e	*Friday*
der Samstag, -e	*Saturday*
der Sonntag, -e	*Sunday*
die Woche, -n	*week*
das Wochenende, -n	*weekend*
montags/dienstags/ mittwochs	*on Mondays/Tuesdays/ Wednesdays*
morgens	*in the morning*
nachmittags	*in the afternoon*
abends	*in the evening*

Suggestion Explain that a **Diplom** is one of the degrees awarded by universities, in addition to others such as the **Magister** and the **Staatsexamen.**

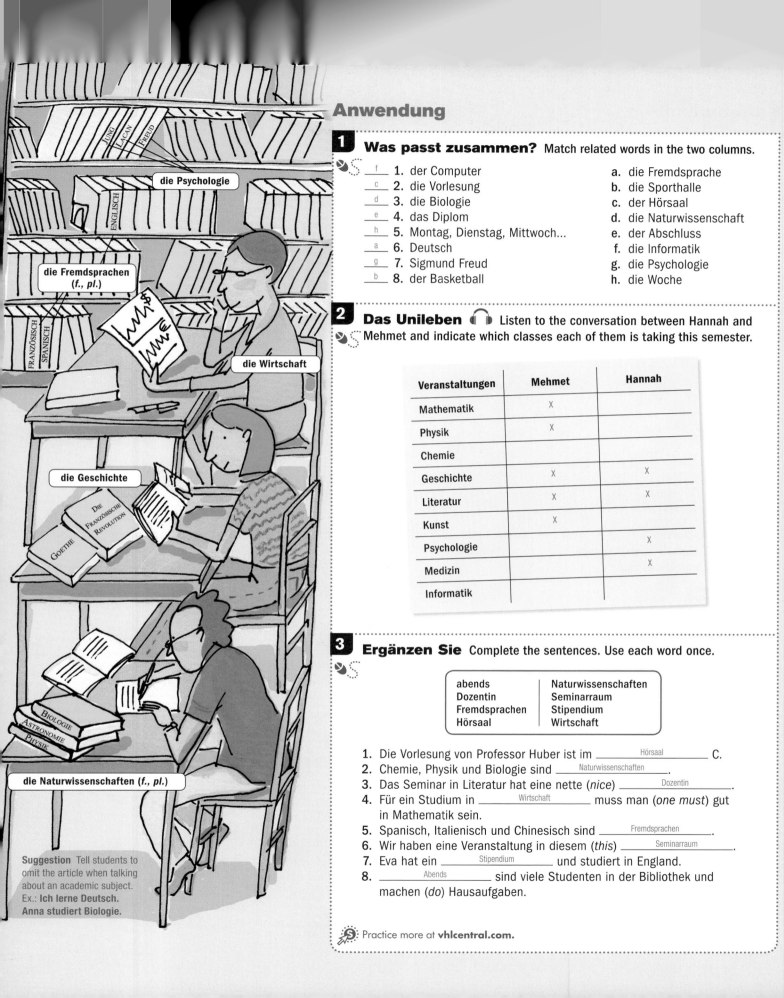

die Psychologie

die Fremdsprachen (f., pl.)

die Wirtschaft

die Geschichte

die Naturwissenschaften (f., pl.)

Suggestion Tell students to omit the article when talking about an academic subject. Ex.: **Ich lerne Deutsch. Anna studiert Biologie.**

Anwendung

1 **Was passt zusammen?** Match related words in the two columns.

_f_ 1. der Computer	a. die Fremdsprache
_c_ 2. die Vorlesung	b. die Sporthalle
_d_ 3. die Biologie	c. der Hörsaal
_e_ 4. das Diplom	d. die Naturwissenschaft
_h_ 5. Montag, Dienstag, Mittwoch...	e. der Abschluss
_a_ 6. Deutsch	f. die Informatik
_g_ 7. Sigmund Freud	g. die Psychologie
_b_ 8. der Basketball	h. die Woche

2 **Das Unileben** 🎧 Listen to the conversation between Hannah and Mehmet and indicate which classes each of them is taking this semester.

Veranstaltungen	Mehmet	Hannah
Mathematik	X	
Physik	X	
Chemie		
Geschichte	X	X
Literatur	X	X
Kunst	X	
Psychologie		X
Medizin		X
Informatik		

3 **Ergänzen Sie** Complete the sentences. Use each word once.

abends	Naturwissenschaften
Dozentin	Seminarraum
Fremdsprachen	Stipendium
Hörsaal	Wirtschaft

1. Die Vorlesung von Professor Huber ist im _____Hörsaal_____ C.
2. Chemie, Physik und Biologie sind _____Naturwissenschaften_____.
3. Das Seminar in Literatur hat eine nette (*nice*) _____Dozentin_____.
4. Für ein Studium in _____Wirtschaft_____ muss man (*one must*) gut in Mathematik sein.
5. Spanisch, Italienisch und Chinesisch sind _____Fremdsprachen_____.
6. Wir haben eine Veranstaltung in diesem (*this*) _____Seminarraum_____.
7. Eva hat ein _____Stipendium_____ und studiert in England.
8. _____Abends_____ sind viele Studenten in der Bibliothek und machen (*do*) Hausaufgaben.

Practice more at **vhlcentral.com**.

Kommunikation

4 Auf dem Campus
Write a caption for each picture. Include one sentence saying what the students are studying and one sentence giving your opinion of the course. In pairs, take turns reading your sentences out of order. Your partner must decide which picture each sentence refers to. Sample answers are provided.

▶ **BEISPIEL** Markus
studiert Informatik.
Informatik ist schwierig.

1. Daniela studiert/belegt Spanisch.
Spanisch ist nützlich.

4 Suggestion Before students do this activity, you may want to have them preview the conjugations of **studieren** and **belegen**. Call on individual students and ask: **Was studierst du?/Was belegst du?**

2. Björn studiert/belegt Psychologie.
Psychologie ist einfach.

3. Anna studiert/belegt Chemie.
Chemie ist nutzlos.

4. Sie (*pl.*) studieren/belegen Architektur.
Architektur ist schwierig.

5 Ihr Studium
Indicate whether each statement is **richtig** or **falsch**, in your opinion. Then, compare your answers with a classmate's. Answers will vary.

BEISPIEL

S1: Chemie ist nützlich. Richtig oder falsch?
S2: Falsch. Chemie ist nutzlos.

	richtig	falsch
1. Mathematik ist schwierig.	☐	☐
2. Fremdsprachen sind einfach.	☐	☐
3. Literatur ist interessant.	☐	☐
4. Ein Abschluss in Psychologie ist nutzlos.	☐	☐
5. Prüfungen in Geschichte sind einfach.	☐	☐

6 Eine Umfrage zum Studium
Your instructor will give you a worksheet. Keep a record of your classmates' answers to share with the class.

BEISPIEL

S1: Ist Mathematik einfach oder (*or*) schwierig?
S2: Mathematik ist schwierig aber (*but*) nützlich.

7 Ein Stundenplan
Your instructor will give you and a partner different worksheets. In pairs, take turns asking each other questions to fill in the missing information on your worksheets.

BEISPIEL

S1: Hat Sarah montags Chemie?
S2: Nein, sie hat mittwochs Chemie.
S1: Hat sie nachmittags Mathematik?
S2: Ja, sie hat nachmittags Mathematik.
S1: Hat sie...?

5 Expansion Read the statements out loud and have students vote on whether each is **richtig** or **falsch**. Then have a class discussion about the results of the poll.

Aussprache und Rechtschreibung

 Audio: Presentation
Record & Compare Activities

🎧 Consonant sounds

The German letter **g** has three different pronunciations. At the end of a syllable or before a **t**, it is pronounced like the *k* in the English word *keep*. In the suffix **-ig**, the **g** is pronounced like the German **ch**. Otherwise, **g** is pronounced like the *g* in the English word *garden*.

Tag	belegt	schwierig	gehen	fragen

The German letter **j** is pronounced very similarly to the letter *y* in the English word *young*. However, in a small number of loanwords from other languages, **j** may be pronounced like the *j* in *job* or the *g* in *mirage*.

jung	Januar	ja	jobben	Journal

The German letter **v** is pronounced like the *f* in the English word *fable*. In a few loanwords from other languages, **v** is pronounced like the *v* in the English word *vase*.

vier	Vorlesung	Vase	Universität	Volleyball

The German letter **w** is pronounced like the *v* in the English word *vote*.

wissen	Mittwoch	Wirtschaft	Wort	Schwester

Although most German consonants sound very similar to their English counterparts, there are five letters that represent different sounds than they do in English: **g**, **j**, **v**, **w**, and initial **c**, which will be discussed in **Vol. 2, 2B**.

Suggestion Tell students that the pronunciation of the final -**ig** sound has several regional variations.

Suggestion Have students look at the sample words and sentences on this page to identify cognates and words they already know. Tell students the meanings of any unfamiliar words or phrases.

1 Sprechen Sie nach Practice saying these words aloud.

1. Garten
2. Essig
3. Weg
4. Jahr
5. Journalist
6. joggen
7. Vater
8. verstehen
9. Violine
10. Wasser
11. zwischen
12. weil

2 Artikulieren Sie Practice saying these sentences aloud.

1. Wir wollen wissen, wie wir das wissen sollen.
2. In vier Wochen wird Veronikas Vater wieder in seiner Villa wohnen.
3. Gestern war Gregors zwanzigster Geburtstag.
4. Jeden Tag soll ich Gemüse und Grünzeug wie Salat essen.
5. Meine Schwester studiert Jura an der Universität Jena.
6. Viele Studenten jobben, um das Studium zu finanzieren.

3 Sprichwörter Practice reading these sayings aloud.

Es ist nicht alles Gold, was glänzt.[1]

Was ich nicht weiß, macht mich nicht heiß.[2]

[1] All that glitters is not gold.

[2] Ignorance is bliss. (lit. *What I don't know, doesn't bother me.*)

Ressourcen

SAM
LM: p. 12

vhlcentral.com

Checkpoint Charlie

 **Video:** *Fotoroman*

George und Hans reden über (*talk about*) das Studium und über Meline und Sabite. Ist Hans in Sabite verliebt (*in love*)?

Vorbereitung Have students look at scene 7 and try to predict what Hans is reacting to. After they have watched the video, have them review their predictions.

1

GEORGE Woher kommst du?
HANS Ich komme aus Straubing. Das ist in Bayern.
GEORGE Wie viele Menschen leben dort?
HANS Hmm... etwa 100.000.

2

HANS Woher kommst du?
GEORGE Milwaukee, Wisconsin.
HANS Wie viel Uhr ist es dort?
GEORGE Wie viel Uhr ist es hier?
HANS Es ist Viertel vor zwei.
GEORGE Der Zeitunterschied ist sieben Stunden. Also Viertel vor sieben morgens.

3

HANS Alles in Ordnung?
GEORGE Ich studiere Architektur, belege Kurse in Städtebau, Physik, Mathematik und Philosophie!

4

HANS Und du belegst einen Deutschkurs, nicht wahr? Studieren ist nicht leicht. George, du bist ein Mitbewohner und Freund. Ich helfe dir.
GEORGE Wann?
HANS Morgens. Um 5.00 Uhr!

5

6

GEORGE Hey! Wir sind da!
HANS Check...
GEORGE ...point Charlie.

GEORGE Sabite kommt aus Prenzlauer Berg. Und Meline?
HANS Was ist mit Meline?
GEORGE Woher kommt sie?
HANS Wien.

ÜBUNGEN

1 **Wer ist das?** Which character does each statement describe: George, Meline, Sabite, or Hans?

1. Er hält ein Referat über Architektur und Kunst. George
2. Sie kommt aus Wien. Meline
3. Er belegt einen Deutschkurs. George
4. Er kommt aus Straubing. Hans
5. Er studiert Architektur. George

6. Er ist Hans' Mitbewohner und Freund. George
7. Sie liest Bücher über Kunst und Mode. Sabite
8. Sie kommt aus Prenzlauer Berg. Sabite
9. Er kommt aus Milwaukee. George
10. Er will George helfen (*wants to help George*). Hans

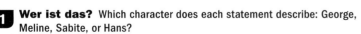

PERSONEN

George   Hans

HANS Sabite ist ganz anders. Sie liest Bücher über Kunst und Mode.
GEORGE Mode ist nutzlos. Ich halte am 20. Oktober ein Referat über Architektur und Kunst in Berlin. Sabite hilft mir.
HANS Was?
GEORGE Sabite studiert Kunst. Ich halte bald das Referat. Sie hilft mir.

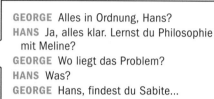

GEORGE Alles in Ordnung, Hans?
HANS Ja, alles klar. Lernst du Philosophie mit Meline?
GEORGE Wo liegt das Problem?
HANS Was?
GEORGE Hans, findest du Sabite...

HANS Sabite ist nur eine Freundin.
GEORGE Okay.
HANS Also, ähm... hat Sabite einen Freund? Nein?
GEORGE Ich glaube nicht, dass sie einen hat.

HANS Du und Sabite, ihr seid nicht...?
GEORGE Nein!
HANS Okay.
GEORGE Okay.

Nützliche Ausdrücke

- **etwa**
  about
- **Wie viel Uhr ist es dort?**
  What time is it there?
- **der Zeitunterschied**
  time difference
- **Und du belegst einen Deutschkurs, nicht wahr?**
  And you're taking a German class, aren't you?
- **Was ist mit Meline?**
  What's with Meline?
- **ein Referat halten**
  to give a presentation
- **Alles klar!**
  All right!
- **Wo liegt das Problem?**
  Where's the problem?
- **Sabite ist nur eine Freundin.**
  Sabite's just a friend.
- **Ich glaube nicht, dass sie einen hat.**
  I don't think she has one.

2A.1
- **Sabite studiert Kunst.**
  Sabite is studying art.

2A.2
- **Woher kommst du?**
  Where are you from?

2A.3
- **Es ist Viertel vor zwei.**
  It's a quarter to two.

---

2 **Zum Besprechen** In this episode, the characters talk about their classes. With a partner, discuss your schedule and course load.
Answers will vary.

3 **Vertiefung** George and Hans visit Checkpoint Charlie on their walk in Berlin. Find out more about this well-known landmark. What is its significance? What streets are nearby? What does "Charlie" refer to?
Sample answers: It was the main crossing point of the Berlin Wall; it is located at the junction of Friedrichstraße, Zimmerstraße, and Mauerstraße; "Charlie" comes from the letter C in the NATO phonetic alphabet.

Ressourcen

SAM VM: p. 3	DVD Folge 3	vhlcentral.com

IM FOKUS

Uni-Zeit, Büffel-Zeit Reading

MOST UNIVERSITIES IN GERMANY are funded by the government. Historically, university education has been free for all students. However, some states have begun charging a tuition fee, usually 500 Euros per semester.

These new fees, along with recent changes to the structure of undergraduate and postgraduate education, have met with resistance from some students. There have been student protests in response to the introduction of tuition fees, as well as issues like overcrowding in lecture halls, and education reform in general. Some students complain that, as a result of the transition from 4- to 6-year **Diplom** and **Magister°** degrees to 3-year **Bachelor** degrees, the original curriculum has simply been compressed into a shorter time frame. Many students also object to the shift toward a heavier workload with more frequent testing.

The unpopularity of these changes may have contributed to an increase in the number of private universities established in Germany. The percentage of students who study at private universities remains very small, but it is gradually increasing. Tuition is quite expensive in comparison to the public university fees, but class size is smaller, and students have more contact with professors. In addition, for people interested in preparing for the international job market, many courses at private universities are offered in English.

Statistische Informationen zum Thema Studium	
Neue Studenten pro Jahr°	ca. 1.000.000
Studenten, die nach dem° Bachelor weiter studieren°	78%
Bachelor-Studenten, die zum Studieren ins Ausland gehen°	15%
Bachelor-Absolventen°, die 1,5 Jahre nach dem Abschluss Arbeit° haben	ca. 97%
Deutsche Studenten, die 2006 in Studentenwohnheimen° wohnen°	ca. 11,3%

QUELLE: Der Tagesspiegel

Uni-Zeit, Büffel-Zeit *University time, cramming time*
Diplom, Magister *degrees available before the education reform* **pro Jahr** *per year* **die nach dem** *who after the* **weiter studieren** *continue their studies* **ins Ausland gehen** *go abroad* **Absolventen** *graduates* **Arbeit** *work* **Studentenwohnheimen** *dormitories* **wohnen** *live*

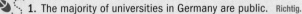

ÜBUNGEN

1 **Richtig oder falsch?** Indicate whether each statement is **richtig** or **falsch**. Then, in pairs, correct the false statements.

1. The majority of universities in Germany are public. Richtig.

2. German universities have always charged tuition fees.
   Falsch. Historically, German universities have not charged tuition fees.
3. Students in Germany have accepted reforms in education wholeheartedly.
   Falsch. There have been protests.
4. It takes more time to earn a **Bachelor**'s degree than it did to earn the **Magister** or the **Diplom**. Falsch. It takes less time.
5. Students now have a lighter workload with fewer tests.
   Falsch. There has been a shift toward a heavier workload with more frequent tests.

6. A small percentage of students study at private universities. Richtig.

7. Private and public universities charge the same tuition fees.
   Falsch. Tuition is higher at private universities.
8. The majority of German students leave school after completing their Bachelor degree. Falsch. The majority of students continue their studies.

9. Most German students study abroad. Falsch. 15% go abroad.

10. In Germany, most students live in dormitories. Falsch. 11.3% live in dormitories.

Practice more at **vhlcentral.com.**

DEUTSCH IM ALLTAG

Die Uni

der Besserwisser, -	know-it-all
der Mitbewohner, - / die Mitbewohnerin, -nen	roommate
das Referat, -e	presentation
das Schwarze Brett	bulletin board
das Studentenwohnheim, -e	dormitory
die Studiengebühr, -en	tuition fee
büffeln	to cram (for a test)

DIE DEUTSCHSPRACHIGE WELT

Der Bologna-Prozess

Bologna, 1999: Bildungsminister° aus der Europäischen Union kommen in Bologna in Italien zusammen°: Wie soll Bildung° in Europa aussehen°? Die Bildungssysteme von Land zu Land sind zu verschieden°. Sie brauchen° international einheitliche° Abschlüsse. Das Resultat ist die Bologna-Erklärung°; 29 Länder unterschreiben° sie. In Europa müssen° Universitäten die Hochschulbildung° standardisieren. Für Deutschland bedeutet° das: Bachelor- und Master-Abschlüsse ersetzen° die Abschlüsse Magister und Diplom.

Bildungsminister *secretaries of education* **zusammen** *together* **Bildung** *education* **soll... aussehen** *should look like* **zu verschieden** *too different* **brauchen** *need* **einheitliche** *standardized* **Erklärung** *declaration* **unterschreiben** *sign* **müssen** *must* **Hochschulbildung** *higher education* **bedeutet** *means* **ersetzen** *replace*

PORTRÄT

Uni Basel

Suggestion Tell students that Paracelsus is famous for his statement: "**Alle Ding' sind Gift, und nichts ohn' Gift; allein die Dosis macht, daß ein Ding kein Gift ist.**" This is often paraphrased in English as "The dose makes the poison", a central principle of toxicology.

Universität Basel (gegründet° 1460): Viele brillante Wissenschaftler° belegen hier Vorlesungen und machen ihren° Abschluss in Medizin, Philosophie oder Psychologie. Der exzentrische Paracelsus (1493–1541) ist hier Professor für Medizin. Auch Holbein (1497–1543), Jung (1875–1961) und Hesse (1877–1962) leben° in Basel. Aber der berühmteste° Professor hier ist der Philosoph Friedrich Nietzsche (1844–1900).

Heute ist die Universität in Basel voller Leben° und sehr modern. 12.000 Studenten sind hier, viele studieren Biowissenschaften°. Andere° lernen Literatur, Wirtschaft oder Mathematik – für 700 Schweizer Franken im Semester.

gegründet *founded* **Wissenschaftler** *scientists* **machen ihren** *make their* **leben** *live* **berühmteste** *most famous* **voller Leben** *bustling life* **Biowissenschaften** *life sciences* **Andere** *Others*

IM INTERNET

Österreichische Universitäten. Wie ist das Studium in Österreich? Ist es mit dem (*with the*) deutschem System vergleichbar (*comparable*)?

For more information on this **Kultur**, go to **vhlcentral.com**.

Expansion Have students search online for more information about the people mentioned in this article, as well as other famous intellectuals from Basel. Have them share their findings with the class.

---

2 **Ergänzen Sie** Ergänzen Sie die Sätze.

1. Nach der Bologna-Erklärung müssen viele Länder in Europa ihre (*their*) Hochschulbildung ___standardisieren___.

2. Der Bachelor und der Master sind zwei neue ___Abschlüsse___ an deutschen Universitäten.

3. Heute lernen Studenten in Basel ___Biowissenschaften___, Literatur, Wirtschaft oder Mathematik.

4. Der berühmteste Professor der Universität Basel ist ___(Friedrich) Nietzsche___.

3 **Studentenleben hier und da** In pairs, discuss the similarities and differences between student life in German-speaking countries and in the United States. Would you like to study in a German-speaking country? Which system do you think is best? Give reasons for your answers.

Answers will vary.

3 **Suggestion** Ask students what they like and dislike about their college experience. Is tuition too high? Is the workload too heavy? Can they imagine studying the same amount of material in three years?

Ressourcen

vhlcentral.com

Regular verbs  Presentation

Startblock Most German verbs follow predictable conjugation patterns in which a set of endings is added to the verb stem.

Ich **studiere** Architektur.

Lernst du Philosophie mit Meline?

QUERVERWEIS

In **Kapitel 1**, you learned the irregular verbs **sein** and **haben**. You will learn more about irregular verbs in **2B.1**.

ACHTUNG

Depending on the context, **sie studiert** can be translated as *she studies*, *she is studying*, or *she does study*.

- To form the present tense of a regular verb, drop the **-en** or **-n** ending from the infinitive and add **-e**, **-st**, **-t**, or **-en/-n** to the stem.

	studieren (*to study*)		wandern (*to hike*)	
ich	studiere	*I study*	wandere	*I hike*
du	studierst	*you study*	wanderst	*you hike*
Sie	studieren	*you study*	wandern	*you hike*
er/sie/es	studiert	*he/she studies*	wandert	*he/she hikes*
wir	studieren	*we study*	wandern	*we hike*
ihr	studiert	*you study*	wandert	*you hike*
Sie	studieren	*you study*	wandern	*you hike*
sie	studieren	*they study*	wandern	*they hike*

Studierst du Physik?
Are you studying physics?

Sie wandern im Sommer.
They go hiking in the summer.

- Regular verbs whose stems end in **-d** or **-t** add an **e** before the endings **-st** or **-t** for ease of pronunciation.

arbeiten (*to work*)			
ich arbeite	*I work*	wir arbeiten	*we work*
du arbeitest	*you work*	ihr arbeitet	*you work*
Sie arbeiten	*you work*	Sie arbeiten	*you work*
er/sie/es arbeitet	*he/she/it works*	sie arbeiten	*they work*

Suggestion Tell students that infinitives consist of a stem and an ending. Reinforce this idea by writing infinitives on the board and modeling the conjugation patterns. Ask students to identify the stem of each verb.

QUERVERWEIS

As in English, the simple present can sometimes be used to talk about a future action. You will learn more about this usage in **2B.2**.

Lena **arbeitet** in der Bibliothek.
*Lena **works** in the library.*

Findest du Mathematik interessant?
Do you find math interesting?

Wartet ihr auf eure Freunde?
*Are you **waiting** for your friends?*

Diese Zeitschrift **kostet** zu viel.
*That magazine **costs** too much.*

- Verbs whose stems end in **-gn** or **-fn** also add an **-e** before the endings **-st** and **-t**.

Es regnet morgen.
It's going to rain tomorrow.

Öffnest du das Fenster?
Are you opening the window?

- If a verb stem ends in **-s**, **-ß**, **-x**, or **-z**, the **-s** is dropped from the second person singular ending.

heißen (*to be named*)			
ich heiße	*I am named*	wir heißen	*we are named*
du heißt	*you are named*	ihr heißt	*you are named*
Sie heißen	*you are named*	Sie heißen	*you are named*
er/sie/es heißt	*he/she/it is named*	sie heißen	*they are named*

Du heißt Jonas, nicht wahr?
Your name is Jonas, right?

Mein Hund **heißt** Fritz.
My dog's name is Fritz.

Martin **reist** oft in die Schweiz.
Martin often travels to Switzerland.

Ihr **grüßt** den Professor nicht?
You're not going to greet the professor?

common regular verbs (present tense)			
antworten	*to answer*	lernen	*to learn; to study*
bauen	*to build*	lieben	*to love*
bedeuten	*to mean*	machen	*to do; to make*
begrüßen	*to greet*	meinen	*to mean; to think*
belegen	*to take (a class)*	öffnen	*to open*
brauchen	*to need*	regnen	*to rain*
bringen	*to bring*	reisen	*to travel*
finden	*to find*	sagen	*to say*
fragen	*to ask*	spielen	*to play*
gehen	*to go*	suchen	*to look for*
hören	*to hear; to listen to*	träumen	*to dream*
kaufen	*to buy*	verstehen	*to understand*
kommen	*to come*	warten	*to wait*
korrigieren	*to correct*	wiederholen	*to repeat*
kosten	*to cost*	wohnen	*to live (somewhere)*

Kaufst du Kaffee im Supermarkt?
Do you buy coffee at the supermarket?

Was **bedeutet** das auf Englisch?
What does that mean in English?

Ich **lerne** Deutsch.
I'm learning German.

Wir **belegen** Biologie.
We're taking Biology.

ACHTUNG

Note that the 2nd-person singular informal (**du**), 3rd-person singular (**er/sie/es**), and 2nd-person plural informal (**ihr**) forms of **heißen** are identical.

Suggestion Remind students that new verbs are also vocabulary items. Tell students that they should be able to recognize these verbs in all of their present-tense forms, but they will learn more about how to use them in later chapters.

QUERVERWEIS

Some verbs, such as **bringen**, **finden**, and **gehen**, are regular in the present tense and irregular in the past tense.

Students will learn more about the past tense forms in **Vol. 2: 1A.1, 1B.1, and 2A.1**.

Ressourcen

SAM
WB: pp. 19–20

SAM
LM: p. 13

S
vhlcentral.com

Jetzt sind Sie dran! **Write the appropriate form of the verb.**

1. Wir ___lernen___ (lernen) Deutsch.
2. Der Student ___wiederholt___ (wiederholen) den Satz (*sentence*).
3. Ich ___warte___ (warten) auf den Bus.
4. Die Lehrerin ___korrigiert___ (korrigieren) die Prüfungen.
5. Du ___belegst___ (belegen) viele (*a lot of*) Veranstaltungen.
6. Das Universitätsstudium ___kostet___ (kosten) sehr viel.

7. Ihr ___versteht___ (verstehen) Mathematik.
8. Wir ___brauchen___ (brauchen) viel Papier und viele Bleistifte für den Unterricht.
9. Anja und Thomas ___begrüßen___ (begrüßen) den Dozenten.
10. Ich ___kaufe___ (kaufen) eine Tasse Kaffee in der Mensa.
11. Wir ___machen___ (machen) nachmittags Hausaufgaben.
12. Du ___öffnest___ (öffnen) die Tür.

Anwendung

1 Wählen Sie Select the verb that best completes each sentence.

1. Astrid und Dominik (wohnen / bedeuten) in Berlin.
2. Marion (träumt / korrigiert) von (*about*) einem Haus in Italien.
3. Ich (baue / studiere) Informatik und Mathematik.
4. Wir (belegen / grüßen) sehr viele Vorlesungen.
5. Du (wanderst / lernst) gern in der Bibliothek.
6. Ihr (macht / kauft) nachmittags Hausaufgaben.
7. Sie (wiederholen / kosten) sehr viel, Professor Meier!
8. Du (sagst / reist) im Sommer nach (*to*) Spanien und Italien.

2 Expansion Have students write their own dialogues about the courses they are taking.

2 Ergänzen Sie Complete the conversation with the correct verb forms.

GISA Hallo, Fritz! Wie ist dein (*your*) Deutschseminar?

FRITZ Ach, es (1) ___geht___ (gehen) ganz gut (*pretty well*), aber ich (2) ___verstehe___ (verstehen) den Lehrer nicht. Und du? Wie ist dein Informatikseminar?

GISA Ich (3) ___liebe___ (lieben) Informatik! Wir (4) ___bauen___ (bauen) heute einen Computer.

FRITZ Vielleicht (*Maybe*) (5) ___belege___ (belegen) ich nächstes Semester auch Informatik. (6) ___Machst___ (Machen) du viele Hausaufgaben?

GISA Ja, leider (*unfortunately*) (7) ___lerne___ (lernen) ich immer (*always*) samstags und sonntags.

FRITZ Oje. Samstags und sonntags (8) ___spielen___ (spielen) Max und ich Computerspiele.

3 Schreiben Sie Write complete sentences using the cues.

1. ich / kaufen / einen Apfel   Ich kaufe einen Apfel.
2. Jürgen / brauchen / das Handy (*cell phone*)   Jürgen braucht das Handy.
3. du / arbeiten / freitags und samstags   Du arbeitest freitags und samstags.
4. Kurt / suchen / das Deutschbuch   Kurt sucht das Deutschbuch.
5. Josef und ich / spielen / in der Sporthalle / Fußball (*soccer*)   Josef und ich spielen in der Sporthalle Fußball.
6. ihr / lernen / in der Bibliothek   Ihr lernt in der Bibliothek.
7. Lara / reisen / nach (*to*) Afrika   Lara reist nach Afrika.
8. Hans und Jana / warten / auf (*for*) den Bus   Hans und Jana warten auf den Bus.

Kommunikation

4 **Was fehlt?** With a partner, say what each person is doing.

▶ **BEISPIEL**

Du ___hörst___ Musik.

1. Herr Becker __arbeitet__.

2. Wir __spielen__ Tennis.

3. Ihr __lernt__ in der Bibliothek.

4. Ich __kaufe__ ein neues Fahrrad.

5. Heinrich __begrüßt__ den Mann.

6. Hans __liebt__ seine Freundin.

5 **Bilden Sie Sätze** In pairs, use items from each column to create six sentences. You may use some items more than once. Answers will vary.

BEISPIEL *Ich höre Musik.*

A	B	C
ich	hören	Deutsch
du	lernen	Hausaufgaben
Alena	lieben	Kunst
Anna und ich	machen	Musik
ihr	spielen	Naturwissenschaft
die Studenten	verstehen	Tennis

6 **Persönliche Fragen** In pairs, take turns asking and answering the questions. Answers will vary.

1. Welche (*Which*) Veranstaltungen belegst du?
2. Welche Fremdsprachen lernst du?
3. Welche Veranstaltungen machen Spaß (*are fun*)?
4. Was machst du morgens?
5. Was machst du nachmittags?
6. Was machst du abends?

6 Expansion Have students write a paragraph about themselves, including their name, age, major, and class schedule.

7 **Gespräch** In pairs, fill in Student 2's half of the dialogue in **Teil** (*part*) **A**. Then continue the conversation with your partner using the cues in **Teil B**. Answers will vary.

Teil A

S1: Hallo! Studierst du hier an der Uni?
S2: …
S1: Ich auch! Was studierst du?
S2: …
S1: Ich verstehe Wirtschaft nicht (*not*). Wirtschaft ist nützlich, aber schwierig.
S2: …
S1: Montags und mittwochs habe ich Geschichte. Und du?
S2: …

Teil B

das Diplom	Psychologie
lernen	sonntags
Literatur	spielen
machen	das Stipendium
nachmittags	wohnen

Interrogative words  Presentation

Startblock Interrogative words, also called question words, are used to ask for information.

Wie viele Menschen leben dort?

Was ist mit Meline?

Suggestion Ask students additional questions using interrogatives from the list, and have students answer. Ex.: **Was ist das? Wer ist sie?**, etc.

interrogatives			
wann?	*when?*	**wie?**	*how?*
warum?	*why?*	**wie viel?**	*how much?*
was?	*what?*	**wie viele?**	*how many?*
welcher/welche/welches?	*which?*	**wo?**	*where?*
wen?	*whom?*	**woher?**	*where (from)?*
wer?	*who?*	**wohin?**	*where (to)?*

Students will learn more about **wohin, woher,** and related words in Vol. 2, 2A.2. **Welcher** is a **der** word. Students will learn about **der** words in Vol. 2, 4B.2.

- To ask an information question (one that cannot be answered with **ja** or **nein**), begin the question with an interrogative word.

Wann beginnen wir?	**Warum** machst du das?	**Wer** ist Frau Schultz?
***When** do we start?*	***Why** are you doing that?*	***Who** is Mrs. Schultz?*

- The form of **welcher** depends on the gender and number of the noun it modifies. Its three forms (**welcher/welche/welches**) have the same endings as the masculine, feminine/plural, and neuter forms of the definite article (**der/die/das**).

Welche Professorin lehrt Mathematik?	**Welcher Student** belegt Mathematik?
***Which professor** teaches mathematics?*	***Which student** is taking math?*

- Like **welcher**, **wie viel** and **wie viele** function like adjectives. Use **wie viel** with a singular noun and **wie viele** with a plural noun.

Wie viel Zeit haben wir?	**Wie viele** Bücher kauft er?
***How much** time do we have?*	***How many** books is he buying?*

Expansion Have students take turns asking each other the questions and giving logical answers, where possible.

ACHTUNG

Use **wer** when the person you're asking about is the grammatical subject of the question and **wen** when the person is the direct object of the verb.

Wer begrüßt den Professor?
Who is greeting the professor?

Wen begrüßt der Professor?
Who(m) is the professor greeting?

QUERVERWEIS

Answers to questions that ask **Wie...?** or **Wo...?** may require the dative case. You will learn about the dative in **4B.1** and **4B.2**.

ACHTUNG

The word **viel(e)** by itself means a *lot (of)/many*.
Ich studiere viele Fächer.
Du arbeitest viel.

Jetzt sind Sie dran! **Select the appropriate interrogative for each question.**

1. (Woher / Wer) kommst du?
2. (Wohin / Wann) haben wir Deutsch?
3. (Was / Wohin) reisen wir?
4. (Wer / Wo) braucht ein Blatt Papier?
5. (Wen / Warum) lernst du so viel?
6. (Warum / Wo) wohnst du?

7. (Welche / Woher) Seminare sind einfach?
8. (Was / Wie viele) machst du samstags?
9. (Wie / Wann) heißt der Dozent?
10. (Wie viele / Wie viel) kostet das Telefon?
11. (Wie viele / Wann) Hausaufgaben haben wir?
12. (Wer / Wen) liebst du?

Anwendung und Kommunikation

1 Ergänzen Sie Complete each sentence with an appropriate interrogative word.

1. _____Wann/Wo_____ spielen wir Tennis?
2. _____Wann/Woher_____ kommt die Dozentin?
3. _____Was_____ kaufst du für das Studium?
4. _____Warum/Wann_____ brauchst du einen Computer?
5. _Wo/Wann/Wie viel/Was_ lernst du?
6. _____Wie_____ alt bist du?
7. _Welche/Wie viele_ Spiele (*games*) spielst du gern?
8. _____Wie viel_____ Zeit haben wir abends?

2 Schreiben Sie Write questions using the cues. Pay attention to word order.

1. der / Hörsaal / wo / ist Wo ist der Hörsaal?
2. wie / Deutschvorlesung / ist / die Wie ist die Deutschvorlesung?
3. gehen / wann / wir / in die Bibliothek Wann gehen wir in die Bibliothek?
4. wer / braucht / Kuli / einen Wer braucht einen Kuli?
5. kauft / was / Patrick / in der Mensa Was kauft Patrick in der Mensa?
6. wohin / die / gehen / nachmittags / Studenten Wohin gehen die Studenten nachmittags?
7. welches / macht / Seminar / Spaß (*fun*) Welches Seminar macht Spaß?
8. nichts (*nothing*) / warum / verstehe / ich Warum verstehe ich nichts?

3 Fragen Sie In pairs, write a question for each response. Sample answers are provided.

BEISPIEL Ich lerne Geschichte in der Bibliothek.
Wo lernst du Geschichte?

1. Karl hat <u>montags, mittwochs und freitags</u> Vorlesungen. Wann hat Karl Vorlesungen?
2. In der Universitätsbibliothek sind <u>3.726</u> Bücher. Wie viele Bücher sind in der Universitätsbibliothek?
3. <u>Kunst, Philosophie und Psychologie</u> machen viel Spaß. Was macht viel Spaß?/Welche Kurse machen viel Spaß?
4. Das Essen in der Mensa kostet nur <u>3,50 €</u>. Wie viel kostet das Essen in der Mensa?
5. Ich brauche das Buch *Die Traumdeutung* von Sigmund Freud
   für die Psychologievorlesung. Welches Buch brauchst du für die Psychologievorlesung?
6. Ich komme <u>aus (*from*) der Schweiz</u>. Woher kommst du?
7. <u>Der Dozent</u> wiederholt die Frage. Wer wiederholt die Frage?
8. Anna liebt <u>den netten (*nice*) Paul</u>. Wen liebt Anna?

4 Interview Prepare six questions about college life using interrogative words. Then, survey your classmates. Answers will vary.

 Practice more at **vhlcentral.com.**

3 Suggestion Point out that the phrase **aus der Schweiz** uses the dative form of the article **die**. Tell students they will learn more about dative articles and dative prepositions in **Lektion 4B**.

4 Expansion Have each group of students make a set of flashcards with interrogative pronouns. One student chooses a card and asks a question with the selected word to someone in the group. That person must answer the question and select the next card.

Talking about time and dates  Presentation

Startblock Like English, German uses cardinal numbers (*one, two, three*) to tell time and ordinal numbers (*first, second, third*) to give dates.

Telling time

- To ask *What time is it?*, say **Wie spät ist es?** or **Wie viel Uhr ist es?**. To answer, say **Es ist** + [*hour*] + **Uhr** + [*minutes*].

Es ist ein Uhr./　　**Es ist zwei Uhr./**　　**Es ist zwölf Uhr./**
Es ist eins.　　　　**Es ist zwei.**　　　　**Es ist Mittag/Mitternacht.**

- Use **vor** and **nach** to indicate minutes before and after the hour. Use **Viertel vor** for *quarter to* and **Viertel nach** for *quarter past*. In these constructions, omit the word **Uhr**.

Es ist **Viertel vor** elf./　　　　　Es ist **zwanzig nach** vier./
Es ist zehn Uhr fünfundvierzig.　　Es ist vier Uhr zwanzig.

- Use **halb** to mean *half an hour before*. Note that it is not equivalent to the English phrase *half past*.

Es ist **halb zehn**.　　　　　　　Es ist **halb sieben**.
Es ist neun Uhr dreißig.　　　　　Es ist sechs Uhr dreißig.

- Use the 24-hour clock when talking about train schedules, movie listings, and official timetables. Do not use the expressions **Viertel vor**, **Viertel nach**, or **halb** with the 24-hour clock.

　　20.30 Uhr = zwanzig Uhr dreißig　　　**18.45 Uhr = achtzehn Uhr fünfundvierzig**
　　8:30 p.m.　　　　　　　　　　　　　　*6:45 p.m.*

- To specify the time at which an event or activity will take place, use **um** + [*time*].

　　—Um wie viel Uhr beginnt der Film?　　—**Um** sechzehn Uhr zehn.
　　—*What time* does the movie start?　　　—*At four-ten p.m.*

Ordinal numbers

- The ordinal numbers (**die Ordinalzahlen**) from 1st to 19th are formed, with a few exceptions, by adding **-te** to the corresponding cardinal numbers. To form all other ordinals, add **-ste** to the cardinal forms. Use a period to indicate the abbreviated form of an ordinal number.

ordinal numbers

1.	**erste**	*first*	7.	**siebte**	*seventh*	19.	neunzehnte	*nineteenth*
2.	**zweite**	*second*	8.	**achte**	*eighth*	20.	zwanzigste	*twentieth*
3.	**dritte**	*third*	9.	neunte	*ninth*	31.	einunddreißigste	*thirty-first*
4.	vierte	*fourth*	10.	zehnte	*tenth*	55.	fünfundfünfzigste	*fifty-fifth*
5.	fünfte	*fifth*	11.	elfte	*eleventh*	100.	hundertste	*hundredth*
6.	sechste	*sixth*	12.	zwölfte	*twelfth*	1000.	tausendste	*thousandth*

der **erste** Dozent
the **first** instructor

die **zweite** Vorlesung
the **second** lecture

das **dritte** Fach
the **third** subject

Dates

die Monate (*months*)

Januar	April	Juli	Oktober
Februar	Mai	August	November
März	Juni	September	Dezember

Januar ist der erste Monat.
January is the first month.

Dezember ist der zwölfte Monat.
December is the twelfth month.

- Answer the question **Der Wievielte ist heute?** (*What is the date today?*) with **Heute ist der** + [*ordinal number* (+ *month*)].

  Heute ist **der erste Mai**.
  *Today is **May first.***

  Heute ist **der einunddreißigste**.
  *Today is **the thirty-first.***

  23. März 2010 ⟶ **23.3.2010**
  March 23rd, 2010 ⟶ *3/23/2010*

  7. Oktober 2014 ⟶ **7.10.2014**
  October 7th, 2014 ⟶ *10/7/2014*

- To specify the day on which an event or activity takes place, use **am** before the date, and add **-n** to the ordinal number. Note that an ordinal number is indicated by putting a period after the number.

  Wer hat **am 7. (siebten) Juli** Geburtstag?
  *Whose birthday is **on July 7th**?*

  Am 1. (ersten) Januar beginnt das neue Jahr.
  *The new year begins **on January 1st**.*

- The pattern **am** + [*time expression*] is also used with days of the week.

  am Montag
  on Monday

  am Dienstag
  on Tuesday

  am Wochenende
  on the weekend

- Like English, German uses cardinal numbers to refer to a particular year.

  1895 = achtzehnhundertfünfundneunzig

  2016 = zweitausendsechzehn

ACHTUNG

To form the accusative of ordinal numbers, add **-n** before masculine nouns. The feminine and neuter forms do not change.

Du trinkst deinen zweiten Kaffee.
You're having your second coffee.

Ich antworte auf die dritte Frage.
I'm answering the third question.

___

In writing, the day also comes before the month. Note that an ordinal number is indicated by putting a period after the number.

Suggestion Show students this alternative question/answer pattern for recognition purposes only: **Den Wievielten haben wir heute? Heute haben wir den zweiundzwanzigsten Juni.** Point out the use of the accusative article and the -n added to the ordinal number.

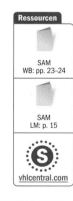

Ressourcen

SAM
WB: pp. 23–24

SAM
LM: p. 15

S
vhlcentral.com

Jetzt sind Sie dran!

Expansion Write some additional times and dates on the board and have students read them aloud.

A. Select the correct time.

1. **7:15 a.m.** Es ist (Viertel nach / Viertel vor) sieben.
2. **2:00 p.m.** Es ist zwei Uhr (morgens / nachmittags).
3. **10:30 a.m.** Es ist (halb zehn / halb elf) vormittags.
4. **12:00 p.m.** Es ist (Mittag / Mitternacht).
5. **7:55 a.m.** Es ist (acht / sieben) Uhr fünfundfünfzig.
6. **8:37 p.m.** Es ist (zwanzig Uhr / achtzehn Uhr) siebenunddreißig.

B. Write the correct date.

7. **14. Februar** Heute ist der ___vierzehnte___ Februar.
8. **28. Dezember** Heute ist der ___achtundzwanzigste___ Dezember.
9. **3. Juli** Heute ist der ___dritte___ Juli.
10. **30. Mai** Heute ist der ___dreißigste___ Mai.
11. **11. Oktober** Heute ist der ___elfte___ Oktober.
12. **7. August** Heute ist der ___siebte___ August.

Anwendung

1 **Wählen Sie** Select the sentence that refers to the time shown.

1. **Es ist zwei Uhr.**/ Es ist drei Uhr.

2. **Es ist Viertel vor eins.**/ **Es ist zwölf Uhr vierzig.**

3. Es ist fünf Uhr zwanzig. / **Es ist zehn** **vor drei.**

4. **Es ist zwei Uhr** **fünfundvierzig.**/ Es ist Viertel vor zwei.

2 **Wie spät ist es?** Write the time shown on each clock. Answers may vary.

▶ **BEISPIEL**

Es ist ein Uhr.

1. Es ist vier Uhr./Es ist _____ sechzehn Uhr.

2. Es ist zehn nach zwei./Es ist zwei Uhr zehn./Es ist vierzehn Uhr zehn.

3. Es ist acht Uhr zwanzig./Es ist zwanzig nach acht./Es ist zwanzig Uhr zwanzig.

4. Es ist Viertel nach vier./Es ist vier Uhr fünfzehn./Es ist sechzehn Uhr fünfzehn.

5. Es ist halb zehn./Es ist _____ neun Uhr dreißig./Es ist einundzwanzig Uhr dreißig.

6. Es ist Viertel vor zwei./Es ist ein Uhr fünfundvierzig./Es ist dreizehn Uhr fünfundvierzig.

7. Es ist zehn vor neun./Es ist acht Uhr fünfzig./Es ist zwanzig Uhr fünfzig.

8. Es ist fünf vor acht./Es ist sieben Uhr fünfundfünfzig./Es ist neunzehn Uhr fünfundfünfzig.

3 **Suggestion** Reinforce the difference between **am elften Oktober** and **der elfte Oktober**. Ex.: **Am elften Oktober haben Sie eine Prüfung. Der elfte Oktober ist ein Samstag.**

WERKZEUG

Heiligabend
Christmas Eve

Neujahrstag
New Year's Day

Heilige Drei Könige
Three Kings Day

Walpurgisnacht
Walpurgis Night
(Spring Festival)

das Augsburger
Friedensfest
Augsburg Peace Festival

der Tag der
deutschen Einheit
Day of German Unity

Martinstag *The Feast*
of St. Martin

Weihnachten *Christmas*

Silvester *New Year's Eve*

3 **Welcher Tag ist es?** Complete each sentence by writing out the date indicated.

BEISPIEL Heiligabend ist am (24.) *vierundzwanzigsten* Dezember.

1. Neujahrstag ist am (1.) ____ersten____ Januar.

2. Heilige Drei Könige ist am (6.) ____sechsten____ Januar.

3. Valentinstag ist am (14.) ____vierzehnten____ Februar.

4. St.-Patricks-Tag ist am (17.) ____siebzehnten____ März.

5. Walpurgisnacht ist am (30.) ____dreißigsten____ April.

6. Das Augsburger Friedensfest ist am (8.) ____achten____ August.

7. Der Tag der deutschen Einheit ist am (3.) ____dritten____ Oktober.

8. Martinstag ist am (11.) ____elften____ November.

9. Weihnachten ist am (25.) ____fünfundzwanzigsten____ Dezember.

10. Silvester ist am (31.) ____einunddreißigsten____ Dezember.

Kommunikation

4 Um wie viel Uhr...?
In pairs, look at the class schedule. Take turns asking and answering questions about the start times of classes. *Answers will vary.*

BEISPIEL

S1: Wann und um wie viel Uhr ist Literatur?
S2: Literatur ist dienstags und donnerstags um halb neun.

	Montag	Dienstag	Mittwoch	Donnerstag	Freitag
8.30		Literatur		Literatur	Chemie
9.25	Biologie	Biologie	Biologie		Chemie
10.20		Kunst		Kunst	
11.15	Informatik		Informatik		Informatik
12.10	Mathematik	Deutsch	Deutsch	Deutsch	Mathematik

5 Der Wievielte ist heute?
In pairs, take turns pointing at different dates on the calendar and having your partner tell you the date. *Answers will vary.*

BEISPIEL

S1: Der Wievielte ist heute?
S2: Heute ist der dritte Oktober.

Oktober						
Sonntag	Montag	Dienstag	Mittwoch	Donnerstag	Freitag	Samstag
		1	2	3	4	5
6	7	8	9	10	11	12
13	14	15	16	17	18	19
20	21	22	23	24	25	26
27	28	29	30	31		

6 Geburtstage
Ask your classmates when their birthdays are. Find out whose birthday is closest to yours. *Answers will vary.*

BEISPIEL

S1: Wann ist dein Geburtstag (*your birthday*)?
S2: Mein Geburtstag ist am siebten Dezember. Und wann ist dein Geburtstag?
S1: Mein Geburtstag ist am neunten Oktober.

7 Partnerinterview
In pairs, take turns asking and answering the questions. *Answers will vary.*

BEISPIEL

S1: Wann hast du Deutschvorlesung?
S2: Montags, mittwochs und freitags um Viertel nach elf. Und du?

1. Welcher Tag ist heute?
2. Wann hast du Geburtstag?
3. Wann ist dein Lieblingsfeiertag (*favorite holiday*)?
4. Wie spät ist es?
5. Um wie viel Uhr ist die Deutschvorlesung vorbei (*over*)?
6. Wann hast du Veranstaltung?

4 Expansion Ask students to describe their own schedules. In pairs, have them take turns asking and answering questions about their own classes and activities.

5 Expansion Bring an example of movie listings, TV schedules, or course schedules from a German university. In pairs, have students ask and answer questions about the schedules.

5 Suggestion Point out that on German calendars and schedules, **Montag** is listed as the first day of the week and **Sonntag** as the last.

Wiederholung

4 Expansion Show a time zone map and ask what time it is in a given place. Ex.: **Wie viel Uhr ist es in Bangkok?**

1 Graffiti
In small groups, take turns drawing items from the lesson vocabulary and guessing what they are. *Answers will vary.*

BEISPIEL

S1: Ist das ein Diplom?
S2: Nein!
S3: Ist das ein Stipendium?
S2: Ja, richtig!

2 Verabredungen
Take turns asking and answering questions using the cues and the images. *Answers will vary.*

reisen

▶ **BEISPIEL**

S1: Wohin reist du im Sommer?
S2: Ich reise nach Spanien.

1. gehen   2. lernen   3. kosten

4. kaufen   5. hören   6. begrüßen

3 Feiertage und Feste
Ask your classmates on what day these holidays fall. Add three additional holidays. *Answers will vary.*

BEISPIEL Weihnachten (*Christmas*)

S1: Wann ist Weihnachten?
S2: Weihnachten ist am 25. Dezember.

3 Suggestion Provide students with a calendar to consult for this activity.

- Boxing-Tag (*day after Christmas*)
- amerikanischer Unabhängigkeitstag (*Independence Day*)
- amerikanischer Tag der Arbeit (*Labor Day*)
- Columbus-Tag
- Halloween
- Veteranentag
- amerikanisches Erntedankfest (*Thanksgiving*)

3 Suggestion Tell students about the German celebrations of **Aprilscherz, der Tag der Arbeit,** and **Erntedankfest** and explain how they differ from their American equivalents.

4 Zeitzonen
In pairs, take turns telling your partner what time it is in each North American city and asking what time it is in a German-speaking country. *Answers will vary.*

BEISPIEL

S1: In Pittsburgh ist es fünfzehn Uhr zwölf. Wie viel Uhr ist es in Österreich?
S2: In Österreich ist es einundzwanzig Uhr zwölf. In Calgary ist es halb vier. Wie viel Uhr ist es in Deutschland?

Uhrzeit in...	Uhrzeit in Deutschland / in Österreich / in der Schweiz
Pittsburgh, PA: 15.12	+ 6 Stunden (*hours*)
Calgary, AB: 3.30	+ 8 Stunden
Fairbanks, AK: 22.54	+ 11 Stunden
Ft. Stockton, TX: 11.45	+ 7 Stunden
Hope, BC: 15.28	+ 9 Stunden
London, ON: 3.09	+ 6 Stunden
Needles, CA: 12.30	+ 9 Stunden
Tifton, FL: 21.36	+ 6 Stunden
Winnipeg, MB: 20.15	+ 7 Stunden

5 Ein Rennen
Your instructor will give you a worksheet. Talk with your classmates to figure out the starting lineup of a race.

BEISPIEL

S1: Der Wievielte bist du im Rennen?
S2: Ich bin der 14.
S1: (*write*) Klaus ist der Vierzehnte.

5 Suggestion Point out to students that **der Wievielte** is the masculine form. Tell them to use **die Wievielte** when addressing a female student.

6 Wann hast du...?
You and your partner each have two schedules. One shows your activities. The other shows a partial list of your partner's activities, with one activity missing each day. Ask and answer questions to complete both schedules.

BEISPIEL

S1: Was machst du am Sonntag um 5.30 Uhr abends?
S2: Ich treffe Markus. Und was machst du am Donnerstag um 7 Uhr morgens?
S1: Ich habe Yoga.

Zapping

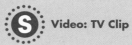 **Video: TV Clip**

TU Berlin

Suggestion After showing students the video, ask questions to facilitate comprehension. Ex.: What types of subjects do students study at the TU? What degrees are offered at the TU?

The **Technische Universität Berlin**, or **TU Berlin**, is a modern-looking institution with a long and impressive history. Founded in 1879, the **TU** is one of the biggest technical universities in Germany, and the only one in Berlin to offer an engineering degree (**Ingenieur-Abschluss**). The TU also has a larger percentage of international students (**Studenten aus dem Ausland**) than any other German university.

Vier Unis hat die Stadt zu bieten°. Die TU ist die zweitälteste°.

Nach vorn° präsentiert sie sich modern und sachlich°.

„Wir haben die Ideen° für die Zukunft°" heißt der Leitspruch°.

---

zu bieten *to offer* **zweitälteste** *second oldest* **Nach vorn** *From the front* **sachlich** *functional* **Ideen** *ideas* **Zukunft** *future* **Leitspruch** *motto*

 Verständnis Circle the correct answers.

1. What percentage of **TU** students come from abroad?
   a. 5   b. 10   (c. 20)   d. 30
2. Which of the following is *not* one of the key subjects (**Schwerpunkte**) offered by the **TU**?
   a. Mathematik   (b. Architektur)   c. Physik   d. Chemie

 Diskussion Discuss the following questions with a partner. Answers will vary.

1. In what ways is the **TU Berlin** similar to your school? How is it different?
2. Would you like to study at the **TU Berlin**? Why or why not?

Communicative Goals

You will learn how to:

- talk about sports
- talk about leisure activities

Wortschatz

Sportarten	*sports*
(der) (American) Football	football
(das) Golf	golf
(das) Hockey	hockey
(der) Volleyball	volleyball
das Schwimmbad, -¨er	swimming pool
das Spiel, -e	game
der Sport	sports
das Stadion, Stadien	stadium
Fahrrad fahren (fährt)	to ride a bicycle
Ski fahren	to ski
schwimmen	to swim
üben/trainieren	to practice
Freizeitaktivitäten	*leisure activities*
der Berg, -e	mountain
das Camping	camping
das Fahrrad, -¨er	bicycle
die Freizeit	free time
das Hobby, -s	hobby
der Park, -s	park
der Strand, -¨e	beach
der Wald, -¨er	forest
angeln gehen	to go fishing
essen gehen	to eat out
spazieren gehen	to go for a walk
klettern	to (rock) climb
kochen	to cook
reiten	to ride (a horse)
schreiben	to write
singen	to sing
tanzen	to dance
wandern	to hike

Suggestion Have students preview the conjugation of **fahren**, which will be covered in **2B.1**. Explain that **fahren** is listed with its third-person singular form because it has a stem change in the present tense.

ACHTUNG

Infinitives can be used as nouns in German. **Freitags habe ich Schwimmen. Samstags habe ich Reiten.** Infinitives used as nouns are neuter.

die Spielerinnen (*sing.* die Spielerin)

Sie spielen Tennis (*n.*).

das Spielfeld, -er/ der Platz, -¨e

die Mannschaft, -en

der Ball, -¨e

der Spieler, -

Er spielt Fußball. (spielen)

Sie verliert. (verlieren)

die Karten (*sing.* die Karte)

Er gewinnt. (gewinnen)

Basketball (*m.*)

der Basketball

Sie spielen Schach (*n.*).

Baseball (*m.*)

Leichtathletik (*f.*)

Anwendung

1 Expansion Have students list additional words that could belong to each grouping.

1 Was passt nicht? Indicate the word that doesn't belong.

1. a. Basketball
   b. Schach
   c. Golf
   d. Tennis

2. a. der Strand
   b. der Spieler
   c. das Stadion
   d. der Platz

3. a. reiten
   b. schwimmen
   c. singen
   d. klettern

4. a. der Rucksack
   b. das Camping
   c. der Berg
   d. das Spielfeld

5. a. spazieren gehen
   b. kochen
   c. wandern
   d. reiten

6. a. die Freizeit
   b. die Schule
   c. die Aktivität
   d. das Hobby

2 Ergänzen Sie Complete the sentences with words from the list.

| kochen | Ski fahren | Spielfeld | Strände | Tennisspielerinnen |

1. Serena und Venus Williams sind ___Tennisspielerinnen___.
2. In den Alpen kann man im Winter ___Ski fahren___.
3. In der Schule *Le Cordon Bleu* lernt man ___kochen___.
4. In einem Fußballspiel sind 22 Spieler auf dem ___Spielfeld___.
5. In Florida gibt es schöne (*beautiful*) ___Strände___.

3 Zuordnungen Write the activity that describes each picture.

Sample answers are provided.

> **BEISPIEL**
>
> *ins Fußballstadion gehen*

3 Expansion Ask students what they do in their free time. Ex.: **Spielen Sie Baseball oder Basketball? Fahren Sie Ski? Gehen Sie im Park spazieren?**

1. ___Ski fahren___

2. ___Camping machen___

3. ___Fahrrad fahren___

4. ___Basketball spielen___

4 Das Wochenende 🎧 Listen to the conversation between Lukas, Max, and Michaela, and indicate who will be doing each activity.

	Lukas	Max	Michaela
1. Tennis spielen		✓	
2. kochen			✓
3. lernen	✓		✓
4. tanzen	✓		✓
5. klettern	✓		
6. Videospiele spielen	✓		

Practice more at **vhlcentral.com**.

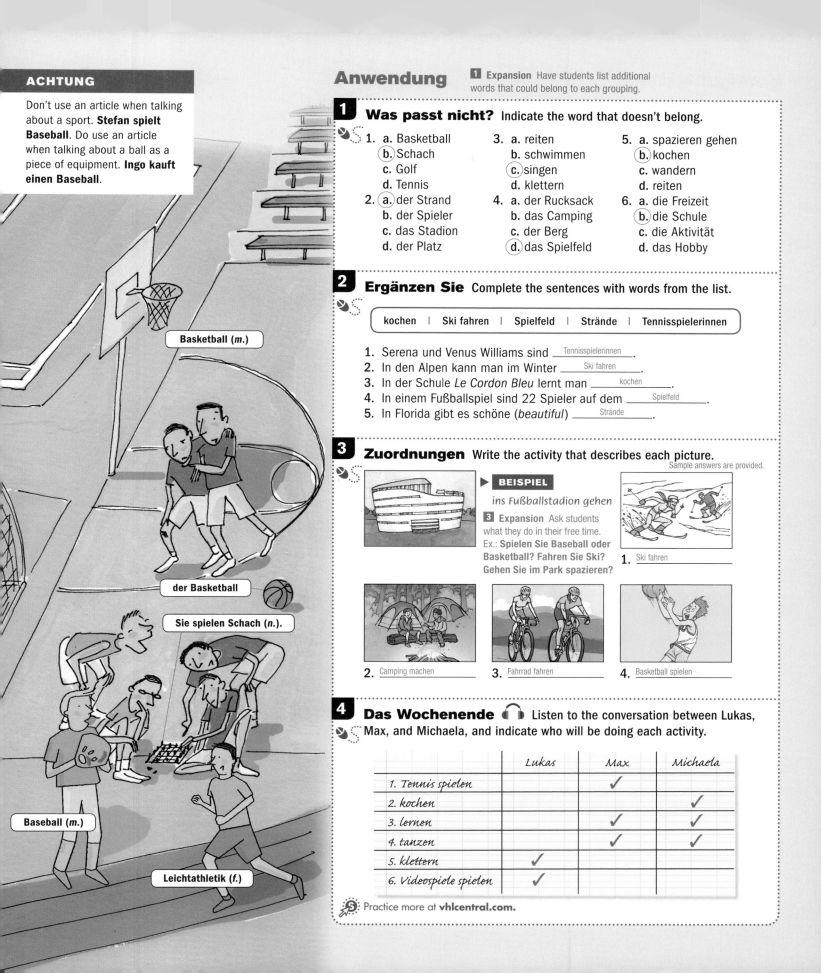

Kommunikation

5 Berühmte Sportler In pairs, match the athletes with the descriptions.

BEISPIEL

S1: *Er spielt Fußball und kommt aus England.*
S2: *Es ist David Beckham.*

___d___ 1. Er kommt aus der Schweiz und spielt Tennis.
___h___ 2. Er spielt Basketball.
___e___ 3. Er fährt in der Formel 1.
___b___ 4. Sie ist eine Tennisspielerin aus Deutschland.
___f___ 5. Er schwimmt und hat viele olympische Medaillen (*medals*).
___c___ 6. Er ist der berühmteste (*most famous*) Baseball-Spieler der Geschichte.
___a___ 7. Sie ist eine Skifahrerin aus Amerika.
___g___ 8. Er spielt Golf.

a. Lindsay Vonn
b. Steffi Graf
c. Babe Ruth
d. Roger Federer
e. Michael Schumacher
f. Michael Phelps
g. Tiger Woods
h. LeBron James

5 Expansion Have students come up with their own prompts, real or fictitious. Ex.: **Sie ist groß und blond und sie spielt Gitarre und singt.** (Taylor Swift) **Er ist Hogwarts-Schüler.** (Harry Potter) **Sein Alter ego heißt „Slim Shady".** (Eminem)

6 Was machst du? Your instructor will give you a worksheet with information about activities. Ask your classmates what they do in their free time.

BEISPIEL Volleyball spielen

S1: *Spielst du Volleyball?*
S2: *Ja. Ich spiele Volleyball./Nein.*

EIN KLEINER TIPP

The verb **fahren** is irregular in the **du** and **er/sie/es** forms of the present tense. Its stem vowel changes from **a** to **ä**.
Ex.: **ich fahre Fahrrad**, but **du fährst Fahrrad, er/sie/es fährt Fahrrad.**

Fahrrad fahren	reiten	Fußball spielen
Ski fahren	schwimmen	Schach spielen
angeln gehen	singen	tanzen
spazieren gehen	Baseball spielen	Tennis trainieren
klettern	Basketball spielen	wandern

6 Suggestion Tell students to find at least one person for each activity.

7 Machst du das gern? In pairs, take turns telling each other whether you like or dislike each activity.

Answers will vary.

BEISPIEL

S1: *Ich schwimme gern (like swimming). Und du?*
S2: *Ich schwimme nicht gern (don't like swimming).*

1. Ich spiele (nicht) gern Schach.
2. Ich koche (nicht) gern.
3. Ich wandere (nicht) gern.
4. Ich gehe (nicht) gern spazieren.
5. Ich klettere (nicht) gern.
6. Ich spiele (nicht) gern Karten.
7. Ich tanze (nicht) gern.
8. Ich trainiere (nicht) gern Leichtathletik (*track and field*).

8 Charade spielen Play charades in groups of four. Take turns acting out activities from the lesson vocabulary. The person who guesses the activity goes next. Answers will vary.

BEISPIEL

S1: *Ist es Baseball?*
S2: *Nein.*
S3: *Ist es Tennis?*
S2: *Ja, es ist Tennis!*

Aussprache und Rechtschreibung

 Audio: Presentation Record & Compare Activities

Diphthongs: *au, ei/ai, eu/äu*

When one vowel sound glides into another vowel sound in the same syllable, the complex sound produced is called a diphthong. In German, this complex sound is said quickly and is not drawn out as it is in English. There are three diphthongs in German: **au**, **ei/ai**, and **eu/äu**.

faul	**aus**	**Leine**	**Mais**	**neun**	**täuschen**

The German diphthong written **au** begins with the vowel sound of the *o* in the English word *pod* and ends with a sound similar to the *oo* in the English word *loose*.

auf	**Frau**	**Bauch**	**Haus**	**auch**

The German diphthong written as **ei** or **ai** is pronounced very similarly to the *i* in the English word *time*. Remember that the German **ie** is not a diphthong, but simply a way of writing the long **i** sound, as in the word **sieben**.

Freitag	**Zeit**	**Mai**	**Eis**	**schreiben**

The German diphthong written as **eu** or **äu** is pronounced very similarly to the *oi* in the English word *coin*.

Zeugnis	**Freund**	**Häuser**	**Europa**	**Deutsch**

1 **Sprechen Sie nach** Practice saying these words aloud.

1. laufen
2. Kaufhaus
3. Rauch
4. Maus
5. mein
6. Wein
7. Mainz
8. reiten
9. treu
10. freuen
11. Leute
12. läuft

2 **Artikulieren Sie** Practice saying these sentences aloud.

1. Die Mäuse laufen einfach im Zimmer herum.
2. Tausende Leute gehen an uns vorbei.
3. Am Freitag habe ich leider keine Zeit.
4. Paul macht eine Europareise mit Freunden.
5. Meine Frau kauft ein neues Haus außerhalb von Mainz.
6. Für den Sauerbraten brauchen wir Rotweinessig.

3 **Sprichwörter** Practice reading these sayings aloud.

Suggestion Have students look at the sample words and sentences on this page to identify cognates and words they already know. Tell students the meanings of any unfamiliar words or phrases.

Schuster, bleib bei deinen Leisten.[1]

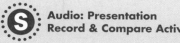

Einem geschenkten Gaul schaut man nicht ins Maul.[2]

[1] Stick with what you know. (lit. Cobbler, stick with your shoe stretchers.)

[2] Don't look a gift horse in the mouth.

 Ressourcen
SAM
LM: p. 17

 vhlcentral.com

Ein Picknick im Park

 Video: *Fotoroman*

George und Meline treffen Sabite und Torsten im Park. Sie sprechen über Sport und ihre Hobbys. Kommt Meline Torsten zu nahe (*too close*)?

Vorbereitung Have students preview the images and write down three questions they want to have answered in the video.

NATIONAL STANDARDS communication cultures

1

TORSTEN Das Fußballspiel beginnt um halb acht.
SABITE Es ist Viertel nach sechs. Niemand ist hier. George kommt von der Uni.

2

TORSTEN Spielt er Fußball?
SABITE Er spielt Baseball in der Freizeit. Er ist in einer Uni-Mannschaft.
TORSTEN Hat Meline Hobbys?
SABITE Sie fährt Ski und spielt Tennis. Sie gewinnt alles.

3

GEORGE Oh, vielen Dank! Wo sind Hans und Meline?
SABITE Meline kommt aus der Bibliothek. Hans hat eine Vorlesung.
GEORGE Studierst du auch, Torsten?
TORSTEN Ja. Ich studiere Chemie und Biologie.

4

MELINE Ich bringe Dessert!
GEORGE Sabite, ich glaube, Hans...
MELINE Hans. Hallo, Torsten, nett dich kennen zu lernen.
TORSTEN Gleichfalls, Meline.

5

MELINE Du studierst Medizin?
TORSTEN Biologie.
MELINE Fährst du Ski?
TORSTEN Nee, meine Familie fährt nicht Ski. Aber ich wandere und klettere.

MELINE Ich komme aus Wien. Alle fahren Ski in den österreichischen Alpen. Wir haben viele Sportarten: Skifahren, Klettern, Fahrradfahren, Golf und Tennis. Spielst du auch Tennis?
SABITE Äh, Meline?
MELINE Hmmm?
SABITE Gehen wir spazieren.

6

ÜBUNGEN

1 Ergänzen Sie Choose the words that best complete the sentences.

1. Torsten und Sabite sind (im Park/ im Café).
2. George kommt (aus dem Stadion / von der Uni).
3. Meline fährt Ski und spielt (Golf / Tennis).
4. Torsten studiert Chemie und (Biologie / Physik).
5. Meline bringt (Kaffee / Dessert).
6. Alle fahren (Ski / Bob) in den österreichischen Alpen.

7. Sabite ist eifersüchtig auf (*jealous of*) (Meline / Torsten).
8. Meline trennt keine (Klassenkameraden / Paare).
9. (Frau Yilmaz / Herr Yilmaz) macht morgen Sauerbraten.
10. Hans weiß nicht, dass Sabite einen (Mitbewohner / Freund) hat.

Expansion Have students write simple sentences with the words that were not chosen.

PERSONEN

 Torsten   Sabite  George   Meline

7

SABITE Meline. Wir sind Mitbewohnerinnen. Freundinnen.
MELINE Und?
SABITE „Spielst du auch Tennis?"

8

MELINE Sabite. Keine Sorge. Ich trenne keine Paare.
SABITE Es ist okay, ich verstehe.

9

SABITE George, Meline, meine Mutter macht morgen Sauerbraten. Kommt ihr zum Abendessen?
MELINE Oh, danke, Sabite. Wir kommen.
TORSTEN Frau Yilmaz ist eine gute Köchin.
GEORGE Wow, vielen Dank. Und Hans?
SABITE Ich frage ihn.

10

MELINE Hans weiß nicht, dass Sabite einen Freund hat, oder?
GEORGE Er hat keine Ahnung.

Nützliche Ausdrücke

- **Niemand ist hier.**
  Nobody's here.
- **die Uni-Mannschaft**
  varsity team
- **Sie gewinnt alles.**
  She wins at everything.
- **glauben**
  to believe
- **aber**
  but
- **Alle fahren Ski in den österreichischen Alpen.**
  Everyone in the Austrian Alps skis.
- **Gehen wir spazieren.**
  Let's go for a walk.
- **Keine Sorge.**
  Don't worry.
- **das Abendessen**
  dinner
- **der Koch / die Köchin**
  cook
- **Hans weiß nicht, dass Sabite einen Freund hat, oder?**
  Hans doesn't know Sabite has a boyfriend, does he?
- **Er hat keine Ahnung.**
  He doesn't have a clue.

2B.1
- **Meine Familie fährt nicht Ski.**
  My family doesn't ski.

2B.2
- **Meine Mutter macht morgen Sauerbraten.**
  My mother is making sauerbraten tomorrow.

2B.3
- **Ich trenne keine Paare.**
  I wouldn't break up a couple.

2 Zum Besprechen In this episode, the characters talk about their favorite sports and pastimes. Interview your classmates to find out who shares your interests. Who likes the same sports? Who has the same hobbies? Answers will vary.

2 Suggestion Refer students to the script for scenes 3, 5, and 6 for model questions they can use to interview their classmates.

3 Vertiefung Fußball (*soccer*) is one of the most popular sports in Germany. What is the name of the German national soccer league? Find the names of four prominent German soccer teams. Which team won last year's championship? (Fußball-)Bundesliga; Sample answers: Bayern München, Borussia Mönchengladbach, Borussia Dortmund, Werder Bremen; Answers will vary.

3 Expansion Have students research popular soccer players from Germany, Austria, and Switzerland and share their names with the class.

Ressourcen — SAM VM: pp. 4 — DVD Folge 4 — vhlcentral.com

Skifahren im Blut

S Reading

IN ALPINE VILLAGES, LEARNING TO SKI is like learning to walk. Almost everyone does it, starting at a very young age. The beginner slopes are full of preschool-aged children taking their first lessons. Skiing courses were required in Austrian schools until 1995, and many schools in Bavaria and Austria still offer **Skiwoche°**, a chaperoned week-long skitrip, as part of their curriculum.

Many of the world's best skiers come from German-speaking countries.

Olympic gold medalist Maria Riesch grew up at the base of the **Zugspitze**, the highest peak in Germany, and began skiing when she was three years old. In 2011, Riesch won the World Cup overall title for best female skier. Austrian Hermann Maier, nicknamed the "Herminator," was told at age 15 that he would never succeed as a professional skier. Maier went on to become a two-time **Olympiasieger°** and a three-time **Weltmeister°**.

While the Alpine skiing tradition remains strong, environmental and economic sustainability have become major concerns. Ski tourism has had a serious impact on the ecology of the Alpine regions. With rising temperatures due to climate change, lack of snow is also becoming an issue. Snowmaking is expensive and uses vast amounts of water. And, while large ski resorts continue to draw visitors from all over the world, skiing is becoming less affordable for locals, with some smaller ski areas struggling to remain in business.

Österreich: Ski-Paradies	
Jährliche Anzahl an° Skitouristen	15,4 Millionen (2010)
Jährliche Einnahmen° durch Skifahren	mehr als° 11 Milliarden Euro (2010)
Arbeitsplätze° im Skitourismus	276.000
Pistenfläche°	25.400 Hektar (254 km²)
Alpine Skiweltmeisterschaft 2011: Medaillen für Österreich	8 (4 Gold, 3 Silber, 1 Bronze)

QUELLE: Trend Wirtschaftsmagazin

Blut *blood* **Skiwoche** *ski week* **Olympiasieger** *Olympic gold medalist* **Weltmeister** *world champion* **Jährliche Anzahl an** *Annual number of* **Einnahmen** *revenue* **mehr als** *more than* **Arbeitsplätze** *jobs* **Pistenfläche** *skiable area*

1 **Ergänzen Sie** Complete the statements.

1. Austrian schools had mandatory ski classes until ____1995____.
2. In Bavaria and Austria, many school classes travel to the mountains for ____Skiwoche____.
3. ____Maria Riesch____ started skiing at age 3.
4. Riesch grew up at the base of the ____Zugspitze____.
5. In 2011, Riesch won the ____World Cup____ title for best female skier.
6. Hermann Maier's nickname is the ____Herminator____.
7. Maier is an **Olympiasieger** and a three-time ____Weltmeister____.
8. ____Snowmaking____ uses excessive quantities of water.
9. Ski tourism accounts for ____276,000____ jobs in Austria.
10. Austria won ____8____ medals in the 2011 Alpine Skiing World Championships.

 Practice more at **vhlcentral.com**.

Mehr Freizeit

der Fan, -s	*fan*
die Meisterschaft, -en	*championship*
das Tor, -e	*goal (in soccer, etc.)*
faulenzen	*to relax; to be lazy*
joggen	*to jog*
lesen	*to read*
fit	*in good shape*
sportlich	*athletic*
Los!	*Start!; Go!*

Die Deutschen und das Fahrrad

In Deutschland hat man im Schnitt° 6 Stunden und 34 Minuten Freizeit am Tag. Populäre Hobbys der Deutschen sind Videospiele, Lesen und natürlich° Sport. Die Deutschen sind leidenschaftliche° Fahrradfahrer. Kilometerlange Radwege° durchkreuzen° das Land, wie etwa° die Romantische Straße° in Bayern: sie führt an Schlössern° und vielseitigen Landschaften° vorbei°.

im Schnitt *on average* **natürlich** *of course* **leidenschaftliche** *passionate* **Radwege** *bike trails* **durchkreuzen** *cross* **wie etwa** *such as* **Straße** *road* **Schlössern** *castles* **vielseitigen Landschaften** *varied landscapes* **führt an... vorbei** *leads past*
Suggestion Tell students that **die Romantische Straße** is a road with an adjacent bike path that runs 418 km from Würzburg to Füssen.

Toooooooor!

Der talentierte und populäre Fußballer **Mesut Özil** spielt international für Deutschland. Am 23. Juni 2010 spielt die deutsche Fußballnationalmannschaft in Johannesburg gegen° Ghana. Es gibt nur° ein Tor im Spiel. Es ist für Deutschland, und es ist von Özil. Dafür wird° er „*Man of the Match*". Er bekommt° auch die Auszeichnung° „*2010 World Cup Most Assists*". Özil ist Deutscher mit türkischer Abstammung° und kommt aus Gelsenkirchen. Er ist Moslem; er betet vor jedem° Spiel. Man sagt, die Familie Özil ist ein gutes Beispiel für erfolgreiche° Integration von Ausländern° in Deutschland. Aber Özil spielt nicht nur° für deutsche Mannschaften. Seit° 2010 spielt er in Spanien, für *Real Madrid*.

gegen *against* **nur** *only* **wird** *becomes* **bekommt** *receives* **Auszeichnung** *award* **mit türkischer Abstammung** *of Turkish descent* **betet vor jedem** *prays before every* **erfolgreiche** *successful* **Ausländern** *foreigners* **nicht nur** *not only* **Seit** *Since*

IM INTERNET

Wandern: Was sind beliebte Wanderwege° in der Schweiz?

beliebte Wanderwege *popular hiking trails*

For more information on this **Kultur**, go to **vhlcentral.com**.

---

2 **Richtig oder falsch?** In pairs, correct the false statements.

	richtig	falsch
1. On average, Germans have more than six hours of leisure time per day.	☑	☐
2. Biking is a popular sport in Germany.	☑	☐
3. Mesut Özil won the 2010 World Cup award for most goals. Özil won the award for most assists.	☐	☑
4. Mesut Özil grew up in Turkey. He grew up in the German town of Gelsenkirchen.	☐	☑

3 **Bekannte Sportler** In pairs, take turns role-playing famous athletes who play each of the sports listed. Your partner must guess who you are.

Answers will vary.

BEISPIEL

S1: *Ich spiele Fußball in Los Angeles.*
S2: *Bist du David Beckham?*

1. Golf
2. Baseball
3. Schwimmen
4. Tennis
5. Basketball
6. Fußball

Stem-changing verbs  Presentation

QUERVERWEIS

See **2A.1** to review the present-tense conjugations of regular verbs.

Startblock Certain irregular verbs follow predictable patterns of spelling changes in their present-tense conjugations. These verbs use the regular endings, but have changes to their stem vowels in the **du** and **er/sie/es** forms. Most stem-changing verbs follow one of four patterns in the present tense.

ACHTUNG

The formal **Sie** forms are the same as the plural **sie** forms for all verbs. Starting in this lesson, **Sie** and **sie** (*pl.*) forms will be listed together in verb tables.

- a ⟶ ä

schlafen (*to sleep*)			
ich schlafe	*I sleep*	wir schlafen	*we sleep*
du schläfst	*you sleep*	ihr schlaft	*you sleep*
er/sie/es schläft	*he/she/it sleeps*	Sie/sie schlafen	*you/they sleep*

Schläfst du jede Nacht acht Stunden?
*Do you **sleep** eight hours every night?*

Sie **schlafen** im Studentenwohnheim.
*They **sleep** in the dormitory.*

- au ⟶ äu

laufen (*to run*)			
ich laufe	*I run*	wir laufen	*we run*
du läufst	*you run*	ihr lauft	*you run*
er/sie/es läuft	*he/she/it runs*	Sie/sie laufen	*you/they run*

Mehmet **läuft** am Strand.
*Mehmet **runs** on the beach.*

Sie **laufen** über das Spielfeld.
*They**'re running** across the field.*

- e ⟶ i

essen (*to eat*)			sprechen (*to speak*)	
ich	esse	*I eat*	spreche	*I speak*
du	isst	*you eat*	sprichst	*you speak*
er/sie/es	isst	*he/she/it eats*	spricht	*he/she/it speaks*
wir	essen	*we eat*	sprechen	*we speak*
ihr	esst	*you eat*	sprecht	*you speak*
Sie/sie	essen	*you/they eat*	sprechen	*you/they speak*

Wir **essen** in der Mensa.
*We**'re eating** in the cafeteria.*

Sprichst du Englisch?
*Do you **speak** English?*

ACHTUNG

Remember: when the verb stem ends in -**s**, drop the -**s** from the second-person singular ending.

- Besides an e ⟶ i vowel change, **nehmen** (*to take*) and **werden** (*to become*) have additional changes in the **du** and **er/sie/es** forms.

nehmen (*to take*)			werden (*to become*)	
ich	nehme	*I take*	werde	*I become*
du	nimmst	*you take*	wirst	*you become*
er/sie/es	nimmt	*he/she/it takes*	wird	*he/she/it becomes*
wir	nehmen	*we take*	werden	*we become*
ihr	nehmt	*you take*	werdet	*you become*
Sie/sie	nehmen	*you/they take*	werden	*you/they become*

Du **nimmst** jeden Tag den Bus.
*You **take** the bus every day.*

Ein Anfänger **wird** mit der Zeit Experte.
*A beginner **becomes** an expert over time.*

- e —→ ie

	lesen (*to read*)		sehen (*to see*)	
ich	lese	*I read*	sehe	*I see*
du	liest	*you read*	siehst	*you see*
er/sie/es	liest	*he/she/it reads*	sieht	*he/she/it sees*
wir	lesen	*we read*	sehen	*we see*
ihr	lest	*you read*	seht	*you see*
Sie/sie	lesen	*you/they read*	sehen	*you/they see*

Du **liest** viele Bücher.
*You **read** a lot of books.*

Seht ihr die Spieler?
*Do you **see** the players?*

- This table summarizes some common verbs with stem changes in the present tense. When a verb with a present-tense stem change is presented in this text, it will be listed with its third-person singular form: **lesen (liest)**.

common stem-changing verbs (present tense)			
a —→ ä		**e —→ i**	
backen	*to bake*	brechen	*to break*
braten	*to fry*	essen	*to eat*
fahren	*to go*	geben	*to give*
fallen	*to fall*	helfen	*to help*
fangen	*to catch*	nehmen	*to take*
lassen	*to let, to allow*	sprechen	*to speak*
schlafen	*to sleep*	treffen	*to hit; to meet*
tragen	*to carry; to wear*	vergessen	*to forget*
waschen	*to wash*	werden	*to become*
		werfen	*to throw*
au —→ äu		**e —→ ie**	
laufen	*to run*	empfehlen	*to recommend*
		lesen	*to read*
		sehen	*to see*
		stehlen	*to steal*

Fährst du nach Berlin?
*Are you **going** to Berlin?*

Es **gibt** dort ein sehr gutes Café.
*There **is** a very good café there.*

Suggestion Remind students that new verbs are also vocabulary items. Tell students that they should be able to recognize these verbs in all of their present-tense forms, but they will learn more about how to use them in later chapters.

ACHTUNG

The verb **geben** is used in certain idiomatic expressions, such as **Es gibt** (*There is/There are*). Idiomatic expressions do not translate literally to English.

Suggestion Tell students that **backen** can be conjugated with or without a present-tense stem change.

Ressourcen

SAM
WB: pp. 27–28

SAM
LM: p. 18

vhlcentral.com

Jetzt sind Sie dran! Write the appropriate form of the verb.

1. Ich ___esse___ (essen) viel Gemüse (*vegetables*).
2. Du ___hilfst___ (helfen) deiner (*your*) Mutter.
3. Wir ___geben___ (geben) dem Lehrer einen Apfel.
4. Peter ___nimmt___ (nehmen) ein Taxi.
5. Ihr ___fahrt___ (fahren) mit dem Fahrrad zur Uni.
6. Sie (*form.*) ___backen___ (backen) eine Torte.

7. Anna ___wird___ (werden) Informatikprofessorin.
8. Du ___liest___ (lesen) viele Bücher.
9. Er ___schläft___ (schlafen) bis 8 Uhr morgens.
10. Ihr ___sprecht___ (sprechen) Deutsch.
11. Die Kinder ___sehen___ (sehen) einen Film.
12. Du ___vergisst___ (vergessen) immer die Hausaufgaben.

Anwendung

1 **Wählen Sie** Select the verb that best completes each sentence.

1. Hannah (schläft / isst) viele Äpfel.
2. Ich (lese / backe) einen Schokoladenkuchen.
3. Du (fährst / triffst) einen Porsche.
4. Wir (helfen / waschen) den Hund in der Badewanne (*bathtub*).
5. Alena und Wolfgang (treffen / sprechen) Deutsch, Englisch und Polnisch.
6. Ihr (lauft / bratet) 8 Kilometer jeden (*every*) Tag.
7. Roland (liest / wird) viele Bücher.
8. Du (gibst / triffst) deine (*your*) Freunde im Café.

2 **Schreiben Sie** Write complete sentences using the cues.

1. der Kellner (*waiter*) / empfehlen / den Sauerbraten und das Schnitzel
   Der Kellner empfiehlt den Sauerbraten und das Schnitzel.
2. ich / helfen / meiner Mutter beim Kochen
   Ich helfe meiner Mutter beim Kochen.
3. du / fahren / das Auto am Wochenende
   Du fährst das Auto am Wochenende.
4. wir / treffen / Katrina und Paul im Restaurant
   Wir treffen Katrina und Paul im Restaurant.
5. Angela / lesen / morgens die Zeitung (*newspaper*)
   Angela liest morgens die Zeitung.
6. du / sprechen / Deutsch in der Vorlesung
   Du sprichst Deutsch in der Vorlesung.
7. eines Tages (*someday*) / werden / ich / Architekt, Pilot oder Astronaut
   Eines Tages werde ich Architekt, Pilot oder Astronaut.
8. Peter / stehlen / einen Apfel / für seinen Bruder (*his brother*)
   Peter stiehlt einen Apfel für seinen Bruder.

3 **Was machen die Personen?** Complete the sentences. Sample answers are provided.

▶ **BEISPIEL**

Peter __läuft__ gern im Park.

1. Sie __schlafen__ in der Hängematte.

2. Tobi __wäscht__ sein Auto.

3. Anja __reist__ nach Mallorca.

4. Hans __liest__ Märchen (*fairy tales*).

5. Er __isst__ eine Bratwurst.

6. Ingrid __trifft__ Rolf im Museum.

 Practice more at **vhlcentral.com**.

Kommunikation

4 **Bilden Sie Sätze** In pairs, create six logical sentences with items
from each column. Some items may be used more than once. Answers will vary.

BEISPIEL *Du empfiehlst den Käsekuchen.*

A	B	C
ich	empfehlen	Fußball im Stadion
du	lesen	Goethes *Faust*
Nina	sehen	den Käsekuchen (*cheesecake*)
Elsa und ich	spielen	23 Jahre alt
Bianca und du	sprechen	viele Sprachen
Olivia und Markus	werden	ein Theaterstück (*play*)

5 **Wer macht was?** Use the cues to ask your classmates whether they
participate in these activities. Answers will vary.

BEISPIEL

S1: *Spielst du Fußball im Stadion?*
S2: *Nein, aber (but) ich laufe im Park. Läufst du im Park oder am Strand?*

in der Bibliothek	im Park	im Stadion
in der Diskothek	im Schwimmbad	am Strand
zu Hause (*at home*)	am See (*lake*)	im Wald

5 Expansion Have students
take notes on their classmates'
answers and report their
findings to the class. Ex.:
**Michael spielt Baseball im
Stadion. Anna fährt Fahrrad
im Park.**

6 **Wie bitte?** Adele is talking to her mother on the phone. You hear
only Adele's side of the conversation. In pairs, reconstruct her
mother's questions. Sample answers are provided.

BEISPIEL Ich fahre am Wochenende nach Hause (*home*).

Wann fährst du nach Hause?

1. Ich kaufe Äpfel und Käse (*cheese*).
   Was kaufst du?
2. Ich esse gewöhnlich (*usually*) um
   7 Uhr abends.
   Wann isst du?
3. Ja, ich koche viel.
   Kochst du viel?
4. Ich sehe Matthias jeden Tag im Café.
   Wann siehst du Matthias?

5. Ja, wir sprechen jeden Tag Deutsch.
   Sprecht ihr jeden Tag Deutsch?
6. Matthias und ich reisen im Sommer
   nach Österreich.
   Wohin reist ihr im Sommer?
7. Matthias kommt aus Bad Tölz.
   Woher kommt Matthias?
8. Ja, ich spiele immer noch (*still*) Tennis.
   Spielst du immer noch Tennis?

7 **Im Park** In pairs, write a paragraph that
describes the activities of the people shown.
You may want to give the people names. Answers will vary.

BEISPIEL

S1: *Die Frauen gehen im Park spazieren.*
S2: *Die Kinder reiten im Park.*

Present tense used as future  Presentation

Startblock In German, as in English, you can use the present tense with certain time expressions to talk about the future.

Heute Abend spielen wir Fußball.

Morgen macht meine Mutter Sauerbraten.

- The adverbs **heute** (*today*), **morgen** (*tomorrow*), and **übermorgen** (*the day after tomorrow*) are commonly used with the present tense to express future ideas. Use them with these time expressions to specify the time of day at which a future action will occur.

common time expressions			
Morgen	*morning*	Nachmittag	*afternoon*
Vormittag	*midmorning*	Abend	*evening*
Mittag	*noon*	Nacht	*night*

Morgen gehen wir einkaufen.
Tomorrow *we're going shopping.*

Heute Nachmittag gehe ich schwimmen.
This afternoon *I'm going swimming.*

- Use **am** with **Morgen, Vormittag, Mittag, Nachmittag, Abend, Wochenende**, or the days of the week to specify when something will occur. When both the day of the week and the time of day are specified, they form a compound noun: **Dienstagmittag, Mittwochabend**.

Am Sonntag gehen wir angeln.
*We're going fishing **on Sunday**.*

Am Freitagnachmittag gehe ich zum Arzt.
*I'm going to the doctor's **Friday afternoon**.*

- Use **im** with months and seasons (**Frühling, Sommer, Herbst, Winter**).

Im Februar fahre ich Ski.
*I'm going skiing **in February**.*

Im Frühling gehe ich wandern.
*I'm going hiking **this spring**.*

- The adjective **nächste** (*next*) can be used with time-related nouns such as days of the week, seasons, and months. In this usage, it takes accusative endings.

nächsten Sommer
next summer

nächste Woche
next week

nächstes Jahr
next year

Jetzt sind Sie dran! Select the appropriate word or phrase.

1. Wir fahren (nächstes /(nächste)) Woche nach Polen.
2. (Am)/ Im) Montagvormittag gehe ich spazieren.
3. (Heute Abend)/ Abend) spielt ihr Karten.
4. Ursula fährt (am / (im)) Februar Ski.
5. Wir wandern ((nächsten)/ nächstes) Freitag im Wald.
6. ((Morgen Nachmittag)/ Nachmittag) fahre ich Fahrrad.
7. Wir gehen (Nacht / (übermorgen)) klettern.
8. (Nächsten / (Nächstes)) Wochenende spielst du Tennis.

Anwendung und Kommunikation

1 **Entscheiden Sie** Select the appropriate time expression.

1. Die nächste Prüfung ist (Nachmittag / übermorgen).
2. Ich fahre (im / am) März in Urlaub.
3. Spielst du (am / im) Abend Hockey?
4. Peter und Bettina fahren (nächstes / nächste) Wochenende in die Berge.
5. Gehst du (Nachmittag / heute Nachmittag) klettern?
6. (Nächstes / Nächsten) Sommer fahren wir an den Strand.

2 **Bilden Sie Sätze** Write sentences using the cues.

1. ich / gehen / heute Nachmittag / angeln   Ich gehe heute Nachmittag angeln.
2. übermorgen / spielen / Roland / Baseball   Übermorgen spielt Roland Baseball.
3. nächstes Jahr / fahren / Anja / an den Strand   Nächstes Jahr fährt Anja an den Strand.
4. Patrick / treffen / Bianca / am Abend   Patrick trifft Bianca am Abend.
5. am Sonntagabend / kochen / wir / Abendessen (*dinner*)   Am Sonntagabend kochen wir Abendessen.
6. du / fahren / im Winter / in den Alpen / Ski   Du fährst im Winter in den Alpen Ski.

3 **Gemischtes** In pairs, use items from each column to make up sentences describing what each person is going to do. Answers will vary.

BEISPIEL

Wir sehen heute Abend einen Film.

A	B	C	D
ich	Fahrrad fahren	am Freitag	für einen Marathonlauf
du	gehen	heute Nacht	im Park
Angelika	spazieren gehen	im Dezember	nach Österreich
wir	reisen	im Frühling	Freunde im Restaurant
ihr	trainieren	morgen Nachmittag	in die Disko
Otto und Gabi	treffen	nächstes Jahr	in den Bergen

3 Expansion Have students ask each other about their own plans for each of the times listed in column C. Ex.: **Was machst du am Freitag?**

4 **Fernsehen** In pairs, decide which TV programs you want to watch, and take turns asking each other when they will be on. Answers will vary.

BEISPIEL

S1: *Wann kommt Sport Aktuell?*
S2: *Sport Aktuell kommt morgen Abend / Mittwochabend.*

	Dienstag (heute)	Mittwoch	Donnerstag
10.00 Uhr	Reisen macht Spaß	Lindenstraße	Türkisch für Anfänger
15.00 Uhr	Otto live!	Das Supertalent	Die Sendung mit der Maus
19.00 Uhr	Formel 1	Kultur und Kunst	Deutschland sucht den Superstar
23.00 Uhr	Bauer sucht Frau	Sport Aktuell	Familien im Brennpunkt

Negation Presentation

Startblock In **1B.2**, you learned to make affirmative statements and ask yes-or-no questions. To negate a statement or ask a negative question, use **nicht** or **kein**.

Nein, meine Familie fährt **nicht** Ski.

Ich trenne **keine** Paare.

Nicht

- In negative statements or questions, place **nicht** after the subject, conjugated verb, direct object, and definite time expressions, but before other sentence elements.

Ich gehe heute in die Sporthalle.
I'm going to the gym today.
▶ Ich gehe heute **nicht** in die Sporthalle.
*I'm **not** going to the gym today.*

Brauchst du den Fußball?
Do you need the soccer ball?
▶ Brauchst du den Fußball **nicht**?
Don't you need the soccer ball?

Die Spieler sind hier.
The players are here.
▶ Die Spieler sind **nicht** hier.
*The players are **not** here.*

ACHTUNG

Ich spiele kein Tennis means *I don't play tennis (at all).* **Ich spiele nicht Tennis** means *I'm not playing tennis (at the moment).*

Kein

- **Kein** is the negative form of the indefinite article **ein**. Use **kein** to negate a noun preceded by an indefinite article or by no article.

—Spielen Sie Tennis?
—*Do you play tennis?*
▶ —Nein, wir spielen **kein** Tennis.
—*No, we **don't** play tennis.*

—Hat er ein Hobby?
—*Does he have a hobby?*
▶ —Nein, er hat **keine** Hobbys.
—*No, he has **no** hobbies.*

QUERVERWEIS

Words that have the same endings as **ein** are often called **ein**-words. You will learn about other **ein**-words in **3A.1**.

Hans weiß **nicht**?

Er hat **keine** Ahnung.

- **Kein** follows the same patterns of gender and case endings as **ein**. Note that, unlike **ein**, **kein** has a plural form.

kein				
	masculine	**feminine**	**neuter**	**plural**
nominative	kein Ball	keine Freizeit	kein Spiel	keine Karten
accusative	keinen Ball	keine Freizeit	kein Spiel	keine Karten

—Hast du **einen** Fußball?
—*Do you have **a** soccer ball?*

▶ —Nein, ich habe **keinen** Fußball.
—*No, I don't have **a** soccer ball.*

—Ist das **ein** Stadion?
—*Is that **a** stadium?*

▶ —Nein, das ist **kein** Stadion.
—*No, that's **not a** stadium.*

—Sind das Basketballspieler?
—*Are those guys basketball players?*

▶ —Nein, das sind **keine** Basketballspieler.
—*No, those are**n't** basketball players.*

Doch

- The conjunction **doch** has no exact equivalent in English. Use it to contradict a negative question or statement.

—Ich habe **keine** Freunde.
—*I don't have **any** friends.*

▶ —**Doch**, du hast viele Freunde!
—***No**, you have lots of friends!*

—Gehst du **nicht** zum Strand?
—*Are**n't** you going to the beach?*

▶ —**Doch**, ich gehe zum Strand.
—***Yes**, I'm going to the beach.*

Suggestion Point out that the responses **Ja**, **Nein**, and **Doch** at the beginning of a sentence do not affect subject-verb word order.

Ressourcen

SAM
WB: pp. 31–32

SAM
LM: p. 20

(S)
vhlcentral.com

 Jetzt sind Sie dran!   **Complete the sentences with the appropriate form of nicht or kein.**

1. Der Volleyballspieler ist ___*nicht*___ sehr fit.

2. Stefan hat ___keinen___ Fußball.

3. Wir machen die Hausaufgaben ___nicht___.

4. Übermorgen habe ich ___keine___ Vorlesung.

5. Uwe trainiert ___nicht___ und verliert das Spiel.

6. Leider (*Unfortunately*) habe ich ___kein___ Foto.

7. Bernhard spielt viel Fußball, aber er gewinnt ___keine___ Spiele.

8. Du schwimmst ___nicht___ im See (*lake*).

9. Wir sehen den Film ___nicht___.

10. Ihr habt ___keine___ Freizeit.

11. Am Donnerstag fahren wir ___nicht___ in die Berge.

12. Es gibt ___kein___ Stadion in der Stadt.

Anwendung

1 **Verneinen Sie** Negate the sentences using **nicht**.

1. Wir haben die Karten.
   Wir haben die Karten nicht.
2. Ich vergesse die Hausaufgaben.
   Ich vergesse die Hausaufgaben nicht.
3. Wir reiten am Wochenende.
   Wir reiten am Wochenende nicht.
4. Ich spiele Schach mit Katrina und Wilfried.
   Ich spiele nicht Schach mit Katrina und Wilfried.

5. Du tanzt in der Disko.
   Du tanzt nicht in der Disko.
6. Ihr verliert das Volleyballspiel.
   Ihr verliert das Volleyballspiel nicht.
7. Thomas und Brigitte schwimmen am Nachmittag.
   Thomas und Brigitte schwimmen am Nachmittag nicht.
8. Am Sonntag gehen wir angeln.
   Am Sonntag gehen wir nicht angeln.

2 **Antworten Sie** Answer the questions using **kein**.

BEISPIEL

S1: *Hast du Hobbys?*
S2: *Nein, ich habe keine Hobbys.*

1. Hat Peter ein schnelles (*fast*) Fahrrad?
   Nein, Peter hat kein schnelles Fahrrad.
2. Habt ihr Freizeit?
   Nein, wir haben keine Freizeit.
3. Sind das Spielerinnen?
   Nein, das sind keine Spielerinnen.
4. Ist Berlin ein Land (*country*)?
   Nein, Berlin ist kein Land.
5. Ist Alexandra eine Hockeyspielerin?
   Nein, Alexandra ist keine Hockeyspielerin.

6. Hast du einen Basketball?
   Nein, ich habe keinen Basketball.
7. Gibt es ein Stadion in der Stadt?
   Nein, es gibt kein Stadion in der Stadt.
8. Spielst du Volleyball?
   Nein, ich spiele keinen Volleyball.
9. Ist Salzburg ein Berg?
   Nein, Salzburg ist kein Berg.
10. Haben Sie Karten?
    Nein, ich habe keine Karten.

3 **Was fehlt?** Complete the conversation with **nicht**, **kein**, or **doch**.

KARIN Hallo, Alina! Geht's dir gut? Warst (*Were*) du (1) ___nicht___ beim Training?

ALINA Gestern (*Yesterday*)? (2) ___Doch___! Aber heute Abend komme ich (3) ___nicht___.

KARIN Schade (*That's too bad*)! Warum (4) ___nicht___?

ALINA Ich habe (5) ___keine___ Fußballschuhe (*soccer shoes*). Die alten (*old*) Fußballschuhe sind zu klein (*too small*).

KARIN Wo kaufst du Schuhe? Nicht bei (*at*) Galeria Kaufhof, oder?

ALINA (6) ___Doch___, die Schuhe dort finde ich schön.

Kommunikation

4 **Partnerinterview** In pairs, take turns asking each other the questions. Contradict your partner's questions using **nicht**, **kein**, or **doch**. Sample answers are provided.

4 **Expansion** Have students create their own questions to ask their partners.

> **BEISPIEL**
>
> **S1:** Hast du einen Basketball?
> **S2:** Nein, ich habe keinen Basketball.
> **S1:** Tanzt du nicht am Wochenende?
> **S2:** Doch, ich tanze am Wochenende.

1. Spielst du Hockey?
   Nein, ich spiele kein Hockey.
2. Wanderst du in den Bergen
   (*in the mountains*)?
   Nein, ich wandere nicht in den Bergen.
3. Fährst du im Dezember an den
   (*to the*) Strand?
   Nein, ich fahre im Dezember nicht an den Strand.
4. Hast du kein Fahrrad?
   Doch, ich habe ein Fahrrad.

5. Trainierst du für
   einen Marathonlauf?
   Nein, ich trainiere für keinen Marathonlauf.
6. Hast du nicht viele
   (*a lot of*) Hausaufgaben?
   Doch, ich habe viele Hausaufgaben.
7. Schwimmst du im Schwimmbad?
   Nein, ich schwimme nicht im Schwimmbad.
8. Bist du ein guter Tennisspieler?
   Nein, ich bin kein guter Tennisspieler.

5 **Das stimmt nicht!** In pairs, take turns making false statements about the photos. Correct your partner's false statements by negating them, then supply the correct answer. Answers will vary.

> ▶ **BEISPIEL**
>
> **S1:** Die Frau fährt Auto.
> **S2:** Nein, sie fährt nicht Auto. Sie fährt Fahrrad.

1.

2.

3.

4.

5.

6.

6 **Ich habe es schlecht** In pairs, take turns coming up with exaggerations using **nicht** and **kein**. Contradict your partner's exaggerations using **doch**. Answers will vary.

> **BEISPIEL**
>
> **S1:** Wir haben keine Freizeit!
> **S2:** Doch, wir haben viele Freizeit!

7 **Trauriger Jörn** In small groups, explain why Jörn is sad, using negative statements. Answers will vary.

> **BEISPIEL**
>
> **S1:** Jörn hat keine Freunde.
> **S2:** Er studiert nächstes Jahr nicht an der Universität.

Wiederholung

1 Expansion Have students add their partner's name to the list and ask questions in order to fill out their partner's row in the chart.

1 Gute Freunde

In pairs, look at the information provided about each person. Decide which of them are friends, based on their interests. Answers will vary.

BEISPIEL Heidi fährt Ski und Florian fährt auch Ski. Heidi und Florian sind Freunde.

	Tennis spielen	Musik hören	Kuchen backen	Ski fahren	Fahrrad fahren	Fremdsprachen sprechen
Heidi	✓			✓		✓
Daniela		✓		✓	✓	✓
Magda		✓	✓	✓		✓
Klaus		✓			✓	✓
Florian	✓			✓	✓	✓
Oliver			✓	✓	✓	

2 Begriffe raten

In small groups, take turns drawing pictures based on words or phrases you learned in **Lektionen 2A** and **2B**. The first person to guess the word or phrase draws next. Answers will vary.

BEISPIEL

S1: Spielt er Schach?
S2: Nein.
S3: Spielt er Karten?
S2: Ja, richtig!

3 Viele Fragen

Start a conversation with a classmate using the questions as prompts. Ask follow-up questions using time expressions. Answers will vary.

BEISPIEL

S1: Machst du deine (your) Hausaufgaben?
S2: Ja, ich mache immer (always) meine Hausaufgaben.
S1: Hast du Hausaufgaben in Geschichte?
S2: Nein, ich habe heute keine Hausaufgaben in Geschichte.

1. Liest du viele Bücher?
2. Reist du im Winter nach Kanada?
3. Sprichst du Deutsch?
4. Verstehst du Mathematik?
5. Machst du viel Sport?
6. Spielst du Schach?
7. Isst du in der Mensa?
8. Fährst du viel Fahrrad?

4 Terminkalender

Your instructor will give you and your partner different worksheets showing schedules. Take turns asking and answering questions to find out the missing information.

BEISPIEL

S1: Wann gehst du ins Stadion?
S2: Nächsten Montag um halb fünf nachmittags.

5 Vermischtes

Use the cues to form questions. Then, in pairs, take turns asking and answering the questions. Answers will vary.

BEISPIEL

S1: Hast du heute Abend Freizeit?
S2: Nein, ich habe heute Abend keine Freizeit.

1. angeln gehen / du / am Sonntag
2. Tennis spielen / du / samstags
3. gehen / du / oft / in die Sporthalle
4. Tennisschuhe / haben / keine / du
5. du / reiten / am Wochenende
6. du / schlafen / bis spät (late) / sonntags
7. für die Prüfung / lernen / nicht / du
8. du / nicht / aus Tennessee / sein

6 Schiffe versenken

Your instructor will give you and your partner each a worksheet. Take turns asking questions to find each other's battleships.

BEISPIEL

S1: Liest Otto ein Buch?
S2: Treffer (Hit)! Er liest ein Buch./ Nein, kein Treffer. Er liest nicht.

	lesen	arbeiten
Otto		
Lukas und Maria		🚢

7 Marias Leben
In pairs, take turns asking and answering questions about Maria's activities. Sample answers are provided.

▶ **BEISPIEL**

Dienstag, 9.15

S1: Was macht Maria am Dienstag um Viertel nach neun morgens?

S2: Am Dienstag um Viertel nach neun morgens macht Maria Hausaufgaben.

1. morgen, 10.30
Was macht Maria morgen um halb elf vormittags? Morgen um halb elf vormittags lernt Maria Deutsch.

2. heute, 12.00
Was macht Maria heute Mittag? Heute Mittag spielt Maria Tennis.

3. Samstag, 14.00
Was macht Maria am Samstag um zwei Uhr nachmittags? Am Samstag um zwei Uhr nachmittags liest Maria ein Buch.

4. heute Nachmittag, 14.25
Was macht Maria heute Nachmittag um fünf vor halb drei? Heute Nachmittag um fünf vor halb drei trinkt Maria einen Kaffee.

5. nächsten Montag, 17.45
Was macht Maria nächsten Montag um Viertel vor sechs nachmittags? Nächsten Montag um Viertel vor sechs nachmittags trifft Maria eine Freundin.

6. Freitag, 23.15
Was macht Maria am Freitag um Viertel nach elf abends? Am Freitag um Viertel nach elf abends schläft Maria.

8 Minigeschichte
In small groups, make up a story about the people in the picture. Be as detailed as possible. You may want to give the people names. Answers will vary.

BEISPIEL

S1: Es ist Samstag und viele Leute sind im Park.

S2: Markus und David spielen nicht mehr Basketball. Sie gehen nach Hause (*home*).

fit	trainieren
gewinnen	treffen
sportlich	verlieren

Mein Wör|ter|buch

Add five words related to the themes **an der Universität** and **Sport und Freizeit** to your personalized dictionary.

die Klausur, -en

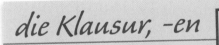

Übersetzung
exam

Wortart
das Substantiv

Gebrauch
Ich muss viel lernen, denn morgen habe ich eine Klausur.

Synonyme
die Prüfung, das Examen, der Test

Antonyme
___

Panorama ⓢ Map

Berlin

Die Stadt in Zahlen

- ▶ **Fläche:** *892 km² (Quadratkilometer)*
- ▶ **Einwohner°** der Stadt Berlin: *3.443.570*
- ▶ **Ausländer°** in Berlin: *474.959 (aus 195 Ländern)*
- ▶ **Touristen (2008):** *7.905.145*
- ▶ **Fastfood:** *Döner Kebap, erfunden° 1961 von Mehmet Aygün in Berlin; etwa 1.600 Verkaufsstellen° Currywurst (70 Millionen pro Jahr), erfunden 1949 von Herta Heuwer in Berlin; etwa 200 Verkaufsstellen*
- ▶ **Touristenattraktionen:** *das Brandenburger Tor, der Reichstag, die Gedächtniskirche, der Gendarmenmarkt, der Alexanderplatz, das Holocaust-Mahnmal, die Museumsinsel, der Potsdamer Platz, das Nikolaiviertel.*

QUELLE: Berlin - offizielles Hauptstadtportal

Berühmte Berliner

- ▶ **Friedrich II. (Friedrich der Große),** *König von Preußen° (1712–1786)*
- ▶ **Alexander von Humboldt,** *Naturforscher° (1769–1859)*
- ▶ **Gustav Langenscheidt,** *Deutschlehrer und Verlagsbuchhändler° (1832–1895)*
- ▶ **Berthold Brecht,** *Dramatiker° (1898–1956)*
- ▶ **Marlene Dietrich,** *Schauspielerin° und Sängerin° (1901–1992)*
- ▶ **Thomas „Icke" Häßler,** *Fußballspieler (1966–)*
- ▶ **Franziska van Almsick,** *Schwimmerin (1978–)*

Suggestion Tell students that Berlin has a Currywurst Museum. You may want to play Herbert Grönemeyer's song *Currywurst* for the class.

Expansion Ask students questions to review numbers. Ex.: **Wie viele Touristen besuchen Berlin 2008? Wie alt ist Franziska von Almsick?**

Expansion Ask students to plan a trip to Berlin for next year. Ask them what sites they will visit and what they will do on their trip.

Einwohner *inhabitants* **Ausländer** *foreigners* **erfunden** *invented* **Verkaufsstellen** *points of sale* **König von Preußen** *King of Prussia* **Naturforscher** *naturalist* **Verlagsbuchhändler** *publisher* **Dramatiker** *playwright* **Schauspielerin** *actress* **Sängerin** *singer* **Weltkrieg** *World War* **in Trümmern** *in ruins* **Gebäude zerstört** *buildings destroyed* **Wohnungen** *apartments* **Krankenhäuser** *hospitals* **beschädigt** *damaged*

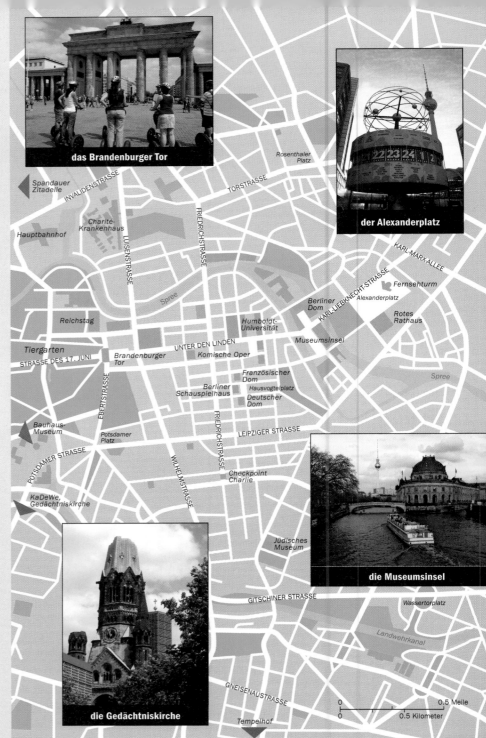

das Brandenburger Tor

der Alexanderplatz

die Museumsinsel

die Gedächtniskirche

Unglaublich aber wahr!

Am 2. Mai 1945 endet der 2. Weltkrieg° in Berlin. 28.5 km² der Stadt liegen in Trümmern°. Im Zentrum sind etwa 50% der Gebäude zerstört°. Etwa 600.000 Wohnungen° sind komplett zerstört. Die Infrastruktur der Stadt, Straßen, Schulen und Krankenhäuser° sind schwer beschädigt°. In Berlin leben noch 2,8 Millionen Menschen, vor dem Krieg sind es 4,3 Millionen.

Symbol

Der Berliner Bär°

Seit 1280 hat Berlin ein offizielles Wappentier°, den Berliner Bären. Jedes Jahr feiern die Berliner am 22. März den Tag des Berliner Bären. Im Jahr 2001 bemalten° Künstler circa 350 Bärenskulpturen. Diese Bären, oder „Buddy Bären", sind alle individuell bemalt. Sie sind so groß wie echte° Bären. Man kann sie in ganz Berlin finden. Es gibt über 1.000 Buddy Bären in der Welt.

Sport

Olympische Spiele 1936

Die Olympischen Sommerspiele 1936 finden vom 1. bis 16. August 1936 in Berlin statt°. 3.961 Athleten aus 49 Nationen nehmen an den Spielen teil° – ein neuer Rekord. Der bekannteste° Sportler dieser Spiele ist der amerikanische Leichtathlet Jesse Owens. Er gewinnt vier Goldmedaillen. Der erfolgreichste° deutsche Athlet ist der Kunstturner° Konrad Frey mit drei Goldmedaillen, einer Silbermedaille und zwei Bronzemedaillen. Die Nationalsozialisten missbrauchen° die Spiele als Propaganda.

Architektur

Der Reichstag°

Zwischen 1884 und 1894 errichtet der Architekt Paul Wallot den Reichstag. Er ist das wichtigste° Gebäude der deutschen Politik: bis 1918 trifft sich hier der Reichstag des Deutschen Kaiserreichs°, danach das Parlament der Weimarer Republik, und seit 1999 der Deutsche Bundestag. 1933 ist der legendäre Reichstagsbrand°. Heute besuchen Touristen oft die Glaskuppel. Sie ist 23,5 Meter hoch°, 38 Meter breit° und 1.200 Tonnen schwer°. Im Sommer 1995 verhüllen° die Künstler Christo und Jeanne-Claude den Reichstag komplett. 5 Millionen Besucher° kommen nach Berlin, um den Reichstag zu sehen.

Kultur

Karneval der Kulturen

Berlin ist eine internationale Stadt mit mehr als 450.000 Menschen aus 195 Ländern. Seit 1996 gibt es jedes Jahr ein Fest, um die Internationalität und Kulturenvielfalt° Berlins zu feiern: den Karneval der Kulturen. Es gibt einen großen Umzug° mit 4.700 Teilnehmern und ein viertägiges Straßenfest mit mehr als 800 Künstlern – Musik, Tanz, Performance – aus über 70 Ländern. 2011 besuchen 1,35 Millionen Menschen das Event in Berlin-Kreuzberg. 750.000 sehen den Umzug. An den vier Tagen kann man viele kulinarische und handwerkliche° Sachen genießen°.

IM INTERNET

1. Suchen Sie Informationen über Marlene Dietrich. Wann beginnt ihre (her) Karriere? Suchen Sie die drei bekanntesten Filme.

2. Was ist die Museumsinsel? Suchen Sie Informationen über mindestens (at least) drei Museen der Museumsinsel.

3. Suchen Sie Beispiele für „Ostalgie" (nostalgia for the East).

For more information on this **Panorama**, go to **vhlcentral.com**.

Bär *bear* **Wappentier** *heraldic animal* **bemalten** *painted* **echte** *real* **finden... statt** *take place* **nehmen... teil** *participate* **bekannteste** *most well-known* **erfolgreichste** *most successful* **Kunstturner** *gymnast* **missbrauchen** *misuse* **Reichstag** *parliament building* **wichtigste** *most important* **des Deutschen Kaiserreichs** *of the German empire* **Reichstagsbrand** *Reichstag fire* **hoch** *high* **breit** *wide* **schwer** *heavy* **verhüllen** *cover with fabric* **Besucher** *visitors* **Kulturenvielfalt** *cultural diversity* **Umzug** *parade* **handwerkliche** *crafts* **genießen** *enjoy*

Was haben Sie gelernt? Complete the sentences.

1. Die Fläche Berlins ist ____892____ Quadratkilometer.

2. Nach dem 2. Weltkrieg sind ____(etwa) 600.000____ Wohnungen in Berlin zerstört.

3. Seit ____1280____ ist der Bär das Wappentier Berlins.

4. In Berlin gibt es etwa 350 von Künstlern bemalte ___Bärenskulpturen/(Buddy) Bären___

5. Der erfolgreichste deutsche Athlet bei den Olympischen Spielen 1936 ist ___Konrad Frey___.

6. An den Olympischen Spielen 1936 nehmen 3.961 ___Athleten___ teil.

7. Paul Wallot errichtet den Reichstag zwischen ____1884____ und 1894.

8. Im Sommer 1995 kommen 5 Millionen ___Besucher___ nach Berlin, um den Reichstag zu sehen.

9. Der Karneval der Kulturen dauert (lasts) ____vier____ Tage.

10. Besucher sehen Künstler – Musiker, Tänzer, etc. – aus über ____70____ Ländern beim Karneval der Kulturen.

 Practice more at **vhlcentral.com**.

Lesen

 **Reading: Audio**

Vor dem Lesen

Strategien

Predicting content through formats

Recognizing the format of a text can help you to predict its content. For example, invitations, greeting cards, and classified ads follow easily identifiable formats, which usually give you a general idea of the information they contain. Look at the text and identify it based on its format.

Uhrzeit	Montag	Dienstag	Mittwoch	Donnerstag	Freitag
7.55	Deutsch	Französisch	Biologie	Religion	Mathe
8.40	Englisch	Musik	Geschichte	Physik	Mathe
9.40	Sport	Geschichte	Mathe	Französisch	Englisch
10.25	Sport	Mathe	Englisch	Französisch	Chemie
11.25	Religion	Physik	Erdkunde	Erdkunde	Musik
12.10	Sozialkunde	Chemie	Deutsch	Deutsch	Bio

If you guessed that this is a page from a student's weekly planner, you are correct. You can now infer that it contains information about a student's weekly schedule, including days, times, classes, and activities.

Texte verstehen

Briefly look at the document. What is its format? What kind of information is given? How is it organized? What are the visual components? What types of documents usually contain these elements?

Verwandte Wörter

You have already learned that you can use cognates, as well as format, to help you predict the content of a document. With a classmate, make a list of all the cognates you find in the reading selection. Based on these cognates and the format of the document, can you guess what this document is and what it is for?

Karlswald-Universität
Studienkolleg Mittelhessen

4 Stunden pro Tag (Montag–Freitag)
2 Tutorien pro Woche

Kurse

- Grundstufe: Anfänger°
- Stufe 1: Einführung° I
- Stufe 2: Einführung II
- Stufe 3: fortgeschritten° I
- Stufe 4: fortgeschritten II
- Stufe 5/6: Vorbereitung° auf die DSH-Prüfung

Kosten

- Einstufungstest: 50 Euro
- Stufe 1, 2, 3 und 4: 410 Euro pro Kurs
- Stufe 5/6: 620 Euro

Unterbringung°

- In Studentenwohnheimen
- In Privatwohnungen

Studienkolleg Mittelhessen
Friedrichstraße 3 | D-35032 Marburg

ausländische *foreign* **die... wollen** *who want* **Anfänger** *beginner* **Einführung** *introduction*
fortgeschritten *advanced* **Vorbereitung** *preparation* **Unterbringung** *accommodations*

Die Deutschkurse an der Karlswald-Universität: Deutschtraining für ausländische° Studenten, die in Karlswald studieren wollen°.

Stufe 1–4 vom 3. Januar bis 14. Februar
Stufe 5/6 vom 3. Januar bis 22. März

Große Auswahl° zusätzlicher Aktivitäten:

- Tagesausflüge° zu Städten der Region (Frankfurt, Eisenach, Heidelberg)
- Besuche von Sehenswürdigkeiten° (Elisabethkirche, Marburger Schloss)
- Besuche von Kulturveranstaltungen° (Theaterproduktionen, Konzerte)
- Sport und andere Aktivitäten

Suggestion Encourage students to record unfamiliar words and phrases that they learn from this reading in their personalized dictionaries.

Intensives Training in Hörverständnis°, Leseverständnis und Textproduktion.

Tel.: (06421) 28 23 651 - Fax.: (06421) 28 23 652
www.uni-karlswald.de/studienkolleg

Auswahl *selection* **Tagesausflüge** *day trips* **Sehenswürdigkeiten** *places of interest*
Kulturveranstaltungen *cultural events* **Hörverständnis** *listening comprehension*

Nach dem Lesen

 Antworten Sie Select the option that best completes the statement.

1. Das ist eine Broschüre für...
   a. ein deutsches Gymnasium.
   (b.) ein Institut für Deutschkurse.
   c. Studenten, die Englisch lernen wollen.

2. Studenten, die kein Deutsch sprechen, nehmen den Kurs...
   (a.) Grundstufe.   b. Stufe 3.   c. Stufe 5/6.

3. Jeden (*Every*) Tag haben Studenten in einem Kurs...
   (a.) 4 Stunden Deutschunterricht.
   b. 4 Stunden Tutorien.
   c. 2 Stunden Deutschunterricht.

4. Der Test am Ende der Stufe 5/6...
   a. ist intensives Training.
   b. hat kein Hörverständnis.
   (c.) heißt DSH-Prüfung.

5. Studenten wohnen...
   a. bei deutschen Familien.
   (b.) im Studentenwohnheim.
   c. in Frankfurt.

6. An Wochenenden besuchen Studenten...
   a. Studentenheime und Privatwohnungen.
   (b.) Frankfurt und andere Städte.
   c. die Universität.

7. Kurse kosten...
   a. 50 Euro.
   b. 1.030 Euro.
   (c.) 410 oder 620 Euro.

Suggestion Go over the answers with the whole class or have students check their answers in pairs.

8. Die Kurse der Stufe 1, 2, 3 und 4 dauern...
   a. 4 Wochen.   (b.) 6 Wochen.   c. 11 Wochen.

 Richtig oder falsch Mark the appropriate box.

	richtig	falsch
1. Das Studienkolleg Mittelhessen ist für deutsche Studenten.	☐	☑
2. Die Deutschkurse sind 5 Stunden jeden Tag.	☐	☑
3. Es gibt Tagesausflüge nach Frankfurt, Eisenach und Heidelberg.	☑	☐
4. Das Studienkolleg ist in der Friedrichstraße 3, D-35032 Marburg.	☑	☐

Hören

Vorbereitung

Based on the photograph, who do you think Julian and Anni are? Where are they? Do they know each other well? Where are they going this morning? What are they talking about?

Zuhören

Listen to the conversation and list any cognates you hear. Listen again and complete the highlighted portions of Julian's schedule.

4. April   Montag

9.30	*Kaffee mit Ingrid in der Cafeteria*	14.30	
10.00	Seminar zur englischen Literatur	15.00	*lernen mit Klaus*
10.30		15.30	
11.00		16.00	
11.30		16.30	
12.00	*Mittagessen mit Karl in der Mensa*	17.00	Fußball spielen
12.30		17.30	
13.00		18.00	
13.30		18.30	
14.00	Englischvorlesung	19.00	*Konzert im Kulturladen*

Verständnis

Richtig oder falsch? Indicate whether each sentence is **richtig** or **falsch**. Then, in pairs, correct any false statements.

1. Anni studiert jeden (*every*) Morgen in der Bibliothek.
   Richtig.

2. Julian und Anni studieren Architektur.
   Falsch. Julian studiert englische Literatur und Anni studiert Architektur.

3. Um 9.30 Uhr trinkt Julian mit Ingrid Kaffee.
   Richtig.

4. Anni hat um 2 Uhr eine Vorlesung.
   Falsch. Julian hat um 2 Uhr eine Vorlesung.

5. Anni findet englische Literatur interessant.
   Falsch. Anni ist kein großer Literaturfan.

6. Anni und Julian haben langweilige Professoren.
   Richtig.

7. Julian und Anni gehen am Nachmittag Fußball spielen.
   Falsch. Julian geht am Nachmittag Fußball spielen.

8. Julian geht am Abend in ein Konzert.
   Richtig.

Pläne In pairs, discuss your plans for this weekend, including where and when you will do each activity.

Suggestion To check answers for **Zuhören**, have students work in pairs and ask each other questions about Julian's schedule.

Schreiben

Strategien

Brainstorming

Brainstorming can help you generate ideas on a specific topic. Before you begin writing, you should spend 10–15 minutes brainstorming, jotting down any ideas about the topic that occur to you. Whenever possible, try to write down your ideas in German. Express your ideas in single words or phrases, and jot them down in any order. While brainstorming, do not worry about whether your ideas are good or bad. Selecting and organizing ideas should be the second stage of your writing. The more ideas you write down while you are brainstorming, the more options you will have to choose from later on, when you start to organize your ideas.

Hobbys...
reiten
angeln gehen
Tennis spielen
kochen
tanzen
Camping
schwimmen
Fahrrad fahren

Thema

 ### Eine persönliche Beschreibung

Write a description of yourself to post on a Web site in order to find a German-speaking e-pal. Your description should include:

- your name and where you are from.
- your birthday.
- the name of your university and where it is located.
- the courses you are currently taking and your opinion of each one.
- your hobbies and pastimes.
- any other information you would like to include.

Hallo!

Ich heiße Markus Schneider und ich komme aus Köln. Ich studiere Physik an der Technischen Universität in Berlin. Ich fahre Ski, spiele Tennis und fahre Fahrrad...

 **Flashcards Audio: Vocabulary**

das Studium

der Abschluss, -̈e/ das Diplom, -e	degree
das Abschlusszeugnis, -se/ das Diplom, -e	diploma
der Dozent, -en / die Dozentin, -nen	college/university instructor
das Fach, -̈er	subject
das Seminar, -e	seminar
das Stipendium, -en	scholarship
die Veranstaltung, -en	class
die Vorlesung, -en	lecture
(die) Architektur	architecture
(die) Biologie	biology
(die) Chemie	chemistry
(die) Fremdsprache, -n	foreign language
(die) Geschichte	history
(die) Informatik	computer science
(die) Kunst, -̈e	art
(die) Literatur	literature
(die) Mathematik	math
(die) Medizin	medicine
(die) Naturwissenschaft, -en	science
(die) Physik	physics
(die) Psychologie	psychology
(die) Wirtschaft	business
belegen	to take (a class)
gehen	to go
lernen	to study; to learn
studieren	to study; to major in

Orte

das Café, -s	café
der Hörsaal, Hörsäle	lecture hall
der Seminarraum, -räume	(college/university) classroom
die Sporthalle, -n	gym

der Stundenplan

der Montag, -e	Monday
der Dienstag, -e	Tuesday
der Mittwoch, -e	Wednesday
der Donnerstag, -e	Thursday
der Freitag, -e	Friday
der Samstag, -e	Saturday
der Sonntag, -e	Sunday
die Woche, -n	week
das Wochenende, -n	weekend
morgens	in the morning
nachmittags	in the afternoon
abends	in the evening
montags	on Mondays
dienstags	on Tuesdays
mittwochs	on Wednesdays
donnerstags	on Thursdays
freitags	on Fridays
samstags	on Saturdays
sonntags	on Sundays

Sportarten

(der) Baseball	baseball
(der) Basketball	basketball
(der) (American) Football	football
(der) Fußball	soccer
(das) Golf	golf
(das) Hockey	hockey
(die) Leichtathletik	track and field
(das) Tennis	tennis
(der) Volleyball	volleyball
der Ball, -̈e	ball
die Mannschaft, -en	team
das Schwimmbad, -̈er	swimming pool
das Spiel, -e	game
der Spieler, - / die Spielerin, -nen	player
das Spielfeld, -er/ der Platz, -̈e	field, court
der Sport	sports
das Stadion, Stadien	stadium
Fahrrad fahren	to ride a bicycle
Ski fahren	to ski
gewinnen	to win
schwimmen	to swim
spielen	to play
üben/trainieren	to practice
verlieren	to lose

zum Beschreiben

einfach	easy
nützlich	useful
nutzlos	useless
schwierig	difficult

Freizeit

der Berg, -e	mountain
das Camping	camping
das Fahrrad, -̈er	bicycle
die Freizeit	free time
die Freizeitaktivität, -en	leisure activity
das Hobby, -s	hobby
die Karte, -n	card
der Park, -s	park
das Schach	chess
der Strand, -̈e	beach
der Wald, -̈er	forest
angeln gehen	to go fishing
essen gehen	to eat out
spazieren gehen	to go for a walk
klettern	to (rock) climb
kochen	to cook
reiten	to ride a horse
schreiben	to write
singen	to sing
tanzen	to dance
wandern	to hike

Regular verbs	See pp. 56–57.
Interrogative words	See p. 60.
Telling time	See p. 62.
Ordinal numbers and dates	See p. 63.
Stem-changing verbs	See pp. 76–77.
Common time expressions	See p. 80.
Negative words	See pp. 82–83.

Ressourcen vhlcentral.com

Suggestion Ask students: Who are the people in the photo and what are they doing?

Communicative Goals

You will learn how to:

- talk about families
- talk about marital status
- describe people
- express ownership

Suggestion Point out to students that **die Eltern** has no singular form. Mention that nouns like **Eltern** and **Leute**, which exist only in the plural, have no grammatical gender in German.

Sabine Schmidts Familie

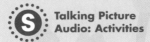

S Talking Picture
Audio: Activities

Walter Gärtner

mein Großvater/Opa (*m.*)

Wortschatz

die Familie	*family*
das Baby, -s	*baby*
die Eltern	*parents*
das Geschwister, -	*sibling*
die Großeltern	*grandparents*
der Halbbruder, -¨	*half brother*
die Halbschwester, -n	*half sister*
das Kind, -er	*child*
der Nachname, -n	*last name*
das Paar, -e	*couple*
der Schwager, -¨	*brother-in-law*
die Schwägerin, -nen	*sister-in-law*
die Schwiegermutter, -¨	*mother-in-law*
der Schwiegervater, -¨	*father-in-law*
der Stiefbruder, -¨	*stepbrother*
die Stiefmutter, -¨	*stepmother*
die Stiefschwester, -n	*stepsister*
der Stiefsohn, -¨e	*stepson*
die Stieftochter, -¨	*stepdaughter*
der Stiefvater, -¨	*stepfather*
der / die Verwandte, -n	*relative*
der Zwilling, -e	*twin*
die Haustiere	*pets*
der Fisch, -e	*fish*
der Hund, -e	*dog*
die Katze, -n	*cat*
der Vogel, -¨	*bird*
der Familienstand	*marital status*
die Witwe, -n	*widow*
der Witwer, -	*widower*
geschieden	*divorced*
getrennt	*separated*
ledig	*single*
verheiratet	*married*
verlobt	*engaged*
heiraten	*to marry*
zum Beschreiben	*to describe*
blaue/grüne/braune Augen	*blue/green/brown eyes*
blonde/braune/ schwarze Haare	*blond/brown/ black hair*
dunkel	*dark*
hell	*light*

Suggestion Point out to students that **Geschwister** is primarily used in the plural. Model this usage by asking individual students whether they have any siblings. Ex.: **Hast du noch Geschwister? Ja, ich habe eine Schwester und zwei Brüder.**

Peter Schmidt   **Marianne Schmidt**

mein Vater (*m.*),
Mariannes Mann (*m.*)

meine Mutter (*f.*),
Walter und Hannas
Tochter (*f.*)

Michaela Schmidt   **Markus Schmidt**   **Sabine Schmidt**

meine Schwägerin   mein Bruder (*m.*)   ich, Peter und
Mariannes Tochter

Jonas Schmidt   **Greta Schmidt**

mein Neffe (*m.*)   meine Nichte (*f.*)
Peter und Mariannes Enkelkinder

ACHTUNG

To say *my big/little brother/sister*,
use **mein großer/kleiner Bruder** or
meine große/kleine Schwester.

Ressourcen

SAM
WB: pp. 33–34

SAM
LM: p. 21

S
vhlcentral.com

Hanna Gärtner

meine Großmutter/Oma *(f.)*

Dieter Gärtner

mein Onkel *(m.)*,
Walter und Hannas
Sohn *(m.)*

Renate Gärtner

meine Tante *(f.)*,
Dieters Frau *(f.)*

Stefan Gärtner

mein Cousin *(m.)*,
Walter und Hannas
Enkelsohn *(m.)*

Sandra Gärtner

meine Cousine *(f.)*,
Stefan und Katjas
Schwester *(f.)*

Katja Gärtner

meine Cousine,
Stefan und Sandras
Schwester,
Walter und Hannas
Enkeltochter *(f.)*

Zeus

Stefan, Sandra und
Katjas Hund

Anwendung

1 **Kombinieren Sie** Match the people with the descriptions.

__g__ 1. Mariannes Bruder
__d__ 2. Markus' Frau
__a__ 3. Marianne und Peter
__c__ 4. Dieter und Renates Sohn
__h__ 5. Mariannes Vater
__f__ 6. Peter und Mariannes Sohn
__e__ 7. Markus' Tochter
__b__ 8. Dieters Frau

a. Sabines Eltern
b. Sabines Tante
c. Sabines Cousin
d. Sabines Schwägerin
e. Sabines Nichte
f. Sabines Bruder
g. Sabines Onkel
h. Sabines Opa

> **1** **Expansion** Get
> students started by
> asking them questions
> about their own
> families. Ex.: **Haben
> Sie Geschwister?**

2 **Identifizieren Sie** Write each person's family relationship to Dieter Gärtner.

BEISPIEL Hanna: ___*die Mutter*___

1. Sandra: ___die Tochter___
2. Marianne: ___die Schwester___
3. Markus: ___der Neffe___
4. Peter: ___der Schwager___
5. Stefan: ___der Sohn___
6. Sabine: ___die Nichte___
7. Walter und Hanna: ___die Eltern___
8. Renate: ___die Frau___

3 **Kategorien** List at least four roles each person could have in a family.

Sample answers are provided.

BEISPIEL eine Frau, 40 Jahre alt
eine Mutter   *eine Tante*   *eine Cousine*   *eine Tochter*

1. ein Mann, 62 Jahre alt:
   ___ein Schwager___   ___ein Großvater___   ___ein Schwiegervater___   ___ein Vater___
2. ein Kind, 3 Jahre alt:
   ___ein Sohn___   ___ein Neffe___   ___ein Enkelsohn___   ___ein Bruder___
3. ein Mädchen, 15 Jahre alt:
   ___eine Cousine___   ___eine Schwester___   ___eine Tochter___   ___eine Enkeltochter___
4. eine Frau, 50 Jahre alt:
   ___eine Oma___   ___eine Tante___   ___eine Schwägerin___   ___eine Mutter___

4 **Hören Sie zu** Listen to Sabine's descriptions and indicate whether each statement is **richtig** or **falsch**, based on her family tree.

	richtig	falsch		richtig	falsch
1.	☑	☐	7.	☐	☑
2.	☐	☑	8.	☐	☑
3.	☑	☐	9.	☑	☐
4.	☑	☐	10.	☐	☑
5.	☐	☑	11.	☐	☑
6.	☑	☐	12.	☑	☐

Practice more at **vhlcentral.com**.

Kommunikation

5 Beschreibungen Use words from the list to describe the images. Compare your answers with a classmate's, and correct each other's work. Sample answers are provided.

> Enkelkinder | Großeltern | Neffe | Sohn | verheiratet | verlobt | Zwillinge

► **BEISPIEL**

Das Paar ist verlobt.

5 Suggestion Give students cues to help them complete this activity. Ask them questions about the pictures. Ex.: **Wer sind die Leute? Wie alt ist das Kind?**

1. Das Kind ist der Neffe.

2. Die Kinder sind Zwillinge.

3. Der Mann und die Frau sind verheiratet.

4. Die Mutter hat einen Sohn.

5. Die Großmutter hat drei Enkelkinder.

6. Die Großeltern grüßen die Familie.

6 Brieffreunde Read Eva's letter. Then, in pairs, take turns answering the questions. Sample answers are provided.

Liebe Andrea,

du möchtest wissen (would like to know), wie groß meine Familie ist? Also, ich habe eine große Schwester Nicole und einen kleinen Halbbruder Peter. Und wir haben einen Hund, Cäsar, und Miezi, unsere kleine Katze.

Nicole studiert Sportmedizin in Heidelberg. Peter ist fünf und geht in den Kindergarten.

Meine Familie ist sehr sportlich. Mein Stiefvater spielt Golf, meine Mutter und Nicole spielen Tennis, Peter spielt Fußball und ich mache Ballett.

Und wie groß ist deine Familie?

Liebe Grüße
deine Eva

6 Expansion Have students write their own responses to Eva's letter. You might provide them with real postcards which they have to "mail" back to you. Encourage volunteers to read their letters aloud to the class.

1. Wie viele Personen wohnen mit Eva zusammen (*together*)? Drei Personen wohnen mit Eva zusammen: der Stiefvater, die Mutter, der Halbbruder.
2. Hat sie auch Haustiere? Ja, sie hat zwei Haustiere: einen Hund und eine Katze.
3. Wie alt ist Peter? Er ist fünf (Jahre alt).
4. Was macht Evas Familie in der Freizeit? Der Stiefvater spielt Golf, die Mutter und die Schwester spielen Tennis, der Halbbruder spielt Fußball und Eva macht Ballett.
5. Ist Ihre (*your, form.*) Familie auch so wie (*like*) Evas? Answers will vary.

7 Wer bin ich? Your instructor will give you a worksheet with statements about family relationships. Use the cues to ask your classmates about their families.

BEISPIEL Ich habe zwei Schwestern.

S1: Hast du zwei Schwestern?
S2: Ja, ich habe zwei Schwestern. (*You write his/her name.*)
OR
S2: Nein, ich habe keine Schwestern. (*You ask another classmate.*)

7 Suggestion Ask volunteers to share their results with the class.

8 Das Wetter ist schön! Use the vocabulary you learned in Kapitel 2 to talk with a classmate about what your family members enjoy doing.

BEISPIEL

S1: Mein Bruder spielt Tennis. Was macht dein Bruder?
S2: Mein Bruder liest Bücher.

Aussprache und Rechtschreibung

🎧 Final consonants

The German consonants **b**, **d**, and **g** generally sound quite similar to their English counterparts.

| **B**all | **B**ru**d**er | **D**ezem**b**er | **b**rin**g**en | **G**olf |

However, when **b** appears at the end of a word or syllable, or before a **t**, it is pronounced like a **p**.

| a**b** | ha**b**t | gel**b** | Stau**b** | lie**b**t |

When **d** appears at the end of a word or syllable, it is pronounced like a **t**. The **-dt** letter combination is also pronounced **t**.

| Gel**d** | Hun**d** | Sta**dt** | sin**d** | Fahrra**d** |

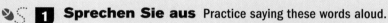

When **g** appears at the end of a word or before a **t**, it is pronounced like a **k**. In standard German, **-ig** at the end of a word is pronounced like the German **ch**.

| klu**g** | brin**g**t | Ta**g** | sa**g**t | zwanz**ig** |

Suggestion Tell students that the pronunciation of the final **-ig** sound has several regional variations. For more about the **ch** sound, see **Vol. 2, Lektion 2A**.

1 Sprechen Sie aus Practice saying these words aloud.

1. Bank
2. sieben
3. Laub
4. lobt
5. danken
6. Boden
7. Abend
8. gehen
9. Junge
10. Berg
11. fragt
12. schwierig

2 Artikulieren Sie Practice saying these sentences aloud.

1. Der Dieb klaut ein Fahrrad.
2. Der Besucher fragt Manfred ruhig um Rat.
3. Bernds Geschwister sind freundlich und großzügig.
4. Viele Diebe klauen viele Fahrräder.
5. Ingrids böser Bruder ist gierig und gemein.
6. Jörg sitzt im Zug und singt ein Lied.

Suggestion Have students look at the sample words and sentences on this page to identify cognates and words they already know. Tell students the meanings of any unfamiliar words or phrases.

3 Sprichwörter Practice reading these sayings aloud.

Kindermund tut Wahrheit kund.[1]

Geld regiert die Welt.[2]

¹ Out of the mouths of babes. (lit. *The mouths of children make known the truth.*)
² Money rules the world.

Ein Abend mit der Familie

S Video: *Fotoroman*

Die Freunde essen bei Familie Yilmaz. Alle wissen (*know*), Torsten ist Sabites Freund. Alle, nur einer nicht.

Vorbereitung Have students scan the images on the pages before they watch the video and try to guess what this episode will be about.

NATIONAL communication cultures STANDARDS

1

ANKE Hallo! Willkommen, ich bin Sabites Mutter.
GEORGE Freut mich sehr, Sie kennen zu lernen, Frau Yilmaz. Ich bin George Bachman.

5

SABITE Hallo, Hans.
HANS Tut mir leid, dass ich zu spät komme.

2

SABITE George, das ist meine jüngere Schwester, Zeynep.
GEORGE Hallo, Zeynep, nett dich kennen zu lernen.
SABITE Und das ist unser Vater.
GEORGE Herr Yilmaz, freut mich.

HANS Hallo!
SABITE Hans, das sind meine Eltern, Anke und Faik.
HANS Guten Abend, Herr Yilmaz. Guten Abend, Frau Yilmaz. Für Sie.
ANKE Danke.
HANS Sehr erfreut.

ANKE Das sind die Patatesli Sigara Böregi von Faiks Großmutter.
MELINE Herr Yilmaz, Ihre Familie kommt aus der Türkei?
FAIK Ja. Ich komme aus Ankara. Ich habe dort Cousins und einen Onkel. Haben Sie Geschwister?
MELINE Ich habe drei ältere Schwestern. Eine ist verheiratet, eine ist getrennt, eine ist verlobt. Ich habe auch eine Nichte, sie heißt Ava und ist 12.

3

6

4

GEORGE Meine Eltern sind geschieden. Meine Urgroßeltern kommen aus Heidelberg.
TORSTEN Mein Onkel lebt in Heidelberg. Er ist Professor. Es ist eine schöne Stadt.

ÜBUNGEN

1 **Richtig oder falsch?** Indicate whether each statement is **richtig** or **falsch**.

1. Als Nachtisch (*dessert*) gibt es Berliner. Falsch.
2. Meline hat zwei ältere Schwestern. Falsch.
3. Melines Nichte heißt Ava. Richtig.
4. Faik kommt aus Ankara. Richtig.
5. Es gibt Sauerbraten bei Familie Yilmaz. Richtig.

6. Georges Eltern sind verheiratet. Falsch.
7. Torstens Onkel lebt in München. Falsch.
8. Georges Urgroßeltern kommen aus Berlin. Falsch.
9. Hans' Familie kommt aus Bayern. Richtig.
10. Max ist 18 und spielt Basketball. Falsch.

PERSONEN

 Anke   Faik   George   Hans   Meline Sabite Torsten Zeynep

7

HANS Bist du ihr Bruder?
TORSTEN Nein, Sabite ist meine Freundin. Ich bin Torsten. Nett dich kennen zu lernen.
HANS Freut mich.
MELINE Börek?
HANS Nein danke.

8

MELINE Frau Yilmaz, Ihr Sauerbraten ist köstlich.
ANKE Danke, Meline. Hans? Alles in Ordnung? Du isst nichts.
HANS Hmm? Ja, danke.

9

FAIK Hans, Ihre Familie kommt aus Bayern?
HANS Ja.
TORSTEN Ich habe eine Tante in München. Hast du Geschwister, Hans?
HANS Mein Bruder, Max, ist 18. Er ist sportlich und spielt gern Fußball.
MELINE Hat er eine Freundin?

10

SABITE Hans, alles in Ordnung?
MELINE Sabite!
SABITE Was?
MELINE Hans.
SABITE Was ist mit Hans? Oh. Ooooh.
ANKE Wir haben Strudel!

Nützliche Ausdrücke

- **Freut mich sehr, Sie kennen zu lernen.**
  Pleased to meet you.
- **Das ist meine jüngere Schwester.**
  This is my younger sister.
- **die Türkei**
  Turkey
- **Haben Sie Geschwister?**
  Do you have any siblings?
- **die Urgroßeltern**
  great-grandparents
- **Tut mir leid, dass ich zu spät komme.**
  Sorry for being late.
- **der Sauerbraten**
  marinated beef
- **Ihr Sauerbraten ist köstlich.**
  Your sauerbraten is delicious.
- **Alles in Ordnung?**
  Everything OK?
- **einladen**
  to invite
- **das Abendessen**
  dinner

3A.1
- **Das is unser Vater.**
  This is our father.

3A.2
- **Es ist eine schöne Stadt.**
  It's a beautiful city.

3A.3
- **Er ist sportlich und spielt gern Fußball.**
  He's athletic and likes to play soccer.

---

2 **Zum Besprechen** Draw your family tree. Include your parents, siblings, aunts, uncles, and grandparents. Then "introduce" your family to a classmate. Answers will vary.

2 **Expansion** Have students present their partners' families to another pair.

3 **Erweiterung** Boreks are a popular Turkish snack with many varieties. In pairs, research another popular Turkish dish, and share your findings with the class. Answers will vary.

Ressourcen

SAM VM: p. 5   DVD Folge 5   vhlcentral.com

Eine deutsche Familie  Reading

Mit wem° die Deutschen leben (%)				
	Eltern	**allein**	**Partner**	**allein mit Kind**	**sonstige°**
18–24	63,5	15,9	15,8	1,4	3,4
25–29	19,8	25,2	48,6	3,1	3,3
30–34	6,8	20,1	66,9	4,5	1,7
35–44	3,3	14,9	74,1	6,3	1,4
45–54	1,3	13,6	78,8	5,0	1,4
55–64	0,3	16,9	79,4	2,2	1,3
65–74	0,1	25,0	70,8	2,1	2,1
75–79	0	41,8	52,0	2,2	3,9
80+	0	58,7	30,1	2,5	3,4

QUELLE: Bundesministerium

HANS UND PETRA SIND EIN deutsches Ehepaar mit zwei Kindern. Sie haben zwei Söhne, Finn und Lukas. Finn ist 11 Jahre alt und in der 5. Klasse. Lukas ist zwei Jahre älter als Finn und geht schon° in die 7. Klasse. Die Familie hat eine große Wohnung° und einen schönen Garten vor dem Haus. Hans arbeitet den ganzen Tag in einem Büro°. Petra arbeitet als Krankenschwester°, aber sie ist nachmittags immer zu Hause, wenn Finn und Lukas um eins von der Schule nach Hause kommen. Abends spielen sie zusammen Fußball im Park oder fahren Fahrrad am Rhein.

In der Familie macht auch Hans Hausarbeit°, aber Petra kocht und putzt° trotzdem mehr. Die Familie fährt einmal im Jahr gemeinsam° in den Urlaub°.

Sind Hans und Petra also eine „typisch" deutsche Familie? Das Leben in Deutschland ist vielfältiger geworden°. In der Wohnung links neben Hans und Petra lebt eine Einwandererfamilie°, rechts von ihnen lebt ein allein erziehender° Vater mit seiner Tochter. Was ist also „typisch" für die deutsche Familie von heute? Vielleicht einfach Zusammenhalt° und Liebe.

schon *already* **Wohnung** *apartment* **Büro** *office* **Krankenschwester** *nurse* **Hausarbeit** *housework* **putzt** *cleans* **gemeinsam** *together* **Urlaub** *vacation* **ist vielfältiger geworden** *has become more diverse* **Einwandererfamilie** *family of immigrants* **allein erziehender** *single parent* **Zusammenhalt** *sticking together* **Mit wem** *With whom* **sonstige** *miscellaneous*

Expansion Have students read the data in the chart aloud to practice saying numbers.

---

1 Ergänzen Sie Complete the statements.

1. Hans' Frau heißt ___Petra___.
2. Ihre (*Their*) ___Söhne___ heißen Finn und Lukas.
3. Am Tag arbeitet ___Hans___ im Büro.
4. Petra ___arbeitet___ als Krankenschwester.
5. Am Vormittag (*In the morning*) sind Finn und Lukas in der ___Schule___.
6. Am Abend (*In the evening*) spielen Hans, Finn, Lukas und Petra Fußball oder 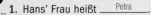 am Rhein.

7. Hans macht in der Familie auch ___Hausarbeit___.
8. Die Familie fährt gemeinsam in den ___Urlaub___.
9. In Deutschland leben die meisten (*most*) 18- bis 24-Jährigen mit ihren (*their*) ___Eltern___.
10. Die meisten Deutschen, die älter als (*older than*) 80 Jahre sind, leben ___allein___.

 Practice more at **vhlcentral.com.**

Die Familie

die Ehe	marriage
das Einzelkind	only child
die Hochzeit	wedding
die Mama	mom
der erste/zweite Mann	first/second husband
der Papa	dad
die Urgroßmutter	great-grandmother
der Urgroßvater	great-grandfather
der / die Verlobte	fiancé(e)
adoptieren	to adopt

Die Liebe

Ein Kuss° ist nicht nur° ein Kuss. In den meisten Teilen° Deutschlands sagt man „Kuss". Aber es gibt andere Möglichkeiten°, „Kuss" in der deutschsprachigen Welt zu sagen. **In der Schweiz/In Liechtenstein** sagt man „Müntschi". **In Österreich/In Bayern** ist ein Kuss ein „Bussi" oder ein „Busserl". **Auf Kölsch** (der Dialekt von Köln) ist das ein „Bütz".

Und wie sagt man „Ich liebe dich"?
Ein paar° Varianten:
In Bayern/In Österreich sagt man „I mog di".
In der Schweiz geht das so: „I liäbä di".
Und die Berliner sagen „Ick liebe Dir".

Kuss kiss **nur** only **meisten Teilen** major parts
Möglichkeiten possibilities **Ein paar** A couple of

Angela Merkel

Seit November 2005 hat Deutschland eine Bundeskanzlerin°: **Angela Merkel**. Viele Deutsche finden Merkel pragmatisch und solide, und im Magazin Forbes steht, sie ist eine der mächtigsten° Frauen der Welt. Die CDU°-Politikerin hat keine Kinder, aber sie hat einen wichtigen Unterstützer°, ihren Mann, Joachim Sauer. Sauer ist Professor für Chemie an der Humboldt-Universität in Berlin. Er hält sich am liebsten von den Medien fern°, aber wenn die mächtigsten Politiker der Welt zusammen essen, ist Sauer oft dabei, neben Michelle Obama und Carla Bruni. Und wer wäscht im Hause Sauer-Merkel die Wäsche°? Beide!

Bundeskanzlerin female chancellor **eine der mächtigsten** one of the most powerful **CDU** Christian Democratic Union **Unterstützer** supporter **hält sich am liebsten von den Medien fern** prefers to stay away from the media **wäscht... die Wäsche** does the laundry

IM INTERNET

 Scheidung (Divorce): Eine Epidemie in den deutschsprachigen Ländern?

For more information on this **Kultur**, go to vhlcentral.com.

---

2 **Richtig oder falsch?** Indicate whether each statement is **richtig** or **falsch**. Then, in pairs, correct the false statements.

1. Der Dialekt, den man in Köln spricht, heißt „Bayerisch".
Falsch. Der Dialekt heißt Kölsch.

 2. „I liäbä di" ist die schweizerische Art (Swiss way), „Ich liebe dich" zu sagen. Richtig.

3. Angela Merkel ist 2005 geboren (was born).
Falsch. Angela Merkel ist seit 2005 Bundeskanzlerin.

4. Joachim Sauer ist mit Angela Merkel verheiratet. Richtig.

5. Joachim Sauer ist der deutsche Bundespräsident.
Falsch. Joachim Sauer ist Professor für Chemie.

3 **Sie sind dran** In pairs, use vocabulary from **Deutsch im Alltag** to write six sentences describing a famous American family. Then share the description with your classmates. Answers will vary.

Possessive adjectives  Presentation

Startblock In both English and German, possessive adjectives indicate ownership or belonging.

QUERVERWEIS

In **Kontext 3A**, you learned some possessive adjectives used with family vocabulary: **mein Großvater**, **meine Mutter**, **meine Eltern**.

- In **1A.1**, you learned about indefinite articles. Possessive adjectives are also referred to as **ein**-words since they take the same endings as the indefinite article **ein**. Each personal pronoun has a corresponding possessive adjective.

personal pronouns and possessive adjectives		
personal pronouns	**possessive adjectives**	
ich	mein	*my*
du	dein	*your* (sing., inf.)
er	sein	*his*
sie	ihr	*her*
es	sein	*its*
wir	unser	*our*
ihr	euer	*your* (pl., inf.)
Sie	Ihr	*your* (sing./pl., form.)
sie	ihr	*their*

Meine Schwester ist 16 Jahre alt.　　　Wo ist **dein** Vater?
My sister is 16 years old.　　　*Where is **your** father?*

- Possessive adjectives always precede the nouns they modify.

meine Mutter	**deine** Mutter	**unsere** Mutter	**seine** Mutter
my mother	*your mother*	*our mother*	*his mother*

Meine Schwester ist sehr sportlich.
My sister is very athletic.

- Like other **ein**-words, their endings change according to the gender, case, and number of the object possessed.

deine Mutter	**dein** Vater	**dein** Kind	**deine** Kinder
your mother	*your father*	*your child*	*your children*

Mein Großvater liebt **seine** Enkelkinder.
*My grandfather loves **his** grandchildren.*

- Like other **ein**-words, possessive adjectives have no added endings before singular masculine or neuter nouns in the nominative, or before singular neuter nouns in the accusative.

nominative and accusative of *ein*-words				
	masculine	**feminine**	**neuter**	**plural**
nominative	**ein** Vater **unser** Vater	**eine** Mutter **unsere** Mutter	**ein** Kind **unser** Kind	**keine** Brüder **unsere** Brüder
accusative	**einen** Vater **unseren** Vater	**eine** Mutter **unsere** Mutter	**ein** Kind **unser** Kind	**keine** Brüder **unsere** Brüder

Ihr Kind ist 3 Jahre alt.
Her child is 3 years old.

Tobias liebt **seinen** Bruder.
*Tobias loves **his** brother.*

- The formal possessive adjective **Ihr** corresponds to the formal personal pronoun **Sie**. The possessive adjective **ihr** can mean either *her* or *their*, depending on context.

Wo sind **Ihre** Eltern?
*Where are **your** parents?*

Rolf und Heike kochen für **ihre** Kinder.
*Rolf and Heike cook for **their** children.*

Christa kocht für **ihre** Enkelkinder.
*Christa cooks for **her** grandchildren.*

- The possessive adjective **euer** drops the second **e** when an ending is added. The possessive adjective **unser** may drop the **e** in the stem when an ending is added, but this form is rare.

euer Enkelsohn *your grandson*	**eure** Familie *your family*	**unser** Sohn *our son*	**uns(e)re** Tochter *our daughter*

Ressourcen

SAM
WB: pp. 35–36

SAM
LM: p. 23

(S)

vhlcentral.com

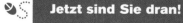

Jetzt sind Sie dran! Write the correct forms of the possessive adjectives.

Nominativ

mein

1. _meine_ Idee

dein

2. _deine_ Eltern

sein

3. _sein_ Wörterbuch

ihr

4. _ihr_ Familienstand

Akkusativ

mein

5. _meinen_ Bruder

dein

6. _deine_ Frage

sein

7. _seine_ Familie

ihr

8. _ihr_ Kind

Nominativ

unser

9. _unser_ Fahrrad

euer

10. _eure_ Mannschaft

Ihr

11. _Ihr_ Nachname

ihr

12. _ihre_ Hausaufgaben

Akkusativ

unser

13. _uns(e)re_ Verwandten

euer

14. _euren_ Sohn

Ihr

15. _Ihre_ Hunde

ihr

16. _ihr_ Problem

Anwendung

1 **Wählen Sie** Select the appropriate form of the possessive adjective.

1. (Mein / Meine) Eltern essen Kuchen (*cake*).
2. (Unser / Unsere) Sohn spielt gut Fußball.
3. Markus und Sabine lieben (ihren / ihre) Eltern.
4. Andrea liebt (euren / euer) Hund.
5. Hat (dein / deinen) Bruder einen Sohn?
6. Sind (Ihr / Ihre) Großeltern reich (*rich*)?
7. Ich lese (mein / meine) Bücher nicht.
8. Mein Vater und (sein / seinen) Freund spielen Schach.

2 **Ergänzen Sie** Complete the sentences with possessive adjectives.

1. ___Unser___ (*Our*) Großvater trinkt Kaffee.
2. Ja, und er fährt ___sein___ (*his*) Fahrrad.
3. ___Meine___ (*My*) Schwägerin hat lange, lockige Haare.
4. Siehst du ___meine___ (*my*) Schwester?
5. Wie heißt ___deine___ (*your*) Freundin?
6. Sie und ___ihre___ (*her*) Tochter heißen beide (*both*) Gertrud.
7. ___Ihre___ (*Her*) Katze heißt Polly.
8. Kinder, wo sind ___eure___ (*your, pl.*) Eltern?

3 Expansion Model using possessive adjectives with students' belongings. Ex.: **Ist das sein Kuli? Nein, das ist ihr Kuli.**

3 **Schreiben Sie** Write a sentence about each item saying whose it is.

▶ **BEISPIEL**

Das sind meine Notizbücher.

ich

1. du Das ist dein Computer.

2. er Das ist sein Fahrrad.

3. wir Das sind unsere Bleistifte.

4. sie Das ist ihr Rucksack.

5. Sie Das ist Ihr Buch.

6. ihr Das ist eure Tafel.

4 **Antworten Sie** Answer the questions with complete sentences. Answers will vary.

1. Wo wohnt Ihre Familie?
2. Wie heißt Ihre Mutter?
3. Wie ist ihr Nachname?
4. Wie alt ist Ihr Vater?
5. Was ist sein Lieblingssport (*favorite sport*)?
6. Spielen Ihre Großeltern Schach?
7. Wie heißt Ihr bester Freund / Ihre beste Freundin?
8. Was ist sein/ihr Lieblingsbuch (*favorite book*)?

Kommunikation

5 **Meine Familie** Use the cues to form questions. Then interview your classmates about their family members. Sample answers are provided.

> **BEISPIEL**
>
> **S1:** *Spricht deine Mutter Deutsch?*
> **S2:** *Ja, meine Mutter spricht Deutsch.*
> **S3:** *Nein, meine Mutter spricht kein Deutsch.*

1. Bruder / spielen / Fußball Spielt dein Bruder Fußball?
2. Vater / haben / ein Hund Hat dein Vater einen Hund?
3. Eltern / lesen / Bücher Lesen deine Eltern Bücher?
4. Großmutter / spielen / Tennis Spielt deine Großmutter Tennis?
5. Schwester / haben / grüne Augen Hat deine Schwester grüne Augen?
6. Onkel und Tante / fahren / Ski Fahren dein Onkel und deine Tante Ski?
7. Verwandte / schreiben / Briefe (*letters*) Schreiben deine Verwandten Briefe?
8. Familie / sein / groß Ist deine Familie groß?

6 **Familie und Freunde** Tell a partner about your family and friends. Answers will vary.

> **BEISPIEL**
>
> **S1:** *Meine Mutter hat zwei Haustiere. Ihre Katze heißt Muffin und ihr Hund heißt Sam.*
> **S2:** *Mein Vater ist Lehrer. Er ist vierzig Jahre alt und hat zwei Brüder.*

1. Meine Mutter hat...
2. Mein Vater ist...
3. Meine Eltern haben...
4. Meine Familie wohnt...
5. Am Samstag gehen meine Freunde...
6. Mein bester Freund studiert...

7 **Ich sehe etwas** Tell the class what you see using a possessive adjective. Then, repeat what the people before you said they saw. Answers will vary.

> **BEISPIEL**
>
> **S1:** *Ich sehe meinen Fußball.*
> **S2:** *Ich sehe mein Buch und Stefan sieht seinen Fußball.*
> **S3:** *Ich sehe meine Fotos, Maria sieht ihr Buch und Stefan sieht seinen Fußball.*

8 **Familienporträt** In small groups, take turns describing your family. Use possessive pronouns in the nominative and accusative case. After everyone has spoken, take turns describing your partners' families to the rest of the class. Answers will vary.

> **BEISPIEL**
>
> **S1:** *Das ist Inga. Ihre Mutter hat grüne Augen und braune Haare.*
> **S2:** *Das ist Michael. Seine Mutter ist Lehrerin.*

Descriptive adjectives and adjective agreement

 **Presentation**

Startblock Adjectives can describe people, places, or things. Here are some adjectives commonly used to describe people and their physical attributes.

physical description			
alt	*old*	hübsch	*pretty*
blond	*blond*	jung	*young*
braunhaarig/brünett	*brown-haired/brunette*	klein	*small; short (stature)*
dick/fett	*fat*	kurz	*short (hair)*
dunkelhaarig	*dark-haired*	lang	*long (hair)*
dünn	*thin*	lockig	*curly*
glatt	*straight (hair)*	rothaarig	*red-headed*
groß	*big; tall*	schlank	*slim*
großartig	*terrific*	schön	*pretty; beautiful*
gut aussehend	*handsome*	schwarzhaarig	*black-haired*
hässlich	*ugly*	sportlich	*athletic*

- Use an adjective with no added endings after the verbs **sein**, **werden**, and **bleiben** (*to remain*).

  Mein Bruder ist **klein**.
  *My brother is **short**.*

  Seine Mutter bleibt **sportlich**.
  *His mother stays **in shape**.*

  Deine Schwester wird **groß**.
  *Your sister is getting **tall**.*

- When you use an adjective before a noun, you need to include an adjective ending.

  Meine **großen** Schwestern spielen Fußball.
  *My **big** sisters play soccer.*

  Das ist eine **hübsche** Katze.
  *That's a **pretty** cat.*

- Adjective endings depend on the case, number, and gender of the noun they modify, and whether they are preceded by a **der**-word, an **ein**-word, or neither.

  Sie lieben ihren **jungen** Sohn.
  *They love their **young** son.*

  Das **kleine** Baby hat **blaue** Augen.
  *The **little** baby has **blue** eyes.*

- Adjectives after a **der**-word have these endings.

after *der*-words				
	masculine	**feminine**	**neuter**	**plural**
nominative	der **groß**e Bruder	die **blond**e Schwester	das **junge** Kind	die **alten** Großeltern
accusative	den **groß**en Bruder	die **blond**e Schwester	das **junge** Kind	die **alten** Großeltern

Der **alte** Mann dort ist mein Opa.
*The **old** man over there is my grandpa.*

Die **große** Frau ist meine Tante.
*The **tall** woman is my aunt.*

Ich liebe die **hübschen** Häuser in dieser Straße.
*I love the **pretty** houses on this street.*

Irene sucht ihren **kleinen** Cousin.
*Irene is looking for her **little** cousin.*

Suggestion Tell students that **der**-words include the definite articles, **dieser** (*this*), **mancher** (*some*), **jeder** (*each*), and **solcher** (*such*), while **ein**-words include the indefinite articles, **kein**, and possessive adjectives.

For more about **der**-words, see **Vol. 2, 4B.2**.

- Adjectives preceded by an **ein**-word have these endings.

after *ein*-words				
	masculine	**feminine**	**neuter**	**plural**
nominative	ein **groß**er Bruder	eine **blond**e Schwester	ein **jung**es Kind	meine **alt**en Großeltern
accusative	einen **groß**en Bruder	eine **blond**e Schwester	ein **jung**es Kind	meine **alt**en Großeltern

Mein **großer** Bruder ist ein **guter** Golfspieler.
*My **big** brother is a **good** golf player.*

Herr Wirth hat eine **sportliche** Tochter.
*Mr. Wirth has an **athletic** daughter.*

Ein **teuerer** Ring ist nicht immer schön.
*An **expensive** ring isn't always beautiful.*

Seine Großmutter hat einen **schönen** Vogel.
*His grandmother has a **beautiful** bird.*

- Unpreceded adjectives have these endings.

unpreceded				
	masculine	**feminine**	**neuter**	**plural**
nominative	**rot**er Wein	**dick**e Milch	**alt**es Brot	**groß**e Fische
accusative	**rot**en Wein	**dick**e Milch	**alt**es Brot	**groß**e Fische

Kleine Kinder brauchen **gute** Eltern.
***Small** children need **good** parents.*

Mein Vater hat **braune** Augen.
*My father has **brown** eyes.*

Altes Brot schmeckt nicht so gut.
***Old** bread doesn't taste so good.*

Unsere Geschwister haben **lockige** Haare.
*Our siblings have **curly** hair.*

- If multiple adjectives precede the same noun, they all take the same ending.

Ist das **kleine**, **rothaarige** Mädchen deine Schwester?
*Is the **little**, **red-headed** girl your sister?*

Sie hat einen **großen**, **gut aussehenden** Bruder.
*She has a **tall**, **good-looking** brother.*

- Some adjectives ending in -**er** or -**el**, such as **teuer** (*expensive*) and **dunkel**, drop the **e** in the stem when an ending is added. Dropping the **e** in **teuer** is optional.

Das ist ein **teu(e)res** Buch.
*That is an **expensive** book.*

Das ist ein **dunkles** Foto.
*That's a **dark** photo.*

Suggestion Point out that most endings for preceded adjectives are either -**e** or -**en**, and that the only other possible endings are -**er**, -**es**, and -**em**.

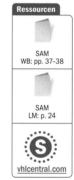

Ressourcen

SAM
WB: pp. 37–38

SAM
LM: p. 24

S
vhlcentral.com

Jetzt sind Sie dran! Write the nominative or accusative form of the adjectives.

Nominativ

1. der _____schlanke_____ (schlank) Vater
2. ein _____verheirateter_____ (verheiratet) Mann
3. die _____große_____ (groß) Familie
4. eine _____alte_____ (alt) Schwägerin
5. das _____verlobte_____ (verlobt) Paar
6. die _____sportlichen_____ (sportlich) Enkelkinder

Akkusativ

7. einen _____jungen_____ (jung) Vater
8. die _____ledigen_____ (ledig) Verwandten
9. einen _____dünnen_____ (dünn) Hund
10. ein _____hübsches_____ (hübsch) Mädchen
11. den _____kleinen_____ (klein) Sohn
12. das _____blonde_____ (blond) Kind

Anwendung

1 **Kombinieren Sie** Match each adjective with its opposite.

_d_ 1. hässlich   **a.** jung
_f_ 2. kurz   **b.** dick
_e_ 3. blond   **c.** klein
_a_ 4. alt   **d.** schön
_c_ 5. groß   **e.** schwarzhaarig
_b_ 6. dünn   **f.** lang
_g_ 7. lockig   **g.** glatt

2 **Was fehlt?** Complete the sentences.

1. Ich habe einen _____großen_____ (groß) Bruder.
2. Mein _____großer_____ (groß) Bruder spielt Fußball.
3. Er hat einen _____kleinen_____ (klein) Hund.
4. Der _____kleine_____ (klein) Hund hat sehr _____kurze_____ (kurz) Beine (*legs*).
5. Seine _____kurzen_____ (kurz) Beine sind auch sehr _____dünn_____ (dünn).
6. Hast du auch so einen _____kleinen_____ (klein), _____schönen_____ (schön) Hund?

3 **Ergänzen Sie** Select the adjective that best completes each sentence.

BEISPIEL Martin arbeitet nicht viel.
Er ist ein _____*fauler*_____ (verantwortlicher, sportlicher, fauler) Junge.

1. Der Vater fährt viel Fahrrad und Ski. Er ist ein _____sportlicher_____ (sportlicher, fauler, blonder) Mann.
2. Deine Schwester hat schöne Haare. Sie ist ein _____hübsches_____ (großes, fettes, hübsches) Mädchen.
3. Die Mutter hat keine lockigen Haare, sondern (*but rather*) _____glatte_____ (kleine, lange, glatte) Haare.
4. Meine Eltern sind nicht mehr zusammen (*together*). Ich habe _____geschiedene_____ (verheiratete, kurze, geschiedene) Eltern.
5. Die Enkeltochter ist 2 Jahre alt. Sie ist ein _____junges_____ (junges, hässliches, dickes) Kind.
6. Die Großeltern sind 80 Jahre alt. Die _____alten_____ (hübschen, alten, kleinen) Großeltern spielen Schach am Wochenende.

4 **Schreiben Sie** Replace the underlined words with the words in parentheses and make any necessary changes.

BEISPIEL Der kleine Junge ist traurig. (die Mädchen)
Die kleinen Mädchen sind traurig.

1. Die rothaarige Tochter spielt Fußball. (der Sohn) Der rothaarige Sohn spielt Fußball.
2. Ihr Großvater liest das alte Buch. (ein Buch) Ihr Großvater liest ein altes Buch.
3. Der fette, dunkelhaarige Onkel sieht den ganzen Tag fern. (mein Onkel) Mein fetter, dunkelhaariger Onkel sieht den ganzen Tag fern.
4. Das fleißige Enkelkind studiert Mathematik. (die Enkelkinder) Die fleißigen Enkelkinder studieren Mathematik.
5. Der Lehrer gibt ihr (*her*) interessante Hausaufgaben. (ein Buch) Der Lehrer gibt ihr ein interessantes Buch.

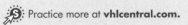 Practice more at **vhlcentral.com**.

Kommunikation

5 **Die Familie Müller** In pairs, take turns describing the members of the Müller family. Answers will vary.

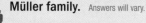

> **BEISPIEL**
> *Moritz ist alt und klein.*

Michael Petra Inez

Rex

Alexander Moritz

6 **Ein guter Freund** Interview a classmate to learn about one of his/her friends. Use the questions below and add three more of your own. Answers will vary.

- Wie heißt er/sie?
- Wie alt ist er/sie?
- Wie groß ist er/sie?
- Welche Eigenschaften (*characteristics*) hat er/sie?
- Ist er ein guter Student? / Ist sie eine gute Studentin?

7 **Raten Sie** Choose a famous person. In small groups, take turns asking yes-or-no questions to determine the identity of each person. Answers will vary.

> **BEISPIEL**
> **S1:** *Ist sie eine Frau?*
> **S2:** *Ja.*
> **S3:** *Hat sie blaue Augen?*
> **S2:** *Nein.*

8 **Beschreiben Sie** In small groups, role-play this situation: you and your friends have new jobs. Describe your new co-workers to each other. Answers will vary.

> **BEISPIEL**
> *Mein Boss ist ein großer Mann. Er hat kurze schwarze Haare...*

- Wie alt ist er/sie?
- Wie ist sein/ihr Familienstand?
- Hat er/sie Kinder?
- Macht er/sie Sport?
- Hat er/sie Haustiere?
- Woher kommt er/sie?

6 Expansions
- Have students bring in photos of their family or friends. Ask students to describe the people in the photos to classmates.
Ex.: **Das ist mein sportlicher Vater und hier ist meine hübsche Mutter.**
- Have students describe their partners' friends to the class.

Gern and *nicht gern*  Presentation

Startblock In English, we use the verb *to like* to convey enjoyment of an activity. In German, the adverb **gern** can be used to convey this idea.

Er spielt **gern** Fußball.

Frau Yilmaz kocht **gern**.

- To say that you like to do something, use the conjugated verb with the adverb **gern**.

  Ich schwimme **gern**.
  *I **like to** swim.*

  Meine Schwester liest **gern** Bücher.
  *My sister **likes to** read books.*

- In an affirmative sentence, place **gern** after the verb it modifies. Note that any direct or indirect objects are placed after **gern**.

  Dein Bruder spielt **gern** Fußball.
  *Your brother **likes to** play soccer.*

  Katzen trinken **gern** Milch.
  *Cats **like to** drink milk.*

- To express dislike for an activity, use **nicht gern** after the verb.

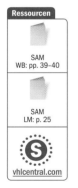

Mein Vater arbeitet **nicht gern** spät.
*My father **doesn't like to** work late.*

Thomas isst **nicht gern** Kuchen.
*Thomas **doesn't like to** eat cake.*

Jetzt sind Sie dran! Complete the sentences using **gern** or **nicht gern**.

1. 👍 Meine Oma bäckt _____*gern*_____ Kuchen.
2. 👎 Die Kinder spielen _____nicht gern_____ Schach.
3. 👎 Ich lese _____nicht gern_____ Lehrbücher.
4. 👍 Meine Brüder fliegen _____gern_____ in Urlaub.
5. 👍 Wir fahren im Sommer (*in the summer*) _____gern_____ nach Deutschland.
6. 👎 Meine Schwester lernt _____nicht gern_____ für ihren Abschluss.
7. 👍 Das Paar geht am Abend (*at night*) _____gern_____ tanzen.
8. 👍 Die Zwillinge spielen _____gern_____ am Strand.
9. 👎 Ich bleibe _____nicht gern_____ lange in der Bibliothek.
10. 👎 Mein Stiefvater geht _____nicht gern_____ spazieren.

Anwendung und Kommunikation

1 Gern oder nicht gern? Write what each person likes or does not like to do.

> **BEISPIEL**
>
> **Elke und Aslan / Ski fahren**
> *Elke und Aslan fahren gern Ski.*

1. das Paar / kochen
Das Paar kocht gern.

2. die Frau und der Hund / spazieren gehen
Die Frau und der Hund gehen nicht gern spazieren.

3. Jens / schwimmen
Jens schwimmt nicht gern.

4. Inge und ihr Mann / sehen / Talkshows
Inge und ihr Mann sehen gern Talkshows.

2 Partnergespräch In pairs, take turns asking and answering the questions. Answers will vary.

> **BEISPIEL**
>
> **S1:** *Sprichst du gern mit deinen Eltern?*
> **S2:** *Ja, ich spreche gern mit meinen Eltern.*

1. Gehst du gern ins Kino?
2. Was machst du gern in deiner Freizeit?
3. Liest du gern Literatur?
4. Machst du gern Sport?

3 Machst du das gern? In pairs, take turns asking and answering the survey questions. Then compare your likes and dislikes. Answers will vary.

> **BEISPIEL**
>
> **S1:** *Spielst du gern Basketball?*
> **S2:** *Ja, ich spiele gern Basketball./*
> *Nein, ich spiele nicht gern Basketball.*

Machst du das gern?	ja	nein
1. angeln	☐	☐
2. reisen	☐	☐
3. Fußball spielen	☐	☐
4. spazieren gehen	☐	☐
5. lesen	☐	☐
6. Physik studieren	☐	☐
7. schwimmen	☐	☐
8. Fahrrad fahren	☐	☐
9. Kuchen backen	☐	☐
10. schlafen	☐	☐

4 Wie ist deine Familie? Interview a classmate to find out the likes and dislikes of his/her family members. Answers will vary.

> **BEISPIEL**
>
> **S1:** *Was macht deine Mutter gern?*
> **S2:** *Sie liest gern, aber sie kocht nicht gern.*

 Practice more at **vhlcentral.com**.

4 Expansion After each pair has completed the activity, have them compare notes with another pair and decide which of their family members will get along, based on their likes and dislikes.

Wiederholung

1

Wer ist wer? In pairs, take turns choosing a person from the list and giving clues to help your partner guess which person you've chosen. Answers will vary.

BEISPIEL

S1: *Mein Vater ist ihr Mann. Meine Schwester ist ihre Tochter. Wer ist sie?*
S2: *Sie ist deine Mutter.*

Bruder	Schwester
Cousin	Schwiegermutter
Enkeltochter	Sohn
Großvater	Tante
Schwager	Vater

2

Saras Familie In pairs, say what each person in Sara's family is like and what he or she likes to do. Use vocabulary from **Kontext 2B.** Answers will vary.

▶ **BEISPIEL**

S1: *Wie ist Saras Bruder?*
S2: *Ihr Bruder ist groß. Er spielt gern Tennis.*

Bruder

1. Cousin

2. Neffe

3. Tante

4. Onkel

5. Großvater

6. Schwägerin

3

Familien-Bingo Your instructor will give you a worksheet with instructions to play Family Bingo. Get eight signatures. Answers will vary.

BEISPIEL

S1: *Paula, hast du einen großen Bruder?*
S2: *Ja, mein Bruder Stefan ist sehr groß.*
S3: *Toll! Bitte unterschreibe (sign) hier!*

4

Verschiedene Menschen In small groups, take turns picking someone in the illustration and describing him/her. The next person repeats the description and adds to it. Keep going around the group, trying to add as many details as possible. Answers will vary.

BEISPIEL

S1: *Die Frau heißt Fatima. Sie ist hübsch.*
S2: *Die Frau heißt Fatima. Sie ist hübsch und liest gern.*
S3: *Die Frau heißt Fatima. Sie ist hübsch und liest gern. Morgen geht sie spazieren.*

Daniel — Fatima — Annika — Murat und Lara — Yusuf und Tobias — Emil und Eva — Uta und Alexander

5

Zwei Familien Your instructor will give you and your partner each a picture of a family. Ask questions to find the six differences between the two pictures. Answers will vary.

BEISPIEL

S1: *Ist die Mutter blond?*
S2: *Nein. Die Mutter ist nicht blond. Sie hat braune Haare.*

6

Stammbaum Create an illustrated family tree, and share it with a classmate. Tell your partner about each of your family members, including their names, how they are related to you, what they are like, and what they like or don't like to do. Answers will vary.

BEISPIEL

S1: *Das ist meine Schwester. Sie heißt Steffi. Sie ist sehr sportlich.*
S2: *Fährt Steffi gern Fahrrad?*

Zapping

(S) **Video: TV Clip**

Volkswagen

Volkswagen (VW) is one of the world's largest automobile manufacturers. The company's headquarters are located in Wolfsburg, Lower Saxony. The name Volkswagen means *car for the people*. Volkswagen cars were initially designed and produced under the Third Reich. However, in post-war Germany, Volkswagen became an important symbol of West Germany's economic recovery. Today, the company also owns Audi, Bentley, Bugatti, and Lamborghini, among others.

Aus Liebe zum Automobil

„Hey! Schickes Auto!"

Kleiner Familienausflug° zum Strand°?

Mit Mutti und den Kleinen?

Familienausflug *family excursion* **zum Strand** *to the beach*

 Verständnis Answer the questions in German.

1. How do the two young men describe the VW Sharan? schickes Auto, Familienauto

2. Who are the members of the older man's family? seine Frau und seine drei Töchter

 Diskussion In pairs, discuss the answers to these questions. Answers will vary.

1. Does your family have a family car? If so, how is it similar to or different from the VW Sharan?

2. What is the message of the commercial? Do you think the commercial is effective in conveying that message? Explain.

Communicative Goals

You will learn how to:

- describe people
- express an attitude about an action
- give instructions

Wortschatz

persönliche Beschreibungen	*personal descriptions*
(un)angenehm	*(un)pleasant*
arm	*poor; unfortunate*
bescheiden	*modest*
dynamisch	*dynamic*
egoistisch	*selfish*
ernst	*serious*
freundlich	*friendly*
gemein	*mean*
gierig	*greedy*
großzügig	*generous*
gut	*good*
intellektuell	*intellectual*
intelligent	*intelligent*
interessant	*interesting*
langsam	*slow*
langweilig	*boring*
Lieblings-	*favorite*
mutig	*brave*
naiv	*naïve*
nervös	*nervous*
nett	*nice*
neugierig	*curious*
schlecht	*bad*
schüchtern	*shy*
schwach	*weak*
stolz	*proud*
toll	*great*
Berufe	*professions*
der Architekt, -en / die Architektin, -nen	*architect*
der Geschäftsmann (*pl.* Geschäftsleute) / die Geschäftsfrau, -en	*businessman / businesswoman*
der Ingenieur, -e / die Ingenieurin, -nen	*engineer*
der Journalist, -en / die Journalistin, -nen	*journalist*
der Rechtsanwalt, -̈e / die Rechtsanwältin, -nen	*lawyer*

Ressourcen

SAM WB: pp. 41–42 | SAM LM: p. 26 | vhlcentral.com

Wie sind sie?

Talking Picture Audio: Activities

Sie sind faul.

Er ist schnell.

Er ist stark.

der Kellner, - (die Kellnerin, -nen)

Er ist fleißig.

der Besitzer, - (die Besitzerin, -nen)

diskret

müde

eifersüchtig

Sie ist besorgt.

Er ist traurig.

ACHTUNG

Note that the plural of **der Geschäftsmann** is **die Geschäftsleute**; **die Leute** means *people*.

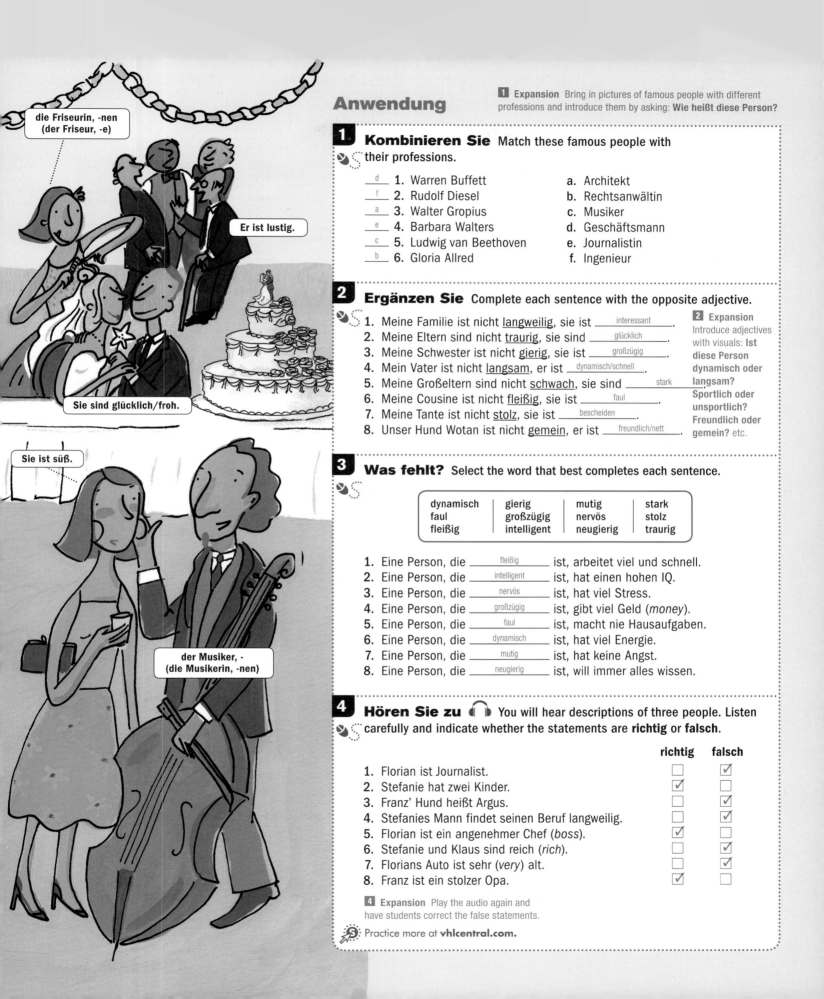

die Friseurin, -nen
(der Friseur, -e)

Er ist lustig.

Sie sind glücklich/froh.

Sie ist süß.

der Musiker, -
(die Musikerin, -nen)

Anwendung

1 **Expansion** Bring in pictures of famous people with different professions and introduce them by asking: **Wie heißt diese Person?**

1 **Kombinieren Sie** Match these famous people with their professions.

_d_	**1.** Warren Buffett	**a.**	Architekt
_f_	**2.** Rudolf Diesel	**b.**	Rechtsanwältin
_a_	**3.** Walter Gropius	**c.**	Musiker
_e_	**4.** Barbara Walters	**d.**	Geschäftsmann
_c_	**5.** Ludwig van Beethoven	**e.**	Journalistin
_b_	**6.** Gloria Allred	**f.**	Ingenieur

2 **Ergänzen Sie** Complete each sentence with the opposite adjective.

1. Meine Familie ist nicht <u>langweilig</u>, sie ist ___interessant___.
2. Meine Eltern sind nicht <u>traurig</u>, sie sind ___glücklich___.
3. Meine Schwester ist nicht <u>gierig</u>, sie ist ___großzügig___.
4. Mein Vater ist nicht <u>langsam</u>, er ist ___dynamisch/schnell___.
5. Meine Großeltern sind nicht <u>schwach</u>, sie sind ___stark___.
6. Meine Cousine ist nicht <u>fleißig</u>, sie ist ___faul___.
7. Meine Tante ist nicht <u>stolz</u>, sie ist ___bescheiden___.
8. Unser Hund Wotan ist nicht <u>gemein</u>, er ist ___freundlich/nett___.

2 **Expansion** Introduce adjectives with visuals: **Ist diese Person dynamisch oder langsam? Sportlich oder unsportlich? Freundlich oder gemein?** etc.

3 **Was fehlt?** Select the word that best completes each sentence.

dynamisch	gierig	mutig	stark
faul	großzügig	nervös	stolz
fleißig	intelligent	neugierig	traurig

1. Eine Person, die ___fleißig___ ist, arbeitet viel und schnell.
2. Eine Person, die ___intelligent___ ist, hat einen hohen IQ.
3. Eine Person, die ___nervös___ ist, hat viel Stress.
4. Eine Person, die ___großzügig___ ist, gibt viel Geld (*money*).
5. Eine Person, die ___faul___ ist, macht nie Hausaufgaben.
6. Eine Person, die ___dynamisch___ ist, hat viel Energie.
7. Eine Person, die ___mutig___ ist, hat keine Angst.
8. Eine Person, die ___neugierig___ ist, will immer alles wissen.

4 **Hören Sie zu** 🎧 You will hear descriptions of three people. Listen carefully and indicate whether the statements are **richtig** or **falsch**.

	richtig	falsch
1. Florian ist Journalist.	☐	☑
2. Stefanie hat zwei Kinder.	☑	☐
3. Franz' Hund heißt Argus.	☐	☑
4. Stefanies Mann findet seinen Beruf langweilig.	☐	☑
5. Florian ist ein angenehmer Chef (*boss*).	☑	☐
6. Stefanie und Klaus sind reich (*rich*).	☐	☑
7. Florians Auto ist sehr (*very*) alt.	☐	☑
8. Franz ist ein stolzer Opa.	☑	☐

4 **Expansion** Play the audio again and have students correct the false statements.

🔧 Practice more at **vhlcentral.com**.

Kommunikation

7 Suggestion Have students brainstorm a list of adjectives to describe themselves and their ideal partner before they start composing their ads.

5 Berufe In pairs, take turns replying to the questions based on the images.

▶ **BEISPIEL**

S1: Ist Karl Musiker?
S2: Nein, er ist Kellner.

1. Ist Helga Ingenieurin?
Nein, sie ist Geschäftsfrau/Rechtsanwältin.

2. Ist Ulrich Architekt?
Nein, er ist Friseur.

3. Sind Markus, Jan und Tobias Rechtsanwälte?
Nein, sie sind Musiker.

4. Ist Birgit Kellnerin?
Nein, sie ist Journalistin.

5. Ist Stefan Friseur?
Nein, er ist Geschäftsmann.

6. Ist Claudia Musikerin?
Nein, sie ist Ingenieurin/Architektin.

---

6 Partnersuche Read Georg's personal ad and discuss with a partner whether Maria or Jessica would be a better match for him. Be ready to defend your opinion to the class. Answers will vary.

Georg, 32 Jahre ✉ ▣ ☺ ⊞

Hallo! Ich heiße Georg, ich bin 32 Jahre alt, 182 cm groß, schlank, dunkelhaarig und habe braune Augen. Ich bin ein netter Mann, optimistisch und dynamisch. Ich habe viele Hobbys, spiele Fußball, Tennis und Handball, sehe gern Filme und koche auch gern und gut. Ich bin geschieden und habe eine kleine Tochter. Meine ideale Partnerin ist zwischen 26 und 32 Jahre alt, nicht zu klein (ca. 168 cm), blond, schlank, aktiv und sportlich. Sie muss gern essen und sie muss Kinder gern haben! Wenn du das bist, dann schicke mir eine E-Mail an nettergeorg@gvz.de.

6 Expansion Ask students to explain their choice of the ideal partner for Georg. Encourage them to use opposite adjectives. Ex.: **Jessica ist nicht groß, sie ist klein**.

Maria
23 Jahre
groß (182 cm)
lustig
schüchtern
aktiv

Jessica
28 Jahre
klein (165 cm)
sportlich
tolerant
schlank

---

7 Wunschpartner Now it's your turn to write a personal ad. Using Georg's ad as a model, describe yourself and your ideal girlfriend or boyfriend. Include details such as profession, age, physical characteristics, and personality. In groups, take turns reading the ads and guessing who wrote them.

EIN KLEINER TIPP

Use these words to help you complete this activity.

ich suche *I am looking for*
ich liebe *I love*
ich hasse *I hate*

---

8 Klatsch und Tratsch Heike is catching up with her cousin Lisa, who is a real **Klatschbase** (*gossip*). With a partner, write a conversation between Heike and Lisa in which Lisa gives her opinion of the guests at a recent family wedding. Use vocabulary you learned in **Lektion 3A**.
Answers will vary.

BEISPIEL

S1: Wie ist Peters Frau?
S2: Sie ist hübsch und sehr schlank, aber eine unangenehme Person und ein bisschen langweilig. Sie ist Journalistin, also der intellektuelle Typ.

8 Expansion Hand out pictures of famous people to pairs or groups of students and ask them to write some gossip about each person.

Aussprache und Rechtschreibung

🎧 Consonant clusters

Some German consonant combinations are not common in English. In the clusters **gn**, **kn**, **pf**, and **ps**, both consonants are pronounced. Do not add a vowel sound between these consonants when you pronounce them.

| **Gnom** | **Knödel** | **Pferd** | **Napf** | **psychisch** |

The German **ng** is always pronounced like the English *ng* in *singer*, never like the consonant combination in *finger*, regardless of where it appears in a word.

| **Ring** | **fangen** | **jung** | **Prüfungen** | **entlang** |

Some German letters represent the sound of a consonant cluster. The letter **x** is pronounced like the consonant combination **ks**. The letter **z** and the consonant combinations **tz** and **ts** are pronounced like the *ts* in the English word *hats*. The letter combination **qu** is pronounced *kv*.

| **extra** | **Zahn** | **Qualität** | **sitzt** | **Äquator** |

1 Sprechen Sie nach Practice saying these words aloud.

1. Gnade
2. knicken
3. Pfeil
4. Topf
5. Pseudonym
6. lang
7. bringen
8. Examen
9. Zoo
10. Mozart
11. Quatsch
12. Aquarell

Suggestion Have students look at the sample words and sentences on this page to identify cognates and words they already know. Tell students the meanings of any unfamiliar words or phrases.

2 Artikulieren Sie Practice saying these sentences aloud.

1. Die Katze streckt sich und legt den Kopf in den Nacken.
2. Felix fängt eine Qualle aus dem Ozean.
3. Der Zoowärter zähmt ein quergestreiftes Zebra.
4. Herr Quast brät Knödel in der Pfanne.
5. Der Gefangene bittet Xerxes um Gnade.
6. Das Taxi fährt kreuz und quer durch die Schweiz.

3 Sprichwörter Practice reading these sayings aloud.

Pferde lassen sich zum Wasser bringen, aber nicht zum Trinken zwingen.[1]

Nachts sind alle Katzen grau.[2]

[1] You can lead a horse to water, but you can't make it drink.
[2] At night, all cats are grey.

Unsere Mitbewohner

 **Video:** *Fotoroman*

George trifft Meline im Museum und Hans trifft Sabite am Brandenburger Tor.
Sie reden über ihre Mitbewohner. Oder über mehr?

Vorbereitung Before showing the video, ask students to brainstorm what adjectives they would use to describe each of the characters. Write these words on the board.

NATIONAL communication cultures STANDARDS

GEORGE Hallo, Meline. Wer ist das?
MELINE Fritz Sommer. Langweilig. George, du sollst nicht immer alles so ernst nehmen.
GEORGE Du bist lustig.
MELINE Und du bist süß, mein kleiner amerikanischer Freund.

HANS Hallo, Sabite!
SABITE Hallo, Hans! Wie geht's? Oh, sei nicht traurig. Du bist nett und großzügig. Können wir Freunde sein?

MELINE Oh, armer Hans!
GEORGE Sei nicht gemein, Meline.
MELINE Bin ich nicht. Sabite ist künstlerisch, lebhaft und verrückt.

MELINE Hans ist intellektuell, aber naiv.
GEORGE Ihn als Mitbewohner zu haben, ist langweilig. Er liest und sieht fern bis um zwei Uhr früh. Ich habe morgens Uni.
MELINE Kann er nicht ohne Fernsehen lernen?
GEORGE Nein, das kann er nicht.

GEORGE Ist Sabite eine gute Mitbewohnerin?
MELINE Sabite ist eine liebenswürdige und bescheidene Person. Ihre Kunst ist hässlich und schlecht!

SABITE Ich bin so stolz auf dich, Hans. Du bist ein echter Freund. Danke, dass du mir hilfst.
HANS Keine Ursache.
SABITE Meline ist gemein.
HANS Meline ist unangenehm.

 Wer ist das? Which character does each statement describe: George, Meline, Sabite, or Hans?

1. Er ist besorgt um seine Noten. George
2. Sie hat schöne Augen. Meline
3. Ihre Kunst ist hässlich und schlecht. Sabite
4. Jungen finden sie geheimnisvoll und faszinierend. Meline
5. Er ist nett und großzügig. Hans

6. Er ist ein echter Freund. Hans
7. Er ist ein netter Typ. George
8. Sie ist künstlerisch, lebhaft und verrückt. Sabite
9. Er ist süß. George
10. Er ist intellektuell, aber naiv. Hans

7

SABITE Ich möchte, dass sie einen neuen Freund hat.
HANS Bist du eifersüchtig?
SABITE Was?
HANS Sie ist lebhaft und hübsch. Sie hat sehr schöne Augen. Jungen finden sie geheimnisvoll und faszinierend.

8

SABITE Ist George ein guter Mitbewohner?
HANS Er ist ein netter Typ. Er ist besorgt um seine Noten. Ich sehe nachts fern und lese und er lernt bis zwei Uhr morgens.

9

SABITE Findest du sie hübsch?
HANS Wen?
SABITE Meline.
HANS Ich weiß nicht.

10

GEORGE Meline, Sabite meint es ernst mit Torsten. Du darfst nicht...
MELINE Ich finde nicht, dass sie gut zusammenpassen. Aber mach dir keine Sorgen. Ich kann sie nicht auseinanderbringen. Sie machen bald Schluss, auch ohne meine Hilfe.

Nützliche Ausdrücke

- **etwas ernst nehmen**
  to take something seriously
- **Du bist lustig.**
  You should talk. (lit. You're funny.)
- **Ihn als Mitbewohner zu haben, ist langweilig.**
  Having him as a roommate is boring.
- **Sei nicht traurig.**
  Don't be sad.
- **Danke, dass du mir hilfst.**
  Thanks for helping me.
- **Keine Ursache.**
  You're welcome.
- **Ich möchte, dass sie einen neuen Freund hat.**
  I want her to get a new boyfriend.
- **Jungen finden sie geheimnisvoll und faszinierend.**
  Boys find her mysterious and fascinating.
- **besorgt sein um**
  to be worried about
- **Du darfst nicht...**
  You mustn't...
- **Ich finde nicht, dass sie gut zusammenpassen.**
  I don't think they're a good match.
- **Schluss machen**
  to break up

3B.1
- **Ich kann sie nicht auseinanderbringen.**
  I can't break them up.

3B.2
- **Er ist besorgt um seine Noten.**
  He's worried about his grades.

3B.3
- **Mach dir keine Sorgen.**
  Don't worry.

---

2 **Zum Besprechen** In pairs, write a brief description of a well-known person in your school or community, using as many descriptive adjectives as you can. Do not mention his/her name. Be prepared to read your description to the class, who will guess this person's identity. Answers will vary.

freundlich	intellektuell	schüchtern
glücklich	lustig	traurig
großzügig	mutig	...

3 **Vertiefung** Research a famous German person and present him/her to the class. Use adjectives to describe his/her physical appearance and personality. Be prepared to share your description with your classmates. Answers will vary.

3 Suggestion You may wish to assign individuals for students to research, such as Diane Kruger, Hermann Hesse, Wilhelm Röntgen, Hugo Boss, etc.

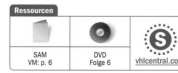

Ressourcen | SAM VM: p. 6 | DVD Folge 6 | vhlcentral.com

Suggestion Encourage students to think about misunderstandings that might arise from the different ways that Americans and Germans use the word "friend".

Auf unsere Freunde!  Reading

EIN KLEINER TIPP

In German, adjectives can often be transformed into nouns.

bekannt → **der / die Bekannte**
known   *acquaintance*

besonders → **(etwas) Besonderes**
special   *something special*

gleich → **das Gleiche**
same   *the same one/the same thing*

IN DIESER° FACEBOOK-ZEIT HABEN wir alle viele „Freunde". Was ist also ein Kumpel°, mit dem Sie hin und wieder auf Partys gehen, und was ist ein echter° Freund? Deutsche sagen nicht so schnell „Freund" wie Amerikaner. In Deutschland ist es etwas Besonderes° ein „Freund" zu sein.

Wirklich gute Freunde hat man in Deutschland wahrscheinlich höchstens° vier oder fünf. Ein echter Freund zu sein bedeutet°, dass man sich sehr gut und vielleicht auch schon sehr lange kennt°. Die meisten Leute in Deutschland sagen, dass sie ihre Freunde schon aus der Schule oder aus der Kinderzeit kennen. Nur

weil man einmal zusammen Kaffee getrunken hat°, ist man noch lange kein Freund.

In der Gruppe kennen sich alle mehr oder weniger gut. Trotzdem° nennen sich die Leute in einer Gruppe „Kumpel", nicht „Freunde". Die anderen Leute, die man kennt, nennt man meistens „Bekannte".

Es gibt also drei Gruppen von Menschen um eine Person: Die meisten Menschen sind Bekannte. Die größere Gruppe sind die Kumpel. Und nur eine sehr kleine Gruppe sind richtige Freunde. Aber mit diesen Freunden kann man alles teilen°. Also: Auf Freunde!

Auf unsere Freunde! *Here's to our friends!* **dieser** *this* **Kumpel** *buddy* **echter** *real* **etwas Besonderes** *something special* **wahrscheinlich höchstens** *probably at most* **bedeutet** *means* **sich... kennt** *know each other* **getrunken hat** *has drunk* **Trotzdem** *Nevertheless* **teilen** *share*

1 **Ergänzen Sie** Complete the statements.

1. In Deutschland sagt man nicht so schnell __Freund__ zu einer neuen Person.

2. Viele Deutsche kennen ihre Freunde aus der __Schule__ und aus der Kinderzeit.

3. Gute __Freunde__ nennt man in Deutschland nur vier oder fünf Personen.

4. __Amerikaner__ gehen relativ locker (*loose*) mit dem Wort „Freund" um.

5. In __Deutschland__ ist ein Freund jemand, den (*whom*) man sehr gut kennt.

6. Einen echten Freund kennt man sehr gut und oft auch sehr __lange__.

7. Es gibt __drei__ Gruppen von Menschen um eine Person.

8. In einer __Gruppe__ sind alle gute Kumpel.

9. Die meisten Menschen, die man kennt, nennt man __Bekannte__.

10. Die Gruppe der Freunde ist eine sehr __kleine__ Gruppe.

 Practice more at **vhlcentral.com**.

Wie wir Menschen sind

aufrichtig	*sincere*
besserwisserisch	*know-it-all (adj.)*
eingebildet	*arrogant*
geduldig	*patient*
geizig	*stingy*
liebevoll	*loving*
locker	*easy-going*
oberflächlich	*superficial*
ruhig	*calm*
weise	*wise*
zuverlässig	*reliable*

Es wird geheiratet!°

Wie wünscht° man dem neuen Paar ein frohes Eheleben? In **Bayern**, **Österreich** und **in der Schweiz** ist das **Brautstehlen°** eine lustige Tradition. Freunde stehlen die Braut und bringen sie von Gaststätte° zu Gaststätte. Der Bräutigam° muss sie finden... und alle Getränke bezahlen°! Die **Deutschen** und die **Österreicher** tragen den Ring meistens an der rechten° Hand. Aber **in der Schweiz** trägt man ihn an der linken° Hand. Das ist dem Herzen näher°.

Es wird geheiratet! *Someone's getting married!* **wünscht** *wishes* **Brautstehlen** *stealing of the bride* **Gaststätte** *restaurant* **Bräutigam** *groom* **Getränke bezahlen** *pay for the drinks* **rechten** *right* **linken** *left* **dem Herzen näher** *closer to the heart*

Ernst August von Hannover

Deutschland hat noch echte Prinzen. **Ernst August**, der Prinz von Hannover, ist einer. Sein Urgroßvater war Kaiser° Wilhelm II., und er ist auch ein Nachkomme° von Georg III. von England. Der Prinz ist 1954 geboren. 1999 hat er seine zweite° Frau geheiratet – Prinzessin **Caroline von Monaco**. Sieben Monate später ist eine kleine Prinzessin, Alexandra, das dritte° Kind des Prinzen, geboren. Die Familie lebt in Hannover und Monaco. Aber auch das Leben eines Prinzen ist nicht immer perfekt. Ernst August hasst° die Paparazzi und hatte° schon ein paar gewalttätige Auseinandersetzungen° mit Kameraleuten. So heißt er in Deutschland auch „Prügelprinz°".

Kaiser *emperor* **Nachkomme** *descendant* **zweite** *second* **dritte** *third* **hasst** *hates* **hatte** *had* **gewalttätige Auseinandersetzungen** *violent disputes* **Prügelprinz** *punching prince*

IM INTERNET

 Sind die Hochzeitsbräuche (*wedding traditions*) anders (*different*) in Deutschland als in den USA?

For more information on this **Kultur**, go to vhlcentral.com.

3 Suggestion You may want to teach students the expression **ich glaube**.

---

2 **Richtig oder falsch?** Indicate whether each statement is **richtig** or **falsch**. Then, in pairs, correct the false statements.

1. In Österreich ist es Tradition, den Bräutigam zu stehlen.
   Falsch. Es ist Tradition, die Braut zu stehlen.
2. In Deutschland trägt man den Ehering an der rechten Hand. Richtig.
3. Prinz Ernst August ist der Sohn von Kaiser Wilhelm II.
   Falsch. Er ist der Urenkelsohn von Kaiser Wilhelm II.
4. Prinz Ernst August mag (*likes*) die Paparazzi. Falsch. Er hasst die Paparazzi.
5. Alexandra ist die Tochter von Prinzessin Caroline von Monaco und Prinz Ernst August von Hannover. Richtig.

3 **Wie sind sie?** In pairs, describe each person in the photo on p. 122. How old do you think they are? What do you think their personalities are like? Are they friends or just classmates? Answers will vary.

Die deutschsprachige Welt Tell students that weddings in Germany typically have two parts: the legal ceremony (which is required) at the **Standesamt**, and the church wedding. After the legal ceremony, friends and family may gather in front of the bride's home to break pottery, because "**Scherben bringen Glück**" (*shards bring happiness*).

Ressourcen

vhlcentral.com

Modals  Presentation

Startblock In both English and German, modal verbs modify the meaning of another verb.

- Modals express an attitude towards an action, such as permission, obligation, ability, desire, or necessity. *May, can,* and *must* are examples of English modals.

modals	
dürfen	*to be allowed to, may*
können	*to be able to, can*
müssen	*to have to, must*
sollen	*to be supposed to*
wollen	*to want to*

- Except for **sollen**, all of the German modals are irregular in their present tense singular forms.

modals in the present tense					
	dürfen	**können**	**müssen**	**sollen**	**wollen**
ich	darf	kann	muss	soll	will
du	darfst	kannst	musst	sollst	willst
er/sie/es	darf	kann	muss	soll	will
wir	dürfen	können	müssen	sollen	wollen
ihr	dürft	könnt	müsst	sollt	wollt
Sie/sie	dürfen	können	müssen	sollen	wollen

- When you use a modal to modify the meaning of another verb, put the conjugated form of the modal in second position. Put the infinitive of the other verb at the end of the sentence.

Ich **muss** Französisch **lernen**.
*I **have to study** French.*

Ich **will** Französisch **lernen**.
*I **want to learn** French.*

- To form a yes-or-no question, move the modal verb to the beginning of the sentence, while the verb it modifies remains at the end.

Willst du Wasser **trinken**?
*Do you **want to drink** water?*

Könnt ihr eurer Mutter **helfen**?
*Can you **help** your mother?*

- **Dürfen** expresses permission.

Mama, **darf** ich heute Nachmittag schwimmen gehen?
*Mom, **may** I go swimming this afternoon?*

Nein, Lina, du **darfst** heute nicht schwimmen gehen.
*No, Lina, you **may** not go swimming today.*

- **Können** expresses ability.

Peter **kann** Ski fahren.
*Peter **can** ski.*

Kannst du Fahrrad fahren?
Can you ride a bicycle?

- **Müssen** expresses obligation.

Anita und Markus **müssen** viel lernen.
*Anita and Markus **have to** study a lot.*

Muss Maria Spanisch lernen?
*Does Maria **have to** learn Spanish?*

- **Sollen** conveys the expectation that a task be completed (*to be supposed to*). Note that, unlike the English *should* or *ought*, **sollen** implies an expectation that comes from someone other than the subject.

Du **sollst** das Buch lesen.
*You **are supposed to** read the book.*

Soll ich nach Hause gehen?
Am I supposed to go home?

- **Wollen** expresses desire.

Sie **wollen** Musikerinnen werden.
*They **want to** become musicians.*

Willst du eine Katze haben?
*Do you **want to** get a cat?*

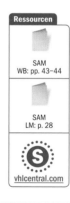

Ressourcen

SAM
WB: pp. 43–44

SAM
LM: p. 28

vhlcentral.com

Jetzt sind Sie dran!   **Complete the sentences.**

1. Die Lehrerin ___soll___ (sollen) den Kindern mit den Hausaufgaben helfen.

2. Ihr ___sollt___ (sollen) eure Hausaufgaben nicht vergessen.

3. Was ___sollen___ (sollen) wir heute machen?

4. Der tolle Musiker ___kann___ (können) Geige (*violin*) spielen.

5. Ich ___kann___ (können) meinen Rucksack nicht finden.

6. ___Kannst___ (Können) du nach Deutschland reisen?

7. Du ___musst___ (müssen) deine Oma morgen besuchen (*visit*).

8. Ein Geschäftsmann ___muss___ (müssen) sehr fleißig sein.

9. Wir ___müssen___ (müssen) das Matheproblem an die Tafel (*on the board*) schreiben.

10. Nur der nette Friseur ___darf___ (dürfen) mir die Haare schneiden (*to cut my hair*).

11. Die Rechtsanwälte ___dürfen___ (dürfen) in der Bibliothek lesen.

12. Du ___darfst___ (dürfen) nicht in das Klassenzimmer gehen.

13. Ich ___will___ (wollen) Architektin werden.

14. Die Kinder ___wollen___ (wollen) Fremdsprachen studieren.

15. ___Wollt___ (Wollen) ihr Schloss (*castle*) Neuschwanstein sehen?

Anwendung

1 Entscheiden Sie Select the correct form of the modal.

1. Ich (sollen / soll) Gitarre spielen.
2. Wir (dürfen / darf) am Nachmittag ein Eis (*ice cream*) essen.
3. (Willst / Wollt) du in die Bibliothek gehen?
4. Ihr (musst / müsst) morgen Abend eure Großeltern anrufen (*call*).
5. Bettina (kann / können) ihre Cousine nicht finden.
6. Rolf und Carsten (kann / können) samstags lange schlafen.

2 Ergänzen Sie Complete the sentences.

1. Die Kellner _____sollen_____ (sollen) das Essen bringen.
2. Du _____kannst_____ (können) Deutsch lernen.
3. Wir _____müssen_____ (müssen) einen Beruf finden.
4. Ihr _____dürft_____ (dürfen) mit dem Besitzer sprechen.
5. Ich _____will_____ (wollen) Journalist werden.

3 Schreiben Sie Rewrite the sentences using the cues.

> **BEISPIEL** Ulrike ist Musikerin. (wollen)
> *Ulrike will Musikerin sein.*

1. Ingenieure lösen (*solve*) viele Probleme. (müssen) Ingenieure müssen viele Probleme lösen.
2. Der Journalist reist nach Deutschland. (dürfen) Der Journalist darf nach Deutschland reisen.
3. Die Geschäftsfrau und der Geschäftsmann verdienen (*earn*) viel Geld. (sollen)
   Die Geschäftsfrau und der Geschäftsmann sollen viel Geld verdienen.
4. Meine Tante und ich tanzen Walzer. (können) Meine Tante und ich können Walzer tanzen.
5. Ich werde Friseurin. (wollen) Ich will Friseurin werden.

4 Fragen Sie Use the cues to form questions about the images.

4 Expansion Have students use these questions as the basis for a partner interview. Instead of using the subjects given, have them pose the questions to one another.
Ex.: **Darfst du schwimmen gehen? Ja, ich darf schwimmen gehen.**

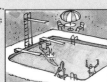

> **BEISPIEL**
> ich / schwimmen
> gehen / dürfen
>
> *Darf ich schwimmen gehen?*

1. ich / ein Stück Kuchen essen / können
Kann ich ein Stück Kuchen essen?

2. du / jetzt studieren / müssen
Musst du jetzt studieren?

3. Erika / Fußball spielen / wollen
Will Erika Fußball spielen?

4. wir / Musik hören / dürfen
Dürfen wir Musik hören?

5. Thomas / Musiker werden / wollen
Will Thomas Musiker werden?

6. ihr / viele Bücher lesen / müssen
Müsst ihr viele Bücher lesen?

Kommunikation

5 **Viele Wünsche** In pairs, take turns saying what each person wants to do. Then, imagine what they must or should do to achieve that goal.

Sample answers are provided.

BEISPIEL mein Bruder / nach Deutschland fahren

S1: *Mein Bruder will nach Deutschland fahren.*
S2: *Er soll Deutsch lernen.*

1. meine Freundin / Architektin werden   Meine Freundin will Architektin werden.
2. ich / das Fußballspiel gewinnen   Ich will das Fußballspiel gewinnen.
3. wir / einen Hund haben   Wir wollen einen Hund haben.
4. mein Vater / ein Stück Kuchen bestellen   Mein Vater will ein Stück Kuchen bestellen.
5. meine Schwester / ein gutes Zeugnis bekommen (*get*)   Meine Schwester will ein gutes Zeugnis bekommen.
6. mein Onkel / kurze Haare haben   Mein Onkel will kurze Haare haben.

5 **Expansion** Have students say what they want to do and let other students give them advice. Ex.: **Ich will gute Noten bekommen. Du must viel lernen.**

6 **Berufe** With a partner, offer advice to help these people get the jobs they want. Answers will vary.

BEISPIEL Muqadessa und Maria / Ingenieurinnen

S1: *Muqadessa und Maria wollen Ingenieurinnen werden.*
S2: *Sie sollen viel studieren.*

1. Edmund und Hakan / Rechtsanwälte
2. Knut und Heidi / Musiker
3. Eren / Architekt
4. Grete und Damla / Geschäftsfrauen

7 **Einladungen** In small groups, take turns inviting each other to take part in these activities. If you turn down an invitation, explain what you want to do, should do, or must do instead, and suggest a different activity. Answers will vary.

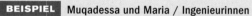

▶ **BEISPIEL**

S1: *Willst du Tennis spielen?*
S2: *Ich kann nicht. Ich muss Hausaufgaben machen. Aber wir können morgen ins Kino gehen.*

1.

2.

3.

4.

5.

6.

3B.2 Prepositions with the accusative  Presentation

Startblock In **1B.1**, you learned the accusative endings for definite and indefinite articles. You also learned that the direct object in German always takes the accusative case. In addition, the objects of certain prepositions are always in the accusative case.

Das Trinkgeld ist **für den Kellner**.
*The tip is **for the waiter**.*

Der Fuchs läuft **durch die Wälder**.
*The fox is running **through the woods**.*

- Prepositions and prepositional phrases describe time, manner, and place, and answer the questions *when*, *how*, and *where*.

um 8 Uhr
at 8 o'clock

ohne das Buch
without the book

gegen die Wand
against the wall

- These are some common accusative prepositions.

Suggestion Help students remember the most common accusative prepositions with the mnemonic **DOGFU: durch, ohne, gegen, für, um**.

prepositions with the accusative							
bis	*until, to*		für	*for*		ohne	*without*
durch	*through*		gegen	*against*		um	*around; at (time)*

Der Besitzer kommt **durch die Tür**.
*The owner is coming **through the door**.*

Was hast du **gegen meinen Freund**?
*What do you have **against my boyfriend**?*

- The prepositions **durch**, **für**, and **um**, when followed by the neuter definite article **das**, may be contracted to **durchs**, **fürs**, and **ums**. These contractions are frequently used in speech and are acceptable in writing.

Das Geschenk ist **fürs** Baby.
*The gift is **for the** baby.*

Die Kinder laufen **ums** Haus.
*The kids are running **around** the house.*

- The accusative preposition **bis** is frequently used with time expressions. When **bis** comes before a proper noun, such as **Samstag** or **März**, no article is necessary.

Ich bin **bis April** in Deutschland.
*I'm in Germany **until April**.*

Wir bleiben **bis nächsten Monat** in Köln.
*We are staying in Cologne **until next month**.*

- **Pro** (*Per*) is also an accusative preposition. The object it precedes takes no article.

Der Kellner verdient 300 Euro **pro Woche**.
*The waiter earns 300 euros **per week**.*

Das Auto fährt 230 Kilometer **pro Stunde**.
*The car goes 230 kilometers **per hour**.*

- The accusative is also used with objects that precede **entlang**.

Wir gehen **den Fluss entlang**.
*We are going **down the river**.*

Ich fahre **die Straße entlang**.
*I'm driving **along the road**.*

Ressourcen

SAM
WB: pp. 45–46

SAM
LM: p. 29

vhlcentral.com

Jetzt sind Sie dran! **Select the preposition that best completes each sentence.**

1. Die Frau geht ((ohne)/ pro) ihren Mann einkaufen.
2. Der Hund läuft ((durch)/ gegen) den Park.
3. Die Mutter braucht ein Geschenk (um / (für)) ihre Tochter.
4. Die Besitzer haben etwas ((gegen)/ ohne) die Musik.
5. Die Kellnerin geht (durch / (um)) den Tisch.

6. Die Friseurin verdient 30 € (für / (pro)) Haarschnitt (*haircut*).
7. Ich gehe den Fluss (*river*) ((entlang)/ bis).
8. Die Journalisten arbeiten (gegen / (bis)) um Mitternacht (*midnight*).

Anwendung und Kommunikation

1 **Wählen Sie** Select the correct preposition.

1. (Durch / Um) 8 Uhr muss ich in die Bibliothek gehen.
2. Der kleine Junge schießt (*kicks*) den Ball (gegen / ohne) die Tür.
3. (Ohne / Entlang) meine Schwester gehe ich nicht auf die Party.
4. Das Auto fährt die Straße (um / entlang).
5. Svenja kauft einen Kaffee (für / gegen) ihre Mutter.
6. Mein Onkel spielt (durch / bis) 6 Uhr Fußball.

2 **Was fehlt?** Complete the paragraph using the appropriate prepositions.

Herr Becker braucht ein Geschenk (*gift*) (1) _____für_____ seine Tochter. Sie hat alles und ist (2) _____gegen_____ teure Geschenke. Er geht in eine Buchhandlung (*bookstore*). Alles auf dem (*on the*) Tisch kostet (3) _____pro_____ Buch nur (*only*) 5 Euro. Er geht (4) _____durch_____ den Park nach Hause. (5) _____Um_____ 8 Uhr gibt er eine kleine Party für seine Tochter.

3 **Umfrage** In pairs, take turns asking and answering the questions. Answers will vary.

 BEISPIEL

S1: *Um wie viel Uhr fährst du zur Uni?*
S2: *Ich fahre um 8 Uhr zur Uni.*

1. Um wie viel Uhr beginnt dein Unterricht?
2. Wie viele Stunden (*hours*) schläfst du pro Nacht?
3. Für wen kaufst du gern Geschenke?
4. Ohne was kannst du nicht leben (*live*)?
5. Gegen welche Mannschaften spielst du gern?

4 **Die Geburtstagsfeier** In small groups, write four sentences describing the illustration. Use at least four prepositions with the accusative.

Possible answers: Der Hund läuft durch das Spielfeld. Die Äpfel sind für die Kinder. Die Jungen spielen ohne ihre Schwester. Die Eltern wollen um Mittag essen.

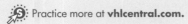

The imperative  Presentation

Startblock Imperatives are used to express commands, requests, suggestions, directions, and instructions.

Sei nicht traurig.

Mach dir keine Sorgen!

- The imperative forms are based on the present-tense conjugation patterns of **du**, **wir**, **ihr**, and **Sie**.

the *Imperativ* conjugation	
Indikativ	**Imperativ**
du kaufst	kauf(e)
ihr kauft	kauft
Sie kaufen	kaufen Sie
wir kaufen	kaufen wir

Mach deine Hausaufgaben!
Do your homework!

Backen wir einen Kuchen!
Let's bake a cake!

- To form an informal singular command, drop the **-st** from the present-tense **du** form of the verb. As in English, omit the subject pronoun with the second-person imperative.

Antworte auf die Frage!
Answer the question!

Schreib deinen Eltern einen Brief.
Write your parents a letter.

- Verbs with an **a** to **ä** vowel change do not retain this change in the imperative. However, **e** to **ie** and **e** to **i** changes are retained in the imperative for **du**.

Fahr langsam!
Drive slowly!

Lies das Buch.
Read the book.

Nimm den Bleistift.
Take the pencil.

- The informal plural **ihr** command is identical to the present-tense form, without the pronoun.

Esst das Gemüse, Kinder!
Eat the vegetables, kids!

Lernt für die Prüfung.
Study for the exam.

- For formal commands, keep the subject **Sie** and invert the subject/verb word order of the present tense. Remember that the singular and plural forms are identical.

Probieren Sie den Kuchen!
Try the cake!

Geben Sie mir den Radiergummi.
Give me the eraser.

- The first person plural command is equivalent to the English *Let's....* As with **Sie**, invert the subject/verb order of the present tense for **wir**.

Essen wir den Kuchen.
Let's eat the cake.

Gehen wir spazieren.
Let's go for a walk.

- In a negative command, **nicht** or **kein** follows the imperative form.

  Fahren Sie nicht so schnell!
  Don't drive so fast!

  Arbeite nicht so langsam!
  Don't work so slowly!

  Hör keine laute Musik!
  Don't listen to loud music!

  Macht kein Theater!
  Don't make a fuss!

- Use **bitte** to soften a command and make it polite. **Bitte** can be placed almost anywhere in a sentence, as long as it doesn't separate the verb from the subject pronoun **wir** or **Sie**.

  Öffnen Sie **bitte** Ihren Rucksack.
  *Open your backpack, **please**.*

  Geh nach Hause, **bitte**.
  *Go home, **please**.*

- The modals **können** and **wollen** are often used instead of the imperative for polite requests.

  Können Sie mir helfen?
  Can you help me?

  Wollen wir gehen?
  Shall we go?

- The verb **sein** has irregular imperative forms.

  Sei lieb!
  Be good! (sing., inf.)

  Seid diskret!
  Be discreet! (pl., inf.)

  Seien Sie mutig!
  Be brave! (form.)

  Seien wir realistisch.
  Let's be realistic.

- Here are some common commands and instructions found on German labels, signs, and in everyday situations. Notice that in some cases, a command is conveyed without using the imperative.

common commands	
Drücken.	*Push.*
Ziehen.	*Pull.*
Bring mir...	*Bring me...*
Langsam fahren.	*Slow down.*
Warte.	*Wait.*
Sprechen Sie bitte langsamer.	*Please speak more slowly.*
Türen schließen.	*Keep doors closed.*
Rauchen verboten.	*No smoking.*
Betreten des Rasens verboten.	*Keep off the grass.*
Keine Zufahrt.	*Do not enter.*
Parkverbot.	*No parking.*

QUERVERWEIS

See **2B.3** to review the use of **nicht** and **kein**.

Suggestion Point out to students that infinitives are often used instead of imperatives on signs and labels, and in recipes.

Jetzt sind Sie dran!   Select the correct imperative form to complete each sentence.

1. Herr Professor Braun, (sprecht / sprechen Sie) bitte langsamer.
2. Anna und Michael, (bringen Sie / bringt) euren Rucksack mit.
3. Patrick, (vergiss / vergessen wir) deine Hausaufgaben nicht!
4. Kinder, (seid / sei) bescheiden und nett!
5. Wir haben morgen eine Prüfung. (Gehen wir / Geht) in die Bibliothek.
6. Roland, (fahrt / fahr) nicht so schnell!
7. Herr und Frau Schmidt, (erklärt / erklären Sie) das Problem.
8. Wir haben Hunger. (Essen wir / Iss) ein Stück Brot.

Anwendung

1 Wählen Sie Select the correct imperative form.

1. Andrea, (spiel / spielt) Tennis mit Klaus!
2. (Gehen wir / Wir gehen) durch den Park!
3. Liebe Schüler, bitte (lies / lest) den Text auf Seite 27.
4. Herr Gärtner, (bleiben Sie / bleib) bitte heute bis 8 Uhr.
5. (Seien Sie / Sei) doch nicht böse, Frau Kampmann.
6. Marius, bitte (kommt / komm) um 6 Uhr nach Hause.

2 Was fehlt? Complete the sentences using the imperative.

BEISPIEL _____Komm_____ (du, kommen)!

1. Herr Schneider, ___wiederholen Sie___ (Sie, wiederholen) bitte.
2. Marie und Lukas, ___esst___ (ihr, essen) euer Gemüse (*vegetables*)!
3. Felix, ___sei___ (du, sein) nicht gemein!
4. Frau Fischer und Herr Wagner, ___essen Sie___ (Sie, essen) ein Stück Kuchen.
5. Paul und Else, ___macht___ (ihr, machen) bitte nicht so viel Krach (*noise*)!
6. ___Sprechen wir___ (wir, sprechen) nur Deutsch!

3 Schreiben Sie Tell these people not to do what they are doing. Sample answers are provided.

BEISPIEL Christa ist eifersüchtig.
Sei nicht eifersüchtig, Christa!

3 Expansion Have students give additional affirmative commands for this activity. Ex.: **1. Seien Sie nicht gierig, Herr Becker! Seien Sie großzügig und nett!**

1. Herr Becker ist gierig.
Seien Sie nicht gierig, Herr Becker!
2. Sie studieren Informatik.
Studieren Sie nicht Informatik!
3. Lukas spielt schlechte Musik.
Spiel keine schlechte Musik, Lukas!
4. Frau Weber kauft hässliche Sachen.
Kaufen Sie keine hässlichen Sachen, Frau Weber!

5. Maximilian und Luca schreiben an die Wand.
Schreibt nicht an die Wand, Maximilian und Luca!
6. Wir bleiben den ganzen Tag an der Universität.
Bleiben wir nicht den ganzen Tag an der Universität!
7. Heike telefoniert 4 Stunden pro Tag.
Heike, telefonier nicht 4 Stunden pro Tag!
8. Otto und Emma essen den Kuchen.
Esst den Kuchen nicht, Otto und Emma!

4 Konjugieren Sie Write a command for each image using the cues. Sample answers are provided.

1. wir Tanzen wir.

2. Julia Julia, zähl.

3. Kinder / eure Bücher
Kinder, öffnet eure Bücher.

4. Frau Schulze / eine Tasse Tee
Frau Schulze, trinken Sie eine Tasse Tee.

5. wir Gehen wir spazieren.

6. Greta / ein Bonbon
(*candy*) Greta, nimm ein Bonbon.

Kommunikation

5 Befehlen Sie In small groups, write eight sentences using **sollen**. Then, trade lists with another group and convert their sentences into commands. Answers will vary.

> **BEISPIEL**
>
> **S1:** *Du sollst deine Hausaufgaben machen.*
> **S2:** *Mach deine Hausaufgaben.*

6 Guter Rat In pairs, use the imperative to give advice to each person or group. Answers will vary.

> **BEISPIEL** deine Professorin
> *Sagen Sie das bitte noch einmal!*

1. deine Klassenkameraden
2. deine beste Freundin
3. deine Eltern
4. dein Bruder
5. dein Friseur
6. deine Katze

7 Ein paar Ratschläge In pairs, list ten pieces of advice that you would give to a new German exchange student at your school. Use the affirmative and negative forms of the imperative. Answers will vary.

> **BEISPIEL**
>
> **S1:** *Sei fleißig, aber nicht zu ernst!*
> **S2:** *Vergiss nicht deine Hausaufgaben!*

8 Simon sagt In groups of five, play Simon Says ("**Simon sagt**"). One student gives commands using the **du**, **Sie**, **ihr**, and **wir** forms. The group members must perform the activity only if the speaker says "**Simon sagt**". The first person to make a mistake becomes the new leader. Answers will vary.

> **BEISPIEL**
>
> **S1:** *Simon sagt: „Tanzen wir!"*
> OR
> **S1:** *Laura und Michael, geht in die Ecke (corner)!*

essen	schlafen
fahren	schreiben
hören	sprechen

8 Suggestion If nobody makes a mistake, tell students to change leaders after three commands.

8 Expansion You may want to introduce students to the traditional German game **Kommando Pimperle**, similar to Simon Says.

Wiederholung

1 Etwas unternehmen
In pairs, make plans for what you will do today in each location. Use prepositions with the accusative. Answers will vary.

BEISPIEL

S1: Um 10 Uhr gehen wir in die Bibliothek.
S2: Ja, dort können wir gute Bücher für das Referat finden.

bis	gegen
durch	ohne
entlang	um
für	

1.

2.

3.

4.

2 Wollen und sollen
In small groups, take turns saying one thing that you want to do today, one thing that you must do, one thing that you can do, one thing that you may do, and one thing that you are supposed to do. Answers will vary.

BEISPIEL

S1: Ich will heute Abend ins Kino gehen, aber ich muss Hausaufgaben machen.
S2: Ich soll für meinen Deutschkurs lernen, aber ich kann auch Tennis spielen.
S3: Ich kann nicht Tennis spielen. Ich muss...

3 Berufliche Eigenschaften
Your instructor will give you and a partner different worksheets with a list of occupations and profiles of several students. Take turns describing the students and matching their qualities to appropriate occupations. Answers will vary.

BEISPIEL

S1: Anke ist kreativ und gut in Mathe.
S2: Ah, dann ist Anke eine gute Architektin.

4 Meine ideale Familie
Survey your classmates about their ideal family situation, and write down their answers. Then, in pairs, compare your results. Answers will vary.

BEISPIEL

S1: Wie ist deine ideale Familie?
S2: Meine ideale Familie ist...

5 Viele Verabredungen
Your instructor will give you a worksheet with several activities listed. Survey your classmates to find someone who would like to do each of the activities with you. When someone says "yes", agree on a time and date. If someone says "no", they must give an excuse, explaining what they have to or are supposed to do instead. Answers will vary.

BEISPIEL

S1: Gehen wir morgen Abend ins Kino!
S2: Ich kann nicht. Ich muss für die Prüfung lernen.
S3: Ich komme gern. Gehen wir morgen um 7 Uhr!

6 Geschwister
In pairs, role-play a conversation between two siblings. The younger sibling asks to do things, and the older sibling tells him/her what to do and what not to do. Answers will vary.

BEISPIEL

S1: Darf ich Fußball spielen?
S2: Nein, das darfst du nicht! Iss dein Abendessen!

7 **Die Familie** With a partner, write a brief description of these five family members. Use the vocabulary you learned in **Lektionen 2A, 2B, 3A,** and **3B** to describe their interests, activities, physical characteristics, and personalities. Answers will vary.

Die Familie

BEISPIEL

Die Tochter heißt Karin. Sie ist zwölf Jahre alt. Sie hat blonde Haare und blaue Augen. Sie ist sehr aktiv und spielt gern Fußball.

der Sohn   die Tochter   der Vater   die Mutter   der Cousin

8 **Am Wochenende** In small groups, prepare a skit in which a group of friends makes plans for the weekend. Use vocabulary from **Kapitel 2.** Answers will vary.

BEISPIEL

S1: *Ich spiele gern Basketball! Können wir morgen Basketball spielen?*
S2: *Nein, bleiben wir hier! Wir müssen unsere Hausaufgaben machen!*
S3: *Ihr könnt hier bleiben, aber ich will...*

Mein Wör|ter|buch

Add five words related to **die Familie** and **persönliche Beschreibungen** to your personalized dictionary.

klug

Übersetzung
clever, smart

Wortart
Adjektiv (Beschreibungswort)

Gebrauch
Der Mann ist klug. Ein kluger Mann spricht nicht zu viel.

Synonyme
schlau, gescheit

Antonyme
dumm, unbegabt

Panorama Map

Die Vereinigten Staaten und Kanada

NATIONAL STANDARDS connections cultures

Anteil der Amerikaner mit deutschen Wurzeln: 17% (51 Millionen)

- ▶ **Kalifornien:** *3.517.470*
- ▶ **Pennsylvania:** *3.491.269*
- ▶ **Ohio:** *3.231.788*
- ▶ **Illinois:** *2.668.955*
- ▶ **Texas:** *2.542.996*
- ▶ **Wisconsin:** *2.455.980*
- ▶ **Michigan:** *2.271.091*
- ▶ **Florida:** *2.270.456*
- ▶ **New York:** *2.231.309*
- ▶ **Minnesota:** *1.949.346*
- ▶ **Indiana:** *1.629.766*
- ▶ **Missouri:** *1.576.813*

QUELLE: U.S. Census 2000

Anteil der Kanadier mit deutschen Wurzeln: 10% (3 Millionen)

- ▶ **Toronto:** *220.135*
- ▶ **Vancouver:** *187.410*
- ▶ **Winnipeg:**: *109.355*
- ▶ **Kitchener:** *93.325*
- ▶ **Montreal:** *83.850*

QUELLE: Canadian Census 2006

Die ersten deutschen Siedler in Kanada kommen zwischen 1750 und 1753 nach Nova Scotia. Die meisten von ihnen° sind Bauern und Kaufleute°. Zwischen 1919 und 1939 kommen fast 100.000 Deutsche nach Kanada. Auch von ihnen sind die meisten Bauern. Sie alle bringen ihre Familien mit und starten ein neues Leben in Nordamerika.

Berühmte Deutschamerikaner und Deutschkanadier

- ▶ **Levi Strauss,** *Unternehmer° (1829–1902)*
- ▶ **Frederick Louis Maytag I,** *Unternehmer (1857–1937)*
- ▶ **Dwight D. Eisenhower,** *Fünf-Sterne General und US-Präsident (1890–1969)*
- ▶ **Lou Gehrig,** *Baseballspieler (1903–1941)*
- ▶ **Henry Kissinger,** *Politiker (1923–)*
- ▶ **Almuth Lütkenhaus,** *Künstlerin° (1930–1996)*
- ▶ **Dany Heatley,** *Eishockeyspieler (1981–)*
- ▶ **Justin Bieber,** *Sänger° (1994–)*

meisten von ihnen *most of them* **Kaufleute** *tradespeople*
Unternehmer *entrepreneur* **Künstlerin** *artist* **Sänger** *singer*
verlässt *leaves* **Flöten** *flutes* **Immobilien** *real estate*
Fellhandel *fur trade* **reichste** *richest*

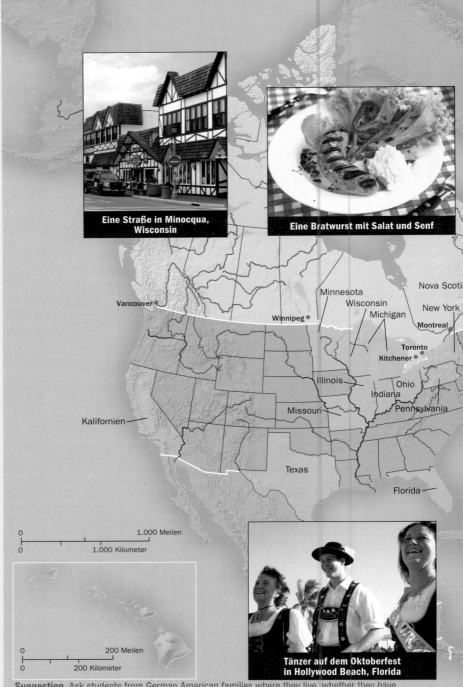

Eine Straße in Minocqua, Wisconsin

Eine Bratwurst mit Salat und Senf

Tänzer auf dem Oktoberfest in Hollywood Beach, Florida

Suggestion Ask students from German American families where they live, whether they have any German traditions in their family, and whether they prepare any German dishes. This is a good opportunity to explore the richness of German American culture in the United States, and also to point out how some German customs have evolved.

Unglaublich, aber wahr!

1784 verlässt° **John Jacob Astor** (1763–1848) das Dorf Walldorf in Deutschland mit $25 und 7 Flöten° in Richtung USA. Durch Immobilien°– und Fellhandel° wird er reich und ist zur Zeit seines Todes der reichste° Mann Amerikas. Sein Vermögen beträgt ungefähr $20 Millionen.

Menschen

Sandra Bullock

Sandra Bullock wurde 1964 in Arlington, Virginia geboren°. Ihre Mutter ist Helga D. Meyer, eine deutsche Opernsängerin. Deshalb verbringt° Bullock, die neben Englisch fließend° Deutsch spricht, auch die ersten 12 Jahre ihres Lebens in der deutschen Stadt Fürth, bevor sie mit ihrer Familie in die USA zieht. Ihre erfolgreiche Karriere beinhaltet Filme wie *Speed*, *Während du schliefst* und *Blind Side – Die große Chance*, für den sie einen Oscar als beste Hauptdarstellerin° erhält.

Essen

Hamburger

Der Hamburger – ein Sandwich aus einer Frikadelle° in einer Semmel° mit einem Salatblatt und einer Scheibe Tomate – hat etwas mit der Stadt Hamburg zu tun. Als deutsche Immigranten und Matrosen° Ende des 18. Jahrhunderts nach New York kommen, bekommen Sie hier „Steak im Hamburger Stil". Diese Steaks damals hatten mit heutigen Hamburgern außer dem Namen noch nicht viel zu tun. Erst mit der Erfindung des Fleischwolfs° im 19. Jahrhunderts werden aus Steaks im Hamburger Stil die heutigen Hamburger.

Feiern

German Fest

Das German Fest in Milwaukee ist das größte „deutsche" Event Nordamerikas. Seit 1981 feiern die Menschen hier am letzten Juliwochenende Kultur deutschsprachiger° Länder und Regionen wie Österreich, Deutschland, Liechtenstein, Südtirol und der Schweiz. Besucher° tragen teilweise Dirndl und Lederhosen, hören traditionelle Blaskapellen° oder moderne Popmusik und bekommen Informationen über ihre deutsche Abstammung°. Im Jahr 2010 essen die Besucher unter anderem 20.000 Bratwürste, 9.000 Knödel°, 200 Spanferkel° und 15.000 Stück Strudel.

Geschichte

Deutsche in Texas

1848 gibt es in Deutschland und vielen anderen europäischen Ländern (Frankreich, Dänemark, Österreich) Revolutionen und Aufstände° auf Grund von sozialen und wirtschaftlichen° Problemen. Nach der Mairevolution verlassen° viele Revolutionäre Deutschland und gehen in die USA. Sie leben in Städten wie zum Beispiel New Braunfels und Fredericksburg in Texas. Diesen deutschen Einfluss° kann man heute hier immer noch sehen. Unter anderem gibt es in Texas eine Form des Deutschen, die man Texas-Deutsch nennt.

IM INTERNET

1. Welche anderen Gerichte (*dishes*) haben ihren Ursprung (*origin*) in deutschsprachigen Ländern?

2. Suchen Sie ein Rezept für ein deutschamerikanisches (oder österreichischamerikanisches) Gericht.

3. Suchen Sie Informationen über eine berühmte deutsch-amerikanische Person.

For more information on this **Panorama**, go to **vhlcentral.com**.

---

wurde... geboren *was born* **verbringt** *spends (time)* **fließend** *fluent* **Hauptdarstellerin** *lead actress* **Aufstände** *uprisings* **wirtschaftlichen** *economic* **verlassen** *leave* **Einfluss** *influence* **Frikadelle** *meatball* **Semmel** *bun* **Matrosen** *sailors* **Erfindung des Fleischwolfs** *invention of the meat grinder* **deutschsprachiger** *German-speaking* **Besucher** *Visitors* **Blaskapellen** *brass bands* **Abstammung** *descent* **Knödel** *dumplings* **Spanferkel** *suckling pigs*

Was haben Sie gelernt? Complete the sentences.

1. Die meisten Amerikaner mit deutschen Wurzeln leben in __Kalifornien__.

2. Ungefähr __17 %__ der amerikanischen Bevölkerung haben deutsche Wurzeln.

3. John Astor verlässt 1784 Deutschland mit __$25__ und 7 Flöten.

4. Eine Schauspielerin, die fließend Deutsch spricht, ist __Sandra Bullock__.

5. Sandra Bullock wohnt in Fürth, bis sie __12 Jahre__ alt ist.

6. Zwei deutsche Städte in Texas sind __New Braunfels__ und Fredericksburg

7. Hamburger haben ihren Namen von der deutschen Stadt __Hamburg__.

8. Die Besucher essen jedes Jahr 200 Spanferkel und 20.000 Bratwürste auf dem __German Fest__.

9. Beim *German Fest* sehen __Besucher__ viele Facetten deutschsprachiger Kultur.

Vor dem Lesen

Predicting content from visuals

When you read in German, look for visual cues that can help you figure out the content and purpose of what you are reading. Photos and illustrations, for example, can give you a good idea of the main points of the reading. You may also encounter helpful visuals that summarize large amounts of data in a way that is easy to comprehend; these visuals include bar graphs, pie charts, flow charts, lists of percentages, and other diagrams.

Die beliebtesten° Haustiere

In Deutschland gibt es Haustiere in mehr als° 12 Millionen Haushalten.

Katzen	**16,5%**	der Haushalte
Hunde	**13,3%**	der Haushalte
Nagetiere°	**6,4%**	der Haushalte
Vögel	**4,9%**	der Haushalte
Aquarien°	**4,4%**	der Haushalte

Auch in Österreich und der Schweiz sind Katzen und Hunde die beliebtesten Haustiere.

beliebtesten *most popular* **mehr als** *more than*
Nagetiere *rodents* **Aquarien** *fish tanks*

Texte verstehen 👥 Take a quick look at the visual elements of the article in order to generate a list of ideas about its content. Then compare your list with a classmate's. What elements did you both notice? What aspects did your partner notice that didn't catch your eye? Discuss your lists and make any changes needed to produce a final list of ideas.

Hunde und Katzen

Für viele Deutsche, Österreicher und Schweizer sind Haustiere sehr wichtig. Allerdings gibt es in diesen Ländern weit weniger vierbeinige Freunde° als in anderen europäischen Ländern. Zum Beispiel hat in Deutschland nur etwa jeder Vierte ein Haustier.

W elche Tiere findet man bei Deutschen, Österreichern und Schweizern am häufigsten°? Oft hört man, der Hund ist des Deutschen bester Freund. Statistiken zeigen allerdings, dass nicht Hunde, sondern Katzen das Haustier Nummer 1 im deutschsprachigen Raum sind. Hunde stehen nur an Nummer 2. Außerdem geht

vierbeinige Freunde *four-legged friends* **am häufigsten** *most frequently*

der allgemeine° Trend hin zu mehr° Katzen und weniger° Hunden. Andere beliebte Tiere sind Nagetiere wie Kaninchen° und Hamster. Vögel singen immer weniger in deutschsprachigen Haushalten°.

Haustiere sind oft ein wichtiger Teil° der Familie. Kinder lernen durch sie, soziale Kontakte zu pflegen°. Großstadtkinder, die mit einem Hund leben, haben später° oft weniger Probleme mit Kriminalität. Vor allem bei Singles sind Katzen beliebt, da sie alleine sein können, aber auch eine Art Partnerersatz sind.

Wer hat welches Haustier?

Status	Katzen	Hunde	Fische	Vögel
Ledig	23%	18%	7%	5%
Verheiratet	18%	18%	6%	5%
Frauen	17%	18%	7%	5%
Männer	17%	18%	6%	5%

allgemeine *general* mehr *more* weniger *fewer* Kaninchen *bunnies* Haushalten *households*
ein wichtiger Teil *an important part* pflegen *to cultivate* später *later*

Nach dem Lesen

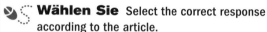

Richtig oder falsch? Indicate whether each statement is **richtig** or **falsch**.
Expansion Have students correct the false statements.

	richtig	falsch
1. Fast jede Familie in Deutschland hat ein Haustier. Jeder Vierte in Deutschland hat ein Haustier.	☐	☑
2. Katzen sind das Haustier Nummer 1.	☑	☐
3. Der Trend in den nächsten Jahren geht zu mehr Hunden. Der Trend in den nächsten Jahren geht zu mehr Katzen.	☐	☑
4. Immer weniger Menschen haben Vögel.	☑	☐
5. Großstadtkinder mit Hunden haben mehr Probleme. Großstadtkinder mit Hunden haben weniger Probleme.	☐	☑
6. Viele Ledige haben Katzen als Haustiere.	☑	☐

Wählen Sie Select the correct response according to the article.

1. Wie viel Prozent der Deutschen besitzen ein Haustier?
   a. 10%–20%   **b.** 20%–30%   c. 30%–40%
2. Welche Haustiere werden immer beliebter?
   a. Katzen   b. Vögel   c. Hunde
3. Welches Tier passt in die Kategorie Nagetiere?
   a. Vögel   b. Hunde   **c.** Hamster
4. Welches Haustier besitzen die meisten Deutschen?
   a. Hunde   b. Fische   **c.** Katzen
5. Welche Bevölkerungsgruppe hat die meisten Haustiere?
   a. Frauen   **b.** Ledige   c. Verheiratete

Meine Haustiere 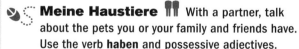 With a partner, talk about the pets you or your family and friends have. Use the verb **haben** and possessive adjectives.

BEISPIEL

S1: *Hast du eine Katze?*
S2: *Nein, ich habe nur einen Fisch, aber mein Onkel hat zwei Katzen…*

Hören

Vorbereitung

Based on the photograph, where do you think Irine and Stefanie are? What do you think they are talking about?

Zuhören

Now you are going to hear Irine and Stefanie's conversation. Write **C** next to adjectives that describe Irine's boyfriend, Christoph. Write **J** next to adjectives that describe Stefanie's boyfriend, Jürgen. Some adjectives will not be used.

_J_	großzügig	_C_	langweilig
___	hübsch	_J_	angenehm
_J_	süß	_C_	egoistisch
___	sportlich	___	langsam
_J_	großartig	_J_	toll
___	ernst	_C_	faul

Vor dem Hören Ask students questions about the two women in the picture to help them guess what they might be talking about. Brainstorm possible topics for the women's conversation and write them on the board. Ex.: **Über was sprechen Irine und Stefanie? Über die Arbeit? Über Familie? Über die Liebe?**

Verständnis

 Wer ist das? Write the name of the person described by each statement.

1. Sie hat ein Problem mit ihrem Freund.
   Irine

2. Videospiele sind sein Hobby.
   Christoph

3. Er ist großzügig und süß.
   Jürgen

4. Sie ist sehr glücklich mit ihrem Freund.
   Stefanie

5. Sie wird bald heiraten.
   Stefanie

6. Er ist der perfekte Freund.
   Jürgen

 Richtig oder falsch? Indicate whether each statement is **richtig** or **falsch**. Correct the false statements.

1. Christoph ist ein großzügiger und großartiger Mann.
   Falsch. Jürgen ist ein großzügiger und großartiger Mann.

2. Irine hat kein Glück mit Männern.
   Richtig.

3. Stefanie ist mit Jürgen verlobt.
   Richtig.

4. Irine kann mit ihrem Freund nichts machen.
   Richtig.

5. Christoph ist sehr interessant.
   Falsch. Christoph ist sehr langweilig.

6. Stefanie kann Irine mit ihrem Männerproblem helfen.
   Falsch. Stefanie kann Irine nicht helfen.

Schreiben

Strategien

Using idea maps

How do you organize ideas for a first draft? Often, the organization of ideas represents the most challenging part of the writing process. Idea maps are useful for organizing information. Here is an example of an idea map you could use when writing.

IDEA MAP

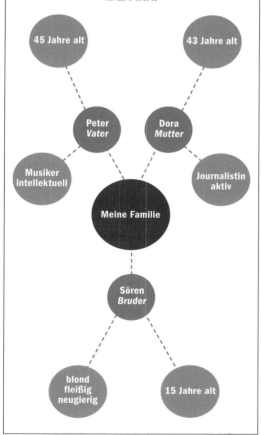

- 45 Jahre alt
- 43 Jahre alt
- Peter *Vater*
- Dora *Mutter*
- Musiker intellektuell
- Journalistin aktiv
- Meine Familie
- Sören *Bruder*
- blond fleißig neugierig
- 15 Jahre alt

Successful Language Learning Remind students to write their notes in German. Emphasize that they should not translate directly from English. Encourage them to use words and phrases they are familiar with and not rely too heavily on the dictionary.

Thema

Briefe schreiben

A German friend you met online wants to know about your family. Using the verbs and grammar structures you learned in this chapter, write a brief description of your family or an imaginary family, including:

- Names and relationships
- Physical characteristics
- Hobbies and interests

Suggestion Tell students that it may be helpful to write their idea maps on note cards, so that they can easily rearrange the ideas if necessary.

Here are some useful expressions for writing a letter or e-mail in German:

Salutations	
Lieber Stefan,	*Dear Stefan,*
Liebe Karin,	*Dear Karin,*

Asking for a response	
Ich hoffe, bald von dir zu hören.	*I hope to hear from you soon.*
Erzähl, was es Neues bei dir gibt.	*Let me know what's new with you.*

Closings	
Bis bald!/Tschüss!	*So long!*
Mach's gut!	*All the best!*
Mit freundlichen Grüßen	*Yours sincerely*
Hochachtungsvoll	*Respectfully*

Suggestion Point out the differences in formality in the closing expressions. For example, **Tschüss!** and **Mach's gut!** should only be used with friends and family, whereas **Mit freundlichen Grüßen** or **Hochachtungsvoll** are more formal.

die Familie

das Baby, -s	baby
der Bruder, -¨	brother
der Cousin, -s	cousin (m.)
die Cousine, -n	cousin (f.)
die Eltern	parents
das Enkelkind, -er	grandchild
der Enkelsohn, -¨e	grandson
die Enkeltochter, -¨	granddaughter
die Frau, -en	wife
das Geschwister, -	sibling
die Großeltern	grandparents
die Großmutter, -¨	grandmother
der Großvater, -¨	grandfather
der Halbbruder, -¨	half brother
die Halbschwester, -n	half sister
das Kind, -er	child
der Mann, -¨er	husband
die Mutter, -¨	mother
der Nachname, -n	last name
der Neffe, -n	nephew
die Nichte, -n	niece
die Oma, -s	grandma
der Onkel, -	uncle
der Opa, -s	grandpa
das Paar, -e	couple
der Schwager, -¨	brother-in-law
die Schwägerin, -nen	sister-in-law
die Schwester, -n	sister
die Schwiegermutter, -¨	mother-in-law
der Schwiegervater, -¨	father-in-law
der Sohn, -¨e	son
der Stiefbruder, -¨	stepbrother
die Stiefmutter, -¨	stepmother
die Stiefschwester, -n	stepsister
der Stiefsohn, -¨e	stepson
die Stieftochter, -¨	stepdaughter
der Stiefvater, -¨	stepfather
die Tante, -n	aunt
die Tochter, -¨	daughter
der Vater, -¨	father
der / die Verwandte, -n	relative
der Zwilling, -e	twin

die Haustiere

der Fisch, -e	fish
der Hund, -e	dog
die Katze, -n	cat
der Vogel, -¨	bird

zum Beschreiben

blaue/grüne/ braune Augen	blue/green/ brown eyes
blonde/braune/ schwarze Haare	blond/brown/ black hair
(un)angenehm	(un)pleasant
arm	poor; unfortunate
bescheiden	modest
besorgt	worried
diskret	discreet
dunkel	dark
dynamisch	dynamic
egoistisch	selfish
eifersüchtig	jealous
ernst	serious
faul	lazy
fleißig	hard-working
freundlich	friendly
froh	happy
gemein	mean
gierig	greedy
glücklich	happy
großzügig	generous
gut	good
hell	light
intellektuell	intellectual
intelligent	intelligent
interessant	interesting
langsam	slow
langweilig	boring
Lieblings-	favorite
lustig	funny
müde	tired
mutig	brave
naiv	naïve
nervös	nervous
nett	nice
neugierig	curious
schlecht	bad
schnell	fast
schüchtern	shy
schwach	weak
stark	strong
stolz	proud
süß	sweet; cute
toll	great
traurig	sad

der Familienstand

die Witwe, -n	widow
der Witwer, -	widower
geschieden	divorced
getrennt	separated
ledig	single
verheiratet	married
verlobt	engaged
heiraten	to marry

Berufe

der Architekt, -en / die Architektin, -nen	architect
der Besitzer, - / die Besitzerin, -nen	owner
der Friseur, -e / die Friseurin, -nen	hairdresser
der Geschäftsmann (pl. Geschäftsleute) / die Geschäftsfrau, -en	businessman / businesswoman
der Ingenieur, -e / die Ingenieurin, -nen	engineer
der Journalist, -en / die Journalistin, -nen	journalist
der Kellner, - / die Kellnerin, -nen	waiter / waitress
der Musiker, - / die Musikerin, -nen	musician
der Rechtsanwalt, -¨e / die Rechtsanwältin, -nen	lawyer

Modalverben

dürfen	to be allowed to, may
können	to be able to, can
müssen	to have to, must
sollen	to be supposed to
wollen	to want to

Possessive adjectives	See p. 104.
Descriptive adjectives	See p. 108.
Gern and *nicht gern*	See p. 112.
Prepositions with the accusative	See p. 128.
Common commands	See p. 131.

Suggestion Have students look at the photo and identify the people and items they see. Ask them what they think this chapter will be about.

Lebensmittel

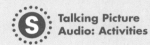

Talking Picture
Audio: Activities

Suggestion Tell students that Germans typically buy fresh bread from a bakery, rather than the supermarket.

Wortschatz

Geschäfte	stores
die Bäckerei, -en	bakery
die Eisdiele, -n	ice cream shop
das Feinkostgeschäft, -e	delicatessen
das Fischgeschäft, -e	fish store
die Konditorei, -en	pastry shop
das Lebensmittelgeschäft, -e	grocery store
der Markt, -¨e	market
die Metzgerei, -en	butcher shop
der Supermarkt, -¨e	supermarket

Essen	food
das Brot, -e	bread
das Brötchen, -	roll
die Butter	butter
der Joghurt, -s	yogurt
der Käse, -	cheese
das Öl, -e	oil
das Olivenöl, -e	olive oil
die Pasta	pasta
der Reis	rice

Suggestion Tell students that some German speakers treat **Joghurt** as a feminine or neuter noun, especially in Austria and Switzerland.

Fleisch und Fisch	meat and fish
die Garnele, -n	shrimp
das Hähnchen, -	chicken
die Meeresfrüchte (pl.)	seafood
das Rindfleisch	beef
der Schinken, -	ham
das Schweinefleisch	pork
der Thunfisch	tuna
das Würstchen, -	sausage

Obst und Gemüse	fruits and vegetables
die Ananas, -	pineapple
die Artischocke, -n	artichoke
die Himbeere, -n	raspberry
die Melone, -n	melon
die Traube, -n	grape

Suggestion Tell students that some words have more than one possible plural form. Ex.: die Ananas/die Ananasse; die Paprika/die Paprikas.

die Orange, -n

die Birne, -n

die Erdbeere, -n

Obst

der Pfirsich, -e

die Banane, -n

der Apfel, ¨-

die Kartoffel, -n

Gemüse

die Zwiebel, -n

die rote Paprika
(pl. die roten Paprika)

die Karotte, -n

die Aubergine, -n

die grüne Bohne
(pl. die grünen Bohnen)

der Knoblauch

der Pilz, -e

die Tomate, -n

Anwendung

ACHTUNG

Note that **der Salat** can refer to either *salad* or *lettuce*. A head of lettuce is **ein Salatkopf** (*m.*).

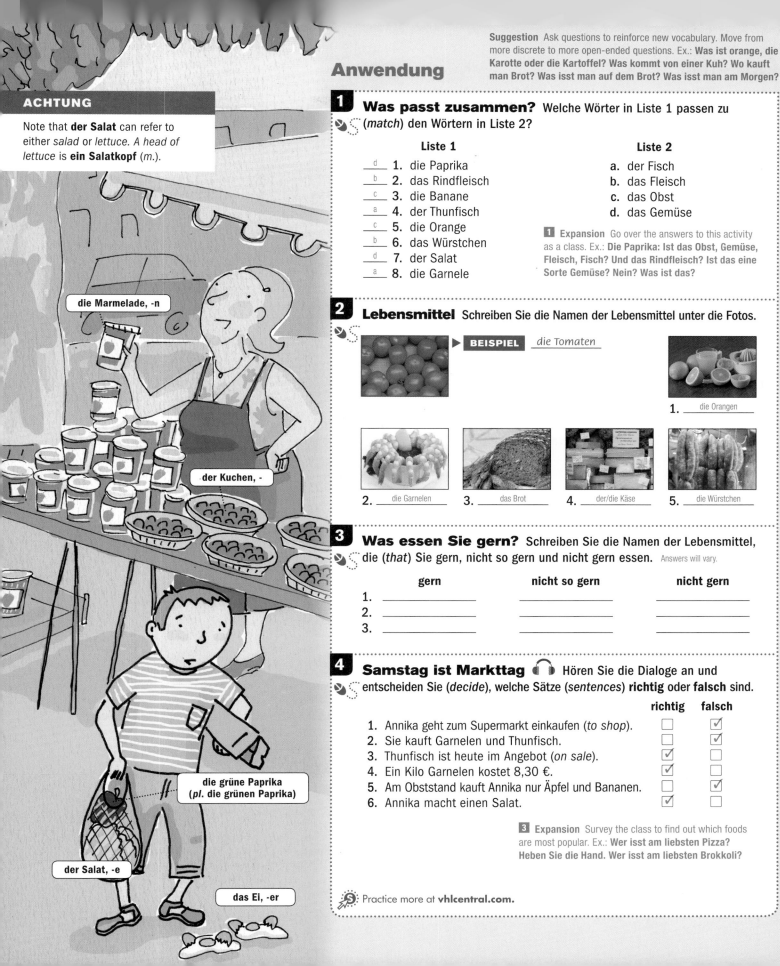

die Marmelade, -n

der Kuchen, -

die grüne Paprika
(*pl.* die grünen Paprika)

der Salat, -e

das Ei, -er

---

1 **Was passt zusammen?** Welche Wörter in Liste 1 passen zu (*match*) den Wörtern in Liste 2?

Liste 1	Liste 2
_d_ 1. die Paprika	a. der Fisch
_b_ 2. das Rindfleisch	b. das Fleisch
_c_ 3. die Banane	c. das Obst
_a_ 4. der Thunfisch	d. das Gemüse
_c_ 5. die Orange	
_b_ 6. das Würstchen	
_d_ 7. der Salat	
_a_ 8. die Garnele	

1 **Expansion** Go over the answers to this activity as a class. Ex.: **Die Paprika: Ist das Obst, Gemüse, Fleisch, Fisch? Und das Rindfleisch? Ist das eine Sorte Gemüse? Nein? Was ist das?**

---

2 **Lebensmittel** Schreiben Sie die Namen der Lebensmittel unter die Fotos.

▶ **BEISPIEL** *die Tomaten*

1. die Orangen

2. die Garnelen   3. das Brot   4. der/die Käse   5. die Würstchen

---

3 **Was essen Sie gern?** Schreiben Sie die Namen der Lebensmittel, die (*that*) Sie gern, nicht so gern und nicht gern essen. Answers will vary.

gern	nicht so gern	nicht gern
1. _____	_____	_____
2. _____	_____	_____
3. _____	_____	_____

---

4 **Samstag ist Markttag** 🎧 Hören Sie die Dialoge an und entscheiden Sie (*decide*), welche Sätze (*sentences*) **richtig** oder **falsch** sind.

	richtig	falsch
1. Annika geht zum Supermarkt einkaufen (*to shop*).	☐	☑
2. Sie kauft Garnelen und Thunfisch.	☐	☑
3. Thunfisch ist heute im Angebot (*on sale*).	☑	☐
4. Ein Kilo Garnelen kostet 8,30 €.	☑	☐
5. Am Obststand kauft Annika nur Äpfel und Bananen.	☐	☑
6. Annika macht einen Salat.	☑	☐

3 **Expansion** Survey the class to find out which foods are most popular. Ex.: **Wer isst am liebsten Pizza? Heben Sie die Hand. Wer isst am liebsten Brokkoli?**

Practice more at **vhlcentral.com**.

Kommunikation

5 Was kann man hier kaufen?
Nennen Sie (*Name*) drei Lebensmittel, die (*which*) Sie in den Geschäften kaufen können. Vergleichen Sie (*Compare*) die Antworten mit einem Partner / einer Partnerin. Answers will vary.

▶ **BEISPIEL**

in der Eisdiele
das Vanilleeis
der Kaffee
die Cola

5 Expansion Check students' answers by asking:
Was kauft man beim Bäcker? Was kauft man in der Metzgerei? Was kauft man auf dem Markt?

1. beim Bäcker
_____
_____
_____

EIN KLEINER TIPP

Auf Deutsch sagt man:

Ich kaufe Brot **beim** Bäcker.

Ich kaufe Fleisch **in der** Metzgerei.

Ich kaufe Fisch **im** Fischgeschäft/ **im** Supermarkt.

Ich kaufe Obst und Gemüse **auf dem** Markt.

2. in der Metzgerei
_____
_____
_____

3. auf dem Markt
_____
_____
_____

4. im Supermarkt
_____
_____
_____

5. im Fischgeschäft
_____
_____
_____

6 Kochen mit Freunden
Sie und Ihre Freunde wollen am Abend zusammen (*together*) kochen. Diskutieren Sie, was Sie alles brauchen und wer was kaufen soll (*who will buy what*). Answers will vary.

BEISPIEL

S1: *Wer bringt Obst und Gemüse?*
S2: *Ich bringe Salat. Thomas, bringst du das Obst?*
S3: *Ja, ich kann Trauben und Birnen bringen.*

7 Geschäftsbesitzer
Sie sind Geschäftsbesitzer (*shop owner*) und Ihre Mitstudenten müssen erraten (*guess*), was man bei Ihnen kaufen kann und welches Geschäft Sie haben.

BEISPIEL

S1: *Verkaufen Sie (Do you sell) Bananen?*
S2: *Nein.*
S3: *Verkaufen Sie Wurst?*
S2: *Ja.*
S1: *Haben Sie eine Metzgerei?*

8 Essen und trinken
Fragen Sie Ihre Mitstudenten, was sie gern oder nicht gern essen und trinken. Finden Sie mindestens (*at least*) eine Person, die denselben Geschmack (*the same taste*) hat wie Sie. Answers will vary.

BEISPIEL

S1: *Ich esse gern Brot und Nutella am Morgen. Isst du auch Nutella?*
S2: *Nein, ich esse nicht gern Nutella.*
S3: *Ich esse gern Brot und Nutella. Und ich trinke morgens Kaffee. Du auch?*

Aussprache und Rechtschreibung

Audio: Presentation
Record & Compare Activities

NATIONAL STANDARDS comparisons

🎧 The German s, z, and c

The *s* sound in German is represented by **s**, **ss**, or **ß**. At the end of a word, **s**, **ss**, and **ß** are pronounced like the *s* in the English word *yes*. Before a vowel, **s** is pronounced like the *s* in the English word *please*.

Rei**s**	Profe**ss**or	wei**ß**	**S**upermarkt	Kä**s**e

The German **z** is pronounced like the *ts* in the English word *bats*, whether it appears at the beginning, middle, or end of a word. The combination **tz** is also pronounced *ts*. The ending **-tion** is always pronounced *-tsion*.

Pil**z**e	**Z**wiebel	Plat**z**	Besit**z**er	Kau**tion**

Only in loan words does the letter **c** appear directly before a vowel. Before **e** or **i**, the letter **c** is usually pronounced *ts*. Before other vowels, it is usually pronounced like the *c* in *cat*. The letter combination **ck** is pronounced like the *ck* in the English word *packer*.

Cent	**C**elsius	**C**omputer	ba**ck**en	Bä**ck**erei

Suggestion Tell students that people in Southern Germany, Austria, and Switzerland typically pronounce **s** like the *s* in *yes*, even before vowels.

🔊 1 Sprechen Sie nach Wiederholen Sie die Wörter, die Sie hören.

1. lassen
2. lasen
3. weißer
4. weiser
5. sinnlos
6. seitens
7. selbst
8. Zeile
9. Katzen
10. letztes
11. Campingplatz
12. Fleck

🔊 2 Artikulieren Sie Wiederholen Sie die Sätze, die Sie hören.

1. Der Musiker geht am Samstag zum Friseur.
2. Es geht uns sehr gut.
3. Die Zwillinge essen eine Pizza mit Pilzen, Zwiebeln und Tomaten.
4. Jetzt ist es Zeit in den Zoo zu gehen.
5. Der Clown sitzt im Café und spielt Computerspiele.
6. Ich esse nur eine Portion Eis.

2 Suggestion Tell students that tuna, eggs, shrimp, and corn are all common pizza toppings in Germany.

🔊 3 Sprichwörter Wiederholen Sie die Sprichwörter, die Sie hören.

Aus den Augen, aus dem Sinn.[1]

Gegensätze ziehen sich an.[2]

[1] Out of sight, out of mind.
[2] Opposites attract.

Ressourcen

SAM
LM: p. 32

vhlcentral.com

Börek für alle Video: *Fotoroman*

George und Hans treffen Meline und Sabite im Supermarkt. George hat eine
Idee: Er macht Börek für seine Freunde. Aber kann George kochen?

Vorbereitung Have students scan the images and try to guess what the characters will buy. Have them create a grocery shopping list for the boys and another one for the girls.

1

GEORGE Was möchtest du heute essen?
HANS Hmmm. Ich esse gerne Fleisch.
  Rindfleisch, Schweinefleisch und Wurst...
GEORGE Los! Auf zur Fleischtheke!
HANS Ja!

5

MELINE Müssen wir mit Hans und
  George essen?
SABITE Ach, Meline, sei nett.

2

SABITE Ich esse gern Tofu mit Pilzen
  und Erdbeeren.
HANS Erdbeeren und was?
SABITE Pilze. Mit Tofu.

3

HANS Muss Meline mit uns essen? Sie ist
  extrem unangenehm. Ich finde, das ist
  eine ausgesprochen schlechte Idee.
GEORGE Meline ist lustig. Du magst
  sie bestimmt.
HANS Das glaube ich kaum.
GEORGE Sie mag dich bestimmt.

GEORGE Sabite, welche Zutaten kommen
  in die Börek von deiner Mutter? Wir können
  sie kochen.
SABITE Hmm. Lass mich überlegen. Kartoffeln,
  Blätterteig, Zwiebeln. Kartoffeln kochen,
  Zwiebeln braten, Teig aufrollen. Backen.

6

4

GEORGE Ich mache heute Abend Börek!
SABITE Wir bringen Käse und Brot mit. Wann
  sollen wir kommen?
GEORGE Kommt um halb sieben vorbei.
SABITE Perfekt.
MELINE Was ist perfekt?

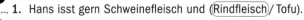

ÜBUNGEN

1 Ergänzen Sie Ergänzen Sie die Sätze mit den richtigen Informationen.

1. Hans isst gern Schweinefleisch und (Rindfleisch / Tofu).
2. Sabite mag Tofu mit Pilzen und (Wurst / Erdbeeren).
3. In die Börek von Frau Yilmaz kommen (Pilze / Zwiebeln).
4. Man muss die Zwiebeln (waschen / braten).
5. Meline und Sabite sollen um (zehn nach sieben / halb sieben)
   bei Hans und George sein.

6. Sie bringen (Käse und Brot / Käse und Wurst) mit.
7. Hans findet die Idee ausgesprochen (schlecht / gut).
8. In den Börek fehlt (*is missing*) (Blätterteig / Schafskäse).
9. Sabite ruft morgen (ihre Mutter / ihre Oma) an.
10. Hans und George haben noch (Milch und Äpfel / Joghurt
    und Bananen).

PERSONEN

 George   Hans   Meline   Sabite

7
GEORGE Tada! Prost!
HANS Prost!

8
SABITE George! Was...
GEORGE Ich weiß es nicht!

9
SABITE Wo ist der Schafskäse? Er gibt ihnen erst noch den Geschmack.
GEORGE Schafskäse? Wieso...
SABITE Oh, nein. Oh, George, es tut mir leid! Ich rufe morgen meine Mutter an und schreibe es dann auf.

10
GEORGE Es ist schon okay. Der Butterkäse und das Brot liegen dort.
MELINE Ich brate Eier und Kartoffeln.
HANS Gute Idee. Wir haben hier oben noch Joghurt und Bananen.
SABITE Hier stehen noch Butter und Marmelade für das Brot!

Nützliche Ausdrücke

- **die Wurst** *cold cuts*
- **Los! Auf zur Fleischtheke!** *Let's go! To the butcher's counter!*
- **die Zutat** *ingredient*
- **der Blätterteig** *phyllo dough*
- **aufrollen** *roll up*
- **Kommt um halb sieben vorbei!** *Come over at half past seven!*
- **Brauchen wir noch etwas?** *Do we need anything else?*
- **Ich finde, das ist eine ausgesprochen schlechte Idee.** *I think it's an extremely bad idea.*
- **der Schafskäse** *Feta cheese*
- **Es tut mir leid!** *I'm sorry!*

4A.1
- **Du magst sie bestimmt.** *You really will like her.*

4A.2
- **Ich mache heute Abend Börek!** *I'm making boreks tonight!*

4A.3
- **Ich rufe morgen meine Mutter an und schreibe es dann auf.** *I'll call my mother tomorrow, and I'll write it down.*

Suggestion Explain to students that **Wurst** can refer to either sausage or cold cuts.

2 Zum Besprechen Sie und ein Freund möchten heute Abend Ihre Klassenkameraden zum Essen einladen (*invite*). Schreiben Sie mit einem Partner einen Dialog. Was wollen Sie servieren? Welche Zutaten brauchen Sie? Wo kaufen Sie ein? Wie kochen Sie das Essen? Answers will vary.

2 Expansion Have students work in groups to talk about German food. Have they ever tried German food? What dishes have they heard of? Are there any German stores or restaurants in your area? Invite students from German-American families to share family recipes with the class.

3 Vertiefung Suchen Sie bekannte Lebensmittelhersteller (*food brands*) in Deutschland, wie Knorr, Maggi oder Haribo. Finden Sie drei bekannte Produkte. Präsentieren Sie der Klasse Ihre Resultate. Answers will vary.

Der Wiener Naschmarkt  Reading

IN DEUTSCHLAND, ÖSTERREICH und der Schweiz hat fast jede Stadt° einen Marktplatz°. Er ist normalerweise im Zentrum der Stadt.

Stände am Naschmarkt	
Lebensmittel	31
Gastronomie°	27
Obst und Gemüse	20
Fleischwaren	9
Backwaren°	8
Fisch	5
Blumen	2
Milchprodukte	2
Wein	1
Bier	1
Sonstiges°	1

QUELLE: Edition moKKa

Große Städte haben oft mehr als einen Marktplatz. Berühmte° Marktplätze sind der Viktualienmarkt in München, der Alexanderplatz in Berlin, der Helvetiaplatz in Zürich und der Naschmarkt in Wien.

Der Naschmarkt ist einer der 26 Märkte in Wien. Er existiert seit über° 80 Jahren und liegt° sehr zentral. Viele Stände° auf dem Naschmarkt sind Montag bis Samstag zwischen° 9 Uhr und 21 Uhr offen. Vor allem° samstagmorgens bei gutem Wetter° findet man alte und junge Menschen an den Ständen. Die Atmosphäre ist lebendig°: Menschen unterhalten sich° und Kunden handeln mit den Verkäufern°.

Märkte wie der Wiener Naschmarkt haben auch viele verschiedene° Waren: Es gibt Käse, Fleisch, Wurst, Obst und Gemüse. Natürlich gibt es auch Milchprodukte wie Käse und Joghurt. Außerdem° kann man Blumen oder Seife° kaufen. Der Markt ist auch sehr international mit italienischen, griechischen, türkischen und asiatischen Ständen.

fast jede Stadt almost every city **Marktplatz** market square **Berühmte** Famous **existiert seit über** has existed for more than **liegt** is located **Viele Stände** Many stands **zwischen** between **Vor allem** Especially **bei gutem Wetter** when the weather is nice **lebendig** lively **unterhalten sich** chat **Kunden handeln mit den Verkäufern** buyers negotiate with the vendors **verschiedene** different **Außerdem** In addition **Seife** soap **Gastronomie** prepared foods **Backwaren** baked goods **Sonstiges** Other

---

1 **Der Wiener Naschmarkt** Ergänzen Sie die Sätze.

1. Jede Stadt in Deutschland, __Österreich__ und der Schweiz hat einen Marktplatz.

2. Der Marktplatz ist normalerweise im __Zentrum__ der Stadt.

3. Ein berühmter Marktplatz in Berlin heißt __Alexanderplatz__.

4. In Wien gibt es __26__ Märkte.

5. Der Naschmarkt existiert seit über __80__ Jahren.

6. Viele Stände sind zwischen 9 und __21__ Uhr offen.

7. Die Atmosphäre auf dem Naschmarkt ist __lebendig__.

8. Der Naschmarkt ist sehr international mit italienischen, griechischen, __türkischen__ und asiatischen Waren.

9. An fünf Ständen kann man __Fisch__ kaufen.

10. Auf dem Naschmarkt gibt es __20__ Obst- und Gemüsestände.

 Practice more at **vhlcentral.com**.

Auf dem Markt

Ich hätte gern...	*I would like...*
ein Dutzend Eier	*a dozen eggs*
ein Pfund Kartoffeln	*a pound of potatoes*
100 Gramm Käse	*100 grams of cheese*
Das macht 3,80 €.	*That's € 3.80.*
Sonst noch etwas?	*Anything else?*
Was wünschen Sie?	*What would you like?*
Wie viel kostet das?	*How much is that?*

Das ist eine Tomate, oder?

Deutsche und Österreicher sprechen Deutsch, aber es gibt verschiedene Vokabeln. Deutsche sagen „Tomate". Was sagen Österreicher? Hier ist eine kurze Liste mit Essensvokabeln:

In Deutschland	In Österreich
die Aprikose°	die Marille
grüne Bohnen	Fisolen
das Brötchen	die Semmel
das Hackfleisch°	das Faschierte
die Kartoffel	der Erdapfel
der Meerrettich°	der Kren
der Quark°	der Topfen
die Sahne°	der Obers
die Tomate	der Paradeiser

Aprikose *apricot* **Hackfleisch** *ground meat* **Meerrettich** *horseradish* **Quark** *curd cheese* **Sahne** *cream*

Wolfgang Puck

Wolfgang Puck ist ein österreichischer Koch°. Er lebt und arbeitet in den USA, hat aber auch Restaurants in Japan. Er ist sehr erfolgreich°: Der Umsatz° seiner Firmen ist mehr als 100 Millionen Dollar pro Jahr. In den USA hat er mehr als 70 Restaurants: Bistros, Cafés und Gourmetrestaurants. Ein sehr berühmtes und sehr teures° Restaurant ist das Spago in Beverly Hills. Das Essen in seinen Restaurants ist nicht nur amerikanisch. In fast jedem Restaurant kann man neben amerikanischen Burgern auch Wiener Schnitzel° und Kärntner Kasnudeln° bestellen.

Koch *chef* **erfolgreich** *successful* **Umsatz** *total revenue* **teures** *expensive* **Wiener Schnitzel** *Viennese schnitzel* **Kärntner Kasnudeln** *South Austrian cheese noodles*

IM INTERNET

Wie viele Christkindlmärkte gibt es in Österreich? Wo sind sie? Welche Christkindlmärkte sind sehr berühmt?

*For more information on this **Kultur**, go to vhlcentral.com.*

---

2 **Richtig oder falsch?** Korrigieren Sie die falschen Aussagen (*statements*) mit einem Partner / einer Partnerin.

1. Das Brötchen heißt Semmel in Österreich. Richtig.
2. Eine Tomate heißt Marille in Österreich. Falsch. Sie heißt ein Paradeiser.
3. Wolfgang Puck ist ein deutscher Koch. Falsch. Er ist ein österreicher Koch.
4. Wolfgang Puck hat Restaurants nur in Amerika. Falsch. Er hat Restaurants in den USA und Japan.
5. In fast jedem Restaurant von Wolfgang Puck kann man Wiener Schnitzel bestellen. Richtig.

3 **Ein Gespräch auf dem Naschmarkt** Spielen Sie ein Gespräch zwischen einem Kunden (*customer*) und einem Verkäufer auf dem Naschmarkt. Integrieren Sie die folgenden Informationen: Grüße, zwei Produkte, Preise, Bezahlung (*payment*), Abschiede. Answers will vary.

BEISPIEL

3 Suggestion Encourage students to use phrases from the **Deutsch im Alltag** box in their role-plays.

S1: *Guten Tag.*
S2: *Grüß Gott. Kann ich Ihnen helfen?*
S1: *Ja. Ich hätte gerne...*

The modal *mögen*  Presentation

Startblock In **3A.3**, you learned to express likes and dislikes using **gern** and **nicht gern.** Another way of expressing liking is with the modal **mögen.**

Hey! Ich **mag** das! Danke.

Meline ist lustig. Du **magst** sie bestimmt.

- Like all the modal verbs, **mögen** is irregular in the singular.

mögen (*to like*)			
ich mag	*I like*	wir mögen	*we like*
du magst	*you like*	ihr mögt	*you like*
er/sie/es mag	*he/she/it likes*	Sie/sie mögen	*you/they like*

- While most modals modify another verb, **mögen** almost always appears on its own.

Die Kinder **mögen** diesen Joghurt.
*The kids **like** this yogurt.*

Magst du Zwiebeln und Knoblauch?
*Do you **like** onions and garlic?*

- **Möchten** is the subjunctive form of **mögen.** Use **möchten** for polite requests and to say what you *would like* to have or do. **Möchten** may be followed by either a verb or a noun.

möchten			
ich möchte	*I would like*	wir möchten	*we would like*
du möchtest	*you would like*	ihr möchtet	*you would like*
er/sie/es möchte	*he/she/it would like*	Sie/sie möchten	*you/they would like*

Wir **möchten** Fußball spielen.
*We **would like** to play soccer.*

Möchten Sie Kaffee oder Tee?
***Would** you **like** coffee or tea?*

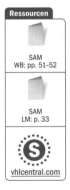

Jetzt sind Sie dran! Ergänzen Sie die Lücken mit den richtigen Formen der Modalverben **mögen** oder **möchten.**

1. Die Kinder __mögen__ (mögen) Schokolade.
2. Ich __mag__ (mögen) Joghurt und Käse.
3. Julia __möchte__ (möchten) in die Konditorei gehen.
4. __Möchtest__ (Möchten) du Pasta oder Reis?
5. Anne __mag__ (mögen) Auberginen nicht.
6. __Möchten__ (Möchten) Sie einen Tisch beim Fenster?
7. Ihr __möchtet__ (möchten) zur Bäckerei gehen.

8. __Magst__ (Mögen) du Meeresfrüchte nicht?
9. Ich __möchte__ (möchten) kein Fleisch essen.
10. Hans und Mark __mögen__ (mögen) Bananen zum Frühstück.
11. __Mögt__ (Mögen) ihr Garnelen?
12. Wir __möchten__ (möchten) ein Stück (*piece of*) Kuchen.

Anwendung und Kommunikation

1 **Ergänzen Sie** Ergänzen Sie die Sätze mit der richtigen Form von **mögen**.

> **BEISPIEL** Hans ___mag___ Fußball.

1. Meine Schwester ___mag___ Schokolade.
2. Meine Eltern ___mögen___ die Komponisten Mozart und Haydn.
3. Ich ___mag___ russische Literatur.
4. Mein Mann und ich ___mögen___ Filme mit Robert De Niro.
5. Unser Hund ___mag___ unsere Katzen nicht.
6. Und du, du ___magst___ deine Hausaufgaben nicht!

2 **Pläne für das Wochenende** Ergänzen Sie die Sätze mit der richtigen Form von **möchten** und mit Wörtern aus der Liste.

2 Expansion Have students write 5 sentences about what *they* would like to do this weekend, using **möchten**.

am Wochenende Fußball spielen	schlafen
ins Restaurant gehen	tanzen
auf Hochzeitsreise (*honeymoon*) gehen	Tennis spielen

▶ **BEISPIEL**
Ben und Christian
möchten am Wochenende Fußball spielen.

1. Elias und Petra
möchten auf Hochzeitsreise gehen

2. Karin, du
möchtest schlafen .

3. Professor Klein
möchte Tennis spielen .

4. Holger und du, ihr
möchtet tanzen .

5. Marie und ich, wir
möchten ins Restaurant gehen .

3 **Was magst du?** Fragen Sie Ihren Partner / Ihre Partnerin, was er/sie (nicht) mag. Fragen Sie auch nach den anderen Personen in seiner/ihrer Familie. Answers will vary.

BEISPIEL
S1: *Magst du Thunfisch?*
S2: *Nein, aber ich mag Käse.*
S1: *Und dein Bruder? Mag er Thunfisch?*
S2: *Nein, aber er mag Würstchen.*

3 Suggestion You may want to teach students the words **igitt** and **lecker** for use in this activity.

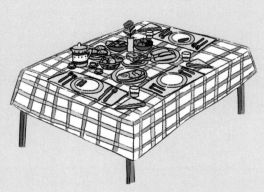

Adverbs  **Presentation**

Startblock In German, as in English, adverbs are words or phrases that modify a verb, an adjective, or another adverb. Adverbs describe *when, how,* or *where* an action takes place.

Ich gehe **wirklich gern** einkaufen.

Ich mache **heute Abend** Börek!

- An adverb usually comes immediately before the adjective or adverb it modifies. Adverbs that frequently modify adjectives or other adverbs include **fast** (*almost*), **nur** (*only*), **sehr** (*very*), **so** (*so*), **wirklich** (*really*), and **zu** (*too*).

  Der Kuchen ist **fast** fertig.
  *The cake is **almost** ready.*

  Du isst **viel zu** schnell.
  *You eat **much too** quickly.*

- When an adverb modifies a verb, it generally comes immediately after the verb it modifies. Adverbs of time or place can also come directly before the verb.

  Ich esse **täglich** Gemüse.
  *I eat vegetables **every day**.*

  Morgens trinken wir **immer** Kaffee.
  *We **always** drink coffee **in the morning**.*

- Here are some common adverbs of time, manner, and place.

adverbs					
Wann?		**Wie?**		**Wo?**	
immer	*always*	allein	*alone*	da/dort	*there*
jetzt	*now*	bestimmt	*definitely*	drüben	*over there*
nie	*never*	leider	*unfortunately*	hier	*here*
oft	*often*	vielleicht	*maybe*	überall	*everywhere*
selten	*rarely*	zusammen	*together*	woanders	*somewhere else*

- Adverbs of time indicate *when* or *how frequently* an event occurs and answer the questions **wann?** and **wie oft?** (*how often?*).

  Wir kaufen **morgen** einen Kuchen.
  *We're getting a cake **tomorrow**.*

  Ich esse **selten** Kuchen.
  *I **rarely** eat cake.*

- If there is more than one time expression in a sentence, general time references are placed before adverbs of specific time.

  Die Bäckerei öffnet **am Sonntag um 9 Uhr**.
  *The bakery opens at **9 o'clock on Sunday**.*

  Samstag morgens um 11 Uhr frühstücke ich mit meinem Vater.
  *I have breakfast with my father **every Saturday morning at 11 o'clock**.*

- Adverbs of manner indicate *how* an action is done. They answer the question **wie?**

  Ich mache das **allein**.
  I'm doing this by myself.

  Du spielst **wirklich gut** Tennis.
  You play tennis really well.

- Adverbs of place describe locations or directions and answer the questions **wo?**, **wohin?**, and **woher?**

  Woher kommst du?
  Where are you from?

  Ich komme **aus Deutschland**.
  I'm from Germany.

  Wo bleibt ihr?
  Where are you staying?

  Wir bleiben **zu Hause**.
  We're staying at home.

- When there is more than one adverbial expression in a sentence, adverbs of time come first, followed by adverbs of manner, then adverbs of place.

  Papa kauft **heute in der Konditorei** eine Geburtstagstorte.
  *Dad is getting a birthday cake **today at the pastry shop**.*

  Wir fahren **zusammen zum Supermarkt**.
  *We're going **to the supermarket together**.*

  Heute Abend esse ich **vielleicht im Restaurant**.
  *Maybe I'll eat **at a restaurant tonight**.*

  Sie essen **morgen Abend bestimmt woanders**.
  *They are **definitely** eating **somewhere else tomorrow night**.*

- In **2B.3** you learned how to negate sentences with **nicht**. In sentences with adverbial expressions, the negation **nicht** usually *precedes* general expressions of time, manner, and place, but *follows* adverbs of specific time.

  Wir kaufen Fleisch **nicht oft** im Supermarkt.
  *We don't **often** buy meat at the supermarket.*

  Ich möchte **am Montag nicht** in die Schule gehen.
  *I don't want to go to school **on Monday**.*

Suggestion Point out to students that adverbs can make their speech and writing more informative and expressive. Give them a sample sentence, such as **Anna geht spazieren**. Ask them to make it more vivid by adding adverbs that describe where, how, and when the action takes place.

Ressourcen

SAM
WB: pp. 53–54

SAM
LM: p. 34

Ⓢ
vhlcentral.com

Jetzt sind Sie dran! Geben Sie an (*Indicate*), ob die Adverbien die Zeit (*time*), die Art und Weise (*manner*) oder den Ort beschreiben.

1. Wir kochen heute Abend <u>zusammen</u>. _Art und Weise_
2. Marina ist <u>immer</u> besorgt. _Zeit_
3. Die Eltern trinken <u>gern</u> Rotwein. _Art und Weise_
4. Das Lebensmittelgeschäft ist <u>dort drüben</u>. _Ort_
5. Meine Schwester isst <u>nie</u> Obst und Gemüse. _Zeit_
6. Ihr trinkt <u>selten</u> Kaffee. _Zeit_

7. Du machst deine Hausaufgaben <u>allein</u>. _Art und Weise_
8. Ich fahre <u>schnell</u> zur Universität. _Art und Weise_
9. Petra hat <u>jetzt</u> keine Zeit. _Zeit_
10. Ich esse <u>oft</u> Käse und Brot. _Zeit_
11. Kann man Auberginen <u>überall</u> kaufen? _Ort_
12. Wir bleiben <u>hier</u> in Berlin. _Ort_

Anwendung

1 Wählen Sie Wählen Sie (*Choose*) das adverbiale Element, das am besten passt.

> **BEISPIEL** Ich gehe (die ganze Nacht / im Restaurant / (morgens)) in den Unterricht.

1. Yusuf macht ((in der Bibliothek)/ im Fitnessstudio / in der Bäckerei) Hausaufgaben.
2. Wir möchten später (selten / beim Bäcker / (im Park)) picknicken.
3. Efe geht (im Hörsaal / (im Supermarkt)/ im Café) einkaufen (*to shop*).
4. Das Restaurant ist ((oft)/ überall / zusammen) voll (*crowded*).
5. Der Schinken ist (jetzt/ fast / (wirklich)) salzig.
6. Thomas isst (dort / (selten) / allein) Fleisch.
7. Der Kuchen schmeckt (abends / am Wochenende / (sehr)) lecker (*delicious*).
8. Zum Mittagessen gehen wir (leider / (in der Mensa) / nie) essen.

2 Alltagsleben auf dem Campus Setzen Sie das Adverb an die richtige Stelle.

> **BEISPIEL** Wir essen um 6 Uhr. (immer)
> *Wir essen immer um 6 Uhr.*

1. David vergisst immer seine Hausaufgaben. (fast)
   David vergisst fast immer seine Hausaufgaben.

2. Ich gehe nach (*after*) meinem Deutschkurs einkaufen. (oft)
   Ich gehe oft nach meinem Deutschkurs einkaufen.

3. Paula geht nachmittags spazieren. (auf dem Campus)
   Paula geht nachmittags auf dem Campus spazieren.

4. Die Studenten essen in der Mensa. (nicht gern)
   Die Studenten essen nicht gern in der Mensa.

5. Ihr lernt in der Bibliothek. (abends)
   Ihr lernt abends in der Bibliothek.

6. Du gehst freitags tanzen. (im Club)
   Du gehst freitags im Club tanzen.

7. Die Professorin korrigiert die Prüfungen. (am Sonntag)
   Die Professorin korrigiert am Sonntag die Prüfungen./Die Professorin korrigiert die Prüfungen am Sonntag.

8. Julius fährt nach Hause (*home*). (am Wochenende)
   Julius fährt am Wochenende nach Hause.

3 Was machen diese Leute? Bilden Sie Sätze mit zwei Adverbien. Setzen Sie die Wörter in die richtige Reihenfolge (*order*). Answers will vary.

3 Suggestion Remind students that they do not need to use words from each column in every sentence. Create one sentence together as a class, before having students work in groups.

Subjekt	Objekt	Verb	Adverbien	
ich	das Auto	backen	gern	selten
du	die Hausaufgaben	fahren	jetzt	im Sommer
mein Vater	den Hund	kaufen	nächstes Jahr	überall
wir	einen Kuchen	machen	nie	um 9 Uhr
du und Dieter	einen Obstsalat	wandern	oft	am Wochenende
meine Freunde	einen Snack	waschen	schnell	zusammen

Kommunikation

4 **Wie und warum?** Was machen die Personen, wie machen Sie das und warum? Erfinden Sie (*Make up*) ein kurzes Szenario. Benutzen Sie jedes der folgenden Adverbien nur einmal (*once*): **allein, langsam, oft, selten, vielleicht, zusammen.** Sample answers are provided.

▶ **BEISPIEL**

S1: Wie geht er?
S2: Er geht schnell. Wohin geht er?
S3: Er geht vielleicht nach Hause.

1. Sie lernen zusammen.

2. Er liest allein. 3. Er kocht vielleicht Reis. 4. Sie fährt langsam. 5. Er fährt oft Fahrrad.

5 **Partnergespräch** Stellen Sie Ihrem Partner / Ihrer Partnerin Fragen. Answers will vary.

BEISPIEL

S1: Wann machst du Hausaufgaben?
S2: Ich mache morgens Hausaufgaben.

1. Wann lernst du?
2. Wann sind deine Kurse?
3. Wie oft gehst du in die Mensa?
4. Wann machst du deine Mittagspause?
5. Wie oft gehst du tanzen?
6. Wie oft fährst du zu den Großeltern?

6 **Meine Mitstudenten** Finden Sie für jede Aktivität eine Person aus Ihrer Veranstaltung.

BEISPIEL

S1: Isst du oft Fisch?
S2: Nein, ich esse nicht oft Fisch.
S3: Und du?

oft / Fisch essen
gut / Gitarre spielen
jeden Tag / in der Sporthalle trainieren
selten / Gemüse essen
gern / am Wochenende tanzen gehen
oft / Schokomilch trinken
nie / samstags zu Hause bleiben
immer / Eier zum Frühstück essen
gut / kochen können

6 Suggestion Before students begin the activity, make sure they know how to form the questions properly. Emphasize that they must answer using complete sentences. During the activity, circulate around the room and interact with students, asking them questions and keeping them on task.

4A.3

Separable and inseparable prefix verbs **Presentation**

Startblock In German, many verbs have a prefix in their infinitive form.

Ich gehe wirklich gern **einkaufen**.

Lass mich **überlegen**.

Suggestion Tell students that separable prefix verbs are the "drama queens" of the grammar world. They like to "break up" and "get back together". They break off from the main verb and move to the end of the clause in the indicative and the imperative, but get back together when used with modals.

- A verb with a prefix has the same conjugations as its base form, but the added prefix changes the meaning.

  Sucht ihr eure Eltern?
  *Are you **looking for** your parents?*

  Besucht ihr eure Verwandten?
  *Do you **visit** your relatives?*

- Some prefixes are always attached to the verb and others can be separated from it.

  Jakob **verkauft** sein Fahrrad.
  *Jakob **is selling** his bike.*

  Ich **kaufe** im Supermarkt **ein**.
  *I **shop** at the supermarket.*

QUERVERWEIS

See **2B.1** to review the present tense of irregular verbs like **fangen** and **schlafen**.

You might want tell the students that the verb **vorstellen** is often used reflexively. Students will learn more about reflexive verbs in **Vol. 3, 1A.1** and **1A.2**.

Suggestion Give students the name of a celebrity and ask them to write sentences about what this celebrity does on a typical Saturday, using 5-6 separable or inseparable prefix verbs. Create the first sentence as a class.

- Here are some of the most common separable and inseparable prefix verbs.

verbs with separable prefixes	
anfangen	*to begin*
ankommen	*to arrive*
anrufen	*to call*
aufstehen	*to get up*
ausgehen	*to go out*
einkaufen	*to shop*
einschlafen	*to fall asleep*
mitbringen	*to bring along*
mitkommen	*to come along*
vorbereiten	*to prepare*
vorstellen	*to introduce*
zuschauen	*to watch*
zurückkommen	*to come back*

verbs with inseparable prefixes	
bestellen	*to order*
besuchen	*to visit*
bezahlen	*to pay (for)*
erklären	*to explain*
verkaufen	*to sell*
überlegen	*to think over*
wiederholen	*to repeat*

ACHTUNG

When speaking, place the stress on the prefix of a separable prefix verb: **an**rufen, **ein**schlafen. The prefix of an inseparable prefix verb is never stressed: ver**kau**fen, wieder**ho**len.

- Separable prefixes are generally prepositions (**an**, **aus**, **mit**) or other parts of speech that carry meaning and can stand alone. In contrast, most inseparable prefixes (**be-**, **er-**, **ver-**) have no independent meaning and never stand alone.

  Heute Abend **gehen** wir zusammen **aus**.
  *Tonight we**'re going out** together.*

  Ich **bestelle** die Pasta mit Garnelen.
  *I**'m ordering** the pasta with shrimp.*

  Stefan **steht** jeden Morgen um 6 Uhr **auf**.
  *Stefan **gets up** at 6 o'clock every morning.*

  Ihr **verkauft** euer Auto?
  *You**'re selling** your car?*

- When using a separable prefix verb in the present tense or the imperative, move the prefix to the end of the sentence or clause.

Wir **kaufen** auf dem Markt **ein**.
We're shopping at the market.

Bitte **stellen** Sie die Frau **vor**.
Please introduce the woman.

Kommst du **zurück**?
Are you coming back?

Ruf deine Eltern **an**!
Call your parents!

Wir **bringen** Käse und Brot **mit**.

Wir **laden** Meline und Sabite zu uns zu Börek **ein**?

- To make the sentence negative, add **nicht** immediately before the separable prefix.

Ich komme **nicht** zurück.
I'm not coming back.

Ruf deine Eltern **nicht** an!
Don't call your parents!

- When using a modal with a separable prefix verb, move the infinitive of the separable prefix verb to the end of the sentence.

Die Mädchen **möchten** morgen Abend **ausgehen**.
The girls want to go out tomorrow night.

Ich **muss** mit meinen Hausaufgaben **anfangen**.
I need to start my homework.

- The prefix of an inseparable prefix verb always remains attached to the beginning of the verb.

Ich **bezahle** die Lebensmittel.
I'll pay for the groceries.

Wiederholen Sie den Satz.
Repeat the sentence.

ACHTUNG

In this book, separable prefix verbs are presented with their third person present-tense form in parentheses: **einkaufen (kauft... ein)**

Expansion Before they begin the **Jetzt sind Sie dran!** activity, have students identify which verbs have separable prefixes and which do not.

Ressourcen

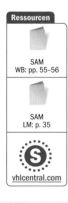

SAM
WB: pp. 55–56

SAM
LM: p. 35

S

vhlcentral.com

Jetzt sind Sie dran! Schreiben Sie die richtige Form des Verbs in Klammern.

1. Ich __wiederhole__ den Satz. (wiederholen)
2. Wir __rufen__ unsere Freunde __an__. (anrufen)
3. Erwin und Marta __verkaufen__ ihr Haus. (verkaufen)
4. Du musst heute Abend noch __einkaufen__. (einkaufen)
5. Der Student __stellt__ seine Eltern __vor__. (vorstellen)
6. __Gehen__ wir am Wochenende __aus__? (ausgehen)
7. Papa __bestellt__ gern Nachtisch (*dessert*). (bestellen)
8. Ich __bezahle__ die Rechnung (*bill*). (bezahlen)
9. Kannst du Brot __mitbringen__? (mitbringen)
10. Wir __besuchen__ unsere Verwandten in Salzburg. (besuchen)

Anwendung

1 Expansion Have students work in pairs to create mini-dialogues using two or three commands from this activity. Ex.: **Frau Meinedienerin, wir haben nichts zu essen. Kaufen Sie ein! Jawohl, Herr Herrschigern!** Have pairs perform their dialogues for the class.

1 Befehle Geben Sie Befehle (*commands*) in der **Sie**-Form.

 BEISPIEL

aufstehen
Stehen Sie auf.

1. anrufen   Rufen Sie an.
2. einkaufen   Kaufen Sie ein.
3. bezahlen   Bezahlen Sie.
4. zuschauen   Schauen Sie zu.
5. nicht mitkommen   Kommen Sie nicht mit.

6. überlegen   Überlegen Sie.
7. anfangen   Fangen Sie an.
8. nicht einschlafen   Schlafen Sie nicht ein.
9. zurückkommen   Kommen Sie zurück.
10. nicht ausgehen   Gehen Sie nicht aus.

2 Fragen Formulieren Sie die Fragen um und verwenden Sie (*use*) dabei die angegebenen (*indicated*) Modalverben.

 BEISPIEL

Kommst du mit? (können)
Kannst du mitkommen?

1. Gehst du aus? (wollen)   Willst du ausgehen?
2. Kaufen wir ein? (sollen)   Sollen wir einkaufen?
3. Kommt Birgit mit? (müssen)   Muss Birgit mitkommen?

4. Fangt ihr an? (möchten)   Möchtet ihr anfangen?
5. Schläfst du ein? (dürfen)   Darfst du einschlafen?
6. Schaut Nils zu? (können)   Kann Nils zuschauen?

3 Was machen diese Personen? Schreiben Sie zu jedem (*each*) Foto einen Satz und benutzen Sie (*use*) Präfixverben.

> Freunde anrufen
> heute Abend ausgehen
> die Bücher bezahlen
> einkaufen
>
> einschlafen
> die Grammatik erklären
> euren Hund mitbringen

 ▶ **BEISPIEL**
Herr Schröder
Herr Schröder erklärt die Grammatik.

ich
1. Ich schlafe ein.

Jana und Lina
2. Jana und Lina rufen Freunde an.

Emma und ihre Freunde
3. Emma und ihre Freunde gehen heute Abend aus.

Stefanie
4. Stefanie bezahlt die Bücher.

Frau Neumann und ihre Tochter
5. Frau Neumann und ihre Tochter kaufen ein.

ihr
6. Ihr bringt euren Hund mit.

Kommunikation

4 Mein Tag

Mein Tag Füllen Sie einen Terminkalender mit Ihren Informationen aus und diskutieren Sie dann mit Ihrem Partner / Ihrer Partnerin, was Sie den ganzen Tag (*all day*) so machen. Answers will vary.

BEISPIEL

S1: Ich stehe um 8 Uhr auf. Und du?
S2: Ich stehe um 8.30 Uhr auf. Meine erste Veranstaltung fängt um 10 Uhr an. Und deine?

8.00	Ich stehe auf.
9.00	
10.00	
11.00	
12.00	
13.00	
14.00	
15.00	

5 Wer ist das?

Wer ist das? Wählen Sie eine Person und schreiben Sie zwei Dinge auf, die diese (*this*) Person macht. Ihre Mitstudenten müssen raten (*guess*), wer es ist. Answers will vary.

BEISPIEL

S1: Sie kommt um 8 Uhr zur Uni.
Sie erklärt uns (*to us*) die Hausaufgaben.
S2: Ist es die Professorin?

anfangen	ausgehen	einkaufen	mitkommen
ankommen	besuchen	erklären	vorbereiten
anrufen	bezahlen	mitbringen	zurückkommen

6 Ein Picknick machen

Ein Picknick machen Sie und Ihre Freunde planen ein Picknick. Diskutieren Sie, wer was kauft, wer was mitbringt und was Sie alles machen müssen. Answers will vary.

BEISPIEL

S1: Sollen wir viele Freunde anrufen?
S2: Ja, und wir müssen auch viel Essen mitbringen.
S3: Ich bringe Wurst und Käse mit!

Wiederholung

1 **Expansion** Ask students to brainstorm other good food combinations and then have the class vote on the best one.

1 Was magst du? Fragen Sie einen Partner / eine Partnerin, was er/sie mag oder nicht mag. *Answers will vary.*

BEISPIEL

S1: *Magst du Hähnchen mit Reis?*
S2: *Ja, ich mag Hähnchen mit Reis. Und du?*
S1: *Nein, ich mag Hähnchen mit Reis nicht. Magst du…?*

Würstchen mit Brot	Schweinefleisch mit Kartoffeln
Thunfisch mit Zwiebeln	Auberginen mit Tomaten
Pasta mit Pilzen	Schinken mit Brot
Hähnchen mit Reis	Pasta mit Käse
Garnelen mit Tomaten	Rindfleisch mit Salat

2 Das Wochenende Sagen Sie, was die Personen am Wochenende machen möchten. Wechseln Sie sich (*Take turns*) mit einem Partner / einer Partnerin ab. *Answers will vary.*

Klara

▶ **BEISPIEL**

S1: *Was möchte Klara am Wochenende machen?*
S2: *Klara möchte am Wochenende gern lesen.*

1. Petra und Klaus

2. Paul, Manfred, Andrea und Monika

3. Inge

4. Robert

3 Was isst du? Fragen Sie Ihre Mitstudenten, wie oft, wie und wo sie diese Lebensmittel essen. *Answers will vary.*

BEISPIEL

S1: *Wie oft isst du Eier in der Mensa?*
S2: *Ich esse selten Eier in der Mensa.*

4 Was machen sie? Ein Student / Eine Studentin spielt eine Aktion. Die anderen Studenten raten (*guess*) die Aktion. Benutzen Sie vollständige (*complete*) Sätze. *Answers will vary.*

BEISPIEL

S1: *Fährst du Fahrrad?*
S2: *Nein.*
S1: *Reitest du ein Pferd (horse)?*
S2: *Ja.*

4 **Suggestion** Remind students of the stem-vowel change in the verbs **backen**, **fahren**, and **schlafen**. Model correct pronunciation in both the **ich** and **du** forms.

aufstehen	im Restaurant	einschlafen
ausgehen	bestellen	Fahrrad fahren
einen Kuchen	einen Freund	ein Pferd reiten
backen	besuchen	Volleyball spielen

5 Wann kaufst du ein? Sie bekommen eine Tabelle von Ihrem Professor / Ihrer Professorin. Fragen Sie einen Partner / eine Partnerin, wann die Personen die Aktivitäten machen.

BEISPIEL

S1: *Wann geht Alex Lebensmittel einkaufen?*
S2: *Alex geht am Samstag Lebensmittel einkaufen.*

6 Der Wochenplan Entscheiden Sie (*Decide*), was Sie diese Woche machen wollen. Suchen Sie andere Studenten in der Gruppe, die das Gleiche machen wollen und finden Sie eine Zeit, wann sie das machen können. *Answers will vary.*

BEISPIEL

S1: *Willst du diese Woche einkaufen gehen?*
S2: *Ja, ich will diese Woche einkaufen gehen.*
S1: *Können wir zusammen einkaufen gehen?*
S2: *Ja, gern.*
S1: *Hast du am Mittwoch Zeit?*
S2: *Nein, am Mittwoch habe ich keine Zeit. Hast du am Donnerstag Zeit?*
S1: *Ja, am Donnerstag habe ich Zeit. Um wie viel Uhr…*

6 **Suggestion** Have students brainstorm activities before they begin the exercise.

6 **Expansion** Instead of working in small groups, have students stand up and circulate throughout the entire class.

Zapping

 S Video: TV Clip

Yello Strom

Die Firma Yello Strom ist eine deutsche Stromfirma°. In Deutschland können Kunden° zwischen verschiedenen° Stromfirmen wählen. Kundenservice° ist deshalb aber auch ein wichtiger Aspekt für das Gewinnen neuer Kunden. Yello Strom ist eine kreative Firma mit neuen Ideen. Kundenservice ist sehr wichtig für diese Firma. In diesem Werbeclip zeigt° die Firma, dass Kunden bei Yello Strom nur mit echten Menschen reden!

Auf dem Wochenmarkt°

„Sie haben drei gelbe° Bananen gewählt°."

„Guter Service geht anders°."

Stromfirma *electric company* **Kunden** *customers* **verschiedenen** *different* **Kundenservice** *customer service* **zeigt** *shows* **Wochenmarkt** *farmer's market* **gelbe** *yellow* **gewählt** *selected* **anders** *differently*

 Verständnis Beantworten Sie die Fragen mit den Informationen aus dem Video.

1. Was möchte die Frau auf dem Markt?
   Sie möchte drei ___Äpfel___.

2. Was versteht der Verkäufer?
   Er versteht drei ___(gelbe) Bananen___.

 Diskussion Diskutieren Sie die folgenden Fragen mit einem Partner / einer Partnerin. Answers will vary.

1. Wie finden Sie Telefonmenüs? Funktionieren sie gut? Sind sie praktisch oder frustrierend?

2. Finden Sie die Werbung (*commercial*) lustig? Warum, oder warum nicht?

Communicative Goals

You will learn how to:

- talk about food and meals
- describe flavors

S Talking Picture
Audio: Activities

der Koch, -¨e
(die Köchin, -nen *f.*)

Die Suppe schmeckt gut.
(schmecken)

der Kellner, -
(die Kellnerin, -nen *f.*)

die Gabel, -n

die Speisekarte, -n

Speisekarte

die Serviette, -n

der Teller, -

das Messer, -

die Tischdecke, -n

Wortschatz

im Restaurant	**at the restaurant**
die Beilage, -n	side dish
das Besteck	silverware
die Flasche, -n	bottle
der erste/zweite Gang	first/second course
die Hauptspeise, -n	main course
die Nachspeise, -n	dessert
die Rechnung, -en	check
die Tasse, -n	cup
das Trinkgeld	tip
die Vorspeise, -n	appetizer
Mahlzeiten	**meals**
das Abendessen	dinner
das Frühstück	breakfast
das Mittagessen	lunch
der Snack, -s	snack
Getränke	**drinks**
das Bier	beer
der Kaffee	coffee
die Milch	milk
das Mineralwasser	sparkling water
der Saft, -¨e	juice
der Tee	tea
das stille Wasser	still water
der Wein	wine
Essen beschreiben	**talking about food**
der Geschmack, -¨e	flavor; taste
fade	bland
lecker	delicious
leicht	light
salzig	salty
scharf	spicy
schwer	rich, heavy
süß	sweet
Ausdrücke	**expressions**
Ich hätte gern(e)...	I would like...
auf Diät sein	to be on a diet
hausgemacht	homemade

Suggestion Point out the compound words **Hauptspeise**, **Nachspeise**, **Vorspeise**, and **Speisekarte**. Ask students for a synonym for **Speise**.

Suggestion Point out that the word **Snack** has come into German from English. Tell students that Germans also use the word **die Zwischenmahlzeit**, while Austrians often say **die Jause**.

Suggestion Point out that the noun **Geschmack** comes from the verb **schmecken**.

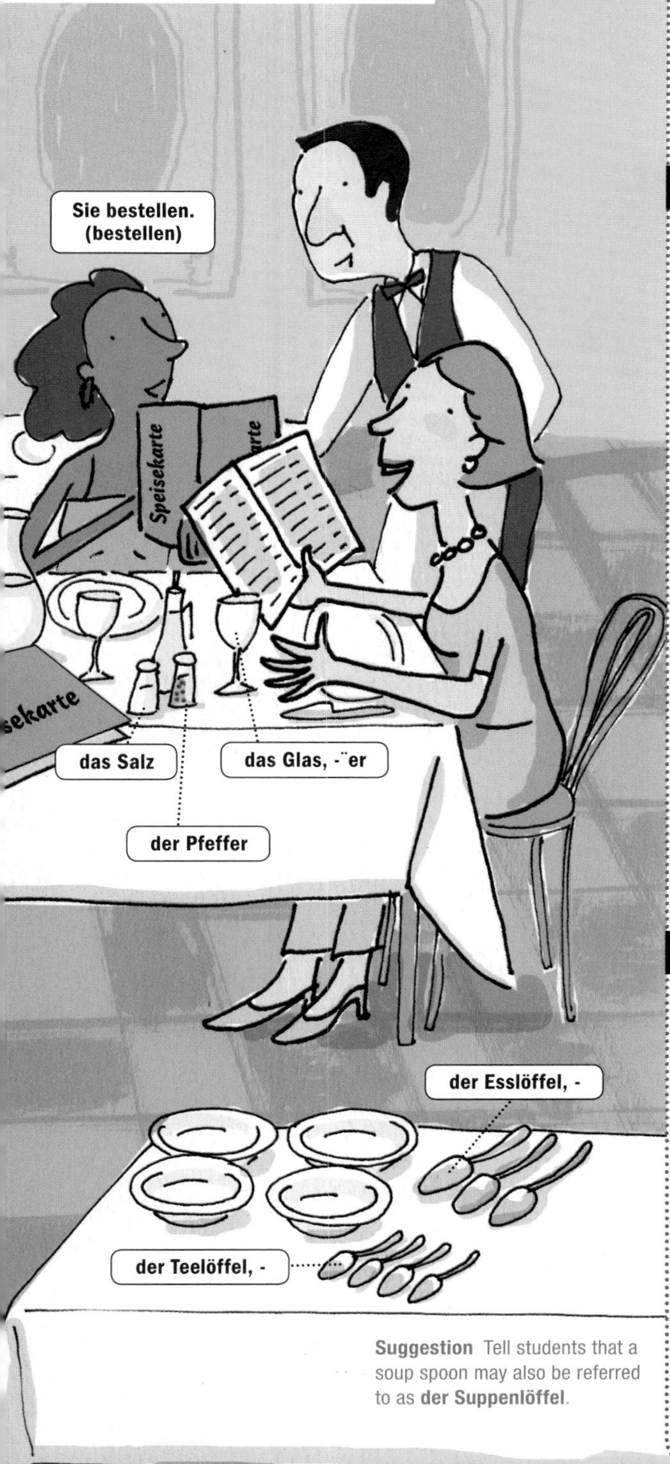

Sie bestellen.
(bestellen)

Speisekarte

das Salz

das Glas, -̈er

der Pfeffer

der Esslöffel, -

der Teelöffel, -

Anwendung

1 Was passt nicht? Welches Wort passt nicht zu den anderen?

1. a. die Gabel
   b. das Messer
   c. (die Serviette)
   d. der Löffel

2. a. die Milch
   b. der Saft
   c. der Kaffee
   d. (das Salz)

3. a. (die Speisekarte)
   b. die Flasche
   c. die Tasse
   d. das Glas

4. a. salzig
   b. (stolz)
   c. scharf
   d. süß

5. a. die Kellnerin
   b. die Köchin
   c. (der Saft)
   d. der Koch

6. a. das Mittagessen
   b. (die Beilage)
   c. das Abendessen
   d. das Frühstück

2 Wie schmeckt's? Beschreiben Sie (*Describe*) den Geschmack der Lebensmittel. Sample answers are provided.

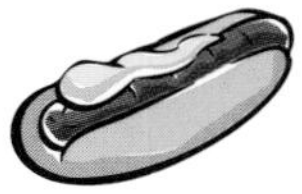

 ▶ **BEISPIEL** Die Bratwurst ist
scharf

 1. Der Saft ist
süß

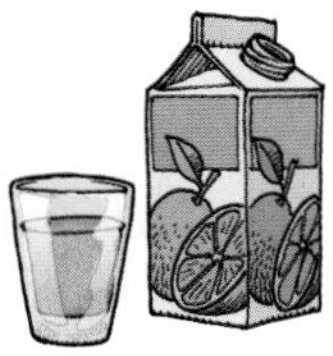

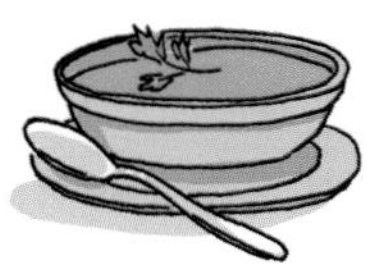

 2. Die Suppe ist
schwer

 3. Der Salat ist
leicht

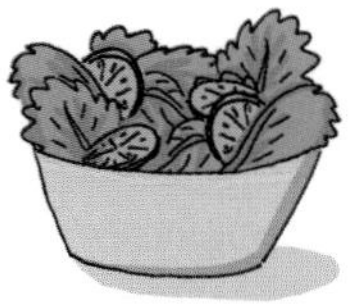

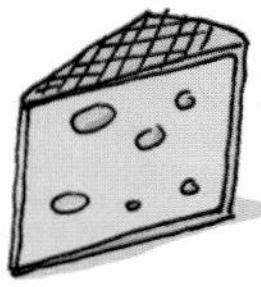

4. Der Käse ist
salzig

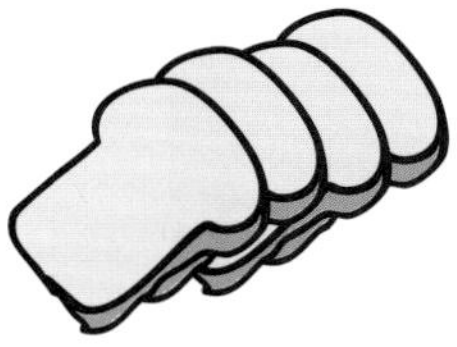

5. Das Brot ist
fade

6. Der Kuchen ist
lecker

3 Was bestellen wir? 🎧 Hören Sie den Dialog an und markieren Sie, was Rolf, Anja und Murat bestellen.

Essen	Rolf	Anja	Murat
1. Steak	☑	☐	☐
2. Cola	☐	☐	☑
3. Meeresfrüchtesalat	☐	☑	☐
4. stilles Wasser	☑	☐	☐
5. gemischter Salat	☑	☐	☐
6. Brot	☐	☑	☐
7. Mineralwasser	☐	☑	☐
8. Rindfleisch	☐	☐	☑

 Practice more at **vhlcentral.com**.

Kommunikation

4 **Verschiedene Mahlzeiten** Fragen Sie Ihren Partner / Ihre Partnerin, welche Mahlzeiten auf den Fotos zu sehen sind. Wechseln Sie sich ab (*Take turns*). Sample answers are provided.

▶ **BEISPIEL**

das Frühstück
S1: Ist das das Frühstück?
S2: Nein, das ist das Abendessen.

1. die Vorspeise
Ist das die Vorspeise?
Nein, das ist die Nachspeise.

2. die Hauptspeise
Ist das die Hauptspeise?
Nein, das ist ein Getränk.

3. die Nachspeise
Ist das die Nachspeise?
Nein, das ist das Mittagessen.

4. das Abendessen
Ist das das Abendessen?
Nein, das ist das Frühstück.

5. ein Snack
Ist das ein Snack?
Nein, das ist das Abendessen.

6. das Mittagessen
Ist das das Mittagessen?
Nein, das ist ein Snack.

5 **Wo möchten wir heute Abend essen?** Sie möchten heute Abend ins Restaurant essen gehen. Lesen Sie die Speisekarte und überlegen Sie, was Sie zu jedem (*for each*) Gang bestellen wollen. Answers will vary.

BEISPIEL

S1: Ich möchte gern den Tomatensalat mit Mozzarella als ersten Gang.
S2: Ich auch! Und als zweiten Gang bestelle ich das Hähnchen mit Reis.
S3: Wollt ihr auch Getränke bestellen?

7 Expansion Have students work in groups to create a commercial for their "ideal restaurant" and present it to the class. You may want to provide prompts. Ex.: **Unser Restaurant ist/hat… Das Essen ist… Wir servieren… In unserem Restaurant kann man… Die Atmosphäre ist… Die Kellner sind…**

Speisekarte

Vorspeisen
Tagessuppe
Chef-Salat mit Schinken, Käse und Ei
Bauern-Salat mit Schafskäse, Zwiebeln und Oliven
Tomatensalat mit Mozzarella

Beilagen
Kartoffelsalat
Karottensalat
Grüner Salat
Kartoffelpuffer
Sauerkraut

Nachspeisen
Apfelkuchen
Bananen mit Schokolade
hausgemachter Joghurt mit Himbeermarmalade
Obstsalat

Hauptspeisen
Würstchen mit Brötchen
Thunfisch mit Salat
Hähnchen mit Reis
Rindfleisch mit Pommes frites
Schweinefleisch mit Kartoffeln
Pasta mit Garnelen
Pasta mit Käse

Getränke
stilles Wasser
Mineralwasser
Orangensaft
Milch
Kaffee
Tee

6 **Stress im Restaurant!** Sie sind im Restaurant und der Kellner bringt Ihre Speisen. Aber auf dem Tisch gibt es kein Besteck, kein Brot, keine Getränke, kein Salz und so weiter. Sagen Sie dem Kellner, was er noch alles bringen soll. Answers will vary.

BEISPIEL

S1: Kann ich bitte auch Gabel und Messer haben?
S2: Und bitte zwei Glas Wasser!
S3: Natürlich. Sofort (*Right away*). Möchten sie noch etwas (*anything else*)?

7 **Wie ist das Restaurant?** Wie sind die Restaurants „Zum Grünen Baum" und „Zur Stadtmauer"? Fragen Sie Ihren Partner / Ihre Partnerin, und ergänzen Sie die fehlenden (*missing*) Informationen.

BEISPIEL

S1: Was für ein Restaurant ist „Zur Stadtmauer"?
S2: Es ist ein vegetarisches Bistro. Und was für ein Restaurant ist „Zum Grünen Baum"?
S1: Es hat deutsche Küche (*cuisine*). Welche Vorspeisen kann man in dem Bistro haben?

Aussprache und Rechtschreibung

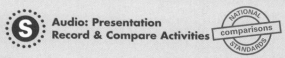

Audio: Presentation
Record & Compare Activities

🎧 The German *s* in combination with other letters

The letter combination **sch** is pronounced like the *sh* in the English word *fish*.

Fisch   **Sch**inken   **Gesch**äft   **Flei**sch   **Sch**ule

---

When an **s** appears at the beginning of a word in front of the letter **p** or **t**, it is also pronounced like the *sh* in *fish*. A prefix added to the word will not change the pronunciation of the **s**. However, if the **sp** or **st** letter combination occurs in the middle or at the end of a word, the **s** is pronounced like the *s* in the English word *restore*.

Speise   **st**oppen   ver**sp**rechen   **A**spirin   Fen**st**er

---

In a few words borrowed from other languages, **sh** and **ch** are also pronounced like the *sh* in *fish*.

Chauffeur   **Ca**shewnuss   **Sh**ampoo   **Ch**ampignon   **ch**armant

---

At the beginning of a word, the letter combination **tsch** is pronounced like the *ch* in *chat*. In the middle or at the end of a word, **tsch** is pronounced like the *tch* in *catch*.

tschüss   **Tsch**ad   **Tsch**echien   Ru**tsch**   Kla**tsch**base

---

🔊 **1** Sprechen Sie nach Wiederholen Sie die Wörter, die Sie hören.

1. Schaft	3. Sport	5. aufstehen	7. Aspekt	9. platschen
2. waschen	4. Strudel	6. Kasten	8. Putsch	10. Kutscher

🔊 **2** Artikulieren Sie Wiederholen Sie die Sätze, die Sie hören.

1. Im Lebensmittelgeschäft kaufst du Schinken und Fisch.
2. In der Schule schwimmen alle Schüler im Schwimmbad.
3. Studenten spielen gern Videospiele.
4. Auf der Speisekarte steht Käsespätzle.
5. Der Tscheche sagt nicht mal tschüss.
6. Ich wünsche dir einen guten Rutsch ins neue Jahr!

🔊 **3** Sprichwörter Wiederholen Sie die Sprichwörter, die Sie hören.

2 Suggestion Point out that **Einen guten Rutsch ins neue Jahr!** is a common New Year's greeting in German.

2 Expansion Item 2 is a tongue twister. Have students take turns trying to say it as quickly as possible. You may also want to teach students the tongue twister **Fischers Fritz fischt frische Fische.**

Besser spät als nie.[1]

Reden ist Silber;
Schweigen ist Gold.[2]

[1] Better late than never.
[2] Talk is silver; silence is golden.

Ressourcen

SAM
LM: p. 37

🅢 vhlcentral.com

Die Rechnung, bitte! Ⓢ Video: *Fotoroman*

Torsten und Sabite sind bei einem romantischen Abendessen in einem
schönen Restaurant. Aber es bleibt nicht so romantisch...

Vorbereitung Have students scan the script to find
words and expressions related to food.

KELLNER Wir bieten eine leckere hausgemachte
Pilzsuppe an. Nicht zu schwer.
SABITE Davon nehme ich einen Teller,
bitte. Und als zweiten Gang nehme ich
die Rindsrouladen.
KELLNER Sehr gerne. Und für Sie, mein Herr?
TORSTEN Als Vorspeise nehme ich den Salat
und als Hauptspeise das Wiener Schnitzel,
mit Salzkartoffeln, bitte.
KELLNER Ausgezeichnet.

SABITE Sie haben sehr gutes Essen in
diesem Restaurant.
TORSTEN Ja. Meine ältere Schwester empfiehlt
es guten Freunden wärmstens.

KELLNER Möchten Sie gerne noch
einen Nachtisch?
MELINE Ach, ich muss auf meine Figur achten!
KELLNER Oh, nein, Sie sind doch extrem...
LORENZO Wir nehmen ein Stück Schwarzwälder
Kirschtorte. Zwei Gabeln.
MELINE Und zwei Kaffee bitte.

SABITE Hallo!
MELINE Sabite! Hallo! Sabite, das ist Lorenzo.
Lorenzo, das ist meine Mitbewohnerin, Sabite.
LORENZO Ciao.

LORENZO Ich komme aus Milano.
MELINE Lorenzo ist geschäftlich in
Berlin. Er arbeitet im Bereich
internationale Finanzen.
LORENZO Bist du auch Studentin?
SABITE Ja, ich studiere Kunst.

SABITE Ich liebe die Kunst von Kandinsky
und Klee. Aber Italien hat die Meister...
Michelangelo... Da Vinci...
LORENZO Ja. Du musst sie mal aus der
Nähe sehen.
SABITE Ich hoffe, sie eines Tages sehen
zu können. Mein Vater kommt aus
der Türkei. Ich möchte dort gern ein
Semester lang studieren.

ÜBUNGEN

1 **Richtig oder falsch?** Entscheiden Sie, ob die folgenden Sätze
richtig oder **falsch** sind.

1. Sabite nimmt die Pilzsuppe und die Roulade. Richtig.
2. Torsten bestellt ein Schnitzel mit Salzkartoffeln. Richtig.
3. Torstens Schwester empfiehlt ihren Freunden das Restaurant. Richtig.
4. Meline und Lorenzo bestellen zwei Stück Schwarzwälder Kirschtorte. Falsch.
5. Lorenzo kommt aus Italien. Richtig.

6. Er studiert Kunst. Falsch.
7. Sabite mag die Kunst von Klee und Picasso. Falsch.
8. Sie möchte ein Jahr in der Türkei studieren. Falsch.
9. Sie möchte Istanbul kennen lernen. Richtig.
10. Sabite findet Torsten egoistisch. Richtig.

1 **Expansion** Have students correct the false sentences.

7

SABITE Torsten, ist alles in Ordnung?
TORSTEN Türkei? Du möchtest in der Türkei studieren?
SABITE Ich möchte Istanbul kennen lernen.

8

SABITE Hör auf. Noch studiert niemand in der Türkei. Entschuldige bitte.
TORSTEN Sabite!

9

SABITE Torsten ist... ist... ist so egoistisch!

10

TORSTEN Frauen. Und du bist also nicht Lukas?
LORENZO Die Rechnung, bitte!

Nützliche Ausdrücke

- **anbieten**
  to offer
- **Davon nehme ich einen Teller, bitte.**
  I would like a bowl of that, please.
- **die Rindsroulade**
  beef roulade
- **die Salzkartoffeln**
  boiled potatoes
- **Ich muss auf meine Figur achten.**
  I have to watch my weight.
- **die Schwarzwälder Kirschtorte**
  Black Forest cake
- **Er ist geschäftlich in Berlin.**
  He's in Berlin on business.
- **Er arbeitet im Bereich internationale Finanzen.**
  He works in international finance.
- **Ich hoffe, sie eines Tages sehen zu können.**
  I hope to see them someday.
- **ein Semester lang**
  for one semester
- **Hör auf!**
  Cut it out!
- **Noch studiert niemand in der Türkei.**
  No one's studying in Turkey today.

4B.1
- **Meine ältere Schwester empfiehlt es guten Freunden wärmstens.**
  My older sister highly recommends it to her close friends.

4B.2
- **Du musst sie mal aus der Nähe sehen.**
  You should see them up close.

2 **Zum Besprechen** Wählen Sie zu dritt ein Gericht aus Deutschland, Österreich oder der Schweiz und machen Sie eine Liste mit Zutaten. Präsentieren Sie der Klasse dann die Liste. Ihre Klassenkameraden müssen das Gericht erraten (*guess*). Answers will vary.

2 **Expansion** Name some well-known German, Austrian or Swiss dishes (**Kaiserschmarrn, Sauerbraten, Knödel,** etc.), and ask students to find the main ingredients. Write any new words on the board.

3 **Vertiefung** In den USA ist Wiener Schnitzel vielleicht das berühmteste (*most famous*) Gericht aus den deutschsprachigen Ländern. Wissen Sie, woher es kommt? Kennen Sie andere Gerichte, die den Namen von Städten haben? Sample answers: Wiener Schnitzel: Wien (*Vienna*); Frankfurter (Würstchen), Hamburger, Nürnberger (Bratwürstchen), Berliner (*jelly doughnut*), Kassler (*smoked pork chop*)

Ressourcen

SAM VM: p. 8 | DVD Folge 8 | vhlcentral.com

IM FOKUS

Wiener Kaffeehäuser Ⓢ Reading

Typische Cafépreise	
Kleiner Schwarzer	2,80 €
Kleiner Brauner	2,90 €
Melange	3,90 €
Großer Schwarzer	4,20 €
Großer Brauner	4,30 €
Einspänner	4,90 €
Kapuziner	4,90 €
Pharisäer	6,60 €

QUELLE: Café Korb in Wien

KAFFEEHÄUSER IN ÖSTERREICH HABEN eine lange Tradition. Kaffeehäuser gibt es seit dem 18. Jahrhundert. In Wien findet man heute mindestens° 1.100 Kaffeehäuser. Typischerweise serviert ein Kellner einen Kaffee auf einem silbernen Tablett° mit einem Löffel, einem Glas Wasser und einem Keks. In den Kaffeehäusern trinkt man aber auch andere Getränke wie Kakao, Wasser und Wein. Zum Kaffee isst man oft Apfelstrudel, Gugelhupf oder Sachertorte°. Oft besuchen Gäste° ein Kaffeehaus, bestellen einen Kaffee und bleiben viele Stunden. Hier diskutieren Gäste auch über Politik, Sport und andere Themen.

Wiener Kaffeehäuser haben spezielle Vokabeln: Sahne° heißt Obers. Ein kleiner oder großer Brauner ist ein Kaffee serviert mit Obers in einer kleinen Schale°. Eine Melange ist halb° Kaffee und halb geschäumte° Milch. Ein Kapuziner ist ein kleiner Mokka (ein Schwarzer oder Espresso pur) mit wenig Milch.

Es gibt auch andere Cafés in Wien. In einer Espresso-Bar trinkt man vor allem° Espresso und Cappuccino wie in Italien. In Stehcafés trinken Gäste Kaffee sehr schnell oder nehmen den Kaffee mit. Café-Konditoreien sind nicht nur Cafés. In der Konditorei kaufen Kunden hausgemachte Kuchen und Süßigkeiten°. Die neueste Version eines Cafés ist der amerikanische Import Starbucks. Hier findet man vor allem jüngere Österreicher.

mindestens *at least* **Tablett** *tray* **Apfelstrudel, Gugelhupf oder Sachertorte** *types of baked goods* **Gäste** *guests* **Sahne** *cream* **Schale** *dish* **halb** *half* **geschäumte** *foamed* **vor allem** *above all* **Süßigkeiten** *sweets*

ÜBUNGEN

1 **Wiener Kaffeehäuser** Ergänzen Sie die Sätze.

1. Wiener Kaffeehäuser haben eine ____lange____ Tradition.

2. In Wien findet man mehr als ____1.100____ Kaffeehäuser.

3. Auf einem Tablett serviert der Kellner den Kaffee, einen Löffel, ein ____Glas Wasser____ und einen Keks.

4. Gäste bleiben oft ____viele____ Stunden.

5. Neben Kaffee kann man auch ____Kakao____, Wasser oder Wein trinken.

6. Typisches Essen in Kaffeehäusern sind ____Apfelstrudel____, Gugelhupf und Sachertorte.

7. Ein Melange ist halb Kaffee und halb ____(geschäumte) Milch____.

8. In Wien gibt es auch Espresso-Bars, ____Stehcafés____ und Café-Konditoreien.

9. In einer Espresso-Bar trinken Gäste Kaffee wie in ____Italien____.

10. Ein Kapuziner im Café Korb kostet ____4,90 €____.

Ⓢ Practice more at **vhlcentral.com**.

DEUTSCH IM ALLTAG

Am Tisch

Die Rechnung, bitte!	*Check, please!*
Die Speisekarte, bitte!	*The menu, please!*
Guten Appetit!	*Enjoy your meal!*
Noch einen Wunsch?	*Anything else?*
Herr Ober!	*Waiter!*
Prost!	*Cheers!*
Zum Wohl!	*Cheers!*

DIE DEUTSCHSPRACHIGE WELT

Ausländische Spezialitäten

In Deutschland besteht die Bevölkerung° ungefähr zu 9% aus° Ausländern°, in der Schweiz sind es fast 20%. Die Ausländer kommen aus vielen Ländern wie Italien, Griechenland°, der Türkei, Nordafrika und dem ehemaligen° Jugoslawien. Deshalb° ist die Restaurantszene in Deutschland, Österreich und der Schweiz auch sehr international. In jeder° Stadt gibt es Restaurants mit italienischen, griechischen und verschiedenen° asiatischen Speisen. Vor allem in Großstädten ist die Auswahl° sehr groß. Die populärsten Restaurants sind definitiv italienisch, aber man findet auch sehr viele asiatische Restaurants.

Bevölkerung *population* **besteht... aus** *consists of* **Ausländern** *foreigners* **Griechenland** *Greece* **ehemaligen** *former* **Deshalb** *Therefore* **jeder** *every* **verschiedenen** *various* **Auswahl** *selection*

Figlmüller

Das Figlmüller ist ein sehr altes Restaurant in Wien. Es ist „die Heimat° des Schnitzels", ein Paradies für Schnitzelfans. Man findet das Restaurant in der Wollzeile im Zentrum Wiens. Das Restaurant existiert seit über 100 Jahren und ist berühmt° für seine Schnitzel, ein Stück Schweinefleisch mit Semmelbröselhülle°. Die Schnitzel sind ziemlich° groß, dünn und sehr knusprig°. Dazu gibt es österreichische Weine. Bier und Kaffee gibt es hier nicht. Auch Süßspeisen finden Gäste nicht auf der Speisekarte. Aber Schnitzel sind hier sehr wichtig. Alle Ober servieren die Schnitzel in einem schwarzen Smoking°!

Heimat *home* **berühmt** *famous* **Semmelbröselhülle** *bread crumb crust* **ziemlich** *relatively* **knusprig** *crisp* **Smoking** *tuxedo*

IM INTERNET

Suchen Sie Informationen über die Mensa an der Universität Wien. Was können Studenten essen? Was können Studenten trinken? Wie viel kostet das Essen?

For more information on this **Kultur**, *go to* vhlcentral.com.

3 **Expansion** After each group creates a menu, have them act out a short restaurant role-play using phrases from the **Deutsch im Alltag** box. Have students request the menu, order their food, and finally pay for it.

---

2 **Richtig oder falsch?** Korrigieren Sie die falschen Aussagen mit einem Partner / einer Partnerin.

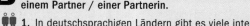

1. In deutschsprachigen Ländern gibt es viele internationale Restaurants. Richtig.
2. Die beliebtesten internationalen Restaurants sind italienisch. Richtig.
3. Das Restaurant Figlmüller ist ein sehr altes Restaurant in Wien. Richtig.
4. Das Restaurant Figlmüller hat eine Spezialität: Apfelstrudel. Falsch. Die Spezialität ist Schnitzel.

3 **Eine Speisekarte** Schreiben Sie eine Speisekarte für ein Restaurant in Deutschland, Österreich oder der Schweiz. Geben Sie die Preise für die Speisen und die Getränke an.

BEISPIEL *Restaurant „Zur Post"*

Hauptspeisen		Nachspeisen	
Schweinebraten	6,90 €	*Obstsalat*	3,10 €
Pizza Marinara	5,50 €	*Tiramisu*	3,50 €

4B.1

QUERVERWEIS

See **1A.3** and **1B.1** to review the use of the nominative and accusative case.

QUERVERWEIS

See **3A.1** to review the use of possessive adjectives.

The dative  Presentation

Startblock In 1B.1, you learned that the direct object of a verb is always in the accusative case. When a verb has an indirect object, it is always in the dative case.

- An object in the dative case indicates *to whom* or *for whom* an action is performed.

  Ich bringe **dem Lehrer** einen Apfel. / *I'm bringing **the teacher** an apple.*

  Zeig **der Professorin** deine Arbeit. / *Show your work **to the professor**.*

- Note that certain verbs in German always take a dative object, even though their English equivalents normally take a direct object.

  Wir helfen **den Kindern**. / *We're helping (giving help to) **the kids**.*

  Sie dankt **dem Kellner**. / *She's thanking (giving thanks to) **the waiter**.*

- The forms of the definite and indefinite articles that accompany dative nouns differ from the forms in the nominative or accusative case.

definite articles				
	masculine	**feminine**	**neuter**	**plural**
nominative	der Kellner	die Kellnerin	das Kind	die Kinder
accusative	den Kellner	die Kellnerin	das Kind	die Kinder
dative	dem Kellner	der Kellnerin	dem Kind	den Kindern

indefinite articles				
	masculine	**feminine**	**neuter**	**plural**
nominative	ein Kellner	eine Kellnerin	ein Kind	keine Kinder
accusative	einen Kellner	eine Kellnerin	ein Kind	keine Kinder
dative	einem Kellner	einer Kellnerin	einem Kind	keinen Kindern

Der Kellner bringt **der Frau** einen Salat. / *The waiter is bringing **the woman** a salad.*

Peter empfiehlt **einem Freund** das Restaurant. / *Peter recommends the restaurant **to a friend**.*

- The endings for possessive adjectives are the same as the endings for the indefinite articles.

possessive adjectives				
	masculine	**feminine**	**neuter**	**plural**
nominative	mein Koch	meine Köchin	mein Kind	meine Kinder
accusative	meinen Koch	meine Köchin	mein Kind	meine Kinder
dative	meinem Koch	meiner Köchin	meinem Kind	meinen Kindern

Der Kellner bringt **meiner Frau** einen Salat. / *The waiter is bringing **my wife** a salad.*

Peter empfiehlt **seinen Freunden** das Restaurant. / *Peter recommends the restaurant **to his friends**.*

- When using plural nouns in the dative case, add **-n** to any noun whose plural form does not already end in **-n** or **-s**.

nominative plural	dative plural
die Teller	den Teller**n**
die Esslöffel	den Esslöffel**n**
die Kaffees	den Kaffees
die Rechnungen	den Rechnungen

- In the dative case, an adjective preceded by an **ein**-word or a **der**-word always ends in **-en**.

Anna kauft **dem kleinen** Jungen ein Eis.
*Anna is buying an ice cream for **the little** boy.*

Ich gebe **meiner kleinen** Schwester eine Banane.
*I'm giving **my little** sister a banana.*

- Adjectives in the dative that are not preceded by an article have endings similar to the definite article endings.

unpreceded adjective endings				
	masculine	**feminine**	**neuter**	**plural**
nominative	süß**er** Kuchen	süß**e** Melone	süß**es** Getränk	süß**e** Äpfel
accusative	süß**en** Kuchen	süß**e** Melone	süß**es** Getränk	süß**e** Äpfel
dative	süß**em** Kuchen	süß**er** Melone	süß**em** Getränk	süß**en** Äpfel**n**

Ich biete **guten** Freunden immer gutes Essen an.
*I always serve good food to **good** friends.*

Die Lehrerin hilft **neuen** Studenten gern.
*The teacher likes to help **new** students.*

- Use the dative question word **wem** to ask *to whom?*

nominative	accusative	dative
wer?	**wen?**	**wem?**

Wem gibst du das Geschenk?
***To whom** are you giving the present?*

Ich gebe **meiner Mutter** das Geschenk.
*I'm giving the present **to my mother**.*

Wem gehört diese Tasse?
***Who** does this cup belong **to**?*

Sie gehört meinem Opa.
*It belongs to **my grandpa**.*

QUERVERWEIS

See **3A.2** to review adjective agreement in the nominative and accusative case.

See **2A.2** to review question words.

ACHTUNG

In sentences with both direct and indirect objects, the dative object comes before the accusative object.

Suggestion Students often forget to add -n in the dative plural. Write sentences on the board in which the n is missing, and ask students to find the mistakes. Ex.: **Der Koch kocht den** Kinder **eine leckere Suppe. Die Kinder bringen ihren** Freunde **viele Geschenke.**

Suggestion Point out to students that these endings are similar to the endings of the definite articles, and also follow the "rese, nese, mrmn" pattern.

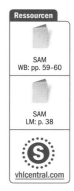

Ressourcen

SAM
WB: pp. 59–60

SAM
LM: p. 38

vhlcentral.com

Jetzt sind Sie dran! **Ergänzen Sie die Sätze mit der richtigen Form im Dativ.**

1. Mama dankt ___*dem Kellner*___ (der Kellner).
2. Die Kellnerin empfiehlt ___meinen Brüdern___ (meine Brüder) die Vorspeise.
3. ___Wem___ (Wer) bringst du die Flasche Wein?
4. Ich gebe ___der Kellnerin___ (die Kellnerin) ein Trinkgeld.
5. Der gute Student hilft ___schlechten Studenten___ (schlechte Studenten) oft.
6. Du gibst ___einem schönen Mädchen___ (ein schönes Mädchen) rote Rosen.
7. Der Koch gibt ___der Köchin___ (die Köchin) das Salz.
8. ___Wem___ (Wer) soll ich das Besteck geben?
9. Kannst du ___meiner Mutter___ (meine Mutter) eine Nachspeise empfehlen?
10. Ich zeige (*show*) ___meinem Freund___ (mein Freund) die Rechnung.
11. Die Kinder helfen ___ihren Eltern___ (ihre Eltern) gern.
12. Der Junge gibt ___den alten Hunden___ (die alten Hunde) Würstchen.

Anwendung

1 Wählen Sie Wählen Sie den richtigen Artikel.

1. Ich gebe (dem / (der)) Professorin die Hausaufgaben.
2. Moritz gibt ((seiner)/ seinem) Mutter ein Parfüm.
3. Die Professorin hilft ((ihren)/ ihrem) Studenten mit der Grammatik.
4. Der Mann bringt ((dem)/ der) Kind ein Glas Milch.
5. Die Großmutter bäckt ((ihrem)/ ihrer) Enkelkind einen Kuchen.
6. Der Vater öffnet (seinem / (seiner)) Tochter die Tür.
7. Ich schreibe ((dem)/ der) Präsidenten eine E-Mail.
8. Sie kauft ((ihrem)/ ihrer) Enkelkind einen Hund.

2 Pluralformen Geben Sie die richtigen Pluralformen im Dativ an.

1. dem alten Hund: _den alten Hunden_
2. seiner lieben Tante: _seinen lieben Tanten_
3. der netten Katze: _den netten Katzen_
4. einem neugierigen Journalisten: _neugierigen Journalisten_
5. dem kleinen Mädchen: _den kleinen Mädchen_
6. keiner stolzen Frau: _keinen stolzen Frauen_
7. dem mutigen Kind: _den mutigen Kindern_
8. ihrem großen Neffen: _ihren großen Neffen_
9. meinem faulen Bruder: _meinen faulen Brüdern_

3 Ergänzen Sie Ergänzen Sie die Sätze mit den richtigen Substantivformen im Dativ.

> **BEISPIEL** deine Freundin: Kaufst du _deiner Freundin_ einen CD-Player?

1. meine Partnerin: Ich zeige _meiner Partnerin_ die Hausaufgaben.
2. ihr Mann: Sie gibt _ihrem Mann_ einen Kuss.
3. die Freunde: Er macht _den Freunden_ ein leckeres Essen.
4. unser Opa: Ich schreibe _unserem Opa_ einen langen Brief (*letter*).
5. die alte Frau: Er bringt _der alten Frau_ ein Mineralwasser.
6. die Kellnerin: Der Koch gibt _der Kellnerin_ eine Tasse Tee.

4 Nettigkeiten Bilden Sie Sätze. Sample answers are provided.

> **BEISPIEL** sie / ihre Eltern / ein Geschenk (*gift*) / geben
> *Sie geben ihren Eltern ein Geschenk.*

1. die Frau / ihre Mutter / ein Kuchen / geben   Die Frau gibt ihrer Mutter einen Kuchen.
2. ich / der Hund / sein Essen / vorbereiten   Ich bereite dem Hund sein Essen vor.
3. der Schüler / die Lehrerin / eine Postkarte / schreiben   Der Schüler schreibt der Lehrerin eine Postkarte.
4. er / seine Tochter / eine Vorspeise / bestellen   Er bestellt seiner Tochter eine Vorspeise.
5. die Köchin / das Kind / ein Brötchen / geben   Die Köchin gibt dem Kind ein Brötchen.
6. meine Frau / die Oma / eine Beilage / mitbringen   Meine Frau bringt der Oma eine Beilage mit.

Kommunikation

5 **Was für ein Chaos!** Ihr Haus ist ein volles Chaos. Fragen Sie Ihren Partner / Ihre Partnerin, wem die Sachen gehören (*belong*), die im Haus herumliegen. Answers will vary.

S1: *Wem gehört der Pullover?*
S2: *Er gehört meiner Schwester.*

meine Eltern	die Köchin
eine Freundin	meine Schwester
der Kellner	ein Student

1.

2.

3.

4.

5.

6.

6 **Geschenke** Machen Sie eine Liste mit Geschenken (*gifts*) für Ihre Familie und Freunde und erzählen Sie Ihrem Partner / Ihrer Partnerin, was Sie wem schenken (*give as a gift*). Answers will vary.

BEISPIEL meine Tante

S1: *Ich schenke meiner Tante ein Buch. Was schenkst du deiner Oma?*
S2: *Ich schenke meiner Oma einen kleinen Vogel!*

1. Mutter/Vater
2. Großeltern
3. Lehrer/Lehrerin
4. Cousin/Cousine

5. Onkel/Tante
6. bester Freund/beste Freundin
7. Hund/Katze
8. Klassenkameraden (*pl.*)

7 **Wem tust du einen Gefallen?** Beantworten Sie die Fragen von Ihrem Partner / Ihrer Partnerin. Answers will vary.

BEISPIEL

S1: *Wem schenkst du Geschenke?*
S2: *Ich schenke meinen Geschwistern Geschenke. Und du?*

1. Wem schreibst du Postkarten im Sommer?
2. Wem kochst du ein Essen?
3. Wem kaufst du ein Buch?

4. Wem hilfst du bei den Hausaufgaben?
5. Wem stellst du deine Eltern vor?
6. Wem bäckst du einen Kuchen?

6 Suggestions
- Even if students have been working well with the accusative and dative in isolation, they often have difficulty when they must use both cases in the same sentence. It may be helpful to have charts on the board, and to emphasize that the person who receives the **Geschenk** will be in the dative, while the gift itself will be in the accusative.
- Give students a moment to generate their lists before they begin working with partners. Encourage students to be creative, and emphasize that they will be working with *both* the accusative and the dative. Ask a student volunteer to put an example on the board.

4B.2

Prepositions with the dative  Presentation

Startblock Certain prepositions are always followed by an object in the dative case.

QUERVERWEIS

See **3B.2** to review prepositions that take an object in the accusative case.

ACHTUNG

The prepositions **nach** and **zu** are also used in the set expressions **nach Hause** (*home*) and **zu Hause** (*at home*). **Ich gehe jetzt nach Hause. Er bleibt immer zu Hause.**

Mein Vater kommt **aus der Türkei**.

Ich glaube, es ist alles okay **mit den beiden**.

- Most dative prepositional phrases provide information about time and location.

prepositions with the dative			
aus	*from*	nach	*after; to*
außer	*except for*	seit	*since; for*
bei	*at; near; with*	von	*from*
mit	*with*	zu	*to; for; at*

Willst du **bei meinen Eltern** essen?
*Do you want to eat **at my parents' house**?*

Zum Geburtstag bekomme ich Geschenke.
*I get presents **on my birthday**.*

- Use **nach** before the names of countries or cities. Use **zu** with people, businesses, or other locations.

Wir fliegen morgen **nach Berlin**.
*We're flying **to Berlin** tomorrow.*

Gehst du **zur Bäckerei**?
*Are you going **to the bakery**?*

- The preposition **seit** is used with time expressions to indicate *since when* or *for how long* something has been taking place.

Seit wann wohnst du in Berlin?
***Since when** have you been living in Berlin?*

Ich wohne **seit einem Jahr** in Berlin.
*I've been living in Berlin **for one year**.*

- The prepositions **bei**, **von**, and **zu** can combine with the definite article **dem** to form contractions. The preposition **zu** also forms a contraction with the definite article **der**.

bei + dem = **beim**
von + dem = **vom**

zu + dem = **zum**
zu + der = **zur**

Wir kaufen oft **beim** Supermarkt ein.
*We often shop **at the** supermarket.*

Ich esse immer Eier **zum** Frühstück.
*I always have eggs **for** breakfast.*

Ressourcen

SAM
WB: pp. 61–62

SAM
LM: p. 39

vhlcentral.com

 Jetzt sind Sie dran! **Wählen Sie die passenden Präpositionen.**

1. Der beste Tisch ist (aus dem / beim) Fenster.
2. Wann fährst du (zum / mit dem) Supermarkt?
3. (Vom / Außer dem) Restaurant ist nichts geöffnet.
4. Deine Familie kommt (mit / aus) den USA.
5. (Seit / Außer) Freitag habe ich Ferien (*vacation*).
6. Tinas Freund fährt (nach der / zur) Universität.
7. Ich wohne (zu / bei) meinen Eltern.
8. Wir essen Pizza (mit / bei) Besteck.

Anwendung und Kommunikation

1 Wählen Sie Wählen Sie die passenden Präpositionen.

BEISPIEL Wir wohnen (seit / um) fünf Jahren hier.

1. Jürgen kommt (mit / aus) Hamburg.
2. Er studiert (bei / seit) sechs Semestern an der Uni Heidelberg.
3. Er wohnt (mit / von) drei Freunden zusammen in einer großen Wohnung.
4. Alle drei Monate fährt er (nach / zu) Hause zu seinen Eltern.
5. Seine Mutter ist immer extrem glücklich, wenn ihr Sohn (nach / zu) Hause ist.
6. Bei schönem Wetter (*weather*) spielt er dann (aus / mit) seinem Vater Tennis.
7. (Außer / Aus) seinen Eltern besucht er auch seine Großeltern.
8. Jürgen hat nächste Woche Geburtstag und er bekommt (nach / von) seinem Opa ein neues Auto.

2 Wer ist das? Setzen Sie die fehlenden Dativpräpositionen ein.

Christoph Waltz kommt (1) ___aus___ Österreich. Seine Großmutter arbeitet als junge Frau als Schauspielerin (*actress*) (2) ___bei___ einem Theater und (3) ___von___ dieser Großmutter hat er sein Talent. In Europa ist Waltz (4) ___seit___ vielen Jahren als ein großartiger Schauspieler berühmt. Den größten Erfolg (*success*) aber hat er erst 2009 als brutaler SS-Offizier in *Inglourious Basterds*, ein Film (5) ___von___ Quentin Tarantino. Waltz wohnt (6) ___mit___ seiner Freundin in Hollywood und auch in London und Berlin.

3 Seit wann? Seit wann macht Ihr Partner / Ihre Partnerin die folgenden Aktivitäten? Answers will vary.

BEISPIEL heute Veranstaltung haben

S1: *Seit wann hast du heute Veranstaltung?*
S2: *Ich habe seit 10 Uhr Veranstaltung. Und du?*

1. hier studieren
2. Deutsch lernen
3. Kaffee trinken
4. einen Computer haben
5. ein Handy haben
6. Auto fahren

4 Wolfgangs Fotoalbum Wer sind die Personen auf den Fotos? Was machen Sie? Woher kommen Sie? Wo wohnen Sie? Answers will vary.

▶ **BEISPIEL**

S1: *Das ist Wolfgangs Opa. Er kommt aus Deutschland.*
S2: *Aber da ist er in Frankreich (France), nicht wahr?*
S3: *Ja, ja. Er reist sehr oft nach Frankreich.*

1.

2.

3.

4.

3 Suggestion Native speakers of English often try to use the present perfect with **seit**. Remind students to use the present tense in this exercise.

4 Suggestion Make sure students understand that they will be talking about the people in the pictures as if they actually knew them.

Wiederholung

1 Ankes Familie hat Durst

Ankes Familie ist in einem Restaurant. Was bringt der Kellner den Familienmitgliedern (*family members*) zu trinken? Answers will vary.

> **BEISPIEL** die Schwester
>
> **S1:** Was bringt der Kellner Ankes Schwester?
> **S2:** Er bringt ihrer Schwester ein Glas Milch.

der Kaffee die Milch	das Mineralwasser der Orangensaft	das stille Wasser der Tee

1. der Onkel
2. die Eltern
3. der Bruder
4. die Oma
5. die Tante
6. der Opa

2 Der Koch

Fragen Sie den Koch, was er den Personen zum Essen macht. Wechseln Sie sich ab. Sample answers are provided.

> **BEISPIEL**
>
> **S1:** Herr Müller, was machen Sie dem Musiker zum Frühstück?
> **S2:** Ich mache dem Musiker ein Schinkenbrot.

der Musiker / das Frühstück

1. die Journalistin / das Abendessen
Herr Müller, was machen Sie der Journalistin zum Abendessen? Ich mache der Journalistin eine Suppe.

2. die Architektin / das Mittagessen
Herr Müller, was machen Sie der Architektin zum Mittagessen? Ich mache der Architektin Rindfleisch.

3. die Friseurin / das Frühstück
Herr Müller, was machen Sie der Friseurin zum Frühstück? Ich mache der Friseurin Eier mit Speck.

4. der Geschäftsmann / der Snack
Herr Müller, was machen Sie dem Geschäftsmann zum Snack? Ich mache dem Geschäftsmann Käse und Wein.

5. die Dozentin / das Abendessen
Herr Müller, was machen Sie der Dozentin zum Abendessen? Ich mache der Dozentin Hähnchen mit Kartoffeln.

6. der Ingenieur / das Mittagessen
Herr Müller, was machen Sie dem Ingenieur zum Mittagessen? Ich mache dem Ingenieur Pasta.

3 Wie schmeckt's?

Sagen Sie einem Partner / einer Partnerin, was die Personen essen und wie sie es finden. Answers will vary.

> **BEISPIEL**
>
> **S1:** Wie findet die Frau die Erdbeeren?
> **S2:** Sie sind der Frau zu süß.

fade	lecker	leicht	salzig	scharf	süß

1. der Mann
2. die Frau
3. das Mädchen

4. die Studenten
5. der Junge
6. die Kinder

4 Chaos im Restaurant

Sie sind Kellner / Kellnerin im Restaurant. Was sollen Sie den Gästen bringen? Fragen Sie Ihren Partner / Ihre Partnerin. Answers will vary.

> **BEISPIEL**
>
> **S1:** Was braucht der junge Mann?
> **S2:** Bring dem jungen Mann eine Serviette.
> **S1:** Was braucht die alte Frau?
> **S2:** Bring der alten Frau eine Gabel.

4 Suggestion Briefly review vocabulary, to make sure students recall the names and genders of all the items pictured before beginning this activity.

5 Was machen Sie?

Sie bekommen von Ihrem Professor / Ihrer Professorin eine Liste mit diversen Aktivitäten. Suchen Sie Klassenkameraden, die diese Aktivitäten machen. Answers will vary.

> **BEISPIEL**
>
> **S1:** Machst du bei einer Lerngruppe mit (*join*)?
> **S2:** Ja, ich mache bei einer Lerngruppe mit.
> OR
> **S1:** Wohnst du bei deinen Eltern?
> **S2:** Nein, ich wohne nicht bei meinen Eltern.

6 Wie lange?

6 Wie lange? Finden Sie vier Dinge heraus, die Ihr Partner / Ihre Partnerin gern macht. Fragen Sie ihn/sie, seit wann er/sie das schon macht.

BEISPIEL

S1: Was spielst du gern?
S2: Ich spiele gern Tennis.
S1: Seit wann spielst du Tennis?
S2: Seit drei Jahren.

7 Interview

7 Interview Führen Sie ein Interview mit einem Partner / einer Partnerin. Wenn eine Person fertig ist, tauschen Sie (*exchange*) Rollen. Answers will vary.

BEISPIEL

S1: Bei wem wohnst du im Sommer?
S2: Ich wohne bei meinen Eltern.

1. Hast du einen Job?
2. Seit wann arbeitest du in diesem (*this*) Job?
3. Was machst du in deinem Job?
4. Mit wem arbeitest du?
5. Bei wem wohnst du im Sommer?
6. Wen triffst du nach der Arbeit?

8 Poetische Präpositionen

8 Poetische Präpositionen Schreiben Sie mit einem Partner / einer Partnerin ein Gedicht aus fünf Sätzen. Außer der letzten Zeile (*line*) soll jede Zeile mit einer Dativ- oder Akkusativpräposition beginnen.

BEISPIEL

Mit dem Ball spiele ich.
Bei dem Metzger kaufen wir ein.
Durch die Stadt läuft die Mutter.
Außer Anton isst die Familie.
Der Hund schläft ein.

Mein Wör | ter | buch

Schreiben Sie noch fünf weitere Wörter in Ihr persönliches Wörterbuch zu den Themen **Lebensmittel** und **im Restaurant**.

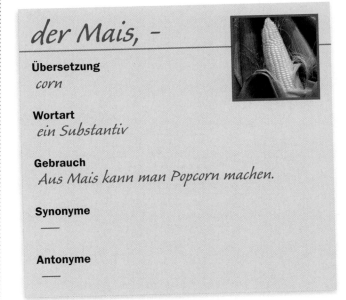

der Mais, -

Übersetzung
corn

Wortart
ein Substantiv

Gebrauch
Aus Mais kann man Popcorn machen.

Synonyme
—

Antonyme
—

Panorama Map

Österreich

Österreich in Zahlen

Suggestion Point out that Austria is slightly smaller than the state of Maine.

► **Fläche°:** *83.855 km² (Quadratkilometer) (60% der Fläche sind gebirgig°)*

► **Bevölkerung:** *8,3 Millionen Menschen*

► **9 Bundesländer°:** *Burgenland, Kärnten, Niederösterreich, Oberösterreich, Salzburg, Steiermark, Tirol, Vorarlberg, Wien*

► **Städte:** *Wien (1,6 Mio. Einwohner), Graz (253.000), Linz (189.000), Salzburg (147.000) und Innsbruck (118.000)*

► **Berge°:** *der Großglockner (3.798 m), die Wildspitze (3.768 m)*

► **Flüsse°:** *die Donau, der Inn*

► **Währung°:** *der Euro (€) (seit 2002)*

► **Wichtige Industriezweige°:** *Banken, Tourismus*

► **Touristenattraktionen:** *Bergsport, Salzburger Festspiele°, Spanische Hofreitschule°, Wintertourismus*

Touristen können in Städten wie Wien und Salzburg viel Kultur genießen° oder in den Alpen Berg- und Wintersport betreiben. Für Firmen ist Österreich interessant, weil die Unternehmenssteuer° sehr niedrig° ist.

QUELLE: Österreichische Botschaft, Washington

Berühmte Österreicher

► **Maria Theresia,** *Kaiserin° (1717–1780)*

► **Wolfgang Amadeus Mozart,** *Komponist (1756–1791)*

► **Sigmund Freud,** *Neurologe (1856–1939)*

► **Gustav Klimt,** *Künstler° (1862–1918)*

► **Lise Meitner,** *Physikerin (1878–1968)*

► **Friedensreich Hundertwasser,** *Architekt (1928–2000)*

► **Elfriede Jelinek,** *Autorin (1946–)*

► **Falco,** *Musiker (1957–1998)*

Suggestion With books closed, tell students: **Wir sprechen sehr oft von Deutschland. Wie heißen die anderen Länder, in denen man Deutsch spricht?** After they answer, ask students what they already know about Austria: rivers, capital, size, money, famous Austrians, dialect, etc. Then have them open the book to p. 180 and review the statistics. Ask comprehension questions: **Wie groß ist Österreich? Wie viele Menschen leben in Österreich?**

Fläche *surface area* **gebirgig** *mountainous* **Bundesländer** *states* **Berge** *mountains* **Flüsse** *rivers* **Währung** *currency* **Wichtige Industriezweige** *Important industries* **Festspiele** *festivals* **Hofreitschule** *Riding School* **genießen** *enjoy* **Unternehmenssteuer** *business tax* **niedrig** *low* **Kaiserin** *empress* **Künstler** *artist* **Pfefferminzbonbons** *peppermint candies* **Geschmacksrichtung** *flavor* **jedem** *every* **Lakritz** *licorice* **Köpfe** *heads* **Spendern** *dispensers*

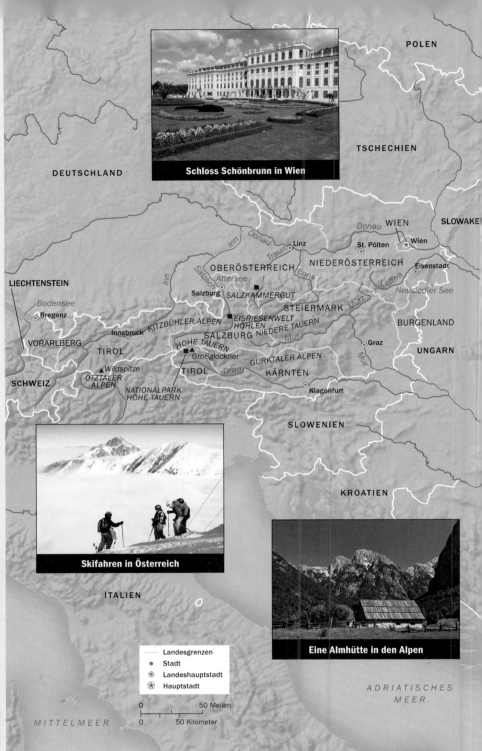

Schloss Schönbrunn in Wien

Skifahren in Österreich

Eine Almhütte in den Alpen

Landesgrenzen
● Stadt
◎ Landeshauptstadt
⊛ Hauptstadt

Unglaublich, aber wahr!

Der Österreicher Eduard Haas III. fängt 1927 an, Pfefferminzbonbons° mit dem Namen PEZ zu verkaufen. Der Name PEZ kommt von der ersten Geschmacksrichtung°, PfeffErminZ. PEZ gibt es heute mit jedem° Geschmack, sogar Chlorophyll und Lakritz°! Seit 1952 gibt es lustige Köpfe° auf den Spendern° wie Mickey Mouse und Donald Duck.

Politik

Internationale Institutionen in Wien

Politisch ist Österreich ein neutrales Land. Es ist Mitglied° in der Europäischen Union, aber nicht in der NATO. Seit 1979 ist Wien einer von vier Hauptsitzen° der Vereinten Nationen°. Die anderen Hauptsitze sind New York, Genf und Nairobi. Andere internationale Organisationen in Wien sind die IAEA (Internationale Organisation für Atomenergie) und die OPEC.

Sport

Olympische Spiele

Olympische Spiele und Österreich bedeuten vor allem° Olympische Winterspiele und alpiner Skisport. 1964 und 1976 treffen sich° Sportler aus aller Welt zu den Olympischen Winterspielen in Innsbruck. Erfolgreiche° österreichische Olympioniken° sind Felix Gottwald (nordischer Kombinierer°) mit drei Gold-, einer Silber- und drei Bronzemedaillen. Der Skispringer° Thomas Morgenstern und der Skifahrer Toni Sailer gewinnen jeweils° drei Goldmedaillen. In alpinen Skidisziplinen gewinnen Österreicher mehr Medaillen als jedes andere Land der Welt (31 Gold-, 35 Silber- und 39 Bronzemedaillen).

Musik

Familie von Trapp in Amerika

Viele kennen° die Familie von Trapp aus dem Film *The Sound of Music*. Aber was passiert° mit der Familie nach der Emigration? 1939 emigriert die Familie mit nur vier Dollar in der Tasche° nach Amerika. Die von Trapps machen als „Trapp Family" Singers Karriere und kaufen 1942 eine Farm in Stowe, Vermont. Auch heute kann man die Farm als Gasthaus° besuchen — und man kann mit den von Trapps Weihnachten° feiern.

Architektur

Friedensreich Hundertwasser

Hundertwasser ist ein kontroverser österreichischer Architekt und Künstler. Er beginnt in den 50er Jahren in Österreich als Künstler mit revolutionären Ideen. Die Beziehung° zwischen Mensch und Natur ist ein zentrales Thema in seiner Kunst. Heute kann man seine Häuser in der ganzen Welt finden: in Magdeburg und Essen (Deutschland), in Napa Valley (USA), in Tel Aviv (Israel) und in Kawakawa (Neuseeland). Das Hundertwasserhaus in Wien ist dabei ein Touristenmagnet und auch die Müllverbrennungsanlage° Spittelau ist sehr berühmt.

IM INTERNET

1. Wer sind die besten österreichischen Frauen bei Olympischen Spielen?
2. Was bedeuten dem Architekten Hundertwasser die Ideen Fensterrecht, Baummieter und Spiralhaus?

For more information on this **Panorama**, go to **vhlcentral.com**.

Mitglied *member* **Hauptsitzen** *head offices* **Vereinten Nationen** *United Nations* **vor allem** *especially* **treffen sich** *meet* **Erfolgreiche** *Successful* **Olympioniken** *Olympic champions* **nordischer Kombinierer** *Nordic combined skier* **Skispringer** *ski jumper* **jeweils** *each* **kennen** *know* **passiert** *happens* **Tasche** *pocket* **Gasthaus** *inn* **Weihnachten** *Christmas* **Beziehung** *relationship* **Müllverbrennungsanlage** *waste incineration plant*

Was haben Sie gelernt? Ergänzen Sie die Sätze.

1. Der Name ___PEZ___ kommt von Pfefferminz.
2. Seit ___1952___ gibt es lustige Köpfe auf den PEZ-Spendern.
3. Offiziell ist Österreich ein ___neutrales___ Land.
4. Wien ist seit ___1979___ einer von vier Hauptsitzen der Vereinten Nationen.
5. 1939 emigriert die Familie ___von Trapp___ nach Amerika.
6. Die Familie von Trapp kauft 1942 eine Farm in ___Stowe___ in Vermont.
7. 1964 und ___1976___ sind die Olympischen Winterspiele in Innsbruck.
8. In alpinen Skidisziplinen gewinnen die Österreicher ___mehr___ Medaillen als jedes andere Land.
9. Hundertwasser ist ein kontroverser österreichischer ___Architekt___ und Künstler.
10. Hundertwassers Häuser kann man in Österreich, Deutschland, den USA, Israel und ___Neuseeland___ finden.

Practice more at **vhlcentral.com**.

Vor dem Lesen

Strategien
Scanning
Scanning involves glancing over a document in search of specific information. For example, you can scan a document to identify its format, to find cognates, to locate visual clues about the document's content, or to find specific facts. Scanning allows you to learn a great deal about a text without having to read it word for word.

Textart Was für ein Text ist das? Erklären Sie Ihre Antwort einem Partner / einer Partnerin.

ein E-Mail	ein Blogeintrag
eine Werbeanzeige	*(blog entry)*
(ad)	ein Memo
eine Einkaufsliste	ein Brief

Auf einen Blick Sehen Sie sich mit einem Partner / einer Partnerin den Text an.

A. Finden Sie drei Aktivitäten, die im Text genannt werden *(are mentioned)*. Sample answers are provided.

schlafen
Inlineskates fahren
klettern

B. Welche Lehnwörter *(loan words)* und Kognate können Sie im Text finden? Diskutieren Sie Ihre Antworten. Sample answers are provided.

Sofas	Musik
Konzerthalle	Brunch
Jamsession	Inlineskates

---

http://www.die-ersten-monate-in-graz.com

Die ersten Monate in Graz

über mich	Hauptseite	Fotos	Kontakt

Besuch!   12. Oktober

Das Kunsthaus

Am Freitag besuchen mich meine Freunde Holger, Klaus und Sepp für ein Wochenende in Graz. Super! Vier Jahre lang haben wir zusammen in Wien studiert. Jetzt sehen wir uns nur selten. Klaus wohnt in Linz, Holger arbeitet in Wien und Sepp studiert immer noch°. Alle können bei mir schlafen. Ich habe ein Gästezimmer° und zwei Sofas im Wohnzimmer°. Das funktioniert prima! Schlafen—nicht an diesem Wochenende! Am Freitag geht's erstmal in die Hopfenlaube, eine tolle Konzerthalle, für eine Jamsession. Da ist die Musik immer toll° und wir können über die guten alten Zeiten° reden. Am Samstag geht's dann ins Café Schwalbennest frühstücken. Nach der langen Nacht ist ein guter Brunch extrem wichtig°. Das Café ist ganz in der Nähe° von meiner Wohnung°. Anschließend° gehen wir bei schönem Wetter° eine Runde im Volksgarten Inlineskates fahren. Der Volksgarten ist total

immer noch *still* **Gästezimmer** *guest bedroom* **Wohnzimmer** *living room* **toll** *great* **guten alten Zeiten** *good old times* **wichtig** *important* **in der Nähe** *near to* **Wohnung** *apartment* **Anschließend** *Afterwards* **bei schönem Wetter** *in nice weather*

schön und sehr zentral gelegen°. Später
können wir auch noch die Treppen° zum
Grazer Schlossberg hochklettern°. Vom
Uhrturm kann man die ganze Stadt super
sehen inklusive der wunderschönen
Innenstadt. Und was machen wir bei
Regen°? Dann können wir das Kunsthaus
Graz besuchen. Dort gibt es immer
moderne Ausstellungen°. Ich freue mich
schon auf° das Wochenende und auf
meine alten Freunde.

Archiv

▶ Prüfungsstress ☹
▶ Glücklich°!
▶ Die Uni
▶ Es ist schon
  wieder° Montag…
▶ September
▶ August
▶ Juli
▶ Juni
▶ Mai
▶ April
▶ März

Der Uhrturm

zentral gelegen *centrally located* **Treppen** *stairs* **hochklettern** *to climb up*
Regen *rain* **Ausstellungen** *exhibits* **freue mich auf** *look forward to*
Glücklich *Happy* **schon wieder** *once again*

Nach dem Lesen

Das richtige Wort Ergänzen Sie
die Aussagen (*statements*) mit den
richtigen Informationen.

1. Am Freitag besuchen drei Freunde die Stadt
   _____Graz_____ für ein Wochenende.

2. Am _____Freitag_____ gehen die Freunde in
   die Hopfenlaube.

3. Am Samstag essen die Freunde _Frühstück/Brunch_
   im Café Schwalbennest.

4. Anschließend gehen sie Inlineskates fahren im
   _____Volksgarten_____.

5. Später können sie die _____Treppen_____ zum Grazer
   Schlossberg hochklettern.

6. Bei Regen besuchen sie _das Kunsthaus Graz_.

Informationen Schreiben Sie die richtigen
Antworten. Schreiben Sie ganze Sätze.
Sample answers are provided.

BEISPIEL Wo wohnt Holger?

Holger wohnt in Wien.

1. Wer besucht Graz am Wochenende?
   Holger, Klaus und Sepp besuchen Graz.

2. Warum wollen die Freunde in die
   Hopfenlaube gehen?
   Die Musik da ist toll.

3. Wann frühstücken die Freunde im
   Café Schwalbennest?
   Sie frühstücken dort am Samstag.

4. Was machen die Freunde im Volksgarten?
   Die Freunde fahren im Volksgarten Inlineskates.

5. Was kann man vom Uhrturm sehen?
   Man kann die ganze Stadt super sehen.

6. Was kann man im Kunsthaus Graz sehen?
   Im Kunsthaus Graz kann man moderne Ausstellungen sehen.

Ihre Heimatstadt Stellen Sie einem
Partner / einer Partnerin Fragen: Was kann oder
soll man in Ihrer Heimatstadt (*hometown*) machen?

BEISPIEL

S1: *Was muss man in deiner Heimatstadt sehen?*
S2: *In meiner Heimatstadt muss man das
Kunstmuseum sehen.*
S1: *Wo kann man gut essen?*

Suggestion Give students a minute to prepare their lists of
sights, and provide them with vocabulary as needed.

Hören

Strategien

Listening for the gist

When you listen to a conversation in German, try to figure out the main ideas that are being expressed, rather than trying to catch every word. Listening for the gist can help you follow what someone is saying, even if you can't hear or understand some of the words.

 To help you practice this strategy, you will listen to three sentences. Jot down a brief summary of what you hear.

Vorbereitung

Schauen Sie sich das Foto an. Wer ist auf dem Foto? Wo sind sie? Was machen sie?

Zuhören

Hören Sie sich den Podcast mit Andrea und der Reporterin an. Lesen Sie dann die Liste. Hören Sie sich den Podcast ein zweites Mal an und markieren Sie die Zutaten (*ingredients*), die Sie hören.

(Pfifferlinge (*chanterelles*))
Kartoffel
(Steinpilz (*porcini*))
(Sahne (*cream*))
Tomaten
(Speck (*bacon*))
Knoblauch

Mehl (*flour*)
(Zwiebeln)
(Salz)
Pfeffer
Butter
(Petersilie (*parsley*))
Pasta

Verständnis

Eine Zusammenfassung Ergänzen Sie die Zusammenfassung (*summary*) von dem Podcast mit Wörtern von der Liste.

alles	die Pfifferlinge	eine Reporterin
findet	frische Pilze	salzig
lecker	einen Podcast	schmeckt
Pfeffer	probieren	Zwiebeln

1. Wir hören _____einen Podcast_____ mit der Köchin Andrea.
2. In der Küche sind Andrea und _____eine Reporterin_____.
3. Laut (*According to*) Andrea kann man im Moment auf dem Markt _____frische Pilze_____ kaufen und sie kocht heute Pfifferlinge.
4. Pfifferlinge sind sehr _____lecker_____.
5. Sie passen gut zu Speck — er ist sehr _____salzig_____.
6. Man braucht auch Sahne und _____Zwiebeln_____.
7. Erst putzt (*cleans*) Andrea _____die Pfifferlinge_____.
8. Dann brät (*fries*) sie _____alles_____ in der Pfanne.
9. Am Ende kommen noch Salz, _____Pfeffer_____ und Petersilie dazu.
10. Die Reporterin _____findet_____ das Gericht (*dish*) lecker!

Und Sie? Erstellen Sie (*Prepare*) mit einem Partner / einer Partnerin ein Rezept für eine Pizza. Welche Zutaten (*ingredients*) sollen auf die Pizza?

BEISPIEL

S1: *Was soll alles auf die Pizza?*
S2: *Pilze, Zwiebeln, Tomaten…*

Schreiben

Strategien

Adding details

How can you make your writing more informative or more interesting? You can add details by answering the "W" questions: Who? What? When? Where? Why? The answers to these questions will provide useful information that can be incorporated into your writing. Here are some useful question words that you have already learned.

Wer?	Wo?
Was?	Warum?
Wann?	Wie?

Compare these two statements.

„Ich muss einkaufen gehen."

„Nach der Schule muss ich Eier kaufen. Mit den Eiern kann ich eine leckere Omelette kochen."

While both statements give the same basic information (the writer needs to go shopping), the details provided in the second statement are much more informative.

Suggestion Remind students that adverbs, like the ones they learned in **4A.2**, can make their speech and writing more informative and expressive.

Thema

 ### Grüße nach Salzburg

Sie entschließen sich (*decide*), ein Jahr in Österreich zu verbringen (*spend*) und bei einer Familie zu leben. Schreiben Sie eine Karte an Ihre Gastfamilie (*host family*). Sagen Sie der Familie, was Sie gern sehen wollen und was Sie machen wollen. Schreiben Sie fünf Sätze. Nennen Sie (*Give*) Details. Beantworten Sie (*Answer*) dabei Fragen mit **wer?**, **was?**, **wo?**, **wie?** und **wann?**

Liebe Gastfamilie, bald kann ich in Salzburg mit euch (*you*) den Uhrturm besuchen...

Expansion Before students start writing, have them come up with an ending to the sample sentence that answers each of the questions **was?**, **wo?**, **wer?**, **wie?**, and **wann?** Write the sentence on the board, underline the answers to each question, and label them with the appropriate interrogative term.

Flashcards
Audio: Vocabulary

Geschäfte

die Bäckerei, -en	bakery
die Eisdiele, -n	ice cream shop
das Feinkostgeschäft, -e	delicatessen
das Fischgeschäft, -e	fish store
die Konditorei, -en	pastry shop
das Lebensmittelgeschäft, -e	grocery store
der Markt, -̈e	market
die Metzgerei, -en	butcher shop
der Supermarkt, -̈e	supermarket

Essen

das Brot, -e	bread
das Brötchen, -	roll
die Butter	butter
das Ei, -er	egg
der Joghurt, -s	yogurt
der Käse, -	cheese
der Kuchen, -	cake; pie
die Marmelade, -n	jam
das Öl, -e	oil
das Olivenöl, -e	olive oil
die Pasta	pasta
der Reis	rice

Fleisch und Fisch

die Garnele, -n	shrimp
das Hähnchen, -	chicken
die Meeresfrüchte (pl.)	seafood
das Rindfleisch	beef
der Schinken, -	ham
das Schweinefleisch	pork
der Thunfisch	tuna
das Würstchen, -	sausage

Mahlzeiten

das Abendessen	dinner
das Frühstück	breakfast
das Mittagessen	lunch
der Snack, -s	snack

Obst und Gemüse

die Ananas, -	pineapple
der Apfel, -̈	apple
die Artischocke, -n	artichoke
die Aubergine, -n	eggplant
die Banane, -n	banana
die Birne, -n	pear
die grüne Bohne (pl. die grünen Bohnen)	green bean
die Erdbeere, -n	strawberry
die Himbeere, -n	raspberry
die Karotte, -n	carrot
die Kartoffel, -n	potato
der Knoblauch	garlic
die Melone, -n	melon
die Orange, -n	orange
die grüne Paprika (pl. die grünen Paprika)	green pepper
die rote Paprika (pl. die roten Paprika)	red pepper
der Pfirsich, -e	peach
der Pilz, -e	mushroom
der Salat, -e	lettuce; salad
die Tomate, -n	tomato
die Traube, -n	grape
die Zwiebel, -n	onion

Getränke

das Bier	beer
der Kaffee	coffee
die Milch	milk
das Mineralwasser	sparkling water
der Saft, -̈e	juice
der Tee	tea
das stille Wasser	still water
der Wein	wine

Essen beschreiben

der Geschmack, -̈e	flavor; taste
fade	bland
lecker	delicious
leicht	light
salzig	salty
scharf	spicy
schwer	rich, heavy
süß	sweet

im Restaurant

die Beilage, -n	side dish
das Besteck	silverware
der Esslöffel, -	soup spoon
die Flasche, -n	bottle
die Gabel, -n	fork
der erste/zweite Gang, -̈	first/second course
das Glas, -̈er	glass
die Hauptspeise, -n	main course
der Kellner, - / die Kellnerin, -nen	waiter / waitress
der Koch, -̈e / die Köchin, -nen	cook
das Messer, -	knife
die Nachspeise, -n	dessert
der Pfeffer	pepper
die Rechnung, -en	check
das Salz	salt
die Serviette, -n	napkin
die Speisekarte, -n	menu
die Suppe, -n	soup
die Tasse, -n	cup
der Teelöffel, -	teaspoon
der Teller, -	plate
die Tischdecke, -n	tablecloth
das Trinkgeld	tip
die Vorspeise, -n	appetizer
bestellen	to order
schmecken	to taste

Ausdrücke

Ich hätte gern(e)... / Ich möchte	I would like...
auf Diät sein	to be on a diet
hausgemacht	homemade
mögen	to like

Adverbs	See p. 154.
Separable and inseparable prefix verbs	See p. 158.
Dative articles and possessive adjectives	See pp. 172–173.
Dative prepositions	See p. 176.

Appendix A

Appendix B

Appendix C

die Welt

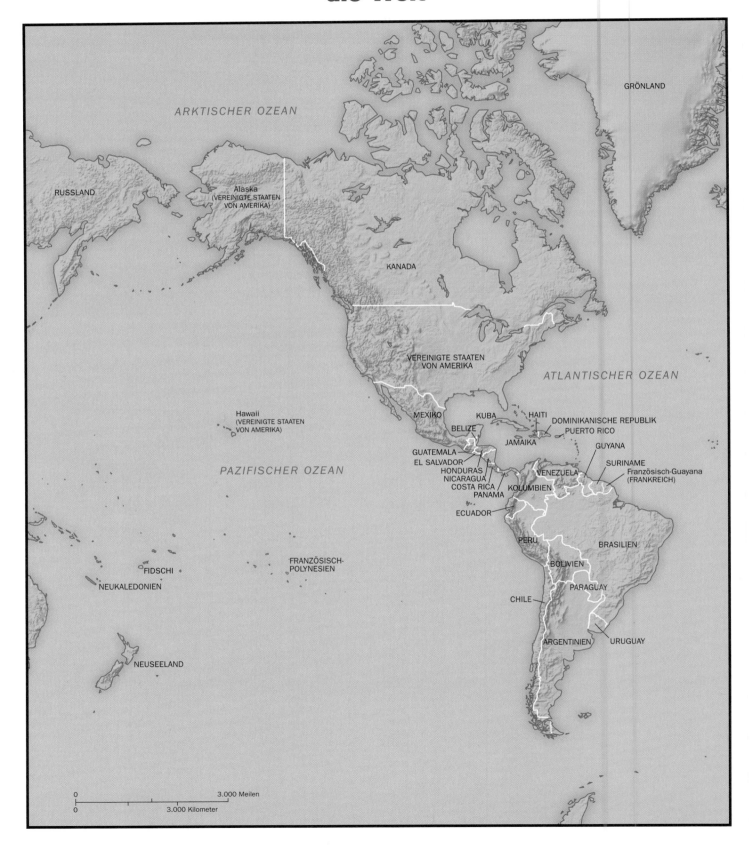

GRÖNLAND

ARKTISCHER OZEAN

RUSSLAND

Alaska
(VEREINIGTE STAATEN
VON AMERIKA)

KANADA

VEREINIGTE STAATEN
VON AMERIKA

ATLANTISCHER OZEAN

Hawaii
(VEREINIGTE STAATEN
VON AMERIKA)

MEXIKO

KUBA

HAITI

DOMINIKANISCHE REPUBLIK
PUERTO RICO

BELIZE

JAMAIKA

GUYANA

PAZIFISCHER OZEAN

GUATEMALA
EL SALVADOR

SURINAME
Französisch-Guayana
(FRANKREICH)

HONDURAS
NICARAGUA

VENEZUELA

COSTA RICA
PANAMA

KOLUMBIEN

ECUADOR

FRANZÖSISCH-
POLYNESIEN

PERU

BRASILIEN

FIDSCHI

BOLIVIEN

NEUKALEDONIEN

PARAGUAY

CHILE

NEUSEELAND

ARGENTINIEN

URUGUAY

0   3.000 Meilen

0   3.000 Kilometer

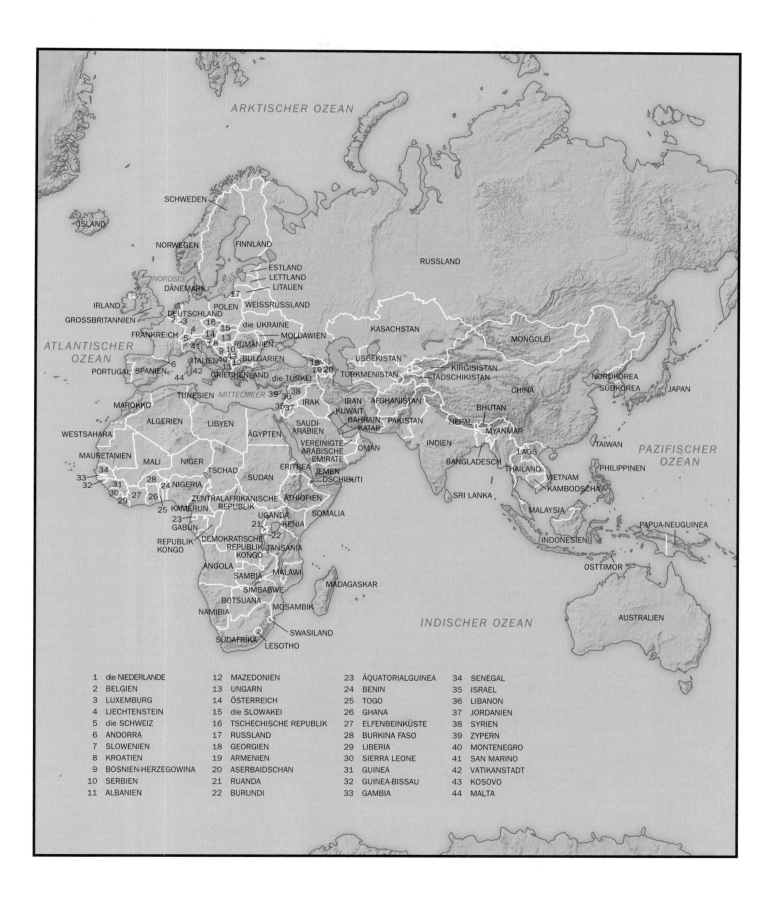

ARKTISCHER OZEAN

ISLAND

SCHWEDEN

NORWEGEN   FINNLAND

RUSSLAND

NORDSEE
DÄNEMARK

ESTLAND
LETTLAND
LITAUEN

IRLAND
GROSSBRITANNIEN

POLEN
DEUTSCHLAND
1
2 3

WEISSRUSSLAND

FRANKREICH

16
4
5   8
41   7
9 10
40 43
12
11
42
44

15   13
die UKRAINE
MOLDAWIEN
RUMÄNIEN
BULGARIEN

KASACHSTAN

MONGOLEI

ATLANTISCHER
OZEAN

PORTUGAL SPANIEN

ANDORRA
6
ITALIEN

GRIECHENLAND
die TÜRKEI

USBEKISTAN

KIRGISISTAN
TADSCHIKISTAN

NORDKOREA
SÜDKOREA   JAPAN

18
19 20
TURKMENISTAN

CHINA

TUNESIEN   MITTELMEER 39 36
35 37

38
IRAK
IRAN AFGHANISTAN

BHUTAN

MAROKKO

KUWAIT
BAHRAIN PAKISTAN
KATAR

NEPAL

MYANMAR

TAIWAN

PAZIFISCHER
OZEAN

WESTSAHARA

ALGERIEN   LIBYEN

ÄGYPTEN

SAUDI-
ARABIEN

VEREINIGTE
ARABISCHE
EMIRATE   OMAN

INDIEN

LAOS
THAILAND

PHILIPPINEN

MAURETANIEN
33   34
32
31
30   27 26
29
25 KAMERUN
23
GABUN
REPUBLIK
KONGO

MALI   NIGER
28
24 NIGERIA
TSCHAD

SUDAN

ERITREA
JEMEN
DSCHIBUTI

BANGLADESCH

SRI LANKA

VIETNAM
KAMBODSCHA

MALAYSIA

PAPUA-NEUGUINEA

ZENTRALAFRIKANISCHE
REPUBLIK

ÄTHIOPIEN

UGANDA
21   KENIA

SOMALIA

INDONESIEN

DEMOKRATISCHE
REPUBLIK
KONGO

22
TANSANIA

OSTTIMOR

ANGOLA

MALAWI
SAMBIA
SIMBABWE
BOTSUANA
NAMIBIA

MOSAMBIK

MADAGASKAR

INDISCHER OZEAN

AUSTRALIEN

SÜDAFRIKA   LESOTHO

SWASILAND

1 die NIEDERLANDE	12 MAZEDONIEN	23 ÄQUATORIALGUINEA	34 SENEGAL
2 BELGIEN	13 UNGARN	24 BENIN	35 ISRAEL
3 LUXEMBURG	14 ÖSTERREICH	25 TOGO	36 LIBANON
4 LIECHTENSTEIN	15 die SLOWAKEI	26 GHANA	37 JORDANIEN
5 die SCHWEIZ	16 TSCHECHISCHE REPUBLIK	27 ELFENBEINKÜSTE	38 SYRIEN
6 ANDORRA	17 RUSSLAND	28 BURKINA FASO	39 ZYPERN
7 SLOWENIEN	18 GEORGIEN	29 LIBERIA	40 MONTENEGRO
8 KROATIEN	19 ARMENIEN	30 SIERRA LEONE	41 SAN MARINO
9 BOSNIEN-HERZEGOWINA	20 ASERBAIDSCHAN	31 GUINEA	42 VATIKANSTADT
10 SERBIEN	21 RUANDA	32 GUINEA-BISSAU	43 KOSOVO
11 ALBANIEN	22 BURUNDI	33 GAMBIA	44 MALTA

Europa

Länder, in denen Deutsch eine Amtssprache ist

BARENTSSEE

ISLAND
Reykjavik

EUROPÄISCHES NORDMEER

SCHWEDEN

FINNLAND

NORWEGEN

Helsinki

Oslo

Stockholm

RUSSLAND

Tallinn
ESTLAND

LETTLAND

Moskau

Riga

DÄNEMARK

NORDSEE

OSTSEE

LITAUEN
Vilnius

Kopenhagen

RUSSLAND

Minsk

WEISSRUSSLAND

ÖSTERREICH
LIECHTENSTEIN
Vaduz
die SCHWEIZ

Dublin
IRLAND

die NIEDERLANDE

GROSS-BRITANNIEN

Amsterdam

London

Berlin

Warschau

POLEN

Kiew

die UKRAINE

Brüssel
BELGIEN

DEUTSCHLAND

die SLOWAKEI

LUXEMBURG

Luxemburg

Paris

Prag
TSCHECHISCHE REPUBLIK

Bratislava

MOLDAWIEN
Kischinau

ATLANTISCHER OZEAN

FRANKREICH

LIECHTENSTEIN

Vaduz

Bern

die SCHWEIZ

Wien
ÖSTERREICH

SLOWENIEN

Budapest

UNGARN

RUMÄNIEN

SCHWARZES MEER

Ljubljana

Zagreb

Bukarest

KROATIEN

Belgrad

ITALIEN

Monaco

BOSNIEN-HERZEGOWINA

SERBIEN

KOSOVO

Andorra la Vella

SAN MARINO

Sarajevo

Pristina

BULGARIEN

Ankara

MONACO

MONTENEGRO

Sofia

PORTUGAL

ANDORRA

Rom

Podgorica

Skopje

Madrid

Korsika

Tirana

MAZEDONIEN

die TÜRKEI

Lissabon

VATIKANSTADT

ALBANIEN

SPANIEN

Sardinien

GRIECHENLAND

Balearische Inseln

Nicosia

Sizilien

Athen

ZYPERN

Algier

Kreta

Tunis

Rabat

Valletta
MALTA

MITTELMEER

MAROKKO

TUNESIEN

Tripolis

ALGERIEN

LIBYEN

Kairo

ÄGYPTEN

0   500 Meilen

0   500 Kilometer

Deutschland

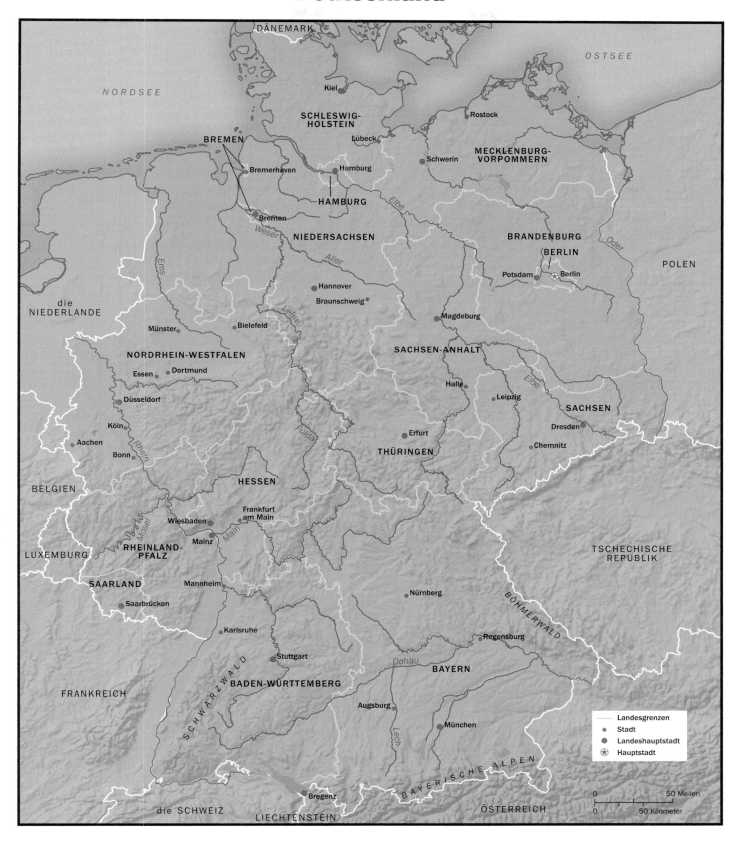

DÄNEMARK

NORDSEE

OSTSEE

Kiel

SCHLESWIG-
HOLSTEIN

Rostock

Lübeck

MECKLENBURG-
VORPOMMERN

BREMEN

Bremerhaven

Hamburg

Schwerin

HAMBURG

Elbe

Bremen

Weser

NIEDERSACHSEN

BRANDENBURG

BERLIN

Oder

Aller

Potsdam

Berlin

POLEN

die
NIEDERLANDE

Ems

Lehne

Hannover

Braunschweig

Magdeburg

Münster

Bielefeld

NORDRHEIN-WESTFALEN

SACHSEN-ANHALT

Essen

Dortmund

Fulda

Halle

Elbe

Leipzig

SACHSEN

Düsseldorf

Dresden

Köln

Erfurt

Chemnitz

Aachen

Bonn

Rhein

THÜRINGEN

BELGIEN

HESSEN

Frankfurt
am Main

TSCHECHISCHE
REPUBLIK

Mosel

Wiesbaden

Main

LUXEMBURG

Mainz

RHEINLAND-
PFALZ

SAARLAND

Mannheim

Nürnberg

BÖHMERWALD

Saarbrücken

Karlsruhe

Regensburg

Donau

SCHWARZWALD

Stuttgart

BAYERN

FRANKREICH

BADEN-WÜRTTEMBERG

Augsburg

Lech

München

	Landesgrenzen
•	Stadt
●	Landeshauptstadt
✪	Hauptstadt

BAYERISCHE ALPEN

50 Meilen

Bregenz

die SCHWEIZ

LIECHTENSTEIN

ÖSTERREICH

0   50 Kilometer

Österreich

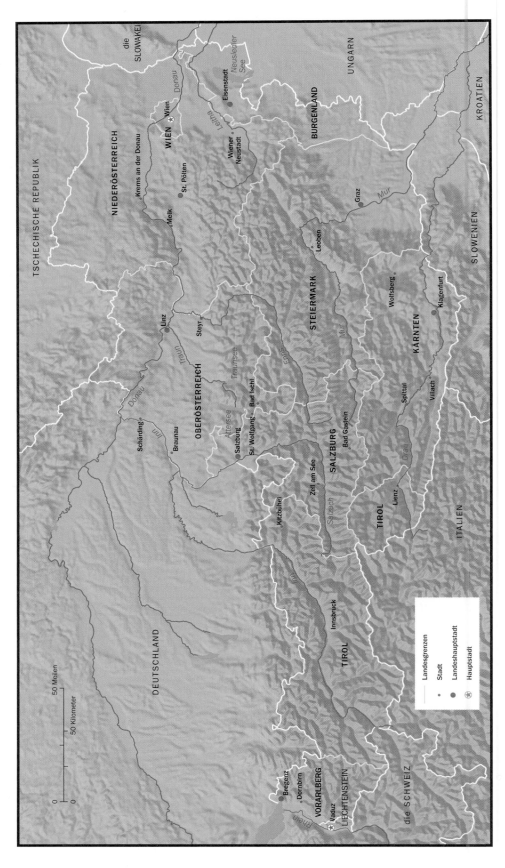

Liechtenstein

die Schweiz

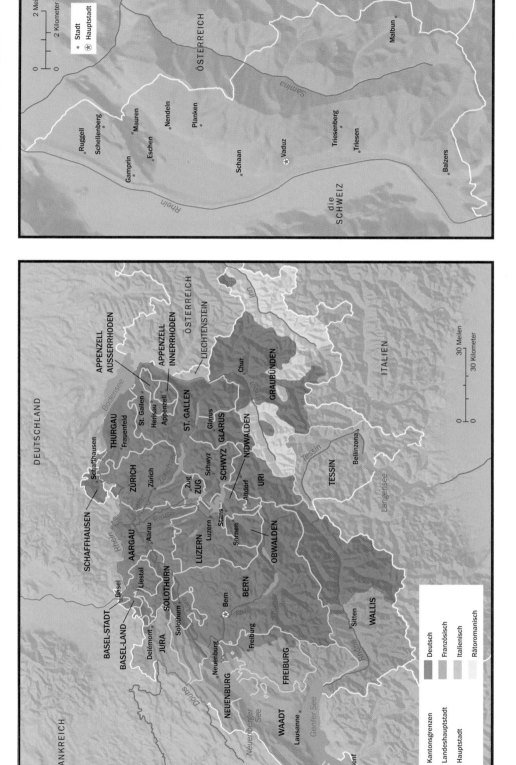

Declension of articles

definite articles			
	masculine	**feminine**	**neuter**	**plural**
nominative	der	die	das	die
accusative	den	die	das	die
dative	dem	der	dem	den
genitive	des	der	des	der

der-words			
	masculine	**feminine**	**neuter**	**plural**
nominative	dieser	diese	dieses	diese
accusative	diesen	diese	dieses	diese
dative	diesem	dieser	diesem	diesen
genitive	dieses	dieser	dieses	dieser

indefinite articles			
	masculine	**feminine**	**neuter**	**plural**
nominative	ein	eine	ein	-
accusative	einen	eine	ein	-
dative	einem	einer	einem	-
genitive	eines	einer	eines	-

ein-words			
	masculine	**feminine**	**neuter**	**plural**
nominative	mein	meine	mein	meine
accusative	meinen	meine	mein	meine
dative	meinem	meiner	meinem	meinen
genitive	meines	meiner	meines	meiner

Declension of nouns and adjectives

nouns and adjectives with *der*-words				
	masculine	feminine	neuter	plural
nominative	der gute Rat	die gute Landschaft	das gute Brot	die guten Freunde
accusative	den guten Rat	die gute Landschaft	das gute Brot	die guten Freunde
dative	dem guten Rat	der guten Landschaft	dem guten Brot	den guten Freunden
genitive	des guten Rates	der guten Landschaft	des guten Brotes	der guten Freunde

nouns and adjectives with *ein*-words				
	masculine	feminine	neuter	plural
nominative	ein guter Rat	eine gute Landschaft	ein gutes Brot	meine guten Freunde
accusative	ein guten Rat	eine gute Landschaft	ein gutes Brot	meine guten Freunde
dative	einem guten Rat	einer guten Landschaft	einem guten Brot	meinen guten Freunden
genitive	eines guten Rates	einer guten Landschaft	eines guten Brotes	meiner guten Freunde

unpreceded adjectives				
	masculine	feminine	neuter	plural
nominative	guter Rat	gute Landschaft	gutes Brot	gute Freunde
accusative	guten Rat	gute Landschaft	gutes Brot	gute Freunde
dative	gutem Rat	guter Landschaft	gutem Brot	guten Freunden
genitive	guten Rates	guter Landschaft	guten Brotes	guter Freunde

Declension of pronouns

personal pronouns										
nominative	ich	du	Sie	er	sie	es	wir	ihr	Sie	sie
accusative	mich	dich	Sie	ihn	sie	es	uns	euch	Sie	sie
accusative reflexive	mich	dich	sich	sich	sich	sich	uns	euch	sich	sich
dative	mir	dir	Ihnen	ihm	ihr	ihm	uns	euch	Ihnen	ihnen
dative reflexive	mir	dir	sich	sich	sich	sich	uns	euch	sich	sich

Glossary of Grammatical Terms

ADJECTIVE Words that describe people, places, or things. An attributive adjective comes before the noun it modifies and takes an ending that matches the gender and case of the noun. A predicate adjective comes after the verb **sein**, **werden**, or **bleiben** and describes the noun that is the subject of the sentence. Predicate adjectives take no additional endings.

Thomas hat eine sehr **gute** Stelle gefunden.
*Thomas found a really **good** job.*

Mein Bruder ist **klein**.
*My brother is **short**.*

Hast du mein **kleines** Adressbuch gesehen?
*Have you seen my **little** address book?*

Deine Schwester wird **groß**.
*Your sister is getting **tall**.*

Possessive adjectives Words that are placed before a noun to indicate ownership or belonging. Each personal pronoun has a corresponding possessive adjective. Possessive adjectives take the same endings as the indefinite article **ein**.

Meine Schwester ist hier.
***My** sister is here.*

Wo ist **dein** Vater?
*Where is **your** father?*

ADVERB Words or phrases that modify a verb, an adjective, or another adverb. Adverbs and adverbial phrases describe *when*, *how*, or *where* an action takes place.

Der Kuchen ist **fast** fertig.
*The cake is **almost** ready.*

Du isst **viel zu** schnell.
*You eat **much too** quickly.*

ARTICLE A word that precedes a noun and indicates its gender, number, and case.

Definite article Equivalent to *the* in English. Its form indicates the gender and case of the noun, and whether it is singular or plural.

der Tisch (*m. s.*)
the table
die Tische (*m. pl.*)
the tables
die Tür (*f. s.*)
the door

die Türen (*f. pl.*)
the doors
das Fenster (*n. s.*)
the window
die Fenster (*n. pl.*)
the windows

Indefinite article Corresponds to *a* or *an* in English. It precedes the noun and matches its gender and case. There is no plural indefinite article in German.

ein Tisch (*m.*)
a table
eine Tür (*f.*)
a door

ein Fenster (*n.*)
a window

CASE There are four cases in German. The case indicates the function of each noun in a sentence. The case of a noun determines the form of the definite or indefinite article that precedes the noun, the form of any adjectives that modify the noun, and the form of the pronoun that can replace the noun.

Nominativ (*nominative*): **Der Professor** ist alt.
***The professor** is old.*

Akkusativ (*accusative*): Ich verstehe **den Professor**.
*I understand **the professor**.*

Dativ (*dative*): Der Assistent zeigt **dem Professor** den neuen Computer.
*The assistant is showing **the professor** the new computer.*

Genitiv (*genitive*): Das ist **des Professors** Assistent.
*This is **the professor's** assistant.*

The nominative case The grammatical subject of a sentence is always in the nominative case. The nominative case is also used for nouns that follow a form of **sein**, **werden**, or **bleiben**. In German dictionaries, nouns, pronouns, and numbers are always listed in their nominative form.

Das ist **eine gute Idee.**
*That's **a good idea.***

Die Kinder schlafen.
***The kids** are sleeping.*

The accusative case A noun that functions as a direct object is in the accusative case.

Der Lehrer hat **den Stift**.
*The teacher has **the pen**.*

Sie öffnet **die Tür**.
*She's opening **the door**.*

Ich kaufe **einen Tisch**.
*I'm going to buy **a table**.*

Ich habe **ein Problem**.
*I have **a problem**.*

The dative case An object in the dative case indicates to whom or for whom an action is performed.

Ich bringe **dem Lehrer** einen Apfel.
*I'm bringing **the teacher** an apple.*

Zeig **der Professorin** deine Arbeit.
*Show your work **to the professor**.*

The genitive case A noun in the genitive case modifies another noun. The genitive case indicates ownership or a close relationship between the genitive noun and the noun it modifies, which may be a subject or an object.

Thorsten hat die Rede **des Bundespräsidenten** heruntergeladen.
*Thorsten downloaded **the president's** speech.*

Das Mikrofon **der Professorin** funktioniert nicht.
***The professor's** microphone doesn't work.*

CLAUSE A group of words that contains both a conjugated verb and a subject, either expressed or implied.

Main (or independent) clause A clause that can stand alone as a complete sentence.

Ich bezahle immer bar, weil ich keine Kreditkarte habe.
I always pay cash, because I don't have a credit card.

Subordinate clause A subordinate clause explains how, when, why, or under what circumstances the action in the main clause occurs. The conjugated verb of a subordinate clause moves to the end of that clause.

Ich lese die Zeitung, **wenn** ich Zeit **habe**.
*I read the newspaper **when** I **have** the time.*

COMPARATIVE The form of an adjective or adverb that compares two or more people or things.

Meine Geschwister sind alle **älter** als ich.
*My siblings are all **older** than I am.*

Die Fahrt dauert mit dem Auto **länger** als mit dem Zug.
*The trip takes **longer** by car than by train.*

CONJUNCTION A word used to connect words, clauses, or phrases.

Coordinating conjunctions Words that combine two related sentences, words, or phrases into a single sentence. There are five coordinating conjunctions in German: **aber** (*but*), **denn** (*because; since*), **oder** (*or*), **sondern** (*but, rather*), **und** (*and*). All other conjunctions are subordinating.

Ich möchte eine große Küche, **denn** ich koche gern.
*I want a big kitchen, **because** I like to cook.*

Lola braucht einen Schrank **oder** eine Kommode.
*Lola needs a closet **or** a dresser.*

Subordinating conjunctions Words used to combine a subordinate clause with a main clause.

Ich lese die Zeitung, **wenn** ich Zeit **habe**.
*I read the newspaper **when** I **have** the time.*

DEMONSTRATIVE Pronouns or adjectives that refer to something or someone that has already been mentioned, or that point out a specific person or thing.

Ist Grete online? –Ja, **die** schreibt eine E-Mail.
*Is Grete online? –Yes, **she's** writing an e-mail.*

Gefällt dir dieser Sessel? –Ja, **der** ist sehr bequem!
*Do you like that chair? –Yes, **it's** very comfortable!*

DER-WORDS Words that take the same endings as the forms of the definite article **der**. These include the demonstrative pronouns **dieser** (*this; that*), **jeder** (*each, every*), **jener** (*that*), **mancher** (*some*), and **solcher** (*such*), and the question word **welcher** (*which*).

Welcher Laptop gefällt dir am besten?
Which laptop do you like best?

Ich finde **diesen** Laptop am schönsten.
*I think **this** laptop is the nicest.*

DIRECT OBJECT A noun or pronoun that directly receives the action of the verb. Direct objects are in the accusative.

Kennst du **diesen Mann**? Ich mache **eine Torte**.
*Do you know **that man**? I'm making **a cake**.*

EIN-WORDS Words that take the same endings as the forms of the indefinite article **ein**. These include the negation **kein** and all of the possessive adjectives.

Hast du **ein** Hund? Ich habe **keinen** Fußball.
*Do you have **a** dog? I don't have **a** soccer ball.*

GENDER The grammatical categorization of nouns, pronouns, and adjectives as masculine, feminine, or neuter.

Masculine
articles: **der, ein**
pronouns: **er, der**
adjectives: **guter, schöner**

Feminine
articles: **die, eine**
pronouns: **sie, die**
adjectives: **gute, schöne**

Neuter
articles: **das, ein**
pronouns: **es, das**
adjectives: **gutes, schönes**

HELPING VERB *See VERB, Auxiliary verb.*

IMPERATIVE Imperatives are verb forms used to express commands, requests, suggestions, directions, or instructions.

Mach deine Hausaufgaben! **Backen wir** einen Kuchen!
Do your homework! Let's bake a cake!

INDIRECT OBJECT A noun or pronoun that receives the action of the verb indirectly. The indirect object is often a person to whom or for whom the action of the sentence is performed. Indirect objects are in the dative case.

Manfred hat **dem Kind** ein Buch geschenkt.
*Manfred gave **the kid** a book.*

INFINITIVE The basic, unconjugated form of a verb. Most German infinitives end in **-en**. A few end in **-ern** or **-eln**.

sehen, essen, lesen, wandern, sammeln
to see, to eat, to read, to hike, to collect

NOUN A word that refers to one or more people, animals, places, things, or ideas. Nouns in German may be masculine, feminine, or neuter, and are either singular or plural.

der **Junge**, die **Katze**, das **Café**
*the **boy**, the **cat**, the **café***

Compound noun Two or more simple nouns can be combined to form a compound noun. The gender of a compound noun matches the gender of the last noun in the compound.

die Nacht + das Hemd = **das Nachthemd**
*night + shirt = **nightshirt***

NUMBER A grammatical term that refers to the quantity of a noun. Nouns in German are either singular or plural. The plural form of a noun may have an added umlaut and/or an added ending. Adjectives, articles, and verbs also have different endings, depending on whether they are singular or plural.

Singular:
der **Mann**, die **Frau**, das **Kind**
*the **man**, the **woman**, the **child***

Plural:
die **Männer**, die **Frauen**, die **Kinder**
*the **men**, the **women**, the **children***

NUMBERS Words that represent quantities.

Cardinal numbers Numbers that indicate specific quantities. Cardinal numbers typically modify nouns, but do not add gender or case endings.

zwei Männer, **fünfzehn** Frauen, **sechzig** Kinder
*two men, **fifteen** women, **sixty** children*

Ordinal numbers Words that indicate the order of a noun in a series. Ordinal numbers add the same gender and case endings as adjectives.

der **erste** Mann, die **zweite** Frau, das **dritte** Kind
*the **first** man, the **second** woman, the **third** child*

PARTICIPLE A participle is formed from a verb but may be used as an adjective or adverb. Present participles are used primarily in written German. Past participles are used in compound tenses, including the **Perfekt** and the **Plusquamperfekt**.

Der **aufgehende** Mond war sehr schön.
*The **rising** moon was beautiful.*

Habt ihr schon **gegessen**?
*Have you already **eaten**?*

PREPOSITION A preposition links a noun or pronoun to other words in a sentence. Combined with a noun or pronoun, it forms a prepositional phrase, which can be used like an adverb to answer the question *when, how,* or *where.* In German, certain prepositions are always followed by a noun in the accusative case, while others are always followed by a noun in the dative case. A small number of prepositions are used with the genitive case.

ohne das Buch **mit** dem Auto
***without** the book* ***by** car*

trotz des Regens
***in spite of** the rain*

Two-way prepositions can be followed by either the dative or the accusative, depending on the situation. They are followed by the accusative when used with a verb that indicates movement toward a destination. With all other verbs, they are followed by the dative.

Stell deine Schuhe nicht **auf den Tisch**!
*Don't put your shoes **on the table**!*

Dein Schal liegt **auf dem Tisch**.
*Your scarf is lying **on the table**.*

PRONOUN A word that takes the place of a noun.

Subject pronouns Words used to replace a noun in the nominative case.

Maria ist nett. **Der Junge** ist groß.
***Maria** is nice.* ***The boy** is tall.*

Sie ist nett. **Er** ist groß.
***She** is nice.* ***He** is tall.*

Accusative pronouns Words used to replace a noun that functions as the direct object.

Wer hat **die Torte** gebacken? Ich habe **sie** gebacken.
*Who baked **the cake**?* *I baked **it**.*

Dative pronouns Words used to replace a noun that functions as the indirect object.

Musst du **deiner Oma** eine E-Mail schicken?
*Do you need to send an e-mail **to your grandma**?*

Nein, ich habe **ihr** schon geschrieben.
*No, I already wrote **to her**.*

Indefinite pronouns Words that refer to an unknown or nonspecific person or thing.

Jemand hat seinen Personalausweis vergessen.
Someone forgot his I.D. card.

Herr Klein will mit **niemandem** sprechen.
Mr. Klein doesn't want to speak with anyone.

Reflexive pronouns The pronouns used with reflexive verbs. When the subject of a reflexive verb is also its direct object, it takes an accusative reflexive pronoun. When the subject of a reflexive verb is not its direct object, it takes a dative reflexive pronoun.

Ich wasche **mich**.
I'm washing (myself).

Ich wasche **mir** das Gesicht.
I'm washing my face.

SUBJUNCTIVE A verb form (**der Konjunktiv II**) used to talk about hypothetical, unlikely or impossible conditions, to express wishes, and to make polite requests. German also has an additional subjunctive tense, der **Konjunktiv I**, used to report what someone else has said without indicating whether the information is true or false.

Ich **hätte** gern viel Geld.
I'd like to have a lot of money.

Wenn er sportlicher **wäre**, **würde** er häufiger trainieren.
If he were more athletic, he would exercise more.

SUPERLATIVE The form of an adjective or adverb used to indicate that a person or thing has more of a particular quality than anyone or anything else.

Welches ist **das größte** Tier der Welt?
What's the biggest animal in the world?

Wie komme ich **am besten** zur Tankstelle?
What's the best way to get to the gas station?

TENSE A set of verb forms that indicates if an action or state occurs in the past, present, or future.

Compound tense A tense made up of an auxiliary verb and a participle or infinitive.

Wir **haben** ihren Geburtstag **gefeiert**.
We celebrated her birthday.

VERB A word that expresses actions or states of being. German verbs are classified as *weak, mixed,* or *strong,* based on the way their past participles are formed.

weak: Ich **habe** eine Torte **gemacht**.
I made a cake.

strong: Wir **haben** Kekse **gegessen**.
We ate cookies.

mixed: Er **hat** eine CD **gebrannt**.
He burned a CD.

Auxiliary verb A conjugated verb used with the participle or infinitive of another verb. The auxiliary verbs **haben** and **sein** are used with past participles to form compound tenses including the **Perfekt** and **Plusquamperfekt**. **Werden** is used with an infinitive to form the future tense, and with a past participle to form a passive construction. Modals are also frequently used as auxiliary verbs.

Habt ihr den Tisch **gedeckt**?
Did you set the table?

Jasmin **war** noch nie nach Zürich **gefahren**.
Jasmin had never been to Zurich.

Wir **werden** uns in einer Woche wieder **treffen**.
We'll meet again in one week.

Es **wird** hier nur Deutsch **gesprochen**.
Only German is spoken here.

Modal verbs Verbs that modify the meaning of another verb. Modals express an attitude toward an action, such as permission, obligation, ability, desire, or necessity.

Ich **muss** Französisch **lernen**.
I have to study French.

Ich **will** Französisch **lernen**.
I want to learn French.

Principal parts German verbs are usually listed in dictionaries by their *principal parts* (**Stammformen**): the infinitive, the third-person singular present tense form (if the verb is irregular in the present), the third-person singular **Präteritum** form, and the past participle. Knowing the principal parts of a verb allows you to produce all of its conjugations in any tense.

geben (gibt)	gab	gegeben
to give (gives)	*gave*	*given*

Reflexive verbs Verbs that indicate an action you do to yourself or for yourself. The subject of a reflexive verb is also its object.

Ich **fühle mich** nicht **wohl**.
I don't feel well.

Wir **haben uns entspannt**.
We've been relaxing.

Reciprocal reflexive verbs Verbs that express an action done by two or more people or things to or for one another.

Wir rufen **uns** jeden Tag an.
We call each other every day.

Meine Großeltern lieben **sich** sehr.
My grandparents love each other very much.

Verb conjugation tables

Here are the infinitives of all verbs introduced as active vocabulary in **Mosaik**. Each verb is followed by a model verb that follows the same conjugation pattern. The number in parentheses indicates where in the verb tables, pages A16–A25, you can find the conjugated forms of the model verb. The word (*sein*) after a verb means that it is conjugated with **sein** in the **Perfekt** and **Plusquamperfekt**. For irregular reflexive verbs, the list may point to a non-reflexive model verb. A full conjugation of the simple forms of a reflexive verb is presented in Verb table 6 on page A17. Verbs followed by an asterisk (*) have a separable prefix.

abbiegen* (*sein*) like schieben (42)
abbrechen* like sprechen (47)
abfahren* (*sein*) like tragen (51)
abfliegen* (*sein*) like schieben (41)
abheben* like heben (30)
abschicken* like machen (3)
abstauben* like machen (3)
(sich) abtrocknen* like arbeiten (1)
adoptieren like probieren (4)
anbieten* like schieben (41)
anfangen* like fangen (23)
angeln like sammeln (5)
ankommen* (*sein*) like kommen (33)
anmachen* like machen (3)
anrufen* like rufen (40)
anschauen* like machen (3)
anstoßen* like stoßen (50)
antworten like arbeiten (1)
(sich) anziehen* like schieben (41)
arbeiten (1)
(sich) ärgern like fordern (26)
aufgehen* (*sein*) like gehen (29)
auflegen* like machen (3)
aufmachen* like machen (3)
aufnehmen* like nehmen (36)
aufräumen* like machen (3)
aufstehen* (*sein*) like stehen (48)
aufwachen* (*sein*) like machen (3)
ausfüllen like machen (3)
ausgehen like gehen (29)
ausmachen like machen (3)
(sich) ausruhen like sich freuen (6)
ausschalten* like arbeiten (1)
(sich) ausziehen* like schieben (41)
backen like waschen (54)
(sich) baden like arbeiten (1)
bauen like machen (3)
beantworten like arbeiten (1)
bedeuten like arbeiten (1)
bedienen like machen (3)
(sich) beeilen like sich freuen (6)
beginnen like schwimmen (44)
behaupten like arbeiten (1)
bekommen like kommen (33)
belegen like machen (3)
benutzen like machen (3)
berichten like arbeiten (1)

beschreiben like bleiben (20)
besprechen like sprechen (47)
bestehen like stehen (48)
bestellen like machen (3)
besuchen like machen (3)
(sich) bewegen like heben (30)
(sich) bewerben like helfen (32)
bezahlen like machen (3)
bieten like schieben (41)
bleiben (*sein*) (19)
braten like schlafen (43)
brauchen like machen (3)
brechen like sprechen (46)
brennen like rennen (17)
bringen like denken (16)
buchen like machen (3)
büffeln like sammeln (5)
bügeln like sammeln (5)
bürsten like arbeiten (1)
danken like machen (3)
decken like machen (3)
denken like denken (16)
drücken like fragen (26)
drucken like machen (3)
durchfallen* (*sein*) like fallen (22)
durchmachen* like machen (3)
dürfen (10)
(sich) duschen like sich freuen (6)
einkaufen* like machen (3)
einladen* like tragen (50)
einschlafen* (*sein*) like schlafen (42)
einzahlen* like machen (3)
empfehlen like stehlen (49)
entdecken like machen (3)
entfernen like machen (3)
entgegennehmen* like nehmen (38)
entlassen like fallen (22)
(sich) entschließen like fließen (25)
(sich) entschuldigen like machen (3)
(sich) entspannen like sich freuen (6)
entwerten like arbeiten (1)
entwickeln like sammeln (5)
erfinden like trinken (52)
erforschen like machen (3)
ergänzen like machen (3)
erhalten like fallen (22)
(sich) erinnern like fordern (26)

(sich) erkälten like arbeiten (1)
erkennen like rennen (17)
erklären like machen (3)
erzählen like machen (3)
essen (21)
fahren (*sein*) like tragen (50)
fallen (*sein*) (22)
fangen (23)
(sich) färben like machen (3)
faulenzen like machen (3)
fegen like machen (3)
feiern (2)
fernsehen* like geben (28)
finden like trinken (52)
fliegen (*sein*) like schieben (41)
folgen (*sein*) like machen (3)
(sich) fragen like machen (3)
(sich) freuen (6)
(sich) fühlen like sich freuen (6)
füllen like machen (3)
funktionieren like probieren (4)
geben (27)
gefallen like fallen (22)
gehen (*sein*) (28)
gehören like machen (3)
genießen like fließen (25)
gewinnen like schwimmen (44)
(sich) gewöhnen like sich freuen (6)
glauben like machen (3)
gratulieren like probieren (4)
grüßen like machen (3)
haben like haben (7)
handeln like sammeln (5)
hängen like machen (3)
heiraten like arbeiten (1)
heißen (30)
helfen (32)
heruntergehen* (*sein*) like gehen (29)
herunterladen* like tragen (50)
(sich) hinlegen* like machen (3)
(sich) hinsetzen* like machen (3)
hinterlassen like fallen (22)
hochgehen* (*sein*) like gehen (28)
hören like machen (3)
husten like arbeiten (1)
(sich) informieren like probieren (4)
(sich) interessieren like probieren (4)

joggen (*sein*) like machen (3)
(sich) kämmen like machen (3)
kaufen like machen (3)
kennen like rennen (17)
klettern (*sein*) like fordern (26)
klingeln like sammeln (5)
kochen like machen (3)
kommen (*sein*) (32)
können (11)
korrigieren like probieren (4)
kosten like arbeiten (1)
küssen like machen (3)
lächeln like sammeln (5)
lachen like machen (3)
laden like tragen (50)
landen (*sein*) like arbeiten (1)
lassen like fallen (22)
laufen (*sein*) (33)
leben like machen (3)
legen like machen (3)
leiten like arbeiten (1)
lernen like machen (3)
lesen like geben (28)
lieben like machen (3)
liegen (35)
löschen like tragen (50)
lügen (36)
machen (3)
meinen like machen (3)
mieten like arbeiten (1)
mitbringen* like denken (16)
mitkommen* (*sein*) like kommen (33)
mitmachen* like machen (3)
mitnehmen* like nehmen (38)
mögen (12)
müssen (13)
nachmachen* like machen (3)
nehmen (38)
(sich) nennen like rennen (17)
niesen like machen (3)
öffnen like arbeiten (1)
packen like machen (3)
parken like machen (3)
passen like machen (3)
passieren (*sein*) like probieren (4)
probieren (4)
putzen like machen (3)

(sich) rasieren like probieren (4)
rauchen like machen (3)
recyceln like sammeln (5)
reden like arbeiten (1)
regnen like arbeiten (1)
reisen (*sein*) like machen (3)
reiten (*sein*) like pfeifen (39)
rennen (*sein*) (17)
reparieren like probieren (4)
retten like arbeiten (1)
sagen like machen (3)
schauen like machen (3)
scheitern (*sein*) like fordern (26)
schenken like machen (3)
schicken like machen (3)
schlafen (43)
schmecken like machen (3)
(sich) schminken like machen (3)
schneien like machen (3)
schreiben like bleiben (20)
schützen like machen (3)
schwänzen like machen (3)
schwimmen (*sein*) (44)
sehen like geben (28)
sein (*sein*) (8)
(sich) setzen like machen (3)
singen like trinken (52)
sitzen (46)

sollen (14)
sortieren like probieren (4)
spazieren (*sein*) like probieren (4)
speichern like fordern (26)
spielen like machen (3)
sprechen (46)
springen (*sein*) like trinken (52)
spülen like machen (3)
starten (*sein*) like arbeiten (1)
staubsaugen like saugen (41)
stehen (48)
stehlen (49)
steigen (*sein*) like bleiben (20)
stellen like machen (3)
sterben (*sein*) like helfen (32)
(sich) streiten like pfeifen (39)
studieren like probieren (4)
suchen like machen (3)
surfen (*sein*) like machen (3)
tanken like machen (3)
tanzen like machen (3)
tragen (51)
träumen like machen (3)
(sich) treffen (*sein*) like sprechen (46)
treiben (*sein*) like bleiben (20)
(sich) trennen like sich freuen (6)
trinken (52)
tun (53)

üben like machen (3)
(sich) überlegen like machen (3)
übernachten like arbeiten (1)
überqueren like machen (3)
überraschen like machen (3)
umtauschen* like machen (3)
(sich) umziehen* (*sein*) like schieben (42)
untergehen* (*sein*) like gehen (28)
(sich) unterhalten* like fallen (22)
unterschreiben like bleiben (20)
(sich) verbessern like fordern (26)
verbringen like denken (16)
verdienen like machen (3)
vereinbaren like machen (3)
vergessen like essen (21)
verkaufen like machen (3)
verkünden like arbeiten (1)
(sich) verlaufen like laufen (34)
(sich) verletzen like machen (3)
(sich) verlieben like machen (3)
verlieren like schieben (42)
verschmutzen (*sein*) like machen (3)
(sich) verspäten like sich freuen (6)
(sich) verstauchen like machen (3)
verstehen like stehen (48)
(sich) vorbereiten* like arbeiten (1)
vormachen* like machen (3)

vorschlagen* like tragen (51)
(sich) vorstellen* like machen (3)
wachsen (*sein*) (54)
wandern (*sein*) like fordern (26)
warten like arbeiten (1)
(sich) waschen (54)
wegräumen* like machen (3)
wegwerfen* like helfen (32)
weinen like machen (3)
werden (*sein*) (9)
wettmachen* like machen (3)
wiederholen like machen (3)
wiegen like schieben (41)
wischen like machen (3)
wissen (55)
wohnen like machen (3)
wollen (15)
(sich) wünschen like machen (3)
zeigen like machen (3)
ziehen (*sein*) like schieben (41)
zubereiten* like arbeiten (1)
zumachen* like machen (3)
(sich) zurechtfinden* like trinken (51)
zurückkommen* (*sein*) like kommen (33)
zuschauen* like machen (3)

Regular verbs: simple tenses

Infinitiv / Partizip I / Partizip II / Perfekt	INDIKATIV Präsens	Präteritum	Plusquamperfekt	KONJUNKTIV I Präsens	KONJUNKTIV II Präsens	Perfekt	IMPERATIV
1 arbeiten (to work) arbeitend gearbeitet gearbeitet haben	arbeite arbeitest arbeitet arbeiten arbeitet arbeiten	arbeitete arbeitetest arbeitete arbeiteten arbeitetet arbeiteten	hatte gearbeitet hattest gearbeitet hatte gearbeitet hatten gearbeitet hattet gearbeitet hatten gearbeitet	arbeite arbeitest arbeite arbeiten arbeitet arbeiten	arbeitete arbeitetest arbeitete arbeiteten arbeitetet arbeiteten	hätte gearbeitet hättest gearbeitet hätte gearbeitet hätten gearbeitet hättet gearbeitet hätten gearbeitet	arbeite arbeiten wir arbeitet arbeiten Sie
2 feiern (to celebrate) feiernd gefeiert gefeiert haben	feiere feierst feiert feiern feiert feiern	feierte feiertest feierte feierten feiertet feierten	hatte gefeiert hattest gefeiert hatte gefeiert hatten gefeiert hattet gefeiert hatten gefeiert	feiere feierest feiere feiern feiert feiern	feierte feiertest feierte feierten feiertet feierten	hätte gefeiert hättest gefeiert hätte gefeiert hätten gefeiert hättet gefeiert hätten gefeiert	feiere feiern wir feiert feiern Sie
3 machen (to make; to do) machend gemacht gemacht haben	mache machst macht machen macht machen	machte machtest machte machten machtet machten	hatte gemacht hattest gemacht hatte gemacht hatten gemacht hattet gemacht hatten gemacht	mache machest mache machen machet machen	machte machtest machte machten machtet machten	hätte gemacht hättest gemacht hätte gemacht hätten gemacht hättet gemacht hätten gemacht	mache/mach machen wir macht machen Sie
4 probieren (to try) probierend probiert probiert haben	probiere probierst probiert probieren probiert probieren	probierte probiertest probierte probierten probiertet probierten	hatte probiert hattest probiert hatte probiert hatten probiert hattet probiert hatten probiert	probiere probierest probiere probieren probieret probieren	probierte probiertest probierte probierten probiertet probierten	hätte probiert hättest probiert hätte probiert hätten probiert hättet probiert hätten probiert	probiere/probier probieren wir probiert probieren Sie
5 sammeln (to collect) sammelnd gesammelt gesammelt haben	sammle sammelst sammelt sammeln sammelt sammeln	sammelte sammeltest sammelte sammelten sammeltet sammelten	hatte gesammelt hattest gesammelt hatte gesammelt hatten gesammelt hattet gesammelt hatten gesammelt	sammle sammlest sammle sammlen sammlet sammlen	sammelte sammeltest sammelte sammelten sammeltet sammelten	hätte gesammelt hättest gesammelt hätte gesammelt hätten gesammelt hättet gesammelt hätten gesammelt	sammle sammeln wir sammelt sammeln Sie

Reflexive verbs

6 — Infinitiv: **sich freuen** (*to be happy*); Partizip I: sich freuend; Partizip II: sich gefreut; Perfekt: sich gefreut haben

	INDIKATIV			KONJUNKTIV I	KONJUNKTIV II		IMPERATIV
	Präsens	Präteritum	Plusquamperfekt	Präsens	Präsens	Perfekt	
	freue mich	freute mich	hatte mich gefreut	freue mich	freute mich	hätte mich gefreut	
	freust dich	freutest dich	hattest dich gefreut	freuest dich	freutest dich	hättest dich gefreut	freue/freu dich
	freut sich	freute sich	hatte sich gefreut	freue sich	freute sich	hätte sich gefreut	
	freuen uns	freuten uns	hatten uns gefreut	freuen uns	freuten uns	hätten uns gefreut	freuen wir uns
	freut euch	freutet euch	hattet euch gefreut	freuet euch	freutet euch	hättet euch gefreut	freut euch
	freuen sich	freuten sich	hatten sich gefreut	freuen sich	freuten sich	hätten sich gefreut	freuen Sie sich

Auxiliary verbs

7 — Infinitiv: **haben** (*to have*); Partizip I: habend; Partizip II: gehabt; Perfekt: gehabt haben

	INDIKATIV			KONJUNKTIV I	KONJUNKTIV II		IMPERATIV
	Präsens	Präteritum	Plusquamperfekt	Präsens	Präsens	Perfekt	
	habe	hatte	hatte gehabt	habe	hätte	hätte gehabt	
	hast	hattest	hattest gehabt	habest	hättest	hättest gehabt	habe/hab
	hat	hatte	hatte gehabt	habe	hätte	hätte gehabt	
	haben	hatten	hatten gehabt	haben	hätten	hätten gehabt	haben wir
	habt	hattet	hattet gehabt	habet	hättet	hättet gehabt	habt
	haben	hatten	hatten gehabt	haben	hätten	hätten gehabt	haben Sie

8 — Infinitiv: **sein** (*to be*); Partizip I: seiend; Partizip II: gewesen; Perfekt: gewesen sein

	INDIKATIV			KONJUNKTIV I	KONJUNKTIV II		IMPERATIV
	Präsens	Präteritum	Plusquamperfekt	Präsens	Präsens	Perfekt	
	bin	war	war gewesen	sei	wäre	wäre gewesen	
	bist	warst	warst gewesen	seiest/seist	wärst/wärest	wärst/wärest gewesen	sei
	ist	war	war gewesen	sei	wäre	wäre gewesen	
	sind	waren	waren gewesen	seien	wären	wären gewesen	seien wir
	seid	wart	wart gewesen	seiet	wärt/wäret	wärt/wäret gewesen	seid
	sind	waren	waren gewesen	seien	wären	wären gewesen	seien Sie

9 — Infinitiv: **werden** (*to become*); Partizip I: werdend; Partizip II: geworden; Perfekt: geworden sein

	INDIKATIV			KONJUNKTIV I	KONJUNKTIV II		IMPERATIV
	Präsens	Präteritum	Plusquamperfekt	Präsens	Präsens	Perfekt	
	werde	wurde	war geworden	werde	würde	wäre geworden	
	wirst	wurdest	warst geworden	werdest	würdest	wärst geworden	werde
	wird	wurde	war geworden	werde	würde	wäre geworden	
	werden	wurden	waren geworden	werden	würden	wären geworden	werden wir
	werdet	wurdet	wart geworden	werdet	würdet	wärt geworden	werdet
	werden	wurden	waren geworden	werden	würden	wären geworden	werden Sie

Compound tenses

Hilfsverb	INDIKATIV		KONJUNKTIV I		KONJUNKTIV II	
	Perfekt	**Plusquamperfekt**	**Präsens**	**Perfekt**	**Präsens**	**Perfekt**
haben	habe	hatte	habe		hätte	
	hast	hattest	habest		hättest	
	hat gemacht	hatte gemacht	habe gemacht	gemacht	hätte gemacht	gemacht
	haben gearbeitet	hatten gearbeitet	haben gearbeitet	gearbeitet	hätten gearbeitet	gearbeitet
	habt studiert	hattet studiert	habet studiert	studiert	hättet studiert	studiert
	haben gefeiert	hatten gefeiert	haben gefeiert	gefeiert	hätten gefeiert	gefeiert
	gesammelt	gesammelt	gesammelt	gesammelt	gesammelt	gesammelt
sein	bin gegangen	war gegangen	sei gegangen		wäre gegangen	
	bist gegangen	warst gegangen	seiest/seist gegangen		wärst/wärest gegangen	
	ist gegangen	war gegangen	sei gegangen		wäre gegangen	
	sind gegangen	waren gegangen	seien gegangen		wären gegangen	
	seid gegangen	wart gegangen	seiet gegangen		wärt/wäret gegangen	
	sind gegangen	waren gegangen	seien gegangen		wären gegangen	

	Futur I/II	**Futur I/II**	**Futur I/II**
werden	werde machen / gemacht haben	werde machen / gemacht haben	würde machen / gemacht haben
	wirst machen / gemacht haben	werdest machen / gemacht haben	würdest machen / gemacht haben
	wird machen / gemacht haben	werde machen / gemacht haben	würde machen / gemacht haben
	werden machen / gemacht haben	werden machen / gemacht haben	würden machen / gemacht haben
	werdet machen / gemacht haben	werdet machen / gemacht haben	würdet machen / gemacht haben
	werden machen / gemacht haben	werden machen / gemacht haben	würden machen / gemacht haben

Modal verbs

Infinitiv / Partizip I / Partizip II / Perfekt	INDIKATIV Präsens	INDIKATIV Präteritum	INDIKATIV Plusquamperfekt	KONJUNKTIV I Präsens	KONJUNKTIV II Präsens	KONJUNKTIV II Perfekt	IMPERATIV
10 dürfen (*to be permitted to*) / dürfend / gedurft/dürfen / gedurft haben	darf / darfst / darf / dürfen / dürft / dürfen	durfte / durftest / durfte / durften / durftet / durften	hatte gedurft / hattest gedurft / hatte gedurft / hatten gedurft / hattet gedurft / hatten gedurft	dürfe / dürfest / dürfe / dürfen / dürfet / dürfen	dürfte / dürftest / dürfte / dürften / dürftet / dürften	hätte gedurft / hättest gedurft / hätte gedurft / hätten gedurft / hättet gedurft / hätten gedurft	*Modal verbs are not used in the imperative.*
11 können (*to be able to*) / könnend / gekonnt/können / gekonnt haben	kann / kannst / kann / können / könnt / können	konnte / konntest / konnte / konnten / konntet / konnten	hatte gekonnt / hattest gekonnt / hatte gekonnt / hatten gekonnt / hattet gekonnt / hatten gekonnt	könne / könnest / könne / können / könnet / können	könnte / könntest / könnte / könnten / könntet / könnten	hätte gekonnt / hättest gekonnt / hätte gekonnt / hätten gekonnt / hättet gekonnt / hätten gekonnt	*Modal verbs are not used in the imperative.*
12 mögen (*to like*) / mögend / gemocht/mögen / gemocht haben	mag / magst / mag / mögen / mögt / mögen	mochte / mochtest / mochte / mochten / mochtet / mochten	hatte gemocht / hattest gemocht / hatte gemocht / hatten gemocht / hattet gemocht / hatten gemocht	möge / mögest / möge / mögen / möget / mögen	möchte / möchtest / möchte / möchten / möchtet / möchten	hätte gemocht / hättest gemocht / hätte gemocht / hätten gemocht / hättet gemocht / hätten gemocht	*Modal verbs are not used in the imperative.*
13 müssen (*to have to*) / müssend / gemusst/müssen / gemusst haben	muss / musst / muss / müssen / müsst / müssen	musste / musstest / musste / mussten / musstet / mussten	hatte gemusst / hattest gemusst / hatte gemusst / hatten gemusst / hattet gemusst / hatten gemusst	müsse / müssest / müsse / müssen / müsset / müssen	müsste / müsstest / müsste / müssten / müsstet / müssten	hätte gemusst / hättest gemusst / hätte gemusst / hätten gemusst / hättet gemusst / hätten gemusst	*Modal verbs are not used in the imperative.*
14 sollen (*to be supposed to*) / sollend / gesollt/sollen / gesollt haben	soll / sollst / soll / sollen / sollt / sollen	sollte / solltest / sollte / sollten / solltet / sollten	hatte gesollt / hattest gesollt / hatte gesollt / hatten gesollt / hattet gesollt / hatten gesollt	solle / sollest / solle / sollen / sollet / sollen	sollte / solltest / sollte / sollten / solltet / sollten	hätte gesollt / hättest gesollt / hätte gesollt / hätten gesollt / hättet gesollt / hätten gesollt	*Modal verbs are not used in the imperative.*
15 wollen (*to want to*) / wollend / gewollt/wollen / gewollt haben	will / willst / will / wollen / wollt / wollen	wollte / wolltest / wollte / wollten / wolltet / wollten	hatte gewollt / hattest gewollt / hatte gewollt / hatten gewollt / hattet gewollt / hatten gewollt	wolle / wollest / wolle / wollen / wollet / wollen	wollte / wolltest / wollte / wollten / wolltet / wollten	hätte gewollt / hättest gewollt / hätte gewollt / hätten gewollt / hättet gewollt / hätten gewollt	*Modal verbs are not used in the imperative.*

Mixed verbs

Infinitiv	INDIKATIV			KONJUNKTIV I	KONJUNKTIV II		IMPERATIV
Partizip I / Partizip II / Perfekt	Präsens	Präteritum	Plusquamperfekt	Präsens	Präsens	Perfekt	
16 denken	denke	dachte	hatte gedacht	denke	dächte	hätte gedacht	
(to think)	denkst	dachtest	hattest gedacht	denkest	dächtest	hättest gedacht	denke/denk
denkend	denkt	dachte	hatte gedacht	denke	dächte	hätte gedacht	
gedacht	denken	dachten	hatten gedacht	denken	dächten	hätten gedacht	denken wir
gedacht haben	denkt	dachtet	hattet gedacht	denket	dächtet	hättet gedacht	denkt
	denken	dachten	hatten gedacht	denken	dächten	hätten gedacht	denken Sie
17 rennen	renne	rannte	war gerannt	renne	rennte	wäre gerannt	
(to run)	rennst	ranntest	warst gerannt	rennest	renntest	wärest gerannt	renne/renn
denkend	rennt	rannte	war gerannt	renne	rennte	wäre gerannt	
gerannt	rennen	rannten	waren gerannt	rennen	rennten	wären gerannt	rennen wir
gerannt sein	rennt	ranntet	wart gerannt	rennet	renntet	wärt gerannt	rennt
	rennen	rannten	waren gerannt	rennen	rennten	wären gerannt	rennen Sie
18 senden	sende	sandte	hatte gesandt	sende	sendete	hätte gesandt	
(to send)	sendest	sandtest	hattest gesandt	sendest	sendetest	hättest gesandt	sende
sendend	sendet	sandte	hatte gesandt	sende	sendete	hätte gesandt	
gesendet	senden	sandten	hatten gesandt	senden	sendeten	hätten gesandt	senden wir
gesendet haben	sendet	sandtet	hattet gesandt	sendet	sendetet	hättet gesandt	sendet
	senden	sandten	hatten gesandt	senden	sendeten	hätten gesandt	senden Sie

Irregular verbs

Infinitiv	INDIKATIV			KONJUNKTIV I	KONJUNKTIV II		IMPERATIV
Partizip I / Partizip II / Perfekt	Präsens	Präteritum	Plusquamperfekt	Präsens	Präsens	Perfekt	
19 bitten	bitte	bat	hatte gebeten	bitte	bäte	hätte gebeten	
(to ask)	bittest	batest	hattest gebeten	bittest	bätest	hättest gebeten	bitte
bittend	bittet	bat	hatte gebeten	bitte	bäte	hätte gebeten	
gebeten	bitten	baten	hatten gebeten	bitten	bäten	hätten gebeten	bitten wir
gebeten haben	bittet	batet	hattet gebeten	bittet	bätet	hättet gebeten	bittet
	bitten	baten	hatten gebeten	bitten	bäten	hätten gebeten	bitten Sie
20 bleiben	bleibe	blieb	war geblieben	bleibe	bliebe	wäre geblieben	
(to stay)	bleibst	bliebst	warst geblieben	bleibest	bliebest	wärest geblieben	bleibe/bleib
bleibend	bleibt	blieb	war geblieben	bleibe	bliebe	wäre geblieben	
geblieben	bleiben	blieben	waren geblieben	bleiben	blieben	wären geblieben	bleiben wir
geblieben sein	bleibt	bliebt	wart geblieben	bleibet	bliebet	wärt geblieben	bleibt
	bleiben	blieben	waren geblieben	bleiben	blieben	wären geblieben	bleiben Sie

	Infinitiv / Partizip I / Partizip II / Perfekt	INDIKATIV Präsens	INDIKATIV Präteritum	INDIKATIV Plusquamperfekt	KONJUNKTIV I Präsens	KONJUNKTIV II Präsens	KONJUNKTIV II Perfekt	IMPERATIV
21	**essen** (to eat) / essend / gegessen / gegessen haben	esse	aß	hatte gegessen	esse	äße	hätte gegessen	
		isst	aßest	hattest gegessen	essest	äßest	hättest gegessen	iss
		isst	aß	hatte gegessen	esse	äße	hätte gegessen	
		essen	aßen	hatten gegessen	essen	äßen	hätten gegessen	essen wir
		esst	aßt	hattet gegessen	esset	äßet	hättet gegessen	esst
		essen	aßen	hatten gegessen	essen	äßen	hätten gegessen	essen Sie
22	**fallen** (to fall) / fallend / gefallen / gefallen sein	falle	fiel	war gefallen	falle	fiele	wäre gefallen	
		fällst	fielst	warst gefallen	fallest	fielest	wärest gefallen	falle/fall
		fällt	fiel	war gefallen	falle	fiele	wäre gefallen	
		fallen	fielen	waren gefallen	fallen	fielen	wären gefallen	fallen wir
		fallt	fielt	wart gefallen	fallet	fielet	wäret gefallen	fallt
		fallen	fielen	waren gefallen	fallen	fielen	wären gefallen	fallen Sie
23	**fangen** (to catch) / fangend / gefangen / gefangen haben	fange	fing	hatte gefangen	fange	finge	hätte gefangen	
		fängst	fingst	hattest gefangen	fangest	fingest	hättest gefangen	fange/fang
		fängt	fing	hatte gefangen	fange	finge	hätte gefangen	
		fangen	fingen	hatten gefangen	fangen	fingen	hätten gefangen	fangen wir
		fangt	fingt	hattet gefangen	fanget	finget	hättet gefangen	fangt
		fangen	fingen	hatten gefangen	fangen	fingen	hätten gefangen	fangen Sie
24	**flechten** (to braid) / flechtend / geflochten / geflochten haben	flechte	flocht	hatte geflochten	flechte	flöchte	hätte geflochten	
		flichst	flochtest	hattest geflochten	flechtest	flöchtest	hättest geflochten	flicht
		flicht	flocht	hatte geflochten	flechte	flöchte	hätte geflochten	
		flechten	flochten	hatten geflochten	flechten	flöchten	hätten geflochten	flechten wir
		flechtet	flochtet	hattet geflochten	flechtet	flöchtet	hättet geflochten	flechtet
		flechten	flochten	hatten geflochten	flechten	flöchten	hätten geflochten	flechten Sie
25	**fließen** (to flow) / fließend / geflossen / geflossen sein	fließe	floss	war geflossen	fließe	flösse	wäre geflossen	
		fließt	flossest/flosst	warst geflossen	fließest	flössest	wärest geflossen	fließe/fließ
		fließt	floss	war geflossen	fließe	flösse	wäre geflossen	
		fließen	flossen	waren geflossen	fließen	flössen	wären geflossen	fließen wir
		fließt	flosst	wart geflossen	fließet	flösset	wärt geflossen	fließt
		fließen	flossen	waren geflossen	fließen	flössen	wären geflossen	fließen Sie
26	**fordern** (to demand) / fordernd / gefordert / gefordert haben	ford(e)re	forderte	hatte gefordert	fordere	forderte	hätte gefordert	
		forderst	fordertest	hattest gefordert	forderest	fordertest	hättest gefordert	fordere/fordre
		fordert	forderte	hatte gefordert	fordere	forderte	hätte gefordert	
		fordern	forderten	hatten gefordert	forderen	forderten	hätten gefordert	fordern wir
		fordert	fordertet	hattet gefordert	forderet	fordertet	hättet gefordert	fordert
		fordern	forderten	hatten gefordert	forderen	forderten	hätten gefordert	fordern Sie
27	**fragen** (to ask) / fragend / gefragt / gefragt haben	frage	fragte	hatte gefragt	frage	fragte	hätte gefragt	
		fragst	fragtest	hattest gefragt	fragest	fragtest	hättest gefragt	frage/frag
		fragt	fragte	hatte gefragt	frage	fragte	hätte gefragt	
		fragen	fragten	hatten gefragt	fragen	fragten	hätten gefragt	fragen wir
		fragt	fragtet	hattet gefragt	fraget	fragtet	hättet gefragt	fragt
		fragen	fragten	hatten gefragt	fragen	fragten	hätten gefragt	fragen Sie

Infinitiv / Partizip I / Partizip II / Perfekt	INDIKATIV Präsens	Präteritum	Plusquamperfekt	KONJUNKTIV I Präsens	KONJUNKTIV II Präsens	KONJUNKTIV II Perfekt	IMPERATIV
28 geben *(to give)* gebend gegeben gegeben haben	gebe gibst gibt geben gebt geben	gab gabst gab gaben gabt gaben	hatte gegeben hattest gegeben hatte gegeben hatten gegeben hattet gegeben hatten gegeben	gebe gebest gebe geben gebet geben	gäbe gäbest gäbe gäben gäbet gäben	hätte gegeben hättest gegeben hätte gegeben hätten gegeben hättet gegeben hätten gegeben	gib geben wir gebt geben Sie
29 gehen *(to go)* gehend gegangen gegangen sein	gehe gehst geht gehen geht gehen	ging gingst ging gingen gingt gingen	war gegangen warst gegangen war gegangen waren gegangen wart gegangen waren gegangen	gehe gehest gehe gehen gehet gehen	ginge gingest ginge gingen ginget gingen	wäre gegangen wärest gegangen wäre gegangen wären gegangen wäret gegangen wären gegangen	gehe/geh gehen wir geht gehen Sie
30 heben *(to lift)* hebend gehoben gehoben haben	hebe hebst hebt heben hebt heben	hob hobst hob hoben hobt hoben	hatte gehoben hattest gehoben hatte gehoben hatten gehoben hattet gehoben hatten gehoben	hebe hebest hebe heben hebet heben	höbe höbest/höbst höbe höben höbet/höbt höben	hätte gehoben hättest gehoben hätte gehoben hätten gehoben hättet gehoben hätten gehoben	hebe/heb heben wir hebt heben Sie
31 heißen *(to be called)* heißend geheißen geheißen haben	heiße heißt heißt heißen heißt heißen	hieß hießest hieß hießen hießt hießen	hatte geheißen hattest geheißen hatte geheißen hatten geheißen hattet geheißen hatten geheißen	heiße heißest heiße heißen heißet heißen	hieße hießest hieße hießen hießet hießen	hätte geheißen hättest geheißen hätte geheißen hätten geheißen hättet geheißen hätten geheißen	heiß/heiße heißen wir heißt heißen Sie
32 helfen *(to help)* helfend geholfen geholfen haben	helfe hilfst hilft helfen helft helfen	half halfst half halfen halft halfen	hatte geholfen hattest geholfen hatte geholfen hatten geholfen hattet geholfen hatten geholfen	helfe helfest helfe helfen helfet helfen	hälfe hälfest/hälfst hälfe hälfen hälfet/hälft hälfen	hätte geholfen hättest geholfen hätte geholfen hätten geholfen hättet geholfen hätten geholfen	hilf helfen wir helft helfen Sie
33 kommen *(to come)* kommend gekommen gekommen sein	komme kommst kommt kommen kommt kommen	kam kamst kam kamen kamt kamen	war gekommen warst gekommen war gekommen waren gekommen wart gekommen waren gekommen	komme kommest komme kommen kommet kommen	käme kämest käme kämen kämet kämen	wäre gekommen wärest gekommen wäre gekommen wären gekommen wäret gekommen wären gekommen	komme/komm kommen wir kommt kommen Sie
34 laufen *(to run)* laufend gelaufen gelaufen sein	laufe läufst läuft laufen lauft laufen	lief liefst lief liefen lieft liefen	war gelaufen warst gelaufen war gelaufen waren gelaufen wart gelaufen waren gelaufen	laufe laufest laufe laufen laufet laufen	liefe liefest liefe liefen liefet liefen	wäre gelaufen wärest gelaufen wäre gelaufen wären gelaufen wäret gelaufen wären gelaufen	laufe/lauf laufen wir lauft laufen Sie

	Infinitiv	INDIKATIV			KONJUNKTIV I	KONJUNKTIV II		IMPERATIV
	Partizip I / Partizip II / Perfekt	Präsens	Präteritum	Plusquamperfekt	Präsens	Präsens	Perfekt	
35	**liegen** (to lie; to be lying) liegend gelegen gelegen haben	liege liegst liegt liegen liegt liegen	lag lagst lag lagen lagt lagen	hatte gelegen hattest gelegen hatte gelegen hatten gelegen hattet gelegen hatten gelegen	liege liegest liege liegen lieget liegen	läge lägest läge lägen läget lägen	hätte gelegen hättest gelegen hätte gelegen hätten gelegen hättet gelegen hätten gelegen	liege/lieg liegen wir liegt liegen Sie
36	**lügen** (to lie) lügend gelogen gelogen haben	lüge lügst lügt lügen lügt lügen	log logst log logen logt logen	hatte gelogen hattest gelogen hatte gelogen hatten gelogen hattet gelogen hatten gelogen	lüge lügest lüge lügen lüget lügen	löge lögest löge lögen löget lögen	hätte gelogen hättest gelogen hätte gelogen hätten gelogen hättet gelogen hätten gelogen	lüge/lüg lügen wir lügt lügen Sie
37	**mahlen** (to grind) mahlend gemahlt/gemahlen gemahlt/gemahlen haben	mahle mahlst mahlt mahlen mahlt mahlen	mahlte mahltest mahlte mahlten mahltet mahlten	hatte gemahlt/gemahlen hattest gemahlt/gemahlen hatte gemahlt/gemahlen hatten gemahlt/gemahlen hattet gemahlt/gemahlen hatten gemahlt/gemahlen	mahle mahlest mahle mahlen mahlet mahlen	mahlte mahltest mahlte mahlten mahltet mahlten	hätte gemahlt/gemahlen hättest gemahlt/gemahlen hätte gemahlt/gemahlen hätten gemahlt/gemahlen hättet gemahlt/gemahlen hätten gemahlt/gemahlen	mahle/mahl mahlen wir mahlt mahlen Sie
38	**nehmen** (to take) nehmend genommen genommen haben	nehme nimmst nimmt nehmen nehmt nehmen	nahm nahmst nahm nahmen nahmt nahmen	hatte genommen hattest genommen hatte genommen hatten genommen hattet genommen hatten genommen	nehme nehmest nehme nehmen nehmet nehmen	nähme nähmest nähme nähmen nähmet nähmen	hätte genommen hättest genommen hätte genommen hätten genommen hättet genommen hätten genommen	nimm nehmen wir nehmt nehmen Sie
39	**pfeifen** (to whistle) pfeifend gepfiffen gepfiffen haben	pfeife pfeifst pfeift pfeifen pfeift pfeifen	pfiff pfiffst pfiff pfiffen pfifft pfiffen	hatte gepfiffen hattest gepfiffen hatte gepfiffen hatten gepfiffen hattet gepfiffen hatten gepfiffen	pfeife pfeifest pfeife pfeifen pfeifet pfeifen	pfiffe pfiffest pfiffe pfiffen pfiffet pfiffen	hätte gepfiffen hättest gepfiffen hätte gepfiffen hätten gepfiffen hättet gepfiffen hätten gepfiffen	pfeife/pfeif pfeifen wir pfeift pfeifen Sie
40	**rufen** (to call) rufend gerufen gerufen haben	rufe rufst ruft rufen ruft rufen	rief riefst rief riefen rieft riefen	hatte gerufen hattest gerufen hatte gerufen hatten gerufen hattet gerufen hatten gerufen	rufe rufest rufe rufen rufet rufen	riefe riefest riefe riefen riefet riefen	hätte gerufen hättest gerufen hätte gerufen hätten gerufen hättet gerufen hätten gerufen	rufe/ruf rufen wir ruft rufen Sie
41	**saugen** (to suck) saugend gesaugt/gesogen gesaugt/gesogen haben	sauge saugst saugt saugen saugt saugen	saugte/sog saugtest/sogst saugte/sog saugten/sogen saugtet/sogt saugten/sogen	hatte gesaugt/gesogen hattest gesaugt/gesogen hatte gesaugt/gesogen hatten gesaugt/gesogen hattet gesaugt/gesogen hatten gesaugt/gesogen	sauge saugest sauge saugen sauget saugen	saugte/söge saugtest/sögest saugte/söge saugten/sögen saugtet/söget saugten/sögen	hätte gesaugt/gesogen hättest gesaugt/gesogen hätte gesaugt/gesogen hätten gesaugt/gesogen hättet gesaugt/gesogen hätten gesaugt/gesogen	sauge/saug saugen wir saugt saugen Sie

	Infinitiv	INDIKATIV			KONJUNKTIV I	KONJUNKTIV II		IMPERATIV
	Partizip I Partizip II Perfekt	Präsens	Präteritum	Plusquamperfekt	Präsens	Präsens	Perfekt	
42	**schieben**	schiebe	schob	hatte geschoben	schiebe	schöbe	hätte geschoben	
	(to push)	schiebst	schobst	hattest geschoben	schiebest	schöbest	hättest geschoben	schiebe/schieb
	schiebend	schiebt	schob	hatte geschoben	schiebe	schöbe	hätte geschoben	
	geschoben	schieben	schoben	hatten geschoben	schieben	schöben	hätten geschoben	schieben wir
	geschoben haben	schiebt	schobt	hattet geschoben	schiebet	schöbet	hättet geschoben	schiebt
		schieben	schoben	hatten geschoben	schieben	schöben	hätten geschoben	schieben Sie
43	**schlafen**	schlafe	schlief	hatte geschlafen	schlafe	schliefe	hätte geschlafen	
	(to sleep)	schläfst	schliefst	hattest geschlafen	schlafest	schliefest	hättest geschlafen	schlafe/schlaf
	schlafend	schläft	schlief	hatte geschlafen	schlafe	schliefe	hätte geschlafen	
	geschlafen	schlafen	schliefen	hatten geschlafen	schlafen	schliefen	hätten geschlafen	schlafen wir
	geschlafen haben	schlaft	schlieft	hattet geschlafen	schlafet	schliefet	hättet geschlafen	schlaft
		schlafen	schliefen	hatten geschlafen	schlafen	schliefen	hätten geschlafen	schlafen Sie
44	**schwimmen**	schwimme	schwamm	war geschwommen	schwimme	schwömme	wäre geschwommen	
	(to swim)	schwimmst	schwammst	warst geschwommen	schwimmest	schwömmest	wärest geschwommen	schwimme/schwimm
	schwimmend	schwimmt	schwamm	war geschwommen	schwimme	schwömme	wäre geschwommen	
	geschwommen	schwimmen	schwammen	waren geschwommen	schwimmen	schwömmen	wären geschwommen	schwimmen wir
	geschwommen sein	schwimmt	schwammt	wart geschwommen	schwimmet	schwömmet	wäret geschwommen	schwimmt
		schwimmen	schwammen	waren geschwommen	schwimmen	schwömmen	wären geschwommen	schwimmen Sie
45	**schwören**	schwöre	schwor	hatte geschworen	schwöre	schwüre	hätte geschworen	
	(to swear)	schwörst	schworst	hattest geschworen	schwörest	schwürest/schwürst	hättest geschworen	schwöre/schwör
	schwörend	schwört	schwor	hatte geschworen	schwöre	schwüre	hätte geschworen	
	geschworen	schwören	schworen	hatten geschworen	schwören	schwüren	hätten geschworen	schwören wir
	geschworen haben	schwört	schwort	hattet geschworen	schwöret	schwüret	hättet geschworen	schwört
		schwören	schworen	hatten geschworen	schwören	schwüren	hätten geschworen	schwören Sie
46	**sitzen**	sitze	saß	hatte gesessen	sitze	säße	hätte gesessen	
	(to sit)	sitzt	saßest	hattest gesessen	sitzest	säßest	hättest gesessen	sitze/sitz
	sitzend	sitzt	saß	hatte gesessen	sitze	säße	hätte gesessen	
	gesessen	sitzen	saßen	hatten gesessen	sitzen	säßen	hätten gesessen	sitzen wir
	gesessen haben	sitzt	saßet	hattet gesessen	sitzet	säßet	hättet gesessen	sitzt
		sitzen	saßen	hatten gesessen	sitzen	säßen	hätten gesessen	sitzen Sie
47	**sprechen**	spreche	sprach	hatte gesprochen	spreche	spräche	hätte gesprochen	
	(to speak)	sprichst	sprachst	hattest gesprochen	sprechest	sprächest	hättest gesprochen	sprich
	sprechend	spricht	sprach	hatte gesprochen	spreche	spräche	hätte gesprochen	
	gesprochen	sprechen	sprachen	hatten gesprochen	sprechen	sprächen	hätten gesprochen	sprechen wir
	gesprochen haben	sprecht	spracht	hattet gesprochen	sprechet	sprächet	hättet gesprochen	sprecht
		sprechen	sprachen	hatten gesprochen	sprechen	sprächen	hätten gesprochen	sprechen Sie
48	**stehen**	stehe	stand	hatte gestanden	stehe	stünde/stände	hätte gestanden	
	(to stand)	stehst	standest/standst	hattest gestanden	stehest	stündest/ständest	hättest gestanden	stehe/steh
	stehend	steht	stand	hatte gestanden	stehe	stünde/stände	hätte gestanden	
	gestanden	stehen	standen	hatten gestanden	stehen	stünden/ständen	hätten gestanden	stehen wir
	gestanden haben	steht	standet	hattet gestanden	stehet	stündet/ständet	hättet gestanden	steht
		stehen	standen	hatten gestanden	stehen	stünden/ständen	hätten gestanden	stehen Sie

49 stehlen (to steal)

Infinitiv: **stehlen** · Partizip I: stehlend · Partizip II: gestohlen · Perfekt: gestohlen haben

	INDIKATIV Präsens	Präteritum	Plusquamperfekt	KONJUNKTIV I Präsens	KONJUNKTIV II Präsens	KONJUNKTIV II Perfekt	IMPERATIV
	stehle	stahl	hatte gestohlen	stehle	stähle/stöhle	hätte gestohlen	
	stiehlst	stahlst	hattest gestohlen	stehlest	stählest/stöhlest	hättest gestohlen	stiehl
	stiehlt	stahl	hatte gestohlen	stehle	stähle/stöhle	hätte gestohlen	
	stehlen	stahlen	hatten gestohlen	stehlen	stählen/stöhlen	hätten gestohlen	stehlen wir
	stehlt	stahlt	hattet gestohlen	stehlet	stählet/stöhlet	hättet gestohlen	stehlt
	stehlen	stahlen	hatten gestohlen	stehlen	stählen/stöhlen	hätten gestohlen	stehlen Sie

50 stoßen (to bump)

Infinitiv: **stoßen** · Partizip I: stoßend · Partizip II: gestoßen · Perfekt: gestoßen haben

	INDIKATIV Präsens	Präteritum	Plusquamperfekt	KONJUNKTIV I Präsens	KONJUNKTIV II Präsens	KONJUNKTIV II Perfekt	IMPERATIV
	stoße	stieß	hatte gestoßen	stoße	stieße	hätte gestoßen	stoße/stoß
	stößt	stießest/stießt	hattest gestoßen	stoßest	stießest	hättest gestoßen	
	stößt	stieß	hatte gestoßen	stoße	stieße	hätte gestoßen	stoße wir
	stoßen	stießen	hatten gestoßen	stoßen	stießen	hätten gestoßen	stoßen wir
	stoßt	stießt	hattet gestoßen	stoßet	stießet	hättet gestoßen	stoßt
	stoßen	stießen	hatten gestoßen	stoßen	stießen	hätten gestoßen	stoßen Sie

51 tragen (to carry)

Infinitiv: **tragen** · Partizip I: tragend · Partizip II: getragen · Perfekt: getragen haben

	INDIKATIV Präsens	Präteritum	Plusquamperfekt	KONJUNKTIV I Präsens	KONJUNKTIV II Präsens	KONJUNKTIV II Perfekt	IMPERATIV
	trage	trug	hatte getragen	trage	trüge	hätte getragen	
	trägst	trugst	hattest getragen	tragest	trügest	hättest getragen	trage/trag
	trägt	trug	hatte getragen	trage	trüge	hätte getragen	
	tragen	trugen	hatten getragen	tragen	trügen	hätten getragen	tragen wir
	tragt	trugt	hattet getragen	traget	trüget	hättet getragen	tragt
	tragen	trugen	hatten getragen	tragen	trügen	hätten getragen	tragen Sie

52 trinken (to drink)

Infinitiv: **trinken** · Partizip I: trinkend · Partizip II: getrunken · Perfekt: getrunken haben

	INDIKATIV Präsens	Präteritum	Plusquamperfekt	KONJUNKTIV I Präsens	KONJUNKTIV II Präsens	KONJUNKTIV II Perfekt	IMPERATIV
	trinke	trank	hatte getrunken	trinke	tränke	hätte getrunken	
	trinkst	trankst	hattest getrunken	trinkest	tränkest	hättest getrunken	trinke/trink
	trinkt	trank	hatte getrunken	trinke	tränke	hätte getrunken	
	trinken	tranken	hatten getrunken	trinken	tränken	hätten getrunken	trinken wir
	trinkt	trankt	hattet getrunken	trinket	tränket	hättet getrunken	trinkt
	trinken	tranken	hatten getrunken	trinken	tränken	hätten getrunken	trinken Sie

53 tun (to do)

Infinitiv: **tun** · Partizip I: tuend · Partizip II: getan · Perfekt: getan haben

	INDIKATIV Präsens	Präteritum	Plusquamperfekt	KONJUNKTIV I Präsens	KONJUNKTIV II Präsens	KONJUNKTIV II Perfekt	IMPERATIV
	tue	tat	hatte getan	tue	täte	hätte getan	
	tust	tatest	hattest getan	tuest	tätest	hättest getan	tue/tu
	tut	tat	hatte getan	tue	täte	hätte getan	
	tun	taten	hatten getan	tuen	täten	hätten getan	tun wir
	tut	tatet	hattet getan	tuet	tätet	hättet getan	tut
	tun	taten	hatten getan	tuen	täten	hätten getan	tun Sie

54 waschen (to wash)

Infinitiv: **waschen** · Partizip I: waschend · Partizip II: gewaschen · Perfekt: gewaschen haben

	INDIKATIV Präsens	Präteritum	Plusquamperfekt	KONJUNKTIV I Präsens	KONJUNKTIV II Präsens	KONJUNKTIV II Perfekt	IMPERATIV
	wasche	wusch	hatte gewaschen	wasche	wüsche	hätte gewaschen	wasche/wasch
	wäschst	wuschest/wuschst	hattest gewaschen	waschest	wüschest/wüschst	hättest gewaschen	
	wäscht	wusch	hatte gewaschen	wasche	wüsche	hätte gewaschen	
	waschen	wuschen	hatten gewaschen	waschen	wüschen	hätten gewaschen	waschen wir
	wascht	wuscht	hattet gewaschen	waschet	wüschet/wüscht	hättet gewaschen	wascht
	waschen	wuschen	hatten gewaschen	waschen	wüschen	hätten gewaschen	waschen Sie

55 wissen (to know)

Infinitiv: **wissen** · Partizip I: wissend · Partizip II: gewusst · Perfekt: gewusst haben

	INDIKATIV Präsens	Präteritum	Plusquamperfekt	KONJUNKTIV I Präsens	KONJUNKTIV II Präsens	KONJUNKTIV II Perfekt	IMPERATIV
	weiß	wusste	hatte gewusst	wisse	wüsste	hätte gewusst	
	weißt	wusstest	hattest gewusst	wissest	wüsstest	hättest gewusst	wisse
	weiß	wusste	hatte gewusst	wisse	wüsste	hätte gewusst	
	wissen	wussten	hatten gewusst	wissen	wüssten	hätten gewusst	wissen wir
	wisst	wusstet	hattet gewusst	wisset	wüsstet	hättet gewusst	wisst
	wissen	wussten	hatten gewusst	wissen	wüssten	hätten gewusst	wissen Sie

Irregular verbs

The following is a list of the principal parts of all strong and mixed verbs that are introduced as active vocabulary in **Mosaik**, as well as other sample verbs. For the complete conjugations of these verbs, consult the verb list on pages **A14–A15** and the verb charts on pages **A16–A25**. The verbs listed here are base forms.

Infinitiv		Präteritum	Partizip II	
backen (bäckt)	*to bake*	backte	gebacken	
beginnen	*to begin*	begann	begonnen	
bieten	*to bid, to offer*	bot	geboten	
binden	*to tie, to bind*	band	gebunden	
bitten	*to request*	bat	gebeten	
bleiben	*to stay*	blieb	(ist) geblieben	
braten (brät)	*to fry, to roast*	briet	gebraten	
brechen (bricht)	*to break*	brach	gebrochen	
brennen	*to burn*	brannte	gebrannt	
bringen	*to bring*	brachte	gebracht	
denken	*to think*	dachte	gedacht	
dürfen (darf)	*to be allowed to*	durfte	gedurft	
empfehlen (empfiehlt)	*to recommend*	empfahl	empfohlen	
essen (isst)	*to eat*	aß	gegessen	
fahren (fährt)	*to go, to drive*	fuhr	(ist) gefahren	
fallen (fällt)	*to fall*	fiel	(ist) gefallen	
fangen (fängt)	*to catch*	fing	gefangen	
finden	*to find*	fand	gefunden	
fliegen	*to fly*	flog	(ist) geflogen	
fließen	*to flow, to pour*	floss	(ist) geflossen	
frieren	*to freeze*	fror	gefroren	
geben (gibt)	*to give*	gab	gegeben	
gehen	*to go, to walk*	ging	(ist) gegangen	
gelten	*to be valid*	galt	gegolten	
genießen	*to enjoy*	genoss	genossen	
geschehen	*to happen*	geschah	(ist) geschehen	
gewinnen	*to win*	gewann	gewonnen	
gleichen	*to resemble*	glich	geglichen	
graben (gräbt)	*to dig*	grub	gegraben	
haben (hat)	*to have*	hatte	gehabt	
halten (hält)	*to hold, to keep*	hielt	gehalten	
hängen	*to hang*	hing	gehangen	
heben	*to raise, to lift*	hob	gehoben	
heißen	*to be called, to mean*	hieß	geheißen	
helfen (hilft)	*to help*	half	geholfen	
kennen	*to know*	kannte	gekannt	
klingen	*to sound, to ring*	klang	geklungen	
kommen	*to come*	kam	(ist) gekommen	
können (kann)	*to be able to, can*	konnte	gekonnt	
laden (lädt)	*to load, to charge*	lud	geladen	
lassen (lässt)	*to let, to allow*	ließ	gelassen	
laufen (läuft)	*to run, to walk*	lief	(ist) gelaufen	

Infinitiv		Präteritum	Partizip II
leiden	*to suffer*	litt	gelitten
leihen	*to lend*	lieh	geliehen
lesen (liest)	*to read*	las	gelesen
liegen	*to lie, to rest*	lag	gelegen
lügen	*to lie, to tell lies*	log	gelogen
meiden	*to avoid*	mied	gemieden
messen	*to measure*	maß	gemessen
mögen (mag)	*to like*	mochte	gemocht
müssen (muss)	*to have, to must*	musste	gemusst
nehmen (nimmt)	*to take*	nahm	genommen
nennen	*to name, to call*	nannte	genannt
preisen	*to praise*	pries	gepriesen
raten (rät)	*to guess*	riet	geraten
reiben	*to rub, to grate*	rieb	gerieben
riechen	*to smell*	roch	gerochen
rufen	*to call, to shout*	rief	gerufen
schaffen (schafft)	*to accomplish*	schuf	geschaffen
scheiden	*to divorce, to depart*	schied	(ist) geschieden
scheinen	*to shine, to appear*	schien	geschienen
schieben	*to push, to shove*	schob	geschoben
schießen	*to shoot*	schoss	geschossen
schlafen (schläft)	*to sleep*	schlief	geschlafen
schlagen (schlägt)	*to beat, to hit*	schlug	geschlagen
schließen	*to close*	schloss	geschlossen
schlingen	*to loop, to gulp*	schlang	geschlungen
schneiden	*to cut*	schnitt	geschnitten
schreiben	*to write*	schrieb	geschrieben
schwimmen	*to swim*	schwamm	(ist) geschwommen
sehen	*to see*	sah	gesehen
sein (ist)	*to be*	war	(ist) gewesen
senden	*to send*	sandte/sendete	gesandt/gesendet
singen	*to sing*	sang	gesungen
sinken	*to sink*	sank	(ist) gesunken
sitzen	*to sit*	saß	gesessen
sollen (soll)	*to be supposed to*	sollte	gesollt
sprechen (spricht)	*to speak*	sprach	gesprochen
stehen	*to stand*	stand	gestanden
stehlen	*to steal*	stahl	gestohlen
steigen	*to climb, to rise*	stieg	gestiegen
sterben	*to die*	starb	(ist) gestorben
stoßen	*to push, to thrust*	stieß	gestoßen
streichen	*to paint, to cancel*	strich	gestrichen
streiten	*to argue*	stritt	gestritten
tragen (trägt)	*to carry*	trug	getragen
treffen (trifft)	*to hit, to meet*	traf	getroffen
treten (tritt)	*to kick*	trat	getreten
trinken	*to drink*	trank	getrunken
tun	*to do*	tat	getan
vergessen (vergisst)	*to forget*	vergaß	vergessen

Infinitiv		Präteritum	Partizip II	
verlieren	*to lose*	verlor	verloren	
wachsen (wächst)	*to grow*	wuchs	(ist) gewachsen	
waschen (wäscht)	*to wash*	wusch	gewaschen	
weisen	*to indicate, to show*	wies	gewiesen	
wenden	*to turn, to flip*	wandte/wendete	gewandt/gewendet	
werben	*to advertise*	warb	geworben	
werden (wird)	*to become*	wurde	(ist) geworden	
werfen (wirft)	*to throw*	warf	geworfen	
winden	*to wind*	wand	gewunden	
wissen	*to know*	wusste	gewusst	
wollen (will)	*to want*	wollte	gewollt	
ziehen	*to pull, to draw*	zog	gezogen	

Abbreviations used in this glossary

acc.	accusative	*gen.*	genitive	*poss.*	possessive
adj.	adjective	*inf.*	informal	*prep.*	preposition
adv.	adverb	*interr.*	interrogative	*pron.*	pronoun
conj.	conjunction	*m.*	masculine noun	*sing.*	singular
dat.	dative	*n.*	neuter noun	*v.*	verb
f.	feminine noun	*nom.*	nominative		
form.	formal	*pl.*	plural		

Understanding the Glossary references

The numbers following each entry can be understood as follows:

(2) 1A = (Mosaik Volume) Chapter, Lesson

So, the entry above would be found in Mosaik 2, Chapter 1, Lesson A.

Deutsch-Englisch

A

abbiegen *v.* to turn (2) **4A**
  rechts/links abbiegen *v.* to turn right/left (2) **4A**
abbrechen *v.* to cancel (2) **3B**
Abend, -e *m.* evening (1) **2B**
  abends *adv.* in the evening (1) **2A**
Abendessen, - *n.* dinner (1) **4B**
aber *conj.* but (2) **2A**
abfahren *v.* to leave (2) **4A**
Abfall, -̈e *m.* waste (3) **4B**
abfliegen *v.* to take off (2) **3B**
Abflug, -̈e *m.* departure (2) **3B**
abheben *v.* to withdraw (money) (3) **2A**
Absatz, -̈e *m.* paragraph (2) **1B**
abschicken *v.* to send (3) **3B**
Abschied, -e *m.* leave-taking; farewell (1) **1A**
Abschluss, -̈e *m.* degree (1) **2A**
  einen Abschluss machen *v.* to graduate (2) **1A**
Abschlusszeugnis, -se *n.* diploma (transcript) (1) **2A**
abstauben *v.* to dust (2) **2B**
sich abtrocknen *v.* to dry oneself off (3) **1A**
acht eight (1) **2A**
Achtung! Attention!
adoptieren *v.* to adopt (1) **3A**
Adressbuch, -̈er *n.* address book (3) **3A**
Adresse, -n *f.* address (3) **2A**
Allee, -n *f.* avenue (3) **2B**
allein *adv.* alone; by oneself (1) **4A**
Allergie, -n *f.* allergy (3) **1B**
allergisch (gegen) *adj.* allergic (to) (3) **1B**
alles *pron.* everything (2) **3B**
  Alles klar? Everything OK? (1) **1A**
  alles Gute all the best (3) **2A**
  Alles Gute zum Geburtstag! Happy birthday! (2) **1A**
Alltagsroutine *f.* daily routine (3) **1A**
  im Alltag in everyday life
als *conj.* as; when (2) **4A**
  als ob as if (3) **2A**
also *conj.* therefore; so (3) **1B**
alt *adj.* old (1) **3A**
Altkleider *f.* second-hand clothing (3) **4B**
Altpapier *n.* used paper (3) **4B**
Amerika *n.* America (3) **2B**
amerikanisch *adj.* American (3) **2B**
Amerikaner, - / Amerikanerin, -nen *m./f.* American (3) **2B**
Ampel, -n *f.* traffic light (3) **2B**

an *prep.* at; on; by; in; to (2) **1B**, (3) **2B**
Ananas, - *f.* pineapple (1) **4A**
anbieten *v.* to offer (3) **4B**
anfangen *v.* to begin (1) **4A**
Angebot, -e *n.* offer
  im Angbot on sale (2) **1B**
angeln gehen *v.* to go fishing (1) **2B**
angenehm *adj.* pleasant (3) **3B**
  Angenehm. Nice to meet you. (1) **1A**
angesagt *adj.* trendy (2) **1B**
Angestellte, -n *m./f.* employee (3) **3A**
Angst, -̈e *f.* fear (2) **3A**
  Angst haben (vor) *v.* to be afraid (of) (2) **3A**
ankommen *v.* to arrive (1) **4A**
Ankunft, -̈e *f.* arrival (2) **3B**
anmachen *v.* to turn on (2) **4B**
Anruf, -e *m.* phone call (3) **3A**
  einen Anruf entgegennehmen *v.* to answer the phone (3) **3A**
Anrufbeantworter *m.* answering machine (2) **4B**
anrufen *v.* to call (1) **4A**
  sich anrufen *v.* to call each other (3) **1A**
anschauen *v.* to watch, look at (2) **3A**
anspruchsvoll *adj.* demanding (3) **3B**
anstatt *prep.* instead of (2) **4B**
anstoßen *v.* to toast (2) **1A**
Antwort, -en *f.* answer
antworten (auf) *v.* to answer (1) **2A**, (2) **3A**
Anwendung *f.* application; usage
anziehen *v.* to put on (2) **1B**
  sich anziehen *v.* to get dressed (3) **1A**
Anzug, -̈e *m.* suit (2) **1B**
Apfel, -̈- *m.* apple (1) **1A**
Apotheke, -n *f.* pharmacy (3) **1B**
April *m.* April (1) **2A**, (2) **3A**
Arbeit, -en *f.* work (3) **3B**
  Arbeit finden *v.* to find a job (3) **3A**
arbeiten (an) *v.* to work (on) (1) **2A**, (2) **3A**
arbeitslos *adj.* unemployed (3) **2A**
Arbeitszimmer, - *n.* home office (2) **2A**
Architekt, -en / Architektin, -nen *m./f.* architect (1) **3B**
Architektur, -en *f.* architecture (1) **2A**
sich ärgern (über) *v.* to get angry (about) (3) **1A**
arm *adj.* poor; unfortunate (1) **3B**
Arm, -e *m.* arm (3) **1A**
Art, -en *f.* species; type (3) **4B**
Artischocke, -n *f.* artichoke (1) **4A**
Arzt, -̈e / Ärztin, -nen *m./f.* doctor (3) **1B**
  zum Arzt gehen *v.* to go to the doctor (3) **1B**
Assistent, -en / Assistentin, -nen *m./f.* assistant (3) **3A**

Aubergine, -n *f.* eggplant (1) **4A**
auch *adv.* also (1) **1A**
auf *prep.* on, onto, to (2) **1B**
  Auf Wiedersehen. Good-bye. (1) **1A**
aufgehen *v.* to rise (sun) (3) **4A**
auflegen *v.* to hang up (3) **3A**
aufmachen *v.* to open (2) **4B**
aufnehmen *v.* to record (2) **4B**
aufräumen *v.* to clean up (2) **2B**
aufregend *adj.* exciting (3) **4A**
aufrichtig *adj.* sincere (1) **3B**
aufstehen *v.* to get up (1) **4A**
aufwachen *v.* to wake up (3) **1A**
Auge, -n *n.* eye (1) **3A**; (3) **1A**
Augenbraue, -n *f.* eyebrow (3) **1A**
August *m.* August (1) **2A**, (2) **3A**
aus *prep.* from (1) **4A**
Ausbildung, - en *f.* education (3) **3A**
Ausdruck *m.* expression
Ausfahrt, -en *f.* exit (2) **4A**
ausfüllen *v.* to fill out (3) **2A**
  ein Formular ausfüllen *v.* to fill out a form (3) **2A**
Ausgang -̈e *m.* exit (2) **3B**
ausgefallen *adj.* offbeat (2) **1B**
ausgehen *v.* to go out (1) **4A**
Ausland *n.* abroad (2) **3B**
ausmachen *v.* to turn off (2) **4B**
sich ausruhen *v.* to rest (3) **1A**
ausschalten *v.* turn out, to turn off (3) **4B**
Aussehen *n.* look (style) (2) **1B**
außer *prep.* except (for) (1) **4B**
außerhalb *prep.* outside of (2) **4B**
Aussprache *f.* pronunciation
Aussterben *n.* extinction (3) **4B**
sich ausziehen *v.* to get undressed (3) **1A**
Auto, -s *n.* car (1) **1A**, (2) **4A**
Autobahn, -en *f.* highway (2) **4A**

B

Baby, -s *n.* baby (1) **3A**
backen *v.* to bake (1) **2B**
Bäckerei, -en *f.* bakery (1) **4A**
Badeanzug, -̈e *m.* bathing suit (2) **1B**
Bademantel, -̈- *m.* bathrobe (3) **1A**
sich baden *v.* to bathe, take a bath (3) **1A**
Badewanne, -n *f.* bathtub (2) **2A**
Badezimmer, - *n.* bathroom (2) **2A**, (3) **1A**
Bahnsteig, -e *m.* track; platform (2) **4A**
bald *adv.* soon
  Bis bald. See you soon. (1) **1A**
Balkon, - e *m.* balcony (2) **2A**

Ball, -̈e *m.* ball (1) **2B**
Ballon, -e *m.* balloon (2) **1A**
Banane, -n *f.* banana (1) **4A**
Bank, -̈e *f.* bench (3) **2B**
Bank, -en *f.* bank (3) **2A**
  auf der Bank *f.* at the bank (3) **2B**
Bankangestellte, -n *m./f.* bank employee (3) **3B**
bar *adj.* cash (3) **2A**
  bar bezahlen *v.* to pay in cash (3) **2A**
Bargeld *n.* cash (3) **2A**
Bart, -̈e *m.* beard (3) **1A**
Baseball *m.* baseball (1) **2B**
Basketball *m.* basketball (1) **2B**
Bauch, -̈e *m.* belly (3) **1A**
Bauchschmerzen *m. pl.* stomachache (3) **1B**
bauen *v.* to build (1) **2A**
Bauer, -n / Bäuerin, -nen *m./f.* farmer (3) **3B**
Bauernhof, -̈e *m.* farm (3) **4A**
Baum, -̈e *m.* tree (3) **4A**
Baumwolle *f.* cotton (2) **1B**
Baustelle, -n *f.* construction zone (2) **4A**
beantworten *v.* to answer (1) **4B**
bedeuten *v.* to mean (1) **2A**
bedeutend *adj.* important (3) **4A**
bedienen *v.* to operate, use (2) **4B**
Bedürfnisse *n./pl.* needs (3) **1B**
sich beeilen *v.* to hurry (3) **1A**
Beförderung, -en *f.* promotion (3) **3B**
beginnen *v.* to begin (2) **2A**
Begrüßung, -en *f.* greeting (1) **1A**
behaupten *v.* to claim (3) **4B**
bei *prep.* at; near; with (1) **4A**
Beilage, -n *f.* side dish (1) **4B**
Bein, -e *n.* leg (3) **1A**
Beitrag-̈e *m.* contribution (3) **4B**
bekannt *adj.* well-known (3) **2A**
bekommen *v.* to get, to receive (2) **1A**
belegen *v.* to take (a class) (1) **2A**
benutzen *v.* to use (2) **4A**
Benutzername, -n *m.* screen name (2) **4B**
Benzin, -e *n.* gasoline (2) **4A**
Berg -e *m.* mountain (1) **2B**, (3) **4A**
berichten *v.* to report (3) **4B**
Beruf, -e *m.* profession; job (1) **3B**, (3) **3A**
Berufsausbildung, -en *f.* professional training (3) **3A**
bescheiden *adj.* modest (1) **3B**
beschreiben *v.* to describe (1) **2A**
Beschreibung, -en *f.* description (1) **3B**
Besen, - *m.* broom (2) **2B**
Besitzer, - / Besitzerin, -nen *m./f.* owner (1) **3B**
besonderes special *adj.* (3) **2A**
  nichts Besonderes *adj.* nothing special (3) **2A**
besorgt worried *adj.* (1) **3B**
Besorgung, -en *f.* errand (3) **2A**
  Besorgungen machen *v.* to run errands (3) **2A**
besprechen *v.* to discuss (2) **4A**
Besprechung, -en *f.* review (2) **4B**, meeting (3) **3B**
besser *adj.* better (2) **4A**
Besserwisser, - / Besserwisserin, -nen *m./f.* know-it-all (1) **2A**
beste *adj.* best (2) **4A**
Besteck *n.* silverware (1) **4B**

bestehen *v.* to pass (a test) (1) **1B**
bestellen *v.* to order (1) **4A**
bestimmt *adv.* definitely. (1) **4A**
besuchen *v.* to visit (1) **4A**
Bett, -en *n.* bed (2) **2A**
  das Bett machen *v.* to make the bed (2) **2B**
  ins Bett gehen *v.* to go bed (3) **1A**
Bettdecke, - n *f.* duvet (2) **2B**
bevor *conj.* before (2) **4A**
sich bewegen *v.* to move (around)
sich bewerben *v.* to apply (3) **3A**
Bewerber, - / die Bewerberin, -nen *m./f.* applicant (3) **3A**
Bewertung, -en *f.* rating (2) **3B**
bezahlen *v.* to pay (for) (1) **4A**
Bibliothek, -en *f.* library (1) **1B**
Bier, -e *n.* beer (1) **4B**
bieten *v.* to offer (3) **1B**
Bild, -er *n.* picture (2) **2A**
Bildschirm, -e *m.* screen (2) **4B**
billig *adj.* cheap (2) **1B**
Bioladen, -̈ *m.* health-food store (3) **1B**
Biologie *f.* biology (1) **2A**
biologisch *adj.* organic (3) **4B**
Birne, -n *f.* pear (1) **4A**
bis *prep.* until (1) **3B**
  Bis bald. See you soon. (1) **1A**
  Bis dann. See you later. (1) **1A**
  Bis gleich. See you soon. (1) **1A**
  Bis morgen. See you tomorrow. (1) **1A**
  Bis später. See you later. (1) **1A**
  bis zu *prep.* up to; until (3) **2B**
Bitte. Please. / You're welcome. (1) **1A**
Blatt, -̈er *n.* leaf (3) **4A**
blau *adj* blue. (1) **3A**
  blaue Fleck, - e *m.* bruise (3) **1B**
bleiben *v.* to stay (2) **1B**
  Bleiben Sie bitte am Apparat. *v.* Please hold. (3) **3A**
Bleistift, -e *m.* pencil (1) **1B**
Blitz, -e *m.* lightning (2) **3A**
blond *adj.* blond (1) **3A**
  blonde Haare *n. pl.* blond hair (1) **3A**
Blume, -n *f.* flower (1) **1A**
Blumengeschäft, -e *n.* flower shop (3) **2A**
Bluse, -n *f.* blouse (2) **1B**
Blutdruck *m.* blood pressure (3) **1B**
Boden, -̈ *m.* floor; ground (2) **2A**
Bohne, -n *f.* bean (1) **4A**
  grüne Bohne *f.* green bean (1) **4A**
Boot, -e *n.* boat (1) **1B**
Bordkarte, -n *f.* boarding pass (2) **3B**
braten *v.* to fry (1) **2B**
brauchen *v.* to need (1) **2A**
braun *adj.* brown (2) **1B**
braunhaarig *adj.* brown-haired, brunette (1) **3A**
brechen *v.* to break (1) **2B**
  sich (den Arm / das Bein) brechen *v.* to break (an arm / a leg) (3) **1B**
Bremse, -n *f.* brake (2) **4A**
brennen *v.* to burn (2) **1A**
Brief, -e *m.* letter (3) **2A**
  einen Brief abschicken *v.* to mail a letter (3) **2A**

Briefkasten, -̈ *m.* mailbox (3) **2A**
Briefmarke, -n *f.* stamp (3) **2A**
Briefträger, - / Briefträgerin, -nen *m./f.* mail carrier (3) **2A**
Briefumschlag, -̈e *m.* envelope (3) **2A**
Brille, -n *f.* glasses (2) **1B**
bringen *v.* to bring (1) **2A**
Brot, -e *n.* bread (1) **4A**
Brötchen, - *n.* roll (1) **4A**
Brücke, -n *f.* bridge (3) **2B**
Bruder, -̈ *m.* brother (1) **1A**
brünett *adj.* brown-haired, brunette (1) **3A**
Brunnen, - *m.* fountain (3) **2B**
Buch, -̈er *n.* book (1) **1A**
buchen *v.* to make a (hotel) reservation (2) **3B**
Bücherregal, -e *n.* bookshelf (2) **2A**
Buchhalter, - / Buchhalterin, -nen *m./f.* accountant (3) **3B**
büffeln *v.* to cram (for a test) (1) **2A**
Bügelbrett, -er *n.* ironing board (2) **2B**
Bügeleisen, - . *n.* iron (2) **2B**
bügeln *v.* to iron (2) **2B**
Bundespräsident, -en / Bundespräsidentin, -nen *m./f.* (federal) president (2) **4B**
bunt *adj.* colorful (3) **2A**
Bürgermeister, - / Bürgermeisterin, -nen *m./f.* mayor (3) **2B**
Bürgersteig, -e *m.* sidewalk (3) **2B**
Büro, -s *n.* office (3) **3B**
Büroklammer, -n *f.* paperclip (3) **3A**
Büromaterial *n.* office supplies (3) **3A**
Bürste, -n *f.* brush (3) **1A**
bürsten *v.* to brush
  sich die Haare bürsten *v.* to brush one's hair (3) **1A**
Bus, -se *m.* bus (2) **4A**
Busch, -̈e *m.* bush (3) **4A**
Bushaltestelle, -n *f.* bus stop (2) **4A**
Businessklasse *f.* business class (2) **3B**
Bußgeld, -er *n.* fine (monetary) (2) **4A**
Butter *f.* butter (1) **4A**

C

Café, -s *n.* café (1) **2A**
Cafeteria (*pl.* Cafeterien) *f.* cafeteria
Camping *n.* camping (1) **2B**
CD, -s *f.* compact disc, CD (2) **4B**
CD-Player, - *m.* CD player (2) **4B**
Chef, -s / Chefin, -nen *m./f.* boss (3) **3B**
Chemie *f.* chemistry (1) **2A**
China *n.* China (3) **2B**
Chinese, -n / Chinesin, -nen *m./f.* Chinese (person) (3) **2B**
Chinesisch *n.* Chinese (language) (3) **2B**
Computer, - *m.* computer (1) **1B**
Cousin, -s / Cousine, -n *m./f.* cousin (3) **3A**

D

da there (1) **1A**
  Da ist/sind... There is/are... (1) **1A**
Dachboden, -̈ *m.* attic (2) **2A**
dafür *adv.* for it (2) **2A**

daher *adv.* from there (2) **2A**
dahin *adv.* there (2) **2A**
damit *conj.* so that (3) **2A**
danach *conj.* Then, after that (3) **1B**
danken *v.* to thank (1) **2A**
   Danke. Thank you. (1) **1A**
dann *adv.* then (2) **3B**
daran *adv.* on it (2) **2A**
darauf *adv.* on it (2) **2A**
darin *adv.* in it (2) **2A**
das *n.* the; this/that (1) **1A**
dass *conj.* that (3) **2A**
Datei, - en *f.* file (2) **4B**
Datum (*pl.* **Daten**) *n.* date (3) **3A**
davon *adv.* of it (2) **2A**
davor *adv.* before it (2) **2A**
Decke, -n *f.* blanket (2) **2B**
decken *v.* to cover (2) **2B**
   den Tisch decken *v.* to set the table (2) **2B**
denken *v.* to think (2) **1A**
   denken an *v.* to think about (2) **3A**
denn *conj.* for; because (2) **2A**
der (*m.*) the (1) **1A**
deshalb *conj.* Therefore; so (3) **1B**
deswegen *conj.* that's why; therefore (3) **1B**
deswegen *conj.* that's why; therefore (3) **1B**
deutsch German *adj.* (3) **2A**
Deutsch German (language) *n.* (3) **2B**
Deutsche *m./f.* German (man/woman) (3) **2B**
Deutschland *n.* Germany (1) **4A**
   deutschsprachig *adj.* German-speaking
Dezember *m.* December (1) **2A**, (2) **3A**
Diät, -en *f.* diet (1) **4B**
   auf Diät sein *v.* to be on a diet (1) **4B**
dick *adj.* fat (1) **3A**
die the (1) **1A**
Dienstag, -e *m.* Tuesday (1) **2A**
   dienstags *adv.* on Tuesdays (1) **2A**
dieser/diese/dieses *pron.* this; these (2) **4B**
diesmal *adv.* this time (2) **3B**
Digitalkamera, -s *f.* digital camera (2) **4B**
Ding, -e *n.* thing
Diplom, -e *n.* diploma (degree) (1) **2A**
diskret *adj.* discreet (1) **3B**
doch *adv.* yes (contradicting a negative statement or question) (1) **2B**
Dokument, -e *n.* document (2) **4B**
Donner, - *m.* thunder (2) **3A**
Donnerstag, -e *n.* Thursday (1) **2A**
   donnerstags *adv.* on Thursdays (1) **2A**
dort *adv.* there (1) **1A**
Dozent, -en / Dozentin, -nen *m./f.* college instructor (1) **2A**
draußen *prep.* outside (2) **2A**, *adv.* out (2) **3A**
   Es ist schön draußen. It's nice out. (2) **3A**
dreckig *adj.* filthy (2) **2B**
drei three (1) **2A**
dritte third *adj.* (1) **2A**
Drogerie, -n *f.* drugstore (3) **2A**
drüben *adv.* over there (1) **4A**
drücken *v.* to push (1) **3B**; to print (2) **4B**
Drucker, - *m.* printer (2) **4B**
du *pron.* (*sing. inf.*) you (1) **1A**

dumm *adj.* dumb (2) **4A**
dunkel *adj.* dark (1) **3A**
dunkelhaarig *adj.* dark-haired (1) **3A**
dünn *adj.* thin (1) **3A**
durch *prep.* through (1) **3B**
durchfallen *v.* to flunk; to fail (1) **1B**
durchmachen *v.* to experience (2) **4B**
dürfen *v.* to be allowed to; may (1) **3B**
(sich) duschen *v.* to take a shower (3) **1A**
Dutzend, -e *n.* dozen (1) **4A**
DVD, -s *f.* DVD (2) **4B**
DVD-Player, - *m.* DVD-player (2) **4B**
dynamisch *adj.* dynamic (1) **3B**

E

Ecke, -n *f.* corner (3) **2B**
egoistisch *adj.* selfish (1) **3B**
Ehe, -n *f.* marriage (2) **1A**
Ehefrau, -en *f.* wife (1) **3A**
Ehemann, -̈er *m.* husband (1) **3A**
Ei, -er *n.* egg (1) **4A**
Eichhörnchen, - *n.* squirrel (3) **4A**
eifersüchtig *adj.* jealous (1) **3B**
ein/eine/ein *m./f./n.* a (1) **1A**
Einbahnstraße, -n *f.* one-way street (2) **4A**
einfach *adj.* easy (1) **2A**
einfarbig *adj.* solid colored (2) **1B**
eingebildet *adj.* arrogant (1) **3B**
einkaufen *v.* to shop (1) **4A**
Einkaufen *n.* shopping (2) **1B**
Einkaufszentrum (*pl.* **Einkaufszentren**) *n.* mall; shopping center (3) **2B**
Einkommensgruppe, -n *f.* income bracket (2) **2B**
einladen *v.* to invite (2) **1A**
einmal *adv.* once (2) **3B**
eins one (1) **2A**
einschlafen *v.* to go to sleep (1) **4A**
einzahlen *v.* to deposit (money) (3) **2A**
Einzelkind, -er *n.* only child (1) **3A**
Eis *n.* ice cream (2) **1A**
Eisdiele, -n *f.* ice cream shop (1) **4A**
Eishockey *n.* ice hockey (2) **2B**
Eiswürfel, - *m.* ice cube (2) **1A**
elegant *adj.* elegant (2) **1B**
Elektriker, - / Elektrikerin, -nen *m./f.* electrician (3) **3B**
elf eleven (1) **2A**
Ellenbogen, - *m.* elbow (3) **1A**
Eltern *pl.* parents (1) **3A**
E-Mail, -s *f.* e -mail (2) **4B**
empfehlen *v.* to recommend (1) **2B**
Empfehlungsschreiben, - *n.* letter of recommendation (3) **3A**
endlich *adv.* finally (3) **1B**
Energie, -n *f.* energy (3) **4B**
energiesparend *adj.* energy-efficient (2) **2B**
eng *adj.* tight (2) **1B**
England *n.* England (3) **2B**
Engländer, - / Engländerin, -nen *m./f.* English (person) (3) **2B**
Englisch *n.* English (language) (3) **2B**
Enkelkind, -er *n.* grandchild. (1) **3A**

Enkelsohn, -̈e *m.* grandson (1) **3A**
Enkeltochter, -̈ *f.* granddaughter (1) **3A**
entdecken *v.* to discover (2) **2B**
entfernen *v.* to remove (2) **2B**
entlang *prep.* along, down (1) **3B**
entlassen *v.* to fire; to lay off (3) **3B**
sich entschließen *v.* to decide (1) **4B**
(sich) entschuldigen *v.* to apologize; to excuse
   Entschuldigen Sie. Excuse me. (form.) (1) **1A**
   Entschuldigung. Excuse me. (1) **1A**
sich entspannen *v.* to relax (3) **1A**
entwerten *v.* to validate (2) **4A**
   eine Fahrkarte entwerten *v.* to validate a ticket (2) **4A**
entwickeln *v.* to develop (3) **4B**
er *pron.* he (1) **1A**
Erdbeben, - *n.* earthquake (3) **4A**
Erdbeere, - n *f.* strawberry (1) **4A**
Erde, -n *f.* earth (3) **4B**
Erderwärmung *f.* global warming (3) **4B**
Erdgeschoss, -e *n.* ground floor (2) **2A**
Erfahrung, -en *f.* experience (3) **3A**
erfinden *v.* to invent (2) **3A**
Erfolg, -e *m.* success (3) **3B**
erforschen *v.* to explore (3) **4A**
ergänzen *v.* complete
Ergebnis, -se *n.* result; score (1) **1B**
erhalten *v.* to preserve (3) **4B**
sich erinnern (an) *v.* to remember (3) **1A**
sich erkälten *v.* to catch a cold (3) **1A**
Erkältung, -en *f.* cold (3) **1B**
erkennen *v.* to recognize (2) **3A**
erklären *v.* to explain (1) **4A**
erneuerbare Energie *f.* renewable energy (3) **4B**
ernst *adj.* serious (1) **3B**
erster/erste/erstes *adj.* first (1) **2A**
erwachsen grown-up *adj.* (3) **2A**
erzählen *v.* to tell (2) **3A**
   erzählen von *v.* to talk about (2) **3A**
es *pron.* it (1) **1A**
   Es gibt... There is/are... (1) **2B**
Essen, - *n.* food (1) **4A**
essen *v.* to eat (1) **2B**
   essen gehen *v.* to eat out (1) **2B**
Esslöffel, - *m.* soup spoon (1) **4B**
Esszimmer, - *n.* dining room (2) **2A**
etwas *pron.* something (2) **3B**
   etwas anderes something else (3) **2A**
euer (*pl. inf.*) *poss. adj.* your (1) **3A**

F

Fabrik, -en *f.* factory (3) **4B**
Fabrikarbeiter, - / Fabrikarbeiterin, -nen *m./f.* factory worker (3) **3B**
Fach, -̈er *n.* subject (1) **2A**
fade *adj.* bland (1) **4B**
fahren *v.* to drive; to go (1) **2B**
   Auto fahren *v.* to drive a car (2) **4A**
   Fahrrad fahren *v.* to ride a bicycle (1) **2B**
   geradeaus fahren *v.* to go straight ahead (2) **4A**
Fahrer, - / Fahrerin, -nen *m./f.* driver (2) **4A**
Fahrgemeinschaft, -en *f.* carpool (3) **4B**

Fahrkarte, -n *f.* ticket (2) **4A**
  eine Fahrkarte entwerten *v.* to validate a ticket (2) **4A**
Fahrkartenschalter, - *m.* ticket office (2) **4A**
Fahrplan, -ˉe *m.* schedule (2) **4A**
Fahrrad, -ˉer *n.* bicycle (1) **2B**, (2) **4A**
Fahrstuhl, -ˉe *m.* elevator (2) **3B**
fallen *v.* to fall (1) **2B**
Familie, -n *f.* family (1) **3A**
Familienstand, -ˉe *m.* marital status (1) **3A**
Fan, -s *m.* fan (1) **2B**
fangen *v.* to catch (1) **2B**
fantastisch *adj.* fantastic (3) **2A**
Farbe, -n *f.* color (2) **1B**
färben *v.* to dye
  sich die Haare färben *v.* to dye one's hair (3) **1A**
fast *adv.* almost (1) **4A**
faul *adj.* lazy (1) **3B**
Faxgerät, -e *n.* fax machine (2) **4B**
Februar *m.* February (1) **2A**, (2) **3A**
fegen *v.* to sweep (2) **2B**
feiern *v.* to celebrate (2) **1A**
Feiertag, -e *m.* holiday (2) **1A**
Feinkostgeschäft, -e *n.* delicatessen (1) **4A**
Feld, -er *n.* field (3) **4A**
Fenster, - *n.* window (1) **1A**
Ferien *pl.* vacation
Fernbedienung *f.* remote control (2) **4B**
fernsehen *v.* to watch television (2) **4B**
Fernseher, - *m.* television (2) **4B**
fertig *adj.* ready; finished (3) **3B**
Fest, -e *n.* festival; celebration (2) **1A**
Festplatte, -n *f.* hard drive (2) **4B**
fett *adj.* fat (1) **3A**
Feuerwehrmann, -ˉer / Feuerwehrfrau, -en (*pl.* **Feuerwehrleute**) *m./f.* firefighter (3) **3B**
Fieber, - *n.* fever (1) **1B**
  Fieber haben *v.* to have a fever (3) **1B**
finden *v.* to find (1) **2A**
Finger, - *m.* finger (3) **1A**
Firma (*pl.* **die Firmen**) *f.* firm; company (3) **3A**
Fisch, -e fish *m.* (1) **4A**, (3) **4A**
Fischgeschäft, -e *n.* fish store (1) **4A**
fit *adj.* in good shape (1) **2B**
Flasche, -n *f.* bottle (1) **4B**
Fleisch *n.* meat (1) **4A**
fleißig *adj.* hard-working (1) **3B**
fliegen *v.* to fly (2) **3B**
Flug, -ˉe *m.* flight (2) **3B**
Flughafen, -ˉ *m.* airport (2) **3B**
Flugticket, -s *n.* (plane) ticket (2) **3B**
Flugzeug, -e *n.* airplane (2) **3B**
Flur, -e *m.* hall (2) **2A**
Fluss, -ˉe *m.* river (1) **3B**, (3) **4A**
folgen *v.* to follow (2) **1A**, (3) **2B**
Form, -en *f.* shape, form
  in guter/schlechter Form sein *v.* to be in/out of shape (3) **1B**
Formular, -e *n.* form (3) **2A**
  ein Formular ausfüllen *v.* to fill out a form (3) **2A**
Foto, -s *n.* photo, picture (1) **1B**
Frage, -n *f.* question (1) **1B**
fragen *v.* to ask (1) **2A**

fragen nach *v.* to ask about (2) **3A**
  sich fragen *v.* to wonder, ask oneself (3) **1A**
Frankreich *n.* France (3) **2B**
Franzose, -n / Französin, -nen *m./f.* French (person) (3) **2B**
Französisch *n.* French (language) (3) **2B**
Frau, -en *f.* woman (1) **1A**; wife (1) **3A**
  Frau... Mrs./Ms. ...(1) **1A**
Freitag, -e *m.* Friday (1) **2A**
  freitags *adv.* on Fridays (1) **2A**
Freizeit, -en *f.* free time, leisure (1) **2B**
Freizeitaktivität, - en *f.* leisure activity (1) **2B**
fremd *adj.* foreign (3) **2A**
Fremdsprache, -n *f.* foreign language (1) **2A**
sich freuen (über) *v.* to be happy (about) (3) **1A**
  Freut mich. Pleased to meet you. (1) **1A**
  sich freuen auf *v.* to look forward to (3) **1A**
Freund, -e / Freundin, - nen *m./f.* friend (1) **1A**
freundlich *adj.* friendly (1) **3B**
  Mit freundlichen Grüßen Yours sincerely (1) **3B**
Freundschaft, -en *f.* friendship (2) **1A**
Frischvermählte, -n *m./f.* newlywed (2) **1A**
Friseur, -e / Friseurin, -nen *m./f.* hairdresser (1) **3B**
froh *adj.* happy (1) **3B**
  Frohe Ostern! Happy Easter! (2) **1A**
  Frohe Weihnachten! Merry Christmas! (2) **1A**
früh *adj.* early; in the morning (1) **2B**
  morgen früh tomorrow morning (1) **2B**
Frühling, -e *m.* spring (1) **2B**, (2) **3A**
Frühstück, -e *n.* breakfast (1) **4B**
fühlen *v.* to feel (1) **2A**
  sich (wohl) fühlen *v.* to feel (well) (3) **1A**
füllen *v.* to fill
fünf five (1) **2A**
funktionieren *v.* to work, function (2) **4B**
für *prep.* for (1) **3B**
furchtbar *adj.* awful (2) **3A**
Fuß, -ˉe *m.* foot (3) **1A**
Fußball *m.* soccer (1) **2B**
Fußgänger, - / Fußgängerin, -nen *m./f.* pedestrian (3) **2B**

G

Gabel, -n *f.* fork (1) **4B**
Gang, -ˉe *m.* course
  erster/zweiter Gang *m.* first/second course (1) **4B**
ganz *adj.* all, total (2) **3B**
ganztags *adj* full-time (3) **3B**
Garage, -n *f.* garage (2) **1B**
Garnele, -n *f.* shrimp (1) **4A**
Gartenabfall, -ˉe *m.* yard waste (3) **4B**
Gärtner, - /Gärtnerin, -nen *m./f.* gardener (3) **3B**
Gast, -ˉe *m.* guest (2) **1A**
Gastfamilie, -n *f.* host family (1) **4B**
Gastgeber, - / Gastgeberin, -nen *m./f.* host/hostess (2) **1A**
Gebäck *n.* pastries; baked goods (2) **1A**
Gebäude, - *n.* building (3) **2A**
geben *v.* to give (1) **2B**
  Es gibt... There is/are... (1) **2B**

Geburt, - en *f.* birth (2) **1A**
Geburtstag, -e *m.* birthday (2) **1A**
  Wann hast du Geburtstag? When is your birthday? (2) **3A**
geduldig *adj.* patient (1) **3B**
Gefahr, -en *f.* danger (3) **4B**
gefährdet *adj.* endangered; threatened (3) **4B**
gefallen *v.* to please (2) **1A**
Gefrierschrank, -ˉe *m.* freezer (2) **2B**
gegen *prep.* against (1) **3B**
gegenüber (von) *prep.* across (from) (3) **2B**
Gehalt, -ˉ er *n.* salary (3) **3A**
  hohes/niedriges Gehalt, -ˉer high/low salary *n.* (3) **3A**
Gehaltserhöhung, -en *f.* raise (3) **3B**
gehen *v.* to go (1) **2A**
  Geht es dir/Ihnen gut? *v.* Are you all right? (*inf./form.*) (1) **1A**
  Wie geht es Ihnen? (*form.*) How are you? (1) **1A**
  Wie geht's (dir)? (*inf.*) How are you? (1) **1A**
gehören *v.* to belong to (2) **1A**
Geländewagen, - *m.* SUV (2) **4B**
gelb *adj.* yellow (2) **1B**
Geld *n.* money (3) **2A**
  Geld abheben/einzahlen *v.* to withdraw/deposit money (3) **2A**
Geldautomat, -en *m.* ATM (3) **2A**
Geldschein, -e *m.* bill (money) (3) **2A**
gemein *adj.* mean (1) **3B**
Gemüse *n.* vegetables (1) **4A**
genau *adv.* exactly
  genauso wie just as (2) **4A**
genießen *v.* to enjoy
geöffnet *adj.* open (3) **2A**
Gepäck *n.* luggage (2) **3B**
geradeaus straight ahead *adv.* (2) **4A**
gern *adv.* with pleasure (1) **3A**
  gern (*+verb*) to like to (*+verb*) (1) **3A**
  ich hätte gern... I would like... (1) **4A**
  Gern geschehen. My pleasure.; You're welcome. (1) **1A**
Geschäft, -e *n.* business (3) **3A**; store (1) **4A**
Geschäftsführer, - / Geschäftsführerin, -nen *m./f.* manager (3) **3A**
Geschäftsmann, -ˉer / Geschäftsfrau, -en (*pl.* **Geschäftsleute**) *m./f.* businessman / businesswoman (1) **3B**
Geschenk, -e *n.* gift (2) **1A**
Geschichte, -n *f.* history (1) **2A**; story
geschieden *adj.* divorced (1) **3A**
Geschirr *n.* dishes (2) **2B**
  Geschirr spülen *v.* to do the dishes (2) **2B**
geschlossen *adj.* closed (3) **2A**
Geschmack, -ˉe *m.* flavor; taste (1) **4B**
Geschwister, - ** *n.* siblings (1) **3A
Gesetz, -e *n.* law (3) **4B**
Gesicht, -er *n.* face (3) **1A**
gestreift *adj.* striped (2) **1B**
gesund *adj.* healthy (2) **4A**; (3) **1B**
  gesund werden *v.* to get better (3) **1B**
Gesundheit *f.* health (3) **1B**
geteilt durch divided by (1) **1B**
Getränk, -e *n.* beverage (1) **4B**
getrennt *adj.* separated (1) **3A**

gewaltfrei *adj.* nonviolent (3) **4B**
Gewerkschaft, -en *f.* labor union (3) **3B**
gewinnen *v.* to win (1) **2B**
sich gewöhnen an *v.* to get used to (3) **1A**
gierig *adj.* greedy (1) **3B**
Giftmüll *m.* toxic waste (3) **4B**
Glas, -¨er *n.* glass (1) **4B**
glatt *adj.* straight (1) **3A**
  glatte Haare *n. pl.* straight hair (1) **3B**
glauben *v.* to believe (2) **1A**
gleich *adj.* same
  ist gleich *v.* equals, is (1) **1B**
Glück *n.* happiness (2) **1A**
glücklich *adj.* happy (1) **3B**
Golf *n.* golf (1) **2B**
Grad *n.* degree (2) **3A**
  Es sind 18 Grad draußen. It's 18 degrees out. (2) **3A**
Gramm, -e *n.* gram (1) **4A**
Granit, -e *m.* granite (2) **2B**
Gras, -¨er *n.* grass (3) **4A**
gratulieren *v.* to congratulate (2) **1A**
grau *adj.* grey (2) **1B**
grausam *adj.* cruel
Grippe, -n *f.* flu (1) **1B**
groß *adj.* big; tall (1) **3A**
großartig *adj.* terrific (1) **3A**
Großeltern *pl.* grandparents (1) **1A**
Großmutter, -¨ *f.* grandmother (1) **3A**
Großvater, -¨ *m.* grandfather (1) **3A**
großzügig *adj.* generous (1) **3B**
grün *adj.* green (2) **1B**
  grüne Bohne, (pl. die grünen Bohnen) *f.* green bean (1) **4A**
Gruß, -¨e *m.* greeting
  Mit freundlichen Grüßen Yours sincerely (1) **3B**
grüßen *v.* to greet (1) **2A**
Gürtel, - *m.* belt (2) **1B**
gut *adj.* good (1) **3B**; *adv.* Well (1) **1A**
  gut aussehend *adj.* handsome (1) **3A**
  gut gekleidet *adj.* well-dressed (2) **1B**
  Gute Besserung! Get well! (2) **1A**
  Guten Appetit! Enjoy your meal! (1) **4B**
  Guten Abend. Good evening. (1) **1A**
  Guten Morgen. Good morning. (1) **1A**
  Gute Nacht. Good night. (1) **1A**
  Guten Tag. Hello. (1) **1A**

H

Haar, -e hair *n.* (1) **3A**, (3) **1A**
Haartrockner, - *m.* hair dryer (3) **1A**
haben to have *v.* (1) **1B**
Hagel *m.* hail (2) **3A**
Hähnchen, - *n.* chicken (1) **4A**
halb *half*; half an hour before (1) **2A**
Halbbruder, -¨ *m.* half-brother (1) **3A**
Halbschwester, -n *f.* half-sister (1) **3A**
halbtags *adj.* part-time (3) **3B**
Hallo. Hello. (1) **1A**
Hals, -¨e *m.* neck (3) **1A**
  Hals- und Beinbruch! Break a leg! (2) **1A**
Halskette, -n *f.* necklace (2) **1B**

Hand, -¨e *f.* hand (3) **1A**
handeln *v.* to act
  handeln von *v.* to be about; have to do with (2) **3A**
Handgelenk, -e *n.* wrist (3) **1B**
Handgepäck *n.* carry-on luggage (2) **3B**
Handschuh, -e *m.* glove (2) **1B**
Handtasche, -n *f.* purse (2) **1B**
Handtuch, -¨er *n.* towel (3) **1A**
Handy, -s *n.* cell phone (2) **4B**
hängen *v.* to hang (2) **1B**
Hase, -n *m.* hare (3) **4A**
hässlich *adj.* ugly (1) **3A**
Hauptspeise, -n *f.* main course (1) **4B**
Hauptstraße, -n *f.* main road (3) **2B**
Haus, -¨er *n.* house (2) **2A**
  nach Hause *adv.* home (2) **1B**
  zu Hause *adv.* at home (1) **4A**
Hausarbeit *f.* housework (2) **2B**
  Hausarbeit machen *v.* to do housework (2) **2B**
Hausaufgabe, -n *f.* homework (1) **1B**
Hausfrau, -en / Hausmann, -¨er *f./m.* homemaker (3) **3B**
hausgemacht *adj.* homemade (1) **4B**
Hausmeister, - / Hausmeisterin, -nen *m./f.* caretaker; custodian (3) **3B**
Hausschuh, -e *m.* slipper (3) **1A**
Haustier, -e *n.* pet (1) **3A**
Heft, -e *n.* notebook (1) **1B**
Hefter, - *m.* stapler (3) **3A**
heiraten *v.* to marry (1) **3A**
heiß *adj.* hot (2) **3A**
heißen *v.* to be named (1) **2A**
  Ich heiße... My name is... (1) **1A**
helfen *v.* to help (1) **2B**
  helfen bei *v.* to help with (2) **3A**
hell *adj.* light (1) **3A**; bright (2) **1B**
Hemd, -en *n.* shirt (2) **1B**
herauf *adv.* up; upwards (2) **2A**
heraus *adv.* out (2) **2A**
Herbst, -e *m.* fall, autumn (1) **2B**, (2) **3A**
Herd, -e *m.* stove (2) **2B**
Herr Mr. (1) **1A**
herunter *adv.* down; downwards (2) **2A**
heruntergehen *v.* to go down (3) **2B**
  die Treppe heruntergehen *v.* to go downstairs (3) **2B**
herunterladen *v.* to download (2) **4B**
Herz, -en *n.* heart
  Herzlichen Glückwunsch! Congratulations! (2) **1A**
heute *adv.* today (1) **2B**
  Heute ist der... Today is the... (1) **2A**
  Welcher Tag ist heute? What day is it today? (2) **3A**
  Der Wievielte ist heute? What is the date today? (1) **2A**
hier *adv.* here (1) **1A**
  Hier ist/sind... Here is/are... (1) **1B**
Himmel *m.* sky (4) **4A**
hin und zurück there and back (2) **3B**
sich hinlegen *v.* to lie down (3) **1A**
sich hinsetzen *v.* to sit down (3) **1A**
hinter *prep.* behind (2) **1B**

hinterlassen *v.* to leave (behind)
  eine Nachricht hinterlassen *v.* to leave a message (3) **3A**
Hobby, -s *n.* hobby (1) **2B**
hoch *adj.* high (2) **4A**
hochgehen *v.* to go up, climb up (3) **2B**
  die Treppe hochgehen *v.* to go upstairs (3) **2B**
Hochwasser, - *n.* flood (3) **4B**
Hochzeit, -en *f.* wedding (2) **1A**
Hockey *n.* hockey (1) **2B**
Höflichkeit, -en *f.* courtesy; polite expression (1) **1A**
Holz *n.* wood (2) **2B**
hören *v.* to hear; listen to (1) **2A**
Hörer, - *m.* receiver (3) **3A**
Hörsaal (*pl.* **Hörsäle**) *m.* lecture hall (1) **2A**
Hose, -n *f.* pants (2) **1B**
  kurze Hose *f.* shorts (1) **1B**
Hotel, -s *n.* hotel (2) **3B**
  Fünf-Sterne-Hotel *n* five-star hotel. (2) **3B**
Hotelgast, -¨e *m.* hotel guest (2) **3B**
hübsch *adj.* pretty (1) **3A**
Hund, -e *m.* dog (1) **3A**
Hundewetter *n.* terrible weather (2) **3A**
husten *v.* to cough (3) **1B**
Hut, -¨e *m.* hat (2) **1B**
Hybridauto, -s *n.* hybrid car (3) **4B**

I

ich *pron.* I (1) **1A**
Idee, -n *f.* idea (1) **1A**
Ihr (*form., sing /pl.*) *poss. adj.* your (1) **3A**
ihr (*inf., pl.*) *pron.* you (1) **1A**; *poss. adj.* her, their (1) **3A**
immer *adv.* always (1) **4A**
Immobilienmakler, - / Immobilienmaklerin, -nen *m./f.* real estate agent (3) **3B**
in *prep.* in (2) **1B**
Inder, - / Inderin, -nen *m./f.* Indian (person) (2) **2B**
Indien *n.* India (3) **2B**
indisch *adj.* Indian (3) **2B**
Informatik *f.* computer science (1) **2A**
sich informieren (über) *v.* to find out (about) (3) **1A**
Ingenieur, -e / Ingenieurin, -nen *m./f.* engineer (1) **3B**
Innenstadt, -¨e *f.* city center
innerhalb *prep.* inside of, within (2) **4B**
Insel, -n *f.* island (3) **4A**
intellektuell *adj.* intellectual (1) **3B**
intelligent *adj.* intelligent (1) **3B**
interessant *adj.* interesting (1) **3B**
sich interessieren (für) *v.* to be interested (in) (3) **1A**
Internet *n.* Web (2) **4B**
  im Internet surfen *v.* to surf the Web (2) **4B**
Internetcafé, -s *n.* internet café (3) **2A**
Italien *n.* Italy (3) **2B**
Italiener, - / Italienerin, -nen *m./f.* Italian (person) (3) **2B**
Italienisch *n.* Italian (language) (3) **2B**

J

ja yes (1) **1B**
Jacke, -n *f.* jacket (2) **1B**
Jahr, -e *n.* year (2) **3A**
    Ein gutes neues Jahr! Happy New Year! (2) **1A**
    Ich bin... Jahre alt. I am... years old (1) **1B**
Jahrestag, -e *m.* anniversary (2) **1A**
Jahreszeit, -en *f.* season (2) **3A**
Januar *m.* January (1) **2A**, (2) **3A**
Jeans *f.* jeans (2) **1B**
jeder/jede/jedes *adj.* any, every, each (2) **4B**
jemand *pron.* someone (2) **3B**
jetzt *adv.* now (1) **4A**
joggen *v.* to jog (1) **2B**
Joghurt, -s *m.* yogurt (1) **4A**
Journalist, -en / Journalistin,
    -nen *m./f.* journalist (1) **3B**
Jugendherberge, -n *f.* youth hostel (2) **3B**
jugendlich *adj.* young; youthful (3) **2A**
Juli *m.* July (1) **2A**, (2) **3A**
jung *adj.* young (1) **3A**
Junge, -n *m.* boy (1) **1A**
Juni *m.* June (1) **2A**, (2) **3A**
Juweliergeschäft, -e *n.* jewelry store (3) **2A**

K

Kaffee, -s *m.* coffee (1) **4B**
Kaffeemaschine, -n *f.* coffeemaker (2) **2B**
kalt *adj.* cold (2) **3A**
sich (die Haare) kämmen *v.* comb
    (one's hair) (3) **1A**
Kanada *n.* Canada (3) **2B**
Kanadier, -/ Kanadierin, -nen *m./f.*
    Canadian (3) **2B**
Kandidat, -en *m.* candidate (3) **3A**
Kaninchen, *n.* rabbit (3) **4A**
Karotte, -n *f.* carrot (1) **4A**
Karriere, -n *f.* career (3) **3B**
Karte, -n *f.* map (1) **1B**, *f.* card (1) **2B**; (2) **1A**
    eine Karte lesen *v.* to read a map (2) **3B**
    mit der Karte bezahlen *v.* to pay by (credit)
        card (3) **2A**
Kartoffel, -n *f.* potato (1) **4A**
Käse, - *m.* cheese (1) **4A**
Katze, -n *f.* cat (1) **3A**
kaufen *v.* to buy (1) **2A**
Kaufhaus, -̈er *n.* department store (3) **2B**
Kaution, -en *f.* security deposit (2) **2A**
kein *adj.* no (1) **2B**
    Keine Zufahrt. Do not enter. (1) **3B**
Keks, -e *m.* cookie (2) **1A**
Keller, - *m.* cellar (2) **2A**
Kellner, -/ Kellnerin, -nen *m./f.* waiter/
    waitress (3) **3B**, (1) **4B**
kennen *v.* to know, be familiar with (2) **1B**
    sich kennen *v.* to know each other (3) **1A**
    (sich) kennen lernen *v.* to meet
        (one another) (1) **1A**
Keramik, -en *f.* ceramic (2) **2B**
Kernenergie *f.* nuclear energy (3) **4B**
Kernkraftwerk, -e *n.* nuclear power plant (3) **4B**

Kind, -er *n.* child (1) **1A**
Kiosk, -e *m.* newspaper kiosk (3) **2A**
Kirche, -n *f.* church (3) **2B**
Kissen, - *n.* pillow (2) **2B**
Klasse, -n *f.* class (1) **1B**
    erste/zweite Klasse, -n first/second class (2) **4A**
Klassenkamerad, -en / Klassenkameradin,
    -nen *m./f.* classmate (1) **1B**
Klassenzimmer, - *n.* classroom (1) **1B**
klassisch *adj.* classical (3) **2A**
Kleid, -er *n.* dress (2) **1B**
Kleidergröße, -n *f.* clothing size (2) **1B**
Kleidung *f. pl.* clothes (2) **1B**
klein *adj.* small; short (stature) (1) **3A**
Kleingeld *n.* change (3) **2A**
Klempner, -/ Klempnerin, -nen *m./f.*
    plumber (3) **3B**
klettern *v.* to climb (mountain) (1) **2B**
klingeln *v.* to ring (2) **4B**
Klippe, -n *f.* cliff (3) **4A**
Knie, - *n.* knee (3) **1A**
Knoblauch, -e *m.* garlic (1) **4A**
Koch, -̈e / Köchin, -nen *m./f.* cook, chef (1) **4B**
kochen *v.* to cook (1) **2B**
Koffer, - *m.* suitcase (2) **3B**
Kofferraum, -̈e *m.* trunk (2) **4A**
Kombi, -s *m.* station wagon (2) **4B**
Komma, -s *n.* comma (1) **1B**
kommen *v.* to come (1) **2A**
Kommode, -n *f.* dresser (2) **2A**
kompliziert *adj.* complicated (3) **2A**
können *v.* to be able, can (1) **3B**
Konditorei, -en *f.* pastry shop (1) **4A**
Konto (pl. Konten) *n.* bank account (3) **2A**
Konzert, -e *n.* concert (2) **1B**
Kopf, -̈e *m.* head (3) **1A**
Kopfhörer, - *m.* headphones (2) **4B**
Kopfschmerzen *(m. pl.)* *f.* headache (3) **1B**
Korea *n.* Korea (3) **2B**
der Koreaner, -/ die Koreanerin,
    -nen *m./f.* Korean (person) (3) **2B**
Koreanisch *n.* Korean (language) (3) **2B**
Körper, - *m.* body (3) **1A**
korrigieren *v.* to correct (1) **2A**
Kosmetiksalon, -s *m.* beauty salon (3) **2A**
kosten *v.* to cost (1) **2A**
    Wie viel kostet das? *v.* How much is that? (1) **4A**
krank *adj.* sick (1) **1B**
    krank werden *v.* to get sick (3) **1B**
Krankenhaus, -̈er *n.* hospital (3) **1B**
Krankenpfleger, -/ Krankenschwester, -n
    m./f. nurse (3) **1B**
Krankenwagen, - *m.* ambulance (3) **1B**
Krawatte, -n *f.* tie (2) **1B**
Kreuzfahrt, -en *f.* cruise (2) **3B**
Kreuzung, -en *f.* intersection (3) **2B**
Küche, -n *f.* kitchen (2) **2A**
Kuchen, - *m.* cake; pie (1) **4A**
Kuh, -̈e *f.* cow (3) **4A**
kühl *adj.* cool (2) **3A**
Kühlschrank, -̈e *m.* refrigerator (2) **2B**
Kuli, -s *m.* (ball-point) pen (1) **1B**
Kunde, -n / Kundin, -nen *m./f.* customers (3) **1B**

kündigen *v.* to resign (3) **3B**
Kunst, -̈e *f.* art (1) **2A**
Kunststoff, -e *m.* plastic (2) **2B**
kurz *adj.* short (1) **3A**
    kurze Haare *n. pl.* short hair
    kurze Hose *f.* shorts (2) **1B**
kurzärmlig *adj.* short-sleeved (2) **1B**
Kurzfilm, -e *m.* short film
Kuss, -̈e *m.* kiss (2) **1A**
küssen *v.* to kiss (2) **1A**
    sich küssen *v.* to kiss (each other) (3) **1A**
Küste, -n *f.* coast (3) **4A**

L

lächeln *v.* to smile (2) **1A**
lachen *v.* to laugh (1) **2A**
Ladegerät, -e *n.* battery charger (2) **4B**
laden *v.* to charge; load (2) **4B**
Lage, -n *f.* location (2) **3B**
Laken, - *n.* sheet (2) **2B**
Lampe, -n *f.* lamp (2) **2A**
Land, -̈er *n.* country (2) **3B**
landen *v.* to land (2) **3B**
Landkarte, -n *f.* map (2) **3B**
Landschaft, -en *f.* landscape (2) **3B**; countryside
    (3) **4A**
lang *adj.* long (1) **3A**
    lange Haare *n. pl.* long hair (1) **3A**
langärmlig *adj.* long-sleeved (2) **1B**
langsam *adj* slow. (1) **3B**
    Langsam fahren. Slow down. (1) **3B**
langweilig *adj.* boring (1) **3B**
Laptop, -s *m./n.* laptop (computer) (2) **4B**
lassen *v.* to let, allow (1) **2B**
laufen *v.* to run (1) **2B**
leben *v.* to live
Lebenslauf, -̈e *m.* résumé; CV (3) **3A**
Lebensmittelgeschäft, -e *n.* grocery store (1) **4A**
lecker *adj.* delicious (1) **4B**
Leder, - *n.* leather (2) **1B**
ledig *adj.* single (1) **3A**
legen *v.* to lay (2) **1B**; *v.* to put; lay (3) **1A**
Lehrbuch, -̈er *n.* textbook (university) (1) **1B**
Lehrer, -/ Lehrerin, -nen *m./f.* teacher (1) **1B**
leicht *adj.* light (1) **4B**; mild (3) **1B**
Leichtathletik *f.* track and field (1) **2B**
leider *adv.* unfortunately (1) **4A**
leiten *v.* to manage (3) **3B**
Lenkrad, -̈er *n.* steering wheel (2) **4A**
lernen *v.* to study; to learn (1) **2A**
lesen *v.* to read (1) **2B**
letzter/letzte/letztes *adj.* last (1) **2B**
Leute *pl.* people (1) **3B**
Licht, -er *n.* light (3) **4B**
Liebe *f.* love (2) **1A**
    Lieber/Liebe *m./f.* Dear (1) **3B**
lieben *v.* to love (1) **2A**
    sich lieben *v.* to love each other (3) **1A**
lieber *adj.* rather (2) **4A**
liebevoll *adj.* loving (1) **3B**
Liebling, -e *m.* darling
    Lieblings- favorite (1) **3B**

liegen *v.* to lie; to be located (2) **1B**
lila *adj.* purple (2) **1B**
Linie, -n *f.* line
Lippe, -n *f.* lip (3) **1A**
Lippenstift, -e *m.* lipstick (3) **1A**
Literatur *f.* literature (1) **2A**
LKW, -s *m.* truck (2) **4A**
LKW-Fahrer, - / LKW-Fahrerin, -nen *m./f.* truck driver (3) **3B**
lockig *adj.* curly (1) **3A**
   lockige Haare *n. pl.* curly hair
Los! Start!; Go! (1) **2B**
löschen *v.* to delete (2) **4B**
Lösung, -en *f.* solution (3) **4B**
   eine Lösung vorschlagen *v.* to propose a solution (3) **4B**
Luft, -̈e *f.* air (3) **4A**
lügen *v.* to lie, tell a lie
Lust, -̈e *f.* desire
   Lust haben *v.* to feel like (2) **3B**
lustig *adj.* funny (1) **3B**

M

machen *v.* to do; make (1) **2A**
   Mach's gut! *v.* All the best! (1) **3B**
Mädchen, - *n.* girl (1) **1A**
Mahlzeit, -en *f.* meal (1) **4B**
Mai *m.* May (1) **2A**, (2) **3A**
Mal, -e *n.* time
   das erste/letzte Mal the first/last time (2) **3B**
   zum ersten/letzten Mal for the first/last time (2) **3B**
mal times (1) **1B**
Mama, -s *f.* mom (1) **3A**
man *pron.* one (2) **3B**
mancher/manche/manches *adj.* some. (2) **4B**
manchmal *adv.* sometimes (2) **3B**
Mann, -̈er *m.* man (1) **1A**; *m.* husband (1) **3A**
Mannschaft, -en *f.* team (1) **2B**
Mantel, -̈ *m.* coat (2) **1B**
Markt, -̈e *m.* market (1) **4A**
Marmelade, -n *f.* jam (1) **4A**
Marmor *m.* marble (2) **2B**
März *m.* March (1) **2A**, (2) **3A**
Material, -ien *n.* material (2) **1B**
Mathematik *f.* mathematics (1) **2A**
Maus, -̈e *f.* mouse (3) **4A**
Mechaniker, - / Mechanikerin, -nen *m./f.* mechanic (2) **4A**
Medikament, -e *n.* medicine (3) **1B**
Medizin *f.* medicine (1) **2A**
Meer, -e *n.* sea; ocean (3) **4A**
Meeresfrüchte *f. pl.* seafood (1) **4A**
mehr *adj.* more (2) **4A**
mein *poss. adj.* my (1) **3A**
meinen *v.* to mean (1) **2A**; to believe; to maintain (3) **4B**
Meisterschaft, -en *f.* championship (1) **2B**
Melone, -n *f.* melon (1) **4A**
Mensa (pl. Mensen) *f.* cafeteria (college/ university) (1) **1B**
Mensch, -en *m.* person
Messer, - *n.* knife (1) **4B**

Metzgerei, -en *f.* butcher shop (1) **4A**
Mexikaner, - / Mexikanerin, -nen *m./f.* Mexican (person) (3) **2B**
mexikanisch *adj.* Mexican (3) **2B**
Mexiko *n.* Mexico (3) **2B**
Miete, -n *f.* rent (2) **2A**
mieten *v.* to rent (2) **2A**
Mikrofon, -e *n.* microphone (2) **4B**
Mikrowelle, -n *f.* microwave (2) **2B**
Milch *f.* milk (1) **4B**
Minderheit, -en *f.* minority (3) **4B**
Mineralwasser *n.* sparkling water (1) **4B**
minus minus (1) **1B**
mir *pron.* myself, me (2) **3A**
   Mir geht's (sehr) gut. *v.* I am (very) well. (1) **1A**
   Mir geht's nicht (so) gut. *v.* I am not (so) well. (1) **1A**
mit with (1) **4B**
Mitbewohner, - / Mitbewohnerin, -nen *m./f.* roommate (1) **2A**
mitbringen *v.* to bring along (1) **4A**
mitkommen *v.* to come along (1) **4A**
mitmachen *v.* to participate (2) **4B**
mitnehmen *v.* to bring with (3) **2B**
   jemanden mitnehmen *v.* to give someone a ride (3) **2B**
Mittag, -e *m.* noon (1) **2A**
Mittagessen *n.* lunch (1) **4B**
Mitternacht *f.* midnight (1) **2A**
Mittwoch, -e *m.* Wednesday (1) **2A**
   mittwochs *adv.* on Wednesdays (1) **2A**
Möbel, - *n.* furniture (2) **2A**
Möbelstück, -e *n.* piece of furniture (2) **2A**
möbliert *adj.* furnished (2) **2A**
modern *adj.* modern (3) **2A**
modisch *adj.* fashionable (2) **1B**
mögen *v.* to like (1) **4B**
   Ich möchte... I would like… (1) **4B**
Monat, -e *m.* month (1) **2A**, (2) **3A**
Mond, -e *m.* moon (3) **4A**
Montag, -e *m.* Monday (1) **2A**
   montags *adv.* on Mondays (1) **2A**
Morgen, - *m.* morning (1) **2B**
   morgens *adv.* in the morning (1) **2A**
morgen *adv.* tomorrow (1) **2B**
   morgen früh tomorrow morning (1) **2B**
Motor, -en *m.* engine (2) **4A**
Motorhaube, -n *f.* hood (of car) (2) **4A**
MP3-Player, - *m.* mp3 player (2) **4B**
müde *adj.* tired (1) **3B**
Müll *m.* trash (2) **2B**; *m.* waste (3) **4B**
   den Müll rausbringen *v.* to take out the trash (2) **2B**
Müllwagen, - *m.* garbage truck (3) **4B**
Mund, -̈er *m.* mouth (3) **1A**
Münze, -n *f.* coin (3) **2A**
Musiker, - / Musikerin, -nen *m./f.* musician (3) **3B**
müssen *v.* to have to; must (1) **3B**
mutig *adj.* brave (1) **3B**
Mutter, -̈ *f.* mother (1) **1A**
Mütze, -n *f.* cap (2) **1B**

N

nach *prep.* after; to; according to (1) **4B**; *prep.* past (time) (1) **2A**
   nach rechts/links to the right/left (2) **2A**
nachdem *conj.* after (3) **2A**
nachmachen *v.* to imitate (2) **4B**
Nachmittag, -e *m.* afternoon (1) **2B**
   nachmittags *adv.* in the afternoon (1) **2A**
Nachname, -n *m.* last name (1) **3A**
Nachricht, -en *f.* message (3) **3A**
   eine Nachricht hinterlassen *v.* to leave a message (3) **3A**
Nachspeise, -n *f.* dessert (1) **4B**
nächster/nächste/nächstes *adj.* next (1) **2B**
Nacht, -̈e *f.* night (1) **2B**
Nachttisch, -e *m.* night table (2) **2A**
nah(e) *adj.* near; nearby (3) **2B**
Nähe *f.* vicinity (3) **2B**
   in der Nähe von *f.* close to (3) **2B**
naiv *adj.* naïve (1) **3B**
Nase, -n *f.* nose (3) **1A**
   verstopfte Nase *f.* stuffy nose (3) **1A**
nass *adj.* wet (3) **4A**
Natur *f.* nature (3) **4A**
Naturkatastrophe, -n *f.* natural disaster (3) **4A**
Naturwissenschaft, -en *f.* science (1) **2A**
Nebel, - *m.* fog; mist (2) **3A**
neben *prep.* next to (2) **1B**
Nebenkosten *pl.* additional charges (2) **2A**
Neffe, -n *m.* nephew (2) **4B**
nehmen *v.* to take (1) **2B**
nein no (1) **1B**
nennen *v.* to call (2) **1A**
nervös *adj.* nervous (1) **3B**
nett *adj.* nice (1) **3B**
neugierig *adj.* curious (1) **3B**
neun nine (1) **1A**
nicht *adv.* not (1) **2B**
   nicht schlecht not bad (1) **1A**
nichts *pron.* nothing (2) **3B**
nie *adv.* never (1) **4A**
niedrig *adj.* low (3) **3A**
niemals *adv.* never (2) **3B**
niemand *pron.* no one (2) **3B**
niesen *v.* to sneeze (3) **1B**
normalerweise *adv.* usually (3) **1B**
Notaufnahme, -n *f.* emergency room (3) **1B**
Note, -n *f.* grade (on an assignment) (1) **1B**
Notfall, -̈e *m.* emergency (3) **3B**
Notiz, -en *f.* note (1) **1B**
November *m.* November (1) **2A**, (2) **3A**
Nummernschild, -er *n.* license plate (2) **4A**
nur *adv.* only (1) **4A**
nützlich *adj.* useful (1) **2A**
nutzlos *adj.* useless (1) **2A**

O

ob *conj.* whether; if (3) **2A**
Obst *n.* fruit (1) **4A**
obwohl *conj.* even though (2) **2A**; *conj.* although (3) **2A**
oder *conj.* or (2) **2A**

Ofen, ¨- *m.* oven (2) **2B**
öffentlich *adj.* public (2) **4A**
  öffentliche Verkehrsmittel *n.* public transportation (2) **4A**
öffnen *v.* to open (1) **2A**
oft *adv.* often (1) **4A**
ohne *prep.* without (1) **3B**
Ohr, -en *n.* ear (3) **1A**
Ökologie *f.* ecology (3) **4B**
ökologisch *adj.* ecological (3) **4B**
Oktober *m.* October (1) **2A**, (2) **3A**
Öl, -e *n.* oil (1) **4A**
Olivenöl, -e *n.* olive oil (1) **4A**
Oma, -s *f.* grandma (1) **3A**
online sein *v.* to be online (2) **4B**
Opa, -s *m.* grandpa (1) **3A**
orange *adj.* orange (2) **1B**
Orange, -n *f.* orange (1) **4A**
ordentlich *adj.* neat, tidy (2) **2B**
Ort, -e *m.* place (1) **1B**
Österreich *n.* Austria (3) **2B**
Österreicher, - / Österreicherin, -nen *m./f.* Austrian (person) (3) **2B**

P

Paar, -e *n.* couple (1) **3A**
packen *v.* to pack (2) **3B**
Paket, -e *n.* package (3) **2A**
Papa, -s *m.* dad (1) **3A**
Papier, -e *n.* paper
  Blatt Papier (*pl.* **Blätter Papier**) *n.* sheet of paper (1) **1B**
Papierkorb, ¨-e *m.* wastebasket (1) **1B**
Paprika, - *f.* pepper (1) **4A**
  grüne/rote Paprika *f.* green/red pepper (1) **4A**
Park, -s *m.* park (1) **1A**
parken *v.* to park (2) **4A**
  Parkverbot. No parking. (1) **3B**
Party, -s *f.* party (2) **1A**
  eine Party geben *v.* to throw a party (2) **1A**
Passagier, -e / Passagierin, -nen *m./f.* passenger (2) **3B**
passen *v.* to fit; to match (2) **1A**
passieren *v.* to happen (2) **1B**
Passkontrolle, -n *f.* passport control (2) **3B**
Passwort, ¨-er *n.* password (2) **4B**
Pasta *f.* pasta (1) **4A**
Patient, -en / Patientin, -nen *m./f.* patient (3) **1B**
Pause, -n *f.* break, recess (1) **1B**
Pension, -en *f.* guesthouse (2) **3B**
Person, -en *f.* person (1) **1A**
Personalausweis, -e *m.* ID card (2) **3B**
Personalchef, -s / die Personalchefin, -nen *m./f.* human resources manager (3) **3A**
persönlich *adj.* personal (1) **3B**
Pfanne, -n *f.* pan (2) **2B**
Pfeffer, - *m.* pepper (1) **4B**
Pferd, -e *n.* horse (3) **4A**
Pfirsich, -e *m.* peach (1) **4A**
Pflanze, -n *f.* plant (2) **2A**
Pfund, -e *n.* pound (1) **4A**
Physik *f.* physics (1) **2A**

Picknick, -s, *n.* picnic (3) **4A**
  ein Picknick machen *v.* to have a picnic (3) **4A**
Pilz, -e *m.* mushroom (1) **4A**
Pinnwand, ¨-e *f.* bulletin board (3) **3A**
Planet, -en *m.* planet (3) **4B**
  den Planeten retten *v.* to save the planet (3) **4B**
Platten, - *m.* flat tire (2) **4A**
  einen Platten haben *v.* to have a flat tire (2) **4A**
Platz, ¨-e *m.* court (1) **1A**
plus *plus* (1) **1B**
Politiker, - / Politikerin, -nen *m./f.* politician (3) **3B**
Polizeiwache, -n *f.* police station (3) **2A**
Polizist, -en / Polizistin, -nen *m./f.* police officer (2) **4A**
Post *f.* post office; mail (3) **2A**
  zur Post gehen *v.* to go to the post office (3) **2A**
Poster, - *n.* poster (2) **2A**
Postkarte, -n *f.* postcard (3) **2A**
Praktikum (*pl.* **die Praktika**) *n.* internship (3) **3A**
prima *adj.* great (1) **1A**
probieren *v.* to try (1) **3B**
  Probieren Sie mal! Give it a try! (1) **3B**
Problem, -e *n.* problem (1) **1A**
Professor, -en / Professorin, -nen *m./f.* professor (1) **1B**
Programm, -e *n.* program (2) **4B**
Prost! Cheers! (1) **4B**
Prozent, - *n.* percent (1) **1B**
Prüfung, -en *f.* exam, test (1) **1B**
Psychologe, -n / Psychologin, -nen *m./f.* psychologist (3) **3B**
Psychologie *f.* psychology (1) **2A**
Pullover, - *m.* sweater (2) **1B**
Punkt, -e *m.* period (1) **1B**
pünktlich *adj.* on time (2) **3B**
putzen *v.* to clean (2) **2B**
  sich die Zähne putzen *v.* to brush one's teeth (3) **1A**

Q

Querverweis, -e *m.* cross-reference

R

Radiergummi, -s *m.* eraser (1) **1B**
Rasen, - *m.* lawn, grass
  Betreten des Rasens verboten. Keep off the grass. (1) **3B**
sich rasieren *v.* to shave (3) **1A**
Rasierer, - *m.* razor (3) **1A**
Rasierschaum, ¨-e *m.* shaving cream (3) **1A**
Rathaus, ¨-er *n.* town hall (3) **2A**
rauchen *v.* to smoke
  Rauchen verboten. No smoking. (1) **3B**
rausbringen *v.* to bring out (2) **2B**
  den Müll rausbringen *v.* to take out the trash (2) **2B**
realistisch *adj.* realistic (3) **2A**
Rechnung, -en *f.* check (1) **4B**
Rechtsanwalt, ¨-e / **Rechtsanwältin, -nen** *m./f.* lawyer (1) **3B**
Rechtschreibung *f.* spelling

recyceln *v.* to recycle (3) **4B**
reden *v.* to talk (2) **1A**
  reden über *v.* to talk about (2) **3A**
Referat, -e *n.* presentation (1) **2A**
Referenz, -en *f.* reference (3) **3A**
Regen *m.* rain (2) **3A**
Regenmantel, - ¨ *m.* raincoat (2) **3A**
Regenschirm, -e *m.* umbrella (2) **3A**
Regierung, -en *f.* government (3) **4B**
regnen *v.* to rain (1) **2A**, (2) **3A**
Reis *m.* rice (1) **4A**
Reise, -n *f.* trip (2) **3B**
Reisebüro, -s *n.* travel agency (2) **3B**
reisen *v.* to travel (1) **2A**
Reisende, -n *m./f.* traveler (2) **3B**
Reiseziel, -e *n.* destination (2) **3B**
reiten *v.* to ride (1) **2B**
rennen *v.* to run (2) **1A**
Rente, -n *f.* pension
  in Rente gehen *v.* to retire (2) **1A**
Rentner, - / Rentnerin, -nen *m./f.* retiree (3) **3B**
reparieren *v.* to repair (2) **4A**
Restaurant, -s *n.* restaurant (1) **4B**
retten *v.* to save (3) **4B**
Rezept, -e *n.* prescription (3) **1B**
Richter, - / Richterin, -nen *m./f.* judge (3) **3B**
Richtung, -en *f.* direction (3) **2B**
  in Richtung *f.* toward (3) **2B**
Rindfleisch *n.* beef (1) **4A**
Rock, - ¨e *m.* skirt (2) **1B**
rosa *adj.* pink (2) **1B**
rot *adj.* red. (1) **3A**
rothaarig *adj.* red-haired (1) **3A**
Rücken, - *m.* back (3) **1A**
Rückenschmerzen *m. pl.* backache (3) **1B**
Rucksack, ¨-e *m.* backpack (1) **1B**
ruhig *adj.* calm (1) **3B**
Russe, -n / Russin, -nen *m./f.* Russian (person) (3) **2B**
Russisch *n.* Russian (language) (3) **2B**
Russland *n.* Russia (3) **2B**

S

Sache, -n *f.* thing (1) **1B**
Saft, - ¨e *m.* juice (1) **4B**
sagen *v.* to say (1) **2A**
Salat, -e *m.* lettuce; salad (1) **4A**
Salz, -e *n.* salt (1) **4B**
salzig *adj.* salty (1) **4B**
Samstag, -e *m.* Saturday (1) **2A**
  samstags *adv.* on Saturdays (1) **2A**
sauber *adj.* clean (2) **2B**
saure Regen *m.* acid rain (3) **4B**
Saustall *n.* pigsty (2) **2B**
  Es ist ein Saustall! It's a pigsty! (2) **2B**
Schach *n.* chess (1) **2B**
Schaf, -e *n.* sheep (3) **4A**
Schaffner, - / Schaffnerin, -nen *m./f.* ticket collector (2) **4A**
Schal, -s *m.* scarf (2) **1B**
scharf *adj.* spicy (1) **4B**
schauen *v.* to look (2) **3A**

Scheibenwischer, - *m.* windshield wiper (2) **4A**
Scheinwerfer, - *m.* headlight (2) **4A**
scheitern *v.* to fail (3) **3B**
schenken *v.* to give (a gift) (2) **1A**
schicken *v.* to send (3) **2A**
Schiff, -e *n.* ship (2) **4A**
Schinken, - *m.* ham (1) **4A**
Schlafanzug, -̈e *m.* pajamas (3) **1A**
schlafen *v.* to sleep (1) **2B**
Schlafzimmer, - *n.* bedroom (2) **2A**
Schlange, -n *f.* line (2) **3B**; *f.* snake (3) **4A**
  Schlange stehen *v.* to stand in line (2) **3B**
schlank *adj.* slim (1) **3A**
schlecht *adj.* bad (1) **3B**
  schlecht gekleidet *adj.* badly dressed (2) **1B**
Schlüssel, - *m.* key (2) **3B**
schmecken *v.* to taste (1) **4B**
Schmerz, -en *m.* pain (1) **1B**
sich duschen *v.* to take a shower (3) **1A**
sich schminken *v.* to put on makeup (3) **1A**
schmutzig *adj.* dirty (2) **2B**
Schnee *m.* snow (2) **3A**
schneien *v.* to snow (2) **3A**
schnell *adj.* fast (1) **3B**
schon *adv.* already, yet (2) **1B**
schön *adj.* pretty; beautiful (1) **3A**
  Schön dich/Sie kennen zu lernen. Nice to meet you. (1) **1A**
  Schönen Tag noch! Have a nice day! (1) **1A**
  Es ist schön draußen. It's nice out. (2) **3A**
Schrank, -̈e *m.* cabinet; closet (2) **2A**
schreiben *v.* to write (1) **2B**
  schreiben an *v.* to write to (2) **3A**
  sich schreiben *v.* to write one another (3) **1A**
Schreibtisch, -e *m.* desk (1) **1B**
Schreibwarengeschäft, -e *n.* paper-goods store (3) **2A**
Schublade, -n *f.* drawer (2) **2A**
schüchtern *adj.* shy (1) **3B**
Schuh, -e *m.* shoe (2) **1B**
Schulbuch, -̈er *n.* textbook (K–12) (1) **1B**
Schule, -n *f.* school (1) **1B**
Schüler, - / Schülerin, -nen (K-12) *m./f.* student (1) **1B**
Schulleiter, - / Schulleiterin, -nen *m./f.* principal (1) **1B**
Schulter, -n *f.* shoulder (3) **1A**
Schüssel, -n *f.* bowl (1) **4B**
schützen *v.* to protect (3) **4B**
schwach *adj.* weak (1) **3B**
Schwager, -̈ *m.* brother-in-law (1) **3A**
Schwägerin, -nen *f.* sister-in-law (1) **3A**
schwanger *adj.* pregnant (3) **1B**
schwänzen *v.* to cut class (1) **1B**
schwarz *adj.* black (2) **1B**
schwarzhaarig *adj.* black-haired (1) **3A**
Schweinefleisch *n.* pork (1) **4A**
Schweiz (die) *f.* Switzerland (2) **3A**
Schweizer, - / Schweizerin, -nen *m./f.* Swiss (person) (3) **2B**
schwer *adj.* rich, heavy (1) **4B**; *adj.* serious, difficult (3) **1B**
Schwester, -n *f.* sister (1) **1A**
Schwiegermutter, -̈ *f.* mother-in-law (1) **3A**

Schwiegervater, -̈ *m.* father-in-law (1) **3A**
schwierig *adj.* difficult (1) **2A**
Schwimmbad, -̈er *n.* swimming pool (1) **2B**
schwimmen *v.* to swim (1) **2B**
schwindlig *adj.* dizzy (3) **1B**
sechs six (1) **2A**
See, -n *m.* lake (3) **4A**
sehen *v.* to see (2) **2B**
sehr *adv.* very (1) **4A**
Seide, -n *f.* silk (2) **1B**
Seife, -n *f.* soap (3) **1A**
sein *v.* to be (1) **1A**
  (gleich) sein *v.* to equal (1) **1B**
sein *poss. adj.* his, its (1) **3A**
seit since; for (1) **4B**
Sekt, -e *m.* champagne (2) **1A**
Sektor, -en *m.* field; sector (3) **3A**
selten *adv.* rarely (1) **4A**
Seminar, -e *n.* seminar (1) **2A**
Seminarraum, -räume *m.* seminar room (1) **2A**
September *m.* September (1) **2A**, (2) **3A**
Serviette, -n *f.* napkin (1) **4B**
Sessel, - *m.* armchair (2) **2A**
setzen *v.* to put, place (2) **1B**; *v.* to put, set (3) **1A**
Shampoo, -s *n.* shampoo (3) **1A**
sicher *adv.* probably (3) **2A**
Sicherheitsgurt, -e *m.* seatbelt (2) **4A**
sie *pron.* she/they (1) **1A**
Sie *pron.* (form., sing./pl.) you (1) **1A**
sieben seven (1) **2A**
Silvester *n.* New Year's Eve (2) **1A**
singen *v.* to sing (1) **2B**
sitzen *v.* to sit (2) **1B**
Ski fahren *v.* to ski (1) **2B**
SMS, - *f.* text message (2) **4B**
Snack, -s *m.* snack (1) **4B**
so *adv.* so (1) **4A**
  so lala so-so (1) **1A**
Socke, -n *f.* sock (2) **1B**
Sofa, -s *n.* sofa; couch (2) **2A**
  Sofa surfen *v.* to couch surf (2) **3B**
Sohn, -̈e *m.* son (1) **3A**
solcher/solche/solches *pron.* such (2) **4B**
sollen *v.* to be supposed to (1) **3B**
Sommer, - *m.* summer (1) **2B**, (2) **3A**
sondern *conj.* but rather; instead (2) **2A**
Sonne, -n *f.* sun (3) **4A**
Sonnenaufgang, -̈e *m.* sunrise (3) **4A**
Sonnenbrand, -̈e *m.* sunburn (3) **1B**
Sonnenbrille, -n *f.* sunglasses (2) **1B**
Sonnenenergie *f.* solar energy (3) **4B**
Sonnenuntergang, -̈e *m.* sunset (3) **4A**
sonnig *adj.* sunny (2) **3A**
Sonntag, -e *m.* Sunday (1) **2A**
  sonntags *adv.* on Sundays (1) **2A**
Spanien *n.* Spain (3) **2B**
Spanier, - / Spanierin, -nen *m./f.* Spanish (person) (3) **2B**
Spanisch *n.* Spanish (language) (3) **2B**
spannend *adj.* exciting (3) **2A**
Spaß *m.* fun (2) **3B**
  Spaß machen *v.* to be fun (2) **3B**

(keinen) Spaß haben *v.* to (not) have fun (2) **1A**
spät *adj.* late
  Wie spät ist es? What time is it? (1) **2A**
spazieren gehen *v.* to go for a walk (1) **2B**
Spaziergang, -̈e *m.* walk
speichern *v.* to save (2) **4B**
Speisekarte, -n *f.* menu (1) **4B**
Spiegel, - *m.* mirror (2) **2A**
Spiel, -e *n.* match, game (1) **2B**
spielen *v.* to play (1) **2A**
Spieler, - / Spielerin, -nen *m./f.* player (1) **2B**
Spielfeld, -er *n.* field (1) **2B**
Spielkonsole, -n *f.* game console (2) **4B**
Spitze! *adj.* great! (1) **1A**
Sport *m.* sports (1) **2B**
  Sport treiben *v.* to exercise (3) **1B**
Sportart, -en *f.* sport; type of sport (1) **2B**
Sporthalle, -n *f.* gym (1) **2A**
sportlich *adj.* athletic (1) **3A**
sprechen *v.* to speak (1) **2B**
  sprechen über *v.* to speak about (2) **3A**
Spritze, -n *f.* shot (3) **1B**
  eine Spritze geben *v.* to give a shot (3) **1B**
Spüle, -n *f.* (kitchen) sink (2) **2B**
spülen *v.* to rinse (2) **2B**
  Geschirr spülen *v.* to do the dishes (2) **2B**
Spülmaschine, -n *f.* dishwasher (2) **2B**
Stadion (pl. Stadien) *n.* stadium (1) **2B**
Stadt, -̈e *f.* city (1) **1B**; *f.* town (3) **2B**
Stadtplan, -̈e *m.* city map (2) **3B**
Stahl *m.* steel (2) **2B**
stark *adj.* strong (1) **3B**
starten *v.* to start (2) **4B**
statt *conj.* instead of
Statue, -n *f.* statue (3) **2B**
staubsaugen *v.* to vacuum (2) **2B**
Staubsauger, - *m.* vacuum cleaner (2) **2B**
stehen *v.* to stand (2) **1B**
  Schlange stehen *v.* to stand in line (2) **3B**
stehlen *v.* to steal (1) **2B**
steif *adj.* stiff (3) **1B**
steigen *v.* to climb (2) **1B**
Stein, -e *m.* rock (3) **4A**
Stelle, -n *f.* place, position (2) **2A**; job (3) **3A**
  an deiner/Ihrer Stelle *f.* if I were you (3) **2A**
  eine Stelle suchen *v.* to look for a job (3) **3A**
stellen *v.* to put, place (2) **2A**
Stellenangebot, -e *n.* job opening (3) **3A**
sterben *v.* to die (2) **1B**
Stereoanlage, -n *f.* stereo system (2) **4B**
Stern -e *m.* star (3) **4A**
Stiefel, - *m.* boot (2) **1B**
Stiefmutter, -̈ *f.* stepmother (1) **3A**
Stiefsohn, -̈e *m.* stepson (1) **3A**
Stieftochter, -̈ *f.* stepdaughter (1) **3A**
Stiefvater, -̈ *m.* stepfather (1) **3A**
Stift, -e *m.* pen (1) **1B**
Stil, -e *m.* style (2) **1B**
still *adj.* still (1) **4B**
  stilles Wasser *n.* still water (1) **4B**
Stipendium, -en *n.* scholarship, grant (1) **2A**
Stock, -̈e *m.* floor (2) **2A**
  erster/zweiter Stock first/second floor (2) **2A**

stolz *adj.* proud (1) **3B**
Stoppschild, -er *n.* stop sign (2) **4A**
Strand, -̈e *m.* beach (1) **2B**
Straße, -n *f.* street (2) **4A**
sich streiten *v.* to argue (3) **1A**
Strom, -̈e *m.* stream (3) **4A**
Student, -en / Studentin, -nen *m./f.* (college/university) student (1) **1A**
Studentenwohnheim, -e *n.* dormitory (1) **2A**
studieren *v.* to study; major in (1) **2A**
Studium (*pl.* **Studien**) *n.* studies (1) **2A**
Stuhl, -̈e *m.* chair (1) **1A**
Stunde, -n *f.* lesson (1) **1B**; hour (1) **2A**
Stundenplan, -̈e *m.* schedule (1) **2A**
Sturm, -̈e *m.* storm (2) **3A**
suchen *v.* to look for (1) **2A**
   eine Stelle suchen *v.* to look for a job (3) **3A**
Supermarkt, -̈e *m.* supermarket (1) **4A**
Suppe, -n *f.* soup (1) **4B**
surfen *v.* to surf (2) **4B**
   im Internet surfen *v.* to surf the Web (2) **4B**
süß *adj.* sweet, cute (1) **3B**, (1) **4B**
Süßigkeit, - en *f.* candy (2) **1A**
Sweatshirt, -s *n.* sweatshirt (2) **1B**
Symptom, -e *n.* symptom (3) **1B**

T

Tablette, -n *f.* pill (3) **1B**
Tafel, -n *f.* board, black board (1) **1B**
Tag, -e *m.* day (1) **1A**, (2) **3A**
   Welcher Tag ist heute? What day is it today? (2) **3A**
täglich *adv.* every day; daily (1) **4A**
Tal, -̈er *n.* valley (3) **4A**
tanken *v.* to fill up (2) **4A**
Tankstelle, -n *f.* gas station (2) **4A**
Tante, -n *f.* aunt (1) **3A**
tanzen *v.* to dance (1) **2B**
Taschenrechner, - *m.* calculator (1) **1B**
Taschentuch, -̈er *n.* tissue (3) **1B**
Tasse, -n *f.* cup (1) **4B**
Tastatur, -en *f.* keyboard (2) **4B**
Taxi, -s *n.* taxi (2) **4A**
Taxifahrer, - / Taxifahrerin, -nen *m./f.* taxi driver (3) **3B**
Technik *f.* technology (2) **4B**
   Technik bedienen *v.* to use technology (2) **4B**
Tee, -s *m.* tea (1) **4B**
Teelöffel, - *m.* teaspoon (1) **4B**
Telefon, -e *n.* telephone (2) **4B**
   am Telefon on the telephone (3) **3A**
Telefonnummer, -n *f.* telephone number (3) **3A**
Telefonzelle, -n *f.* phone booth (2) **2B**
Teller, - *m.* plate (1) **4B**
Tennis *n.* tennis (1) **2B**
Teppich, -e *m.* rug (2) **2A**
Termin, -e *m.* appointment (3) **3A**
   einen Termin vereinbaren *v.* to make an appointment (3) **3A**
Terminkalender, - *m.* planner (1) **1B**
teuer *adj.* expensive (1) **3A**
Thermometer, - *n.* thermometer (3) **1B**
Thunfisch *m.* tuna (1) **4A**
Tier, -e *n.* animal (3) **4A**

Tierarzt, -̈e / Tierärztin, -nen *m./f.* veterinarian (3) **3B**
Tisch, -e *m.* table, desk (1) **1B**
   den Tisch decken *v.* to set the table (2) **2B**
Tischdecke, -n *f.* tablecloth (1) **4B**
Toaster, - *m.* toaster (2) **2B**
Tochter, -̈ *f.* daughter (1) **3A**
Toilette, -n *f.* toilet (2) **2A**
Tomate, -n *f.* tomato (1) **4A**
Topf, -̈e *m.* pot (2) **2B**
Tor, -e *n.* goal (in soccer, etc.) (1) **2B**
Tornado, -s *m.* tornado (3) **4A**
Torte, -n *f.* cake (2) **1A**
Touristenklasse *f.* economy class (2) **3B**
tragen *v.* to carry; wear (1) **2B**
Trägerhemd, -en *n.* tank top (2) **1B**
trainieren *v.* to practice (1) **2B**
Traube, -n *f.* grape (1) **4A**
träumen *v.* to dream (1) **2A**
traurig *adj.* sad (1) **3B**
treffen *v.* to meet; to hit (1) **2B**
   sich treffen *v.* to meet (each other) (3) **1A**
treiben *v.* to float; to push
   Sport treiben *v.* to exercise (3) **1B**
Treibsand *m.* quicksand (3) **4A**
sich trennen *v.* to separate, split up (3) **1A**
Treppe, -n *f.* stairway (2) **2A**
trinken *v.* to drink (1) **3B**
Trinkgeld, -er *n.* tip (1) **4B**
trocken *adj.* dry (3) **4A**
trotz *prep.* despite, in spite of (2) **4B**
Tschüss. Bye. (1) **1A**
T-Shirt, -s *n.* T-shirt (2) **1B**
tun *v.* to do (3) **1B**
   Es tut mir leid. I'm sorry. (1) **1A**
   weh tun *v.* to hurt (3) **1B**
Tür, -en *f.* door (1) **1B**
   Türen schließen. Keep doors closed. (1) **3B**
Türkei (die) *f.* Turkey (3) **2B**
Türke, -n / die Türkin, -nen *m./f.* Turkish (person) (3) **2B**
Türkisch *n.* Turkish (language) (3) **2B**
Turnschuhe *m. pl.* sneakers (2) **1B**

U

U-Bahn *f.* subway (2) **4A**
übel *adj.* nauseous (3) **1B**
üben *v.* to practice (1) **2B**
über *prep.* over, above (2) **1B**
übernachten *v.* to spend the night (2) **3B**
überall *adv.* everywhere (1) **4A**
Überbevölkerung *f.* overpopulation (3) **4B**
überlegen *v.* to think over (1) **4A**
übermorgen *adv.* the day after tomorrow (1) **2B**
überqueren *v.* to cross (3) **2B**
überraschen *v.* to surprise (2) **1A**
Überraschung, -en *f.* surprise (2) **1A**
überzeugend *adj.* persuasive (1) **1B**
Übung, -en *f.* practice
Uhr, -en *f.* clock (1) **1B**
   um... Uhr at... o'clock (1) **2A**
   Wie viel Uhr ist es? *v.* What time is it? (1) **2A**
um *prep.* Around; at (time) (1) **3B**
   um... zu in order to (2) **3B**

Umleitung, -en *f.* detour (2) **4A**
umtauschen *v.* to exchange (2) **2B**
Umwelt, -en *f.* environment (3) **4B**
umweltfreundlich *adj.* environmentally friendly (3) **4B**
Umweltschutz *m.* environmentalism (3) **4B**
umziehen *v.* to move (2) **2A**, (3) **1A**
   sich umziehen *v.* to change clothes (3) **1A**
unangenehm *adj.* unpleasant (1) **3B**
und *conj.* and (2) **2A**
Unfall, -̈e *m.* accident (2) **4A**
   einen Unfall haben *v.* to have an accident (2) **4A**
Universität, -en *f.* university; college (1) **1B**
unmöbliert *adj.* unfurnished (2) **2A**
unser *poss. adj.* our (1) **3A**
unter *prep.* under, below (2) **1B**
untergehen *v.* to set (sun) (3) **4A**
sich unterhalten *v.* to chat, have a conversation (3) **1A**
Unterkunft, -̈e *f.* accommodations (2) **3B**
Unterricht, -e *m.* class (1) **1B**
unterschreiben *v.* to sign (3) **2A**
Unterwäsche *f.* underwear (2) **1B**
Urgroßmutter, -̈ *f.* great grandmother (1) **3A**
Urgroßvater, -̈ *m.* great grandfather (1) **3A**
Urlaub, -e *m.* vacation (2) **3B**
   Urlaub machen *v.* to go on vacation (2) **3B**
   Urlaub nehmen *v.* to take time off (3) **3B**
USA (die) *pl.* U.S.A. (3) **2B**

V

Vase, -n *f.* vase (2) **2A**
Vater, -̈ *m.* father (1) **3A**
Veranstaltung, -en *f.* class (1) **2A**
Verb, -en *n.* verb (3) **1A**
verbessern *v.* to improve (3) **4B**
verbringen *v.* to spend (2) **3A**
verdienen *v.* to earn (3) **3B**
Vereinigten Staaten (die) *pl.* United States (3) **2B**
vergessen *v.* to forget (1) **2B**
Vergangenheit *f.* past (3) **4A**
verheiratet *adj.* married (1) **3A**
verkaufen *v.* to sell (1) **4A**
Verkäufer, - / Verkäuferin, -nen *m./f.* salesperson (2) **1B**
Verkehr *m.* traffic (2) **4A**
Verkehrsmittel *n.* transportation (2) **4A**
   öffentliche Verkehrsmittel *n. pl.* public transportation (2) **4A**
verkünden *v.* to announce (3) **4B**
sich verlaufen *v.* to get lost (3) **2B**
sich verletzen *v.* to hurt oneself (3) **1B**
Verletzung, -en *f.* injury (3) **1B**
sich verlieben (in) *v.* to fall in love (with) (3) **1A**
verlieren *v.* to lose (1) **2B**
verlobt *adj.* engaged (1) **3A**
Verlobte, -n *m./f.* fiancé(e) (1) **3A**
verschmutzen *v.* to pollute (3) **4B**
Verschmutzung *f.* pollution (3) **4B**
sich verspäten *v.* to be late (3) **1A**
Verspätung, -en *f.* delay (2) **3B**
Verständnis, -se *n.* comprehension
sich (das Handgelenk / den Fuß) verstauchen *v.* to sprain (one's wrist/ankle) (3) **1B**

verstehen *v.* to understand (1) **2A**
verstopfte Nase *f.* stuffy nose (3) **1B**
verwandt *adj.* related (3) **2A**
Verwandte, -n *m.* relative (1) **3A**
viel *adv.* much, a lot (of) (1) **4A**
  Viel Glück! Good luck! (2) **1A**
  Vielen Dank. Thank you very much. (1) **1A**
vielleicht *adv.* maybe (1) **4A**
vier *four* (1) **2A**
Viertel, - *n.* quarter (1) **2A**
  Viertel nach/vor quarter past/to (1) **2A**
Visum (*pl.* **Visa**) *n.* visa (2) **3B**
Vogel, -̈ *m.* bird (1) **3A**
voll *adj.* full (2) **3B**
  voll besetzt *adj.* fully occupied (2) **3B**
Volleyball *m.* volleyball (1) **2B**
von *prep.* from (1) **4B**
vor *prep.* in front of, before (2) **1B**; *prep.* to (1) **2A**
vorbei *adv.* over, past (2) **3A**
vorbereiten *v.* to prepare (1) **4A**
  sich vorbereiten (auf) *v.* to prepare oneself (for) (3) **1A**
Vorbereitung, -en *f.* preparation
Vorhang, -̈e *m.* curtain (2) **2A**
Vorlesung, -en *f.* lecture (1) **2A**
vormachen *v.* to fool (2) **4B**
Vormittag, -e *m.* midmorning (1) **2B**
vormittags *adv.* before noon (1) **2A**
Vorspeise, -n *f.* appetizer (1) **4B**
vorstellen *v.* to introduce (3) **1A**
  sich vorstellen *v.* to introduce oneself (3) **1A**
  sich (etwas) vorstellen *v.* to imagine (something) (3) **1A**
Vorstellungsgespräch, -e *n.* job interview (3) **3A**
Vortrag, -̈e *m.* lecture (2) **2B**
Vulkan, -e *m.* volcano (3) **4A**

W

wachsen *v.* to grow (2) **1B**
während *prep.* during (2) **4B**
wahrscheinlich *adv.* probably (3) **2A**
Wald, -̈er *m.* forest (1) **2B**, (3) **4A**
Wand, -̈e *f.* wall (2) **1B**
wandern *v.* to hike (1) **2A**
wann *interr.* when (1) **2A**
  Wann hast du Geburtstag? When is your birthday? (2) **3A**
warm *adj.* warm (3) **2A**
warten *v.* to wait (for) (1) **2A**
  warten auf *v.* to wait for (2) **3A**
  in der Warteschleife sein *v.* to be on hold (3) **3B**
warum *interr.* why (1) **2A**
was *interr.* what (1) **2A**
  Was geht ab? What's up? (1) **1A**
  Was ist das? What is that? (1) **1B**
Wäsche *f.* laundry (2) **2B**
waschen *v.* to wash (1) **2B**
  sich waschen *v.* to wash (oneself) (3) **1A**
  Wäsche waschen *v.* to do laundry (2) **2B**
Wäschetrockner, - *m.* dryer (2) **2B**
Waschmaschine, -n *f.* washing machine (2) **2B**
Waschsalon, -s *m.* laundromat (3) **2A**
Wasser *n.* water (1) **4B**
Wasserfall, -̈e *m.* waterfall (3) **4A**
Wasserkrug, -̈e *m.* water pitcher (1) **4B**

Website, -s *f.* web site (2) **4B**
Weg, -e *m.* path (3) **4A**
wegen *prep.* because of (2) **4B**
wegräumen *v.* to put away (2) **2B**
wegwerfen *v.* to throw away (3) **4B**
weh tun *v.* to hurt (3) **1B**
Weihnachten, - *n.* Christmas (2) **1A**
weil *conj.* because (3) **2A**
Wein, -e *m.* wine (1) **4B**
weinen *v.* to cry (3) **1B**
weise *adj.* wise (1) **3B**
weiß *adj.* white (2) **1B**
weit *adj.* loose; big (2) **1B**; *adj.* far (3) **2B**
  weit von *adj.* far from (3) **2B**
  weiter geht's moving forward
welcher/welche/welches *interr.* which (1) **2A**
  Welcher Tag ist heute? What day is it today? (2) **3A**
Welt, -en *f.* world (3) **4B**
wem *interr.* whom (dat.) (1) **4B**
wen *interr.* whom (acc.) (1) **2A**
Wende, -n *f.* turning point (3) **4B**
wenig *adj.* little; not much (3) **2A**
wenn *conj.* when; whenever; if (3) **2A**
  wenn... dann if... then (3) **2A**
  wenn... nur if... only (3) **2A**
wer *interr.* who (1) **2A**
  Wer ist das? Who is it? (1) **1B**
  Wer spricht? Who's calling? (3) **3A**
werden *v.* to become (1) **2B**
werfen *v.* to throw (1) **2B**
Werkzeug, -e *n.* tool kit
wessen *interr.* whose (4) **4B**
Wetter *n.* weather (2) **3A**
  Wie ist das Wetter? What's the weather like? (2) **3A**
wichtig *adj.* important (2) **3B**
wie *interr.* how (2) **2A**
  wie viel? *interr.* how much? (1) **2A**
  wie viele? *interr.* how many? (1) **2A**
  Wie alt bist du? How old are you? (1) **1B**
  Wie heißt du? *(inf.)* What's your name? (1) **1A**
wiederholen *v.* to repeat (1) **2A**
Wiederholung, -en *f.* repetition; revision
wiegen *v.* to weigh (1) **4B**
willkommen welcome (1) **1A**
  Herzlich willkommen! Welcome! (1) **1A**
Windenergie *f.* wind energy (3) **4B**
windig *adj.* windy (2) **3A**
Windschutzscheibe, -n *f.* windshield (2) **4A**
Winter, - *m.* winter (1) **2B**, (2) **3A**
wir *pron.* we (1) **1A**
wirklich *adv.* really (1) **4A**
Wirtschaft, -en *f.* business; economy (1) **2A**
wischen *v.* to wipe, mop (2) **2B**
wissen *v.* to know (information) (2) **1B**
Wissenschaftler, - / **Wissenschaftlerin, -nen** *m./f.* scientist (3) **3B**
Witwe, -n *f.* widow (1) **3A**
Witwer, - *m.* widower (1) **3A**
wo *interr.* where (1) **2A**
woanders *adv.* somewhere else (1) **4A**
Woche, -n *f.* week (1) **2A**
Wochenende, -n *n.* weekend (1) **2A**
woher *interr.* from where (1) **2A**; (2) **2A**
wohin *interr.* where to (1) **2A**

wohl *adv.* probably (3) **2A**
wohnen *v.* to live (somewhere) (1) **2A**
Wohnung, -en *f.* apartment (2) **2A**
Wohnzimmer, - *n.* living room (2) **2A**
Wolke, -n *f.* cloud (2) **3A**
wolkig *adj.* cloudy (2) **3A**
Wolle *f.* wool (2) **1B**
wollen *v.* to want (1) **3B**
Wörterbuch, -̈er *n.* dictionary (1) **1B**
Wortschatz, -̈e *m.* vocabulary
wünschen *v.* to wish (3) **1A**
  sich (etwas) wünschen *v.* to wish (for something) (3) **1A**
Würstchen, - *n.* sausage (1) **4A**

Z

Zahn, -̈e *m.* tooth (3) **1A**
  sich die Zähne putzen *m.* to brush one's teeth (3) **1A**
Zahnarzt, -̈e / **Zahnärztin, -nen** *m./f.* dentist (3) **1B**
Zahnbürste, -n *f.* toothbrush (3) **1A**
Zahnpasta (*pl.* **Zahnpasten**) *f.* toothpaste (3) **1A**
Zahnschmerzen *m. pl.* toothache (3) **1B**
Zapping *n.* channel surfing
Zebrastreifen, - *m.* crosswalk (3) **2B**
Zeh, -en *m.* toe (3) **1A**
zehn ten (1) **2A**
zeigen *v.* to show (1) **2B**
Zeit, -en *f.* time (3) **3B**
Zeitschrift, -en *f.* magazine (3) **2A**
Zeitung, -en *f.* newspaper (2) **3B**, (3) **2A**
Zelt, -e *n.* tent (2) **3B**
Zeltplatz, -̈e *m.* camping area (2) **3B**
Zeugnis, -se *n.* report card, grade report (1) **1B**
ziehen *v.* to pull (1) **3B**
ziemlich *adv.* quite
  ziemlich gut pretty well (1) **1A**
Zimmer, - *n.* room (1) **1A**
  Zimmer frei vacancy (2) **2A**
Zimmerservice *m.* room service (2) **3B**
Zoll *m.* customs (2) **3B**
zu *adv.* too (1) **4A**; *prep.* to; for; at (1) **4B**
  bis zu *prep.* up to; until (3) **2B**
  um... zu (in order) to (2) **3B**
  Zum Wohl! Cheers! (1) **4B**
zubereiten *v.* to prepare (2) **3A**
zuerst *adv.* first (2) **3B**
Zug, -̈e *m.* train (2) **4A**
zumachen *v.* to close (2) **4B**
sich zurechtfinden *v.* to find one's way (3) **2B**
zurückkommen *v.* to come back (1) **4A**
zusammen *adv.* together (1) **4A**
zuschauen *v.* to watch (1) **4A**
zuverlässig *adj.* reliable (3) **3B**
zwanzig twenty (1) **2A**
zwei two (1) **2A**
zweite *adj.* second (1) **2A**
Zwiebel, -n *f.* onion (1) **4A**
Zwilling, -e *m.* twin (1) **3A**
zwischen *prep.* between (2) **1B**
zwölf twelve (1) **2A**

Englisch-Deutsch

A

a ein/eine (1) **1A**
able: to be able to können *v.* (1) **3B**
about über *prep.* (2) **1B**
  to be about handeln von *v.* (2) **3A**
above über *prep.* (2) **1B**
abroad Ausland *n.* (2) **3B**
accident Unfall, -¨e *m.* (2) **4A**
  to have an accident einen Unfall haben *v.* (2) **4A**
accommodation Unterkunft, -¨e *f.* (2) **3B**
according to nach *prep.* (1) **4B**
accountant Buchhalter, - / Buchhalterin, -nen *m./f* (3) **3B**
acid rain saurer Regen *m.* (3) **4B**
across (from) gegenüber (von) *prep.* (3) **2B**
address Adresse, -n *f.* (3) **2A**
address book Adressbuch, -¨er *n.* (3) **3A**
adopt adoptieren *v.* (1) **3A**
afraid: to be afraid of Angst haben vor *v.* (2) **3A**
after nach *prep.* (1) **4B**; nachdem *conj.* (3) **2A**
afternoon Nachmittag, -e *m.* (1) **2B**
  in the afternoon nachmittags *adv.* (1) **2A**
against gegen *prep.* (1) **3B**
air Luft, -¨e *f.* (3) **4A**
airplane Flugzeug, -e *n.* (2) **3B**
airport Flughafen, -¨ *m.* (2) **3B**
all ganz *adj.* (2) **3B**; alle *pron.* (2) **3B**
allergic (to) allergisch (gegen) *adj.* (3) **1B**
allergy Allergie, -n *f.* (3) **1B**
allow lassen *v.* (1) **2B**
  to be allowed to dürfen *v.* (1) **3B**
almost fast *adv* (1) **4A**
alone allein *adv.* (1) **4A**
along entlang *prep.* (1) **3B**
already schon (2) **1B**
alright: Are you alright? Alles klar? (1) **1A**;
also auch *adv.* (1) **4A**
although obwohl *conj.* (3) **2A**
always immer *adv.* (1) **4A**
ambulance Krankenwagen, - *m.* (3) **1B**
America Amerika *n.* (3) **2B**
American amerikanisch *adj.* (3) **2B**; (person) Amerikaner, - / Amerikanerin, -nen *m./f.* (3) **2B**
  American football American Football *m.* (1) **2B**
and und *conj.* (2) **2A**
animal Tier, -e *n.* (3) **4A**
angry böse *adj.*
  to get angry (about) sich ärgern (über) *v.* (3) **1A**
anniversary Jahrestag, -e *m.* (2) **1A**
announce verkünden *v.* (3) **4B**
answer antworten *v.* (1) **2A**; beantworten *v.* (1) **4B**; Antwort, -en *f.*
  to answer the phone einen Anruf entgegennehmen *v.* (3) **3A**
answering machine Anrufbeantworter, - *m.* (2) **4B**
anything: Anything else? Noch einen Wunsch? (1) **4B**; Sonst noch etwas? (1) **4A**
apartment Wohnung, -en *f.* (2) **2A**
appetizer Vorspeise, -n *f.* (1) **4B**
apple Apfel, ¨- *m.* (1) **1A**

applicant Bewerber, - / Bewerberin, -nen *m./f.* (3) **3A**
apply sich bewerben *v.* (3) **3A**
appointment Termin, -e *m.* (3) **3A**
April April *m.* (1) **2A**
architect Architekt, -en / Architektin, -nen *m./f.* (1) **3B**
architecture Architektur, -en *f.* (1) **2A**
argue sich streiten *v.* (3) **1A**
arm Arm, -e *m.* (3) **1A**
armchair Sessel, - *m.* (2) **2A**
around um *prep.* (1) **3B**
arrival Ankunft, -¨e *f.* (2) **3B**
arrive ankommen *v.* (1) **4A**
arrogant eingebildet *adj.* (1) **3B**
art Kunst, -¨e *f.* (1) **2A**
artichoke Artischocke, -n *f.* (1) **4A**
as als *conj.* (2) **4A**
  as if als ob (3) **2A**
ask fragen *v.* (1) **2A**
  to ask about fragen nach *v.* (2) **3A**
assistant Assistent, -en / Assistentin, -nen *m./f.* (3) **3A**
at um *prep.* (1) **3B**; bei *prep.* (1) **4A**; an *prep.* (2) **1B**
  at... o'clock um... Uhr (1) **2A**
athletic sportlich *adj.* (1) **2B**
ATM Geldautomat, -en *m.* (3) **2A**
Attention! Achtung!
attic Dachboden, -¨ *m.* (2) **2A**
August August *m.* (1) **2A**
aunt Tante, -n *f.* (1) **3A**
Austria Österreich *n.* (3) **2B**
Austrian österreichisch *adj.* (3) **2B**; (person) Österreicher, - / Österreicherin, -nen *m./f.* (3) **2B**
autumn Herbst, -e *m.* (1) **2B**
avenue Allee, -n *f.*
awful furchtbar *adj.* (2) **3A**

B

baby Baby, -s *n.* (1) **3A**
back Rücken, - *m.* (3) **1A**
backache Rückenschmerzen *m. pl.* (3) **1B**
backpack Rucksack, -¨e *m.* (1) **1B**
bad schlecht *adj.* (1) **3B**
  badly dressed schlecht gekleidet *adj.* (2) **1B**
bake backen *v.* (1) **2B**
baked goods Gebäck *n.* (2) **1A**
bakery Bäckerei, -en *f.* (1) **4A**
balcony Balkon, - e *m.* (2) **2A**
ball Ball, -¨e *m.* (1) **2B**
balloon Ballon, -e *m.* (1) **1A**
ball-point pen Kuli, -s *m.* (1) **1B**
banana Banane, -n *f.* (1) **4A**
bank Bank, -en *f.* (3) **2A**
  at the bank auf der Bank *f.* (3) **2B**
bank account Konto (*pl.* Konten) *n.* (3) **2A**
bank employee Bankangestellte, -n *m./f.* (3) **3B**
baseball Baseball *m.* (1) **2B**
basketball Basketball *m.* (1) **2B**
bath: to take a bath sich baden *v.* (3) **1A**
bathing suit Badeanzug, -¨e *m.* (2) **1B**

bathrobe Bademantel, ¨- *m.* (3) **1A**
bathroom Badezimmer, - *n.* (3) **1A**
bathtub Badewanne, -n *f.* (2) **2A**
battery charger Ladegerät, -e *n.* (2) **4B**
be sein *v.* (1) **1A**
  Is/Are there... Ist/Sind hier...? *v.* (1) **1B**; Gibt es...? (1) **2B**
  There is/are... Da ist/sind... *v.* (1) **1A**; Es gibt... (1) **2B**
beach Strand, -¨e *m.* (1) **2B**
bean Bohne, -n *f.*
beard Bart, -¨e *m.* (3) **1A**
beautiful schön *adj.* (1) **3A**
beauty salon Kosmetiksalon, -s *m.* (3) **2A**
because denn *conj.* (2) **2A**; weil *conj.* (3) **2A**
  because of wegen *prep.* (2) **4B**
become werden *v.* (1) **1A**
bed Bett, -en *n.* (2) **2A**
  to go to bed ins Bett gehen *v.* (3) **1A**
  to make the bed das Bett machen *v.* (2) **2B**
bedroom Schlafzimmer, - *n.* (2) **2A**
beef Rindfleisch *n.* (1) **4A**
beer Bier, -e *n.* (1) **4B**
before vor *prep.* (2) **1B**; bevor *conj.* (2) **4A**
  before noon vormittags *adv.* (1) **2A**
begin anfangen *v.* (1) **4A**; beginnen *v.* (2) **2A**
behind hinter *prep.* (2) **1B**
believe glauben *v.* (2) **1A**; meinen *v.* (3) **4B**
belly Bauch, -¨e *m.* (3) **1A**
belong gehören *v.* (2) **1A**
below unter *prep.* (2) **1B**
belt Gürtel, - *m.* (2) **1B**
bench Bank, -¨e *f.* (3) **2B**
best beste/bester/bestes *adj.* (2) **4A**
  All the best! Mach's gut! *v.* (1) **3B**; alles Gute (3) **2A**
better besser *adj.* (2) **4A**
  to get better gesund werden *v.* (3) **1B**
between zwischen *prep.* (2) **1B**
beverage Getränk, -e *n.* (1) **4B**
bicycle Fahrrad, -¨er *n.* (1) **2B**
big groß, weit *adj.* (1) **3A**
bill (money) Geldschein, -e *m.* (3) **2A**
biology Biologie *f.* (1) **2A**
bird Vogel, -¨ *m.* (1) **3A**
birth Geburt, -en *f.* (2) **1A**
birthday Geburtstag, -e *m.* (2) **1A**
  When is your birthday? Wann hast du Geburtstag? (2) **3A**
black schwarz *adj.* (2) **1B**
  black board Tafel, -n *f.* (1) **1B**
  black-haired schwarzhaarig *adj.* (1) **3A**
bland fade *adj.* (1) **4B**
blanket Decke, -n *f.* (2) **2B**
blond blond *adj.* (1) **3A**
  blond hair blonde Haare *n. pl.* (1) **3A**
blood pressure Blutdruck *m.* (1) **1B**
blouse Bluse, -n *f.* (2) **1B**
blue blau *adj.* (1) **3A**
board Tafel, -n *f.* (1) **1B**
boarding pass Bordkarte, -n *f.* (2) **3B**
boat Boot, -e *n.* (2) **4A**
body Körper, - *m.* (3) **1A**

book Buch, -¨er *n.* (1) **1A**
bookshelf Bücherregal, -e *n.* (2) **2A**
boot Stiefel, - *m.* (2) **1B**
boring langweilig *adj.* (1) **3B**
boss Chef, -s / Chefin, -nen *m./f.* (3) **3B**
bottle Flasche, -n *f.* (1) **4B**
bowl Schüssel, -n *f.* (1) **4B**
boy Junge, -n *m.* (1) **1A**
brakes Bremse, -n *f.* (2) **4A**
brave mutig *adj.* (1) **3B**
bread Brot, -e *n.* (1) **4A**
break brechen *v.* (1) **2B**
　to break (an arm / a leg) sich (den Arm /Bein) brechen *v.* (3) **1B**
　Break a leg! Hals- und Beinbruch! (2) **1A**
breakfast Frühstück, -e *n.* (1) **4B**
bridge Brücke, -n *f.* (3) **2B**
bright hell *adj.* (2) **1B**
bring bringen *v.* (1) **2A**
　to bring along mitbringen *v.* (1) **4A**
　to bring out rausbringen (2) **2B**
　to bring with mitnehmen *v.* (3) **2B**
broom Besen, - *m.* (2) **2B**
brother Bruder, -¨ *m.* (1) **1A**
brother-in-law Schwager, -¨ *m.* (1) **3A**
brown braun *adj.* (2) **1B**
　brown-haired braunhaarig *adj.;* brünett *adj.* (1) **3A**
bruise blauer Fleck, -e *m.* (3) **1B**
brunette brünett *adj.* (1) **3A**
brush Bürste, -n *f.* (3) **1A**
　to brush one's hair sich die Haare bürsten *v.* (3) **1A**
　to brush one's teeth sich die Zähne putzen *v* (3) **1A**
build bauen *v.* (1) **2A**
building Gebäude, - *n.* (3) **2A**
bulletin board Pinnwand, -¨e *f.* (3) **3A**
burn brennen *v.* (1) **1A**
bus Bus, -se *m.* (2) **4A**
bus stop Bushaltestelle, -n *f.* (2) **4A**
bush Busch, -¨e *m.* (3) **4A**
business Wirtschaft, -en *f.* (1) **2A**; Geschäft, -e *n.* (3) **3A**
　business class Businessklasse *f.* (2) **3B**
businessman / businesswoman Geschäftsmann, -¨er / Geschäftsfrau, -en *m./f.* (*pl.* Geschäftsleute) (1) **3B**
but aber *conj.* (2) **2A**
　but rather sondern *conj.* (2) **2A**
butcher shop Metzgerei, -en *f.* (1) **4A**
butter Butter *f.* (1) **4A**
buy kaufen *v.* (1) **2A**
by an *prep.* (1) **1B**; bei; von (1) **4B**
Bye! Tschüss! (1) **1A**

<hr>

C

cabinet Schrank, -¨e *m.* (2) **2A**
café Café, -s *n.* (1) **2A**
cafeteria Cafeteria, (*pl.* Cafeterien) *f.;* (**college/university**) Mensa, Mensen *f.* (1) **1B**
cake Kuchen, - *m.* (1) **4A**
cake Torte, -n *f.* (2) **1A**

calculator Taschenrechner, - *m.* (1) **1B**
call anrufen *v.* (1) **4A**; sich anrufen (3) **1A**; nennen *v.* (2) **1A**
　Who's calling? Wer spricht? (3) **3A**
calm ruhig *adj.* (1) **3B**
camping Camping *n.* (1) **2B**
camping area Zeltplatz, -¨e *m.* (2) **3B**
can können *v.* (1) **3B**
Canada Kanada *n.* (3) **2B**
Canadian kanadisch *adj.* (3) **2B**; (**person**) Kanadier, - / Kanadierin, -nen *m./f.* (3) **2B**
cancel abbrechen *v.* (2) **3B**
candidate Kandidat, -en *m.* (3) **3A**
candy Süßigkeit, -en *f.* (2) **1A**
cap Mütze, -n *f.* (2) **1B**
car Auto, -s *n.* (1) **1A**
　to drive a car Auto fahren *v.* (2) **4A**
card Karte, -n *f.* (1) **4B**
career Karriere, -n *f.* (3) **3B**
caretaker Hausmeister, - / Hausmeisterin, -nen *m./f.* (3) **3B**
carpool Fahrgemeinschaft, -en *f.* (3) **4B**
carrot Karotte, -n *f.* (1) **4A**
carry tragen *v.* (1) **2B**
carry-on luggage Handgepäck *n.* (2) **3B**
cash bar *adj.* (3) **2A**; Bargeld *n.* (3) **2A**
　to pay in cash bar bezahlen *v.* (3) **2A**
cat Katze, -n *f.* (1) **3A**
catch fangen *v.* (1) **2B**
　to catch a cold sich erkälten *v.* (3) **1A**
CD player CD-Player, - *m.* (2) **4B**
celebrate feiern *v.* (2) **1A**
celebration Fest, -e *n.* (2) **1A**
cell phone Handy, -s *n.* (2) **4B**
cellar Keller, - *m.* (2) **2A**
ceramic Keramik, -en *f.* (2) **2B**
chair Stuhl, -¨e *m.* (1) **1A**
champagne Sekt, -e *m.* (2) **1A**
championship Meisterschaft, -en *f.* (1) **2B**
change Kleingeld *n.* (3) **2A**
　to change clothes sich umziehen *v.* (3) **1A**
channel Sender, - *m.* (2) **4B**
　channel surfing Zapping *n.*
charge laden *v.* (2) **4B**
chat sich unterhalten *v.* (3) **1A**
cheap billig *adj.* (2) **1B**
check Rechnung, -en *f.* (1) **4B**
Cheers! Prost! (1) **4B**; Zum Wohl! (1) **4B**
cheese Käse, - *m.* (1) **4A**
chemistry Chemie *f.* (1) **2A**
chess Schach *n* (1) **2B**
chicken Huhn,-¨er *n.* 12A; (**food**) Hähnchen, - *n.* (1) **4A**
child Kind, -er *n.* (1) **1A**
China China *n.* (3) **2B**
Chinese (**person**) Chinese, -n / Chinesin, -nen *m./f.* (3) **2B**; (**language**) Chinesisch *n.* (3) **2B**
Christmas Weihnachten, - *n.* (2) **1A**
church Kirche, -n *f.* (3) **2B**
city Stadt, -¨e *f.* (2) **1B**
　city center Innenstadt, -¨e *f.*
claim behaupten *v.* (3) **4B**
class Klasse, -n *f.* (1) **1B**; Unterricht *m.* (1) **1B**;

Veranstaltung, -en *f.* (1) **2A**
　first/second class erste/zweite Klasse (2) **4A**
classical klassisch *adj.* (3) **2A**
classmate Klassenkamerad, -en / Klassenkameradin, -nen *m./f.* (1) **1B**
classroom Klassenzimmer, - *n.* (1) **1B**
clean sauber *adj.* (2) **2B**; putzen *v.* (2) **2B**
　to clean up aufräumen *v.* (2) **2B**
cliff Klippe, -n *f.* (3) **4A**
climb steigen *v.* (2) **1B**
　to climb (mountain) klettern *v.* (1) **2B**
　to climb (stairs) (die Treppe) hochgehen *v.* (3) **2B**
clock Uhr, -en *f.* (1) **1B**
　at... o'clock um... Uhr (1) **2A**
close zumachen *v.* (2) **4B**; nah *adj.* (3) **2B**
　close to in der Nähe von *prep.* (3) **2B**
closed geschlossen *adj.* (3) **2A**
closet Schrank, -¨e *m.* (2) **2A**
clothes Kleidung *f.* (2) **1B**
cloud Wolke, -n *f.* (2) **3A**
cloudy wolkig *adj.* (2) **3A**
coast Küste, -n *f.* (3) **4A**
coat Mantel, -¨ *m.* (2) **1B**
coffee Kaffee, -s *m.* (1) **4B**
coffeemaker Kaffeemaschine, -n *f.* (2) **2B**
coin Münze, -n *f.* (3) **2A**
cold kalt *adj.* (2) **3A**; Erkältung, -en *f.* (3) **1B**
　to catch a cold sich erkälten *v.* (3) **1A**
college Universität, -en *f.* (1) **1B**
college instructor Dozent, -en / Dozentin, -nen *m./f.* (1) **2A**
color Farbe, -n *f.* (2) **1B**
　solid colored einfarbig *adj.* (2) **1B**
colorful bunt *adj.* (3) **2A**
comb Kamm, -¨e *m.* (3) **1A**
　to comb (one's hair) sich (die Haare) kämmen *v.* (3) **1A**
come kommen *v.* (1) **2A**
　to come along mitkommen *v.* (1) **4A**
　to come back zurückkommen *v.* (1) **4A**
comma Komma, -s *f.* (1) **1B**
compact disc CD, -s *f.* (2) **4B**
company Firma (*pl.* die Firmen) *f.* (3) **3A**
complicated kompliziert *adj.* (3) **2A**
computer Computer, - *m.* (1) **1B**
computer science Informatik *f.* (1) **2A**
concert Konzert, -e *n.* (2) **1B**
congratulate gratulieren *v.* (2) **1A**
　Congratulations! Herzlichen Glückwunsch! (2) **1A**
construction zone Baustelle, -n *f.* (2) **4A**
conversation: to have a conversation sich unterhalten *v.* (3) **1A**
cook kochen *v.* (1) **2B**; Koch, -¨e / Köchin, -nen *m./f.* (1) **4B**
cookie Keks, -e *m.* (2) **1A**
cool kühl *adj.* (2) **3A**
corner Ecke, -n *f.* (3) **2B**
correct korrigieren *v.* (1) **2A**
cost kosten *v.* (1) **2A**
cotton Baumwolle *f.* (2) **1B**
couch Sofa, -s *n.* (2) **3B**
　to couch surf Sofa surfen *v.* (2) **3B**

cough husten *v.* **(3) 1B**
country Land, -¨er *n.* **(2) 3B**
countryside Landschaft, -en *f.* **(3) 4A**
couple Paar, -e *n.* **(1) 3A**
courageous mutig *adj.*
course Gang, -¨e *m.* **(1) 4B**
  first/second course erster/zweiter Gang *m.* **(1) 4B**
  main course Hauptspeise, -en *f.* **(1) 4B**
court Platz, -¨e *m.* **(1) 1A**
cousin Cousin, -s / Cousine, -n *m./f.* **(1) 3A**
cover decken *v.* **(2) 2B**
cow Kuh, -¨e *f.* **(3) 4A**
cram (for a test) büffeln *v.* **(1) 2A**
cross überqueren *v.* **(3) 2B**
  to cross the street die Straße überqueren *v.* **(3) 2B**
cross-reference Querverweis, -e *m.*
crosswalk Zebrastreifen, - *pl.* **(3) 2B**
cruel grausam *adj.;* gemein *adj.* **(1) 3B**
cruise Kreuzfahrt, -en *f.* **(2) 3B**
cry weinen *v.* **(1) 1B**
cup Tasse, -n *f.* **(1) 4B**
curious neugierig *adj.* **(1) 3B**
curly lockig *adj.* **(1) 3A**
curtain Vorhang, -¨e *m.* **(2) 2A**
custodian Hausmeister, - / Hausmeisterin, -nen *m./f.* **(3) 3B**
customer Kunde, -n /Kundin, -nen *m./f.* **(3) 1B**
customs Zoll *m.* **(2) 3B**
cut Schnitt, -e *m.* **(2) 1B**
  to cut class schwänzen *v.* **(1) 1B**
cute süß *adj.* **(1) 3B**
CV Lebenslauf, -¨e *m.* **(3) 3A**

D

dad Papa, -s *m.* **(1) 3A**
daily täglich *adv.* **(1) 4A**
  daily routine Alltagsroutine *f.* **(3) 1A**
dance tanzen *v.* **(1) 2B**
danger Gefahr, -en *f.* **(3) 4B**
dark dunkel *adj.* **(1) 3A**
  dark-haired dunkelhaarig *adj.* **(1) 3A**
darling Liebling, -e *m.*
date Datum (*pl.* Daten) *n.* **(2) 3A**
  What is the date today? Der wievielte ist heute? *v.* **(1) 2A**
daughter Tochter, -¨ *f.* **(1) 3A**
day Tag, -e *m.* **(1) 1A**
  every day täglich *adv.* **(1) 4A**
Dear Lieber/Liebe *m./f.* **(1) 3B**
December Dezember *m.* **(1) 2A**
decide sich entschließen *v.* **(1) 4B**
definitely bestimmt *adv.* **(1) 4A**
degree Abschluss, -¨e *m.* **(1) 2A**; Grad *n.* **(3) 3A**
  It's 18 degrees out. Es sind 18 Grad draußen. **(2) 3A**
delay Verspätung, -en *f.* **(2) 3B**
delete löschen *v.* **(2) 4B**
delicatessen Feinkostgeschäft, -e *n.* **(1) 4A**
delicious lecker *adj.* **(1) 4B**
demanding anspruchsvoll *adj.* **(3) 3B**

dentist Zahnarzt, -¨e / Zahnärztin, -nen *m./f.* **(3) 1B**
department store Kaufhaus, -¨er *n.* **(3) 2B**
departure Abflug, -¨e *m.* **(2) 3B**
deposit (money) (Geld) einzahlen *v.* **(3) 2A**
describe beschreiben *v.* **(1) 2A**
description Beschreibung, -en *f.* **(1) 3B**
desk Schreibtisch, -e *m.* **(1) 1B**
despite trotz *prep.* **(2) 4B**
dessert Nachspeise, -n *f.* **(1) 4B**
destination Reiseziel, -e *n.* **(2) 3B**
detour Umleitung, -en *f.* **(2) 4A**
develop entwickeln *v.* **(3) 4B**
dictionary Wörterbuch, -¨er *n.* **(1) 1B**
die sterben *v.* **(2) 1B**
diet Diät, -en *f.* **(1) 4B**
  to be on a diet auf Diät sein *v.* **(1) 4B**
difficult schwierig *adj.* **(1) 2A**
digital camera Digitalkamera, -s *f.* **(2) 4B**
dining room Esszimmer, - *n.* **(2) 2A**
dinner Abendessen, - *n.* **(1) 4B**
diploma Abschlusszeugnis, -se *n.* **(1) 2A**; Diplom, -e *n.* **(2) 2A**
direction Richtung, -en *f.* **(3) 2B**
dirty schmutzig *adj.* **(2) 2B**
discover entdecken *v.* **(2) 2B**
discreet diskret *adj.* **(1) 3B**
discuss besprechen *v.* **(2) 3A**
dishes Geschirr *n.* **(2) 2B**
  to do the dishes Geschirr spülen **(2) 2B**
dishwasher Spülmaschine, -n *f.* **(2) 2B**
dislike nicht gern (*+verb*) **(1) 3A**
divided by geteilt durch **(1) 1B**
divorced geschieden *adj.* **(1) 3A**
dizzy schwindlig *adj.* **(3) 1B**
do machen *v.* **(1) 2A**; tun *v.* **(3) 1B**
  to do laundry Wäsche waschen *v.* **(2) 2B**
  to do the dishes Geschirr spülen *v.* **(2) 2B**
  to have to do with handeln von **(2) 3A**
doctor Arzt, -¨e / Ärztin, -nen *m./f.* **(3) 1B**
  to go to the doctor zum Arzt gehen *v.* **(3) 1B**
document Dokument, -e *n.* **(2) 4B**
dog Hund, -e *m.* **(1) 3A**
door Tür, -en *f.* **(1) 1B**
dormitory Studentenwohnheim, -e *n.* **(1) 2A**
down entlang *prep.* **(1) 3B**; herunter *adv.* **(2) 2A**
  to go down heruntergehen *v.* **(3) 2B**
download herunterladen *v.* **(2) 4B**
dozen Dutzend, -e *n.* **(1) 4A**
  a dozen eggs ein Dutzend Eier **(1) 4A**
drawer Schublade, -n *f.* **(2) 2A**
dream träumen *v.* **(1) 2A**
dress Kleid, -er *n.* **(2) 1B**
  to get dressed sich anziehen *v.* **(3) 1A**
  to get undressed sich ausziehen *v.* **(3) 1A**
dresser Kommode, -n *f.* **(2) 2A**
drink trinken *v.* **(1) 3B**
drive fahren *v.* **(2) 4A**
  to drive a car Auto fahren *v.* **(2) 4A**
driver Fahrer, - / Fahrerin, -nen *m./f.* **(2) 4A**
drugstore Drogerie, -n *f.* **(3) 2A**
dry trocken *adj.* **(3) 4A**
  to dry oneself off sich abtrocknen *v.* **(3) 1A**

dryer Wäschetrockner, - *m.* **(2) 2B**
dumb dumm *adj.* **(2) 4A**
during während *prep.* **(2) 4B**
dust abstauben *v.* **(2) 2B**
duvet Bettdecke, - *n f.* **(2) 2B**
DVD DVD, -s *f.* **(2) 4B**
DVD-player DVD-Player, - *m.* **(2) 4B**
dye (one's hair) sich (die Haare) färben *v.* **(3) 1A**
dynamic dynamisch *adj.* **(1) 3B**

E

ear Ohr, -en *n.* **(3) 1A**
early früh *adj.* **(1) 2B**
earn verdienen *v.* **(3) 3B**
earth Erde, -n *f.* **(3) 4B**
earthquake Erdbeben, - *n.* **(3) 4A**
easy einfach *adj.* **(1) 2A**
eat essen *v.* **(1) 2B**
  to eat out essen gehen *v.* **(1) 2B**
ecological ökologisch *adj.* **(3) 4B**
ecology Ökologie *f.* **(3) 4B**
economy Wirtschaft, -en *f.* **(1) 2A**
  economy class Touristenklasse *f.* **(2) 3B**
education Ausbildung, -en *f.* **(3) 3A**
egg Ei, -er *n.* **(1) 4A**
eggplant Aubergine, -n *f.* **(1) 4A**
eight acht **(1) 2A**
elbow Ellenbogen, - *m.* **(3) 1A**
electrician Elektriker, - / Elektrikerin, -nen *m./f.* **(3) 3B**
elegant elegant *adj.* **(2) 1B**
elevator Fahrstuhl, -¨e *m.* **(2) 3B**
eleven elf **(1) 2A**
e-mail E-Mail, -s *f.* **(2) 4B**
emergency Notfall, -¨e *m.* **(3) 3B**
emergency room Notaufnahme, -n *f.* **(3) 1B**
employee Angestellte, -n *m./f.* **(3) 3A**
endangered gefährdet *adj.* **(3) 4B**
energy Energie, -n *f.* **(3) 4B**
energy-efficient energiesparend *adj.* **(2) 2B**
engaged verlobt *adj.* **(1) 3A**
engine Motor, -en *m.* **(2) 4A**
engineer Ingenieur, -e / Ingenieurin, -nen *m./f.* **(1) 3B**
England England *n.* **(3) 2B**
English (person) Engländer, - / Engländerin, -nen *m./f.* **(3) 2B**; **(language)** Englisch *n.* **(3) 2B**
enjoy genießen *v.*
  Enjoy your meal! Guten Appetit! **(1) 4B**
envelope Briefumschlag, -¨e *m.* **(3) 2A**
environment Umwelt, -en *f.* **(3) 4B**
  environmentally friendly umweltfreundlich *adj.* **(2) 4B**
environmentalism Umweltschutz *m.* **(3) 4B**
equal (gleich) sein *v.* **(1) 1B**
eraser Radiergummi, -s *m.* **(1) 1B**
errand Besorgung, -en *f.* **(3) 2A**
  to run errands Besorgungen machen *v.* **(3) 2A**
even though obwohl *conj.* **(2) 2A**
evening Abend, -e *m.* **(1) 2B**
  in the evening abends *adv.* **(1) 2A**
every jeder/jede/jedes *adv.* **(2) 4B**

everything alles *pron.* (2) **3B**
  Everything OK? Alles klar? (1) **1A**
everywhere überall *adv.* (1) **4A**
exam Prüfung, -en *f.* (1) **1B**
except (for) außer *prep.* (1) **4B**
exchange umtauschen *v.* (2) **2B**
exciting spannend *adj.* (3) **2A**; aufregend *adj.* (3) **4A**
Excuse me. Entschuldigung. (1) **1A**
exercise Sport treiben *v.* (3) **1B**
exit Ausgang, -¨e *m.* (2) **3B**; Ausfahrt, -en *f.* (2) **4A**
expensive teuer *adj.* (1) **3A**
experience durchmachen *v.* (2) **4B**; Erfahrung, -en *f.* (3) **3A**
explain erklären *v.* (1) **4A**
explore erforschen *v.* (3) **4A**
expression Ausdruck, -¨e *m.*
extinction Aussterben *n.* (3) **4B**
eye Auge, -n *n.* (1) **3A**
eyebrow Augenbraue, -n *f.* (3) **1A**

F

face Gesicht, -er *n.* (3) **1A**
factory Fabrik, -en *f.* (3) **4B**
factory worker Fabrikarbeiter, - / Fabrikarbeiterin, -nen *m./f.* (3) **3B**
fail durchfallen *v.* (1) **1B**; scheitern *v.* (3) **3B**
fall fallen *v.* (1) **2B**; (**season**) Herbst, -e *m.* (1) **2B**
  to fall in love (with) sich verlieben (in) *v.* (3) **1A**
familiar bekannt *adj.*
  to be familiar with kennen *v.* (2) **1B**
family Familie, -n *f.* (1) **3A**
fan Fan, -s *m.* (1) **2B**
fantastic fantastisch *adj.* (3) **2A**
far weit *adj.* (3) **2B**
  far from weit von *adj.* (3) **2B**
farm Bauernhof, -¨e *m.* (3) **4A**
farmer Bauer, -n / Bäuerin, -nen *m./f.* (3) **3B**
fashionable modisch *adj.* (2) **1B**
fast schnell *adj.* (1) **3B**
fat dick *adj.* (1) **3A**
father Vater, -¨ *m.* (1) **3A**
father-in-law Schwiegervater, -¨ *m.* (1) **3A**
favorite Lieblings- (1) **3B**
fax machine Faxgerät, -e *n.* (2) **4B**
fear Angst, -¨e *f.* (2) **3A**
February Februar *m.* (1) **2A**
feel fühlen *v.* (2) **2A**; sich fühlen *v.* (3) **1A**
  to feel like Lust haben *v.* (2) **3B**
  to feel well sich wohl fühlen *v.* (3) **1A**
fever Fieber, - *n.* (3) **1B**
  to have a fever Fieber haben *v.* (3) **1B**
fiancé(e) Verlobte, -n *m./f.* (1) **3A**
field Spielfeld, -er *n.* (1) **2B**; Feld, -er *n.* (3) **4A**; Sektor, -en *m.* (3) **3A**
file Datei, -en *f.* (2) **4B**
fill füllen *v.*
  to fill out ausfüllen *v.* (3) **2A**
  to fill up tanken *v.* (2) **4A**
filthy dreckig *adj.* (2) **2B**
find finden *v.* (1) **2A**
  to find one's way sich zurechtfinden *v.* (3) **2B**

to find out (about) sich informieren (über) *v.* (3) **1A**
fine (monetary) Bußgeld, -er *n.* (2) **4A**
  I'm fine. Mir geht's gut. (1) **1A**
finger Finger, - *m.* (3) **1A**
fire entlassen *v.* (3) **3B**; Feuer, - *n.*
firefighter Feuerwehrmann, -¨er / Feuerwehrfrau, -en (*pl.* Feuerwehrleute) *m./f.* (3) **3B**
firm Firma (*pl.* die Firmen) *f.* (3) **3A**
first erster/erste/erstes *adj.* (1) **2A**; zuerst *adv.* (2) **3B**
  first course erster Gang *m.* (1) **4B**
  first class erste Klasse *f.* (2) **4A**
fish Fisch, -e *m.* (1) **4A**
  to go fishing angeln gehen *v.* (1) **2B**
fish store Fischgeschäft, -e *n.* (1) **4A**
fit passen *v.* (2) **1A**; fit *adj.* (1) **2B**
five fünf (1) **2A**
flat tire Platten, - *m.* (2) **4A**
  to have a flat tire einen Platten haben *v.* (2) **4A**
flavor Geschmack, -¨e *m.* (1) **4B**
flight Flug, -¨e *m.* (2) **3B**
flood Hochwasser, - *n.* (3) **4B**
floor Stock, -¨e *m.*; Boden, -¨ *m.* (2) **2A**
  first/second floor erster/zweiter Stock (2) **2A**
flower Blume, -n *f.* (1) **1A**
  flower shop Blumengeschäft, -e *n.* (3) **2A**
flu Grippe, -n *f.* (3) **1B**
flunk durchfallen *v.* (1) **1B**
fly fliegen *v.* (2) **3B**
fog Nebel, - *m.* (2) **3A**
follow folgen *v.* (2) **1A**
food Essen, - *n.* (1) **4A**
foot Fuß, -¨e *m.* (3) **1A**
football American Football *m.* (1) **2B**
for für *prep.* (1) **3B**; seit; zu *prep.* (1) **4B**
foreign fremd *adj.* (3) **2A**
foreign language Fremdsprache, -n *f.* (1) **2A**
forest Wald, -¨er *m.* (1) **2B**
forget vergessen *v.* (1) **2B**
fork Gabel, -n *f.* (1) **4B**
form Formular, -e *n.* (3) **2A**
  to fill out a form ein Formular ausfüllen *v.* (3) **2A**
fountain Brunnen, - *m.* (3) **2B**
four vier (1) **2A**
France Frankreich *n.* (3) **2B**
French (person) Franzose, -n / Französin, -nen *m./f.* (3) **2B**; (**language**) Französisch *n.* (3) **2B**
free time Freizeit, -en *f.* (1) **2B**
freezer Gefrierschrank, -¨e *m.* (2) **2B**
Friday Freitag, -e *m.* (1) **2A**
  on Fridays freitags *adv.* (1) **2A**
friend Freund, -e / Freundin, -nen *m./f.* (1) **1A**
friendly freundlich *adj.* (1) **3B**
friendship Freundschaft, -en *f.* (2) **1A**
from aus *prep.* (1) **4A**; von *prep.* (1) **4B**
  where from woher *interr.* (1) **2A**
front: in front of vor *prep.* (2) **1B**
fruit Obst *n.* (1) **4A**
fry braten *v.* (1) **2B**
full voll *adj.* (2) **3B**
full-time ganztags *adv.* (3) **3B**

fully occupied voll besetzt *adj.* (2) **3B**
fun Spaß *m.* (2) **3B**
  to be fun Spaß machen *v.* (2) **3B**
  to (not) have fun (keinen) Spaß haben *v.* (2) **1A**
function funktionieren *v.* (2) **4B**
funny lustig *adj.* (1) **3B**
furnished möbliert *adj.* (2) **2A**
furniture Möbel, - *n.* (2) **2A**
  piece of furniture Möbelstück, -e *n.* (2) **2A**

G

game Spiel, -e *n.* (1) **2B**
game console Spielkonsole, -en *f.* (2) **4B**
garage Garage, -n *f.* (2) **1B**
garbage truck Müllwagen, - *m.* (3) **4B**
gardener Gärtner, - / Gärtnerin, -nen *m./f.* (3) **3B**
garlic Knoblauch *m.* (1) **4A**
gas Benzin, -e *n.* (2) **4A**
gas station Tankstelle, -n *f.* (2) **4A**
generous großzügig *adj.* (1) **3B**
German (person) Deutsche *m./f.* (3) **2B**; (**language**) Deutsch *n.* (3) **2B**
Germany Deutschland *n.* (1) **4A**
get bekommen *v.* (2) **1A**
  to get up aufstehen *v.* (1) **4A**
  to get sick/better krank/gesund werden *v.* (3) **1B**
gift Geschenk, -e *n.* (2) **1A**
girl Mädchen, - *n.* (1) **1A**
give geben *v.* (1) **2B**
  to give (a gift) schenken *v.* (2) **1A**
glass Glas, -¨er *n.* (1) **4B**
glasses Brille, -n *f.* (2) **1B**
global warming Erderwärmung *f.* (3) **4B**
glove Handschuh, -e *m.* (2) **1B**
go gehen *v.* (1) **2A**; fahren *v.* (1) **2B**
  to go out ausgehen *v.* (1) **4A**
  Go! Los! (1) **2B**
goal (in soccer) Tor, -e *n.* (1) **2B**
golf Golf *n.* (1) **2B**
good gut *adj.* (1) **3B**; nett *adj.*
  Good evening. Guten Abend. (1) **1A**
  Good morning. Guten Morgen. (1) **1A**
  Good night. Gute Nacht. (1) **1A**
  Good-bye. Auf Wiedersehen. (1) **1A**
  Good luck! Viel Glück! (2) **1A**
government Regierung, -en *f.* (3) **4B**
grade Note, -n *f.* (1) **1B**
grade report Zeugnis, -se *n.* (1) **1B**
graduate Abschluss machen, -¨e *v.* (2) **1A**
graduation Abschluss, -¨e *m.* (1) **1B**
gram Gramm, -e *n.* (1) **4A**
  100 grams of cheese 100 Gramm Käse (1) **4A**
granddaughter Enkeltochter, -¨ *f.* (1) **3A**
grandson Enkelsohn, -¨e *m.* (1) **3A**
grandchild Enkel, - *m.* (1) **3A**; Enkelkind, -er *n.* (1) **3A**
grandfather Großvater, -¨ *m.* (1) **3A**
grandma Oma, -s *f.* (1) **3A**
grandmother Großmutter, -¨ *f.* (1) **3A**
grandpa Opa, -s *m.* (1) **3A**
grandparents Großeltern *pl.* (1) **1A**

grape Traube, -n *f.* **(1) 4A**
grass Gras, -¨er *n.* **(3) 4A**
gray grau *adj.* **(2) 1B**
great toll *adj.* **(1) 3B**; prima *adj.*; spitze *adj.* **(1) 1A**
great grandfather Urgroßvater, -¨ *m.* **(1) 3A**
great grandmother Urgroßmutter, -¨ *f.* **(1) 3A**
greedy gierig *adj.* **(1) 3B**
green grün *adj.* **(2) 1B**
green bean grüne Bohne (*pl.* die grünen Bohnen), -n *f.* **(1) 4A**
greet grüßen *v.* **(1) 2A**
greeting Begrüßung, -en *f.* **(1) 1A**; Gruß, -¨e *m.* **(1) 1A**
grocery store Lebensmittelgeschäft, -e *n.* **(1) 4A**
ground floor Erdgeschoss, -e *n.* **(2) 2A**
grow wachsen *v.* **(2) 1B**
grown-up erwachsen *adj.* **(3) 2A**
guest Gast, -¨e *m.* **(2) 1A**
  hotel guest Hotelgast, -¨e *m.* **7B**
guesthouse Pension, -en *f.* **(2) 3B**
gym Sporthalle, -n *f.* **(1) 2A**

H

hail Hagel *m.* **(2) 3A**
hair Haar, -e *n* **(1) 3A**
hair dryer Haartrockner, - *m.* **(3) 1A**
hairdresser Friseur, -e / Friseurin, -nen *m./f.* **(1) 3B**
half halb *adj.* **(1) 2A**
half brother Halbbruder, -¨ *m.* **(1) 3A**
half sister Halbschwester, -n *f.* **(1) 3A**
hall Flur, -e *m.* **(2) 2A**
ham Schinken, - *m.* **(1) 4A**
hand Hand, -¨e *f.* **(3) 1A**
handsome gut aussehend *adj.* **(3) 3A**
hang hängen *v.* **(2) 1B**
  to hang up auflegen *v.* **(3) 3A**
happen passieren *v.* **(2) 1B**
happiness Glück *n.* **(2) 1A**
happy glücklich *adj.* **(1) 3B** froh *adj.* **(1) 3B**
  Happy birthday! Alles Gute zum Geburtstag! **(2) 1A**
  Happy Easter! Frohe Ostern! **(2) 1A**
  Happy New Year! Ein gutes neues Jahr! **(2) 1A**
  to be happy (about) sich freuen (über) *v.* **(3) 1A**
hard schwer *adj.* **(3) 1B**
hard drive Festplatte, -en *f.* **(2) 4B**
hard-working fleißig *adj.* **(1) 3B**
hare Hase, -n *m.* **(3) 4A**
hat Hut, -¨e *m.* **(2) 1B**
have haben *v.* **(1) 1B**
  Have a nice day! Schönen Tag noch! **(1) 1A**
  to have to müssen *v.* **(1) 3B**
he er *pron.* **(1) 1A**
head Kopf, -¨e *m.* **(3) 1A**
headache Kopfschmerzen *m. pl.* **(3) 1B**
headlight Scheinwerfer, -e *m.* **(2) 4A**
headphones Kopfhörer, - *m.* **(2) 4B**
health Gesundheit *f.* **(3) 1B**
health-food store Bioladen, -¨ *m.* **(3) 1B**
healthy gesund *adj.* **(2) 4A**
hear hören *v.* **(1) 2A**
heat stroke Hitzschlag, -¨e *m.* **(3) 1B**

heavy schwer *adj.* **(1) 4B**
hello Guten Tag.; Hallo. **(1) 1A**
help helfen *v.* **(1) 2B**
  to help with helfen bei *v.* **(2) 3A**
her ihr *poss. adj.* **(1) 3A**
here hier *adv.* **(1) 1A**
  Here is/are... Hier ist/sind... **(1) 1B**
high hoch *adj.* **(2) 4A**
highway Autobahn, -en *f.* **(2) 4A**
hike wandern *v.* **(1) 2A**
his sein *poss. adj.* **(1) 3A**
history Geschichte, -en *f.* **(1) 2A**
hit treffen *v.* **(1) 2B**
hobby Hobby, -s *n.* **(1) 2B**
hockey Hockey *n.* **(1) 2B**
hold: to be on hold in der Warteschleife sein *v.* **(3) 3B**
  Please hold. Bleiben Sie bitte am Apparat. **(3) 3A**
holiday Feiertag, -e *m.* **(2) 1A**
home Haus, -¨er *adv.* **(2) 1B**
  at home zu Hause *adv.* **(1) 4A**
home office Arbeitszimmer, - *n.* **(2) 2A**
homemade hausgemacht *adj.* **(1) 4B**
homemaker Hausfrau, -en / Hausmann, -¨er *f./m.* **(3) 3B**
homework Hausaufgabe, -n *f.* **(1) 1B**
hood Motorhaube, -en *f.* **(2) 4A**
horse Pferd, -e *n.* **(3) 4A**
hospital Krankenhaus, -¨er *n.* **(3) 1B**
host / hostess Gastgeber, - / Gastgeberin, -nen *m./f.* **(2) 1A**
host family Gastfamilie, -n *f.* **(1) 4B**
hot heiß *adj.* **(2) 3A**
hotel Hotel, -s *n.* **(2) 3B**
  five-star hotel Fünf-Sterne-Hotel *n.* **(2) 3B**
hour Stunde, -n *f.* **(1) 2A**
house Haus, -¨er *n.* **(2) 2A**
housework Hausarbeit *f.* **(2) 2B**
  to do housework Hausarbeit machen *v.* **(2) 2B**
how wie *interr.* **(1) 2A**
  How are you? *(form.)* Wie geht es Ihnen? **(1) 1A**
  How are you? *(inf.)* Wie geht's (dir)? **(1) 1A**
  how many wie viele *interr.* **(1) 2A**
  how much wie viel *interr.* **(1) 2A**
human resources manager Personalchef, -s / die Personalchefin, -nen *m./f.* **(3) 3A**
humble bescheiden *adj.*
hurry sich beeilen *v.* **(3) 1A**
hurt weh tun *v.* **(3) 1B**
  to hurt oneself sich verletzen *v.* **(3) 1B**
husband Ehemann, -¨er *m.* **(1) 3A**
hybrid car Hybridauto, -s *n.* **(3) 4B**

I

I ich *pron.* **(1) 1A**
ice cream Eis *n.* **(2) 1A**
ice cream shop Eisdiele, -n *f.* **(1) 4A**
ice cube Eiswürfel, - *m.* **(2) 1A**
ice hockey Eishockey *n.* **(1) 2B**
ID card Personalausweis, -e *m.* **(2) 3B**
idea Idee, -n *f.* **(1) 1A**
if wenn *conj.*; ob *conj.* **(3) 2A**

as if als ob **(3) 2A**
if I were you an deiner/Ihrer Stelle *f.* **(3) 2A**
if... only wenn... nur **(3) 2A**
if... then wenn... dann **(3) 2A**
imagine sich (etwas) vorstellen *v.* **(3) 1A**
imitate nachmachen *v.* **(2) 4B**
important wichtig *adj.* **(2) 3B**; bedeutend *adj.* **(3) 4A**
improve verbessern *v.* **(3) 4B**
in in *prep.* **(2) 1B**
  in the afternoon nachmittags *adv.* **(1) 2A**
  in the evening abends *adv.* **(1) 2A**
  in the morning morgens *adv.* **(1) 2A**
  in spite of trotz *prep.* **(2) 4B**
India Indien *n.* **(3) 2B**
Indian indisch *adj.* **(3) 2B**; **(person)** Inder, - / Inderin, -nen *m./f.* **(3) 2B**
injury Verletzung, -en *f.* **(3) 1B**
inside (of) innerhalb *prep.* **(2) 4B**
instead sondern *conj.* **(2) 2A**
  instead of statt *prep.*; anstatt *prep.* **(2) 4B**
intellectual intellektuell *adj.* **(1) 3B**
intelligent intelligent *adj.* **(1) 3B**
interested: to be interested (in) sich interessieren (für) *v.* **(3) 1A**
interesting interessant *adj.* **(1) 3B**
internet café Internetcafé, -s *n.* **(3) 2A**
internship Praktikum (*pl.* die Praktika) *n.* **(3) 3A**
intersection Kreuzung, -en *f.* **(3) 2B**
introduce: to introduce (oneself) (sich) vorstellen *v.* **(3) 1A**
invent erfinden *v.* **(2) 3A**
invite einladen *v.* **(2) 1A**
iron Bügeleisen, - *n.* **(2) 2B**; bügeln *v.* **(2) 2B**
ironing board Bügelbrett, -er *n.* **(2) 2B**
island Insel, -n *f.* **(3) 4A**
it es *pron.* **(1) 1A**
Italian (person) Italiener, - / Italienerin, -nen *m./f.* **(3) 2B**; **(language)** Italienisch *n.* **(3) 2B**
Italy Italien *n.* **(3) 2B**
its sein *poss. adj.* **(1) 3A**

J

jacket Jacke, -n *f.* **(2) 1B**
jam Marmelade, -n *f.* **(1) 4A**
January Januar *m.* **(1) 2A**
jealous eifersüchtig *adj.* **(1) 3B**
jeans Jeans *f.* **(2) 1B**
jewelry store Juweliergeschäft, -e *n.* **(3) 2A**
job Beruf, -e *m.* **(3) 3B**; Stelle, -n *f.* **(3) 3A**
  to find a job Arbeit finden *v.* **(3) 3A**
job interview Vorstellungsgespräch, -e *n.* **(3) 3A**
job opening Stellenangebot, -e *n.* **(3) 3A**
jog joggen *v.* **(1) 2B**
journalist Journalist, -en / Journalistin, -nen *m./f.* **(1) 3B**
judge Richter, - / Richterin, -nen *m./f.* **(3) 3B**
juice Saft, -¨e *m.* **(1) 4B**
July Juli *m.* **(1) 2A**
June Juni *m.* **(1) 2A**
just as genauso wie **(2) 4A**

K

key Schlüssel, - *m.* (2) **3B**
keyboard Tastatur, -en *f.* (2) **4B**
kind nett *adj.*
kiosk Kiosk, -e *m.* (3) **2A**
kiss Kuss, -̈e *m.* (2) **1A**; küssen *v.* (2) **1A**
 to kiss (each other) sich küssen *v.* (3) **1A**
kitchen Küche, -n *f.* (2) **2A**
knee Knie, - *n.* (3) **1A**
knife Messer, - *n.* (1) **4B**
know kennen *v.* (2) **1B**; wissen *v.* (2) **1B**
 to know each other sich kennen *v.* (3) **1A**
know-it-all Besserwisser, - / Besserwisserin
 -nen *m./f.* (1) **2A**
Korea Korea *n.* (3) **2B**
Korean (person) Koreaner, - / Koreanerin,
 -nen *m./f.* (3) **2B**; **(language)** Koreanisch *n.* (3)
 2B

L

labor union Gewerkschaft, -en *f.* (3) **3B**
lake See, -n *m.* (3) **4A**
lamp Lampe, -n *f.* (2) **2A**
land landen *v.* (2) **3B**; Land, -̈er *n.* (2) **3B**
landscape Landschaft, -en *f.* (3) **4A**
laptop (computer) Laptop, -s *m./n.* (4) **4B**
last letzter/letzte/letztes *adj.* (1) **2B**
last name Nachname, -n *m.* (1) **3A**
late spät *adj.* (1) **2A**
 to be late sich verspäten *v.* (3) **1A**
laugh lachen *v.* (1) **2A**
laundromat Waschsalon, -s *m.* (3) **2A**
laundry Wäsche *f.* (2) **2B**
 to do laundry Wäsche waschen *v.* (2) **2B**
law Gesetz, -e *n.* (3) **4B**
lawyer Rechtsanwalt, -̈e / Rechtsanwältin,
 -nen *m./f.* (1) **3B**
lay legen *v.* (2) **1B**
lazy faul *adj.* (1) **3B**
leaf Blatt, -̈er *n.* (3) **4A**
learn lernen *v.* (1) **2A**
leather Leder, - *n.* (2) **1B**
leave abfahren *v.* (2) **4A**
lecture Vorlesung, -en *f.* (1) **2A**; Vortrag, -̈e *m.*
 (2) **2B**
lecture hall Hörsaal (*pl.* Horsale) *m.* (1) **2A**
leg Bein, -e *n.* (3) **1A**
leisure Freizeit *f.* (1) **2B**
lesson Stunde, -n *f.* (1) **1B**
let lassen *v.* (1) **2B**
letter Brief, -e *m.* (3) **2A**
 to mail a letter einen Brief abschicken *v.* (3) **2A**
 letter of recommendation
 Empfehlungsschreiben, - *n.* (3) **3A**
lettuce Salat, -e *m.* (1) **4A**
library Bibliothek, -en *f.* (1) **1B**
license plate Nummernschild, -er *n.* (2) **4A**
lie liegen *v.* (2) **1B**
 to lie down sich (hin)legen *v.* (3) **1A**
 to tell a lie lügen *v.*
light hell *adj.* (1) **3A**; leicht *adj.* (1) **4B**; Licht, -er
 n. (3) **4B**

M

lightning Blitz, -e *m.* (2) **3A**
like mögen *v.* (1) **4B**; gern (+*verb*) *v.* (1) **3A**;
 gefallen *v.* (2) **1A**
 I would like... ich hätte gern… (1) **4A**; Ich
 möchte... (1) **4B**
line Schlange, -n *f.* (2) **3B**; Linie, -n *f.*
 to stand in line Schlange stehen *v.* (2) **3B**
lip Lippe, -n *f.* (3) **1A**
lipstick Lippenstift, -e *m.* (3) **1A**
listen (to) hören *v.* (1) **2A**
literature Literatur *f.* (1) **2A**
little klein *adj.* (1) **3A**; wenig *adj.* (3) **2A**
live wohnen *v.* (1) **2A**; leben *v.*
living room Wohnzimmer, - *n.* (2) **2A**
load laden *v.* (2) **4B**
location Lage, -n *f.* (2) **3B**
long lang *adj.* (1) **3A**
 long-sleeved langärmlig *adj.* (2) **1B**
look schauen *v.* (2) **3A**
 to look at anschauen *v.* (2) **3A**
 to look for suchen *v.* (1) **2A**
 to look forward to sich freuen auf *v.* (3) **1A**
loose weit *adj.* (2) **1B**
lose verlieren *v.* (1) **2B**
 to get lost sich verlaufen *v.* (2) **2B**
love lieben *v.* (1) **2A**; Liebe *f.* (2) **1A**
 to fall in love (with) sich verlieben (in) *v.* (3) **1A**
 to love each other sich lieben *v.* (3) **1A**
loving liebevoll *adj.* (1) **3B**
low niedrig *adj.* (3) **3A**
luggage Gepäck *n.* (2) **3B**
lunch Mittagessen, - *n.* (1) **4B**

M

magazine Zeitschrift, -en *f.* (3) **2A**
mail Post *f.* (3) **2A**
 to mail a letter einen Brief abschicken *v.* (3) **2A**
mail carrier Briefträger, - / Briefträgerin,
 -nen *m.* (3) **2A**
mailbox Briefkasten, -̈ *m.* (3) **2A**
main course Hauptspeise, -n *f.* (1) **4B**
main road Hauptstraße, -n *f.* (3) **2B**
major: to major in studieren *v.* (1) **2A**
make machen *v.* (1) **2A**
makeup: to put on makeup sich schminken *v.* (3)
 1A
mall Einkaufszentrum (*pl.* Einkaufszentren) *n.* (3)
 2B
man Mann, -̈er *m.* (1) **1A**
manage leiten *v.* (3) **3B**
manager Geschäftsführer, - / die
 Geschäftsführerin, -nen *m./f.* (3) **3A**
map Karte, -n *f.* (1) **1B**; Landkarte, -n *f.* (2) **3B**
 city map Stadtplan, -̈e *m.* (2) **3B**
 to read a map eine Karte lesen *v.* (2) **3B**
marble Marmor *m.* (2) **2B**
March März *m.* (1) **2A**
marital status Familienstand, -̈e *m.* (3) **3A**
market Markt, -̈e *m.* (1) **4A**
marriage Ehe, -n *f.* (2) **1A**
married verheiratet *adj.* (1) **3A**
marry heiraten *v.* (1) **3A**
match Spiel, -e *n.* (1) **2B**; passen *v.* (2) **1A**

M

material Material, -ien *n.* (2) **1B**
mathematics Mathematik *f.* (1) **2A**
May Mai *m.* (1) **2A**
may dürfen *v.* (1) **3B**
maybe vielleicht *adv.* (1) **4A**
mayor Bürgermeister, - / Bürgermeisterin,
 -nen *m./f.* (3) **2B**
meal Mahlzeit, -en *f.* (1) **4B**
mean bedeuten *v.* (1) **2A**; meinen *v.* (1) **2A**;
 gemein *adj.* (1) **3B**
meat Fleisch *n.* (1) **4A**
mechanic Mechaniker, - / Mechanikerin,
 -nen *m./f.* (2) **4A**
medicine Medizin *f.* (1) **2A**; Medikament, -e *n.* (3)
 1B
meet (sich) treffen *v.* (1) **2B**; **(for the first time)**
 (sich) kennen lernen *v.* (3) **1A**
 Pleased to meet you. Schön dich/Sie kennen zu
 lernen. (1) **1A**
meeting Besprechung, -en *f.* (3) **3B**
melon Melone, -n *f.* (1) **4A**
menu Speisekarte, -n *f.* (1) **4B**
Merry Christmas! Frohe Weihnachten! (2) **1A**
message Nachricht, -en *f.* (3) **3A**
Mexico Mexiko *n.* (3) **2B**
Mexican mexikanisch *adj.* (3) **2B**; **(person)**
 Mexikaner, - / Mexikanerin, -nen *m./f.* (3) **2B**
microphone Mikrofon, -e *n.* (2) **4B**
microwave Mikrowelle, -n *f.* (2) **2B**
midmorning Vormittag, -e *m.* (1) **2B**
midnight Mitternacht *f.* (1) **2A**
mild leicht *adj.* (3) **1B**
milk Milch *f.* (1) **4B**
minority Minderheit, -en *f.* (3) **4B**
minus minus (1) **1B**
mirror Spiegel, - *m.* (2) **2A**
mist Nebel, - *m.* (2) **3A**
modern modern *adj.* (3) **2A**
modest bescheiden *adj.* (1) **3B**
mom Mama, -s *f.* (3) **3A**
Monday Montag, -e *n.* (1) **2A**
 on Mondays montags *adv.* (1) **2A**
money Geld *n.* (3) **2A**
month Monat, -e *m.* (1) **2A**
moon Mond, -e *m.* (3) **4A**
mop wischen *v.* (2) **2B**
more mehr *adj.* (2) **4A**
morning Morgen, - *m.* (1) **2B**
 in the morning vormittags (1) **2A**
 tomorrow morning morgen früh (1) **2B**
mother Mutter, -̈ *f.* (1) **1A**
mother-in-law Schwiegermutter, -̈ *f.* (3) **3A**
mountain Berg, -e *m.* (1) **2B**; (3) **4A**
mouse Maus, -̈e *f.* (3) **4A**
mouth Mund, -̈er *m.* (3) **1A**
move umziehen *v.* (2) **2A**; sich bewegen *v.*
mp3 player MP3-Player, - *m.* (2) **4B**
Mr. Herr (1) **1A**
Mrs. Frau (1) **1A**
Ms. Frau (1) **1A**
much viel *adv.* (1) **4A**
mushroom Pilz, -e *m.* (1) **4A**
musician Musiker, - / Musikerin, -nen *m./f.* (1) **3B**
must müssen *v.* (1) **3B**

my mein *poss. adj.* (1) **3A**
myself mir *pron.* (2) **3A**

N

naïve naiv *adj.* (1) **3B**
name Name, -n *m.* (1) **1A**
  to be named heißen *v.* (1) **2A**
  What's your name? Wie heißen Sie? *(form.)* /
    Wie heißt du? *(inf.) v.* (1) **1A**
napkin Serviette, -n *f.* (1) **4B**
natural disaster Naturkatastrophe, -n *f.* (3) **4A**
nature Natur, -en *f.* (3) **4A**
nauseous übel *adj.* (3) **1B**
near bei *prep.* (1) **4B**; nah *adj.* (3) **2B**
neat ordentlich *adj.* (2) **2B**
neck Hals, -̈e *m.* (3) **1A**
necklace Halskette, -n *f.* (2) **1B**
need brauchen *v.* (1) **2A**
  to need to müssen *v.* (1) **3B**
nephew Neffe, -n *m.* (2) **4B**
nervous nervös *adj.* (1) **3B**
never nie *adv.* (1) **4A**; niemals *adv.* (2) **3B**
New Year's Eve Silvester *n.* (2) **1A**
newlywed Frischvermählte, -n *m./f.* (2) **1A**
newspaper Zeitung, -en *f.* (2) **3B**
next nächster/nächste/nächstes *adj.* (1) **2B**
  next to neben *prep.* (2) **1B**
nice nett *adj.* (1) **3B**
  It's nice out. Es ist schön draußen. (2) **3A**
  Nice to meet you. Schön dich/Sie kennen zu
    lernen. (1) **1A**
  The weather is nice. Das Wetter ist gut. (2) **3A**
night Nacht, -̈e *f.* (1) **2B**
  to spend the night übernachten *f.* (2) **3B**
night table Nachttisch, -e *m.* (2) **2A**
nine neun (1) **2A**
no nein (1) **1B**; kein *adj.* (1) **2B**
no one niemand *pron.* (2) **3B**
nonviolent gewaltfrei *adj.* (3) **4B**
noon Mittag, -e *m.* (1) **2A**
nose Nase, -n *f.* (3) **1A**
not nicht *adv.* (1) **2B**
  Do not enter. Keine Zufahrt. (1) **3B**
  not bad nicht schlecht (1) **1A**
  not much wenig *adj.* (3) **2A**
note Notiz, -en *f.* (1) **1B**
notebook Heft, -e *n.* (1) **1B**
nothing nichts *pron.* (2) **3B**
November November *m.* (1) **2A**
now jetzt *adv.* (1) **4A**
nuclear energy Kernenergie *f.* (3) **4B**
nuclear power plant Kernkraftwerk, -e *n.* (3) **4B**
nurse Krankenpfleger, - / Krankenschwester,
  -n *m./f.* (3) **1B**

O

ocean Meer, -e *n.* (3) **4A**
October Oktober *m.* (1) **2A**
offer Angebot, -e *n.* (2) **1B**; bieten *v.* (3) **1B**;
  anbieten *v.* (3) **4B**
office Büro, -s *n.* (3) **3B**

office supplies Büromaterial, -ien *n.* (3) **3A**
often oft *adv.* (1) **4A**
oil Öl, -e *n.* (1) **4A**
old alt *adj.* (1) **3A**
  How old are you? Wie alt bist du? (1) **1B**
  I am... years old. Ich bin... Jahre alt. (1) **1B**
olive oil Olivenöl, -e *n.* (1) **4A**
once einmal *adv.* (2) **3B**
one eins (1) **2A**; man *pron.* (2) **3B**
  by oneself allein *adv.* (1) **4A**
one-way street Einbahnstraße, -n *f.* (2) **4A**
onion Zwiebel, -n *f.* (1) **4A**
online: to be online online sein *v.* (2) **4B**
only nur *adv.* (1) **4A**
  only child Einzelkind, -er *n.* (1) **3A**
on-time pünktlich *adj.* (2) **3B**
onto auf *prep.* (2) **1B**
open öffnen *v.* (1) **2A**; aufmachen *v.* (2) **4B**;
  geöffnet *adj.* (3) **2A**
or oder *conj.* (2) **2A**
orange Orange, -n *f.* (1) **4A**; orange *adj.* (2) **1B**
order bestellen *v.* (1) **4A**
organic biologisch *adj.* (3) **4B**
our unser *poss. adj.* (1) **3A**
out draußen *adv.* (2) **3A**; heraus *adv.* (2) **2A**
  It's nice out. Es ist schön draußen. (2) **3A**
  to go out ausgehen *v.* (1) **4A**
  to bring out rausbringen (2) **2B**
outside draußen *prep.* (2) **2A**
  outside of außerhalb *prep.* (2) **4B**
oven Ofen, -̈ *m.* (2) **2B**
over über *prep.* (2) **1B**; vorbei *adv.* (2) **3A**
  over there drüben *adv.* (1) **4A**
overpopulation Überbevölkerung *f.* (3) **4B**
owner Besitzer, - / Besitzerin, -nen *m./f.* (1) **3B**

P

pack packen *v.* (2) **3B**
package Paket, -e *n.* (3) **2A**
pain Schmerz, -en *m.* (3) **1B**
pajamas Schlafanzug, -̈e *m.* (3) **1A**
pan Pfanne, -n *f.* (2) **2B**
pants Hose, -n *f.* (2) **1B**
paper Papier, -e *n.* (1) **1B**
  sheet of paper Blatt Papier *(pl.* Blätter Papier)
    n. (1) **1B**
paperclip Büroklammer, -n *f.* (3) **3A**
paper-goods store Schreibwarengeschäft,
  -e *n.* (3) **2A**
paragraph Absatz, -̈e *m.* (2) **1B**
parents Eltern *pl.* (1) **3A**
park Park, -s *m.* (1) **1A**; parken *v.* (2) **4A**
  No parking. Parkverbot. (1) **3B**
participate mitmachen *v.* (2) **4B**
part-time halbtags *adj.* (3) **3B**
party Party, -s *f.* (2) **1A**
  to go to a party auf eine Party gehen *prep.* (3) **2B**
  to throw a party eine Party geben *v.* (2) **1A**
pass (a test) bestehen *v.* (1) **1B**
passenger Passagier, -e *m.* (2) **3B**
passport control Passkontrolle, -n *f.* (3) **3B**

password Passwort, -̈er *n.* (2) **4B**
past Vergangenheit *f.* (3) **4A**; nach *prep.* (1) **2A**
pasta Pasta *f.* (1) **4A**
pastries Gebäck *n.* (2) **1A**
pastry shop Konditorei, -en *f.* (1) **4A**
path Weg, -e *m.* (3) **4A**
patient geduldig *adj.* (1) **3B**; Patient, -en /
  Patientin, -nen *m./f.* (3) **1B**
pay (for) bezahlen *v.* (1) **4A**
  to pay by (credit) card mit der Karte
    bezahlen *v.* (3) **2A**
  to pay in cash bar bezahlen *v.* (3) **2A**
peach Pfirsich, -e *m.* (1) **4A**
pear Birne, -n *f.* (1) **4A**
pedestrian Fußgänger, - / Fußgängerin,
  -nen *m./f.* (3) **2B**
pen Kuli, -s *m.* (1) **1B**
pencil Bleistift, -e *m.* (1) **1B**
people Leute *pl.* (1) **3B**; Menschen *pl.*
pepper Paprika, - *f.* (1) **4A**; Pfeffer, - *m.* (1) **4B**
percent Prozent *n.* (1) **1B**
period Punkt, -e *m.* (1) **1B**
person Person, -en *f.* (1) **1A**; Mensch, -en *m.*
personal persönlich *adj.* (1) **3B**
pet Haustier, -e *n.* (1) **3A**
pharmacy Apotheke, -n *f.* (3) **1B**
phone booth Telefonzelle, -n *f.* (3) **2B**
photo Foto, -s *n.* (1) **1B**
physics Physik *f.* (1) **2A**
picnic Picknick, -s *n.* (3) **4A**
  to have a picnic ein Picknick machen *v.* (3) **4A**
picture Foto, -s *n.* (1) **1B**; Bild, -er *n.* (2) **2A**
pie Kuchen, - *m.* (1) **4A**
pigsty Saustall, -̈e *n.* (2) **2B**
  It's a pigsty! Es ist ein Saustall! (2) **2B**
pill Tablette, -n *f.* (3) **1B**
pillow Kissen, - *n.* (2) **2B**
pineapple Ananas, - *f.* (1) **4A**
pink rosa *adj.* (2) **1B**
place Ort, -e *m.* (1) **1B**; Lage, -n *f.* (2) **3B**; setzen
  v. (1) **1B**
  in your place an deiner/Ihrer Stelle *f.* (3) **2A**
planner Terminkalender, - *m.* (1) **1B**
plant Pflanze, -n *f.* (2) **2A**
plastic Kunststoff, -e *m.* (2) **2B**
plate Teller, - *m.* (1) **4B**
platform Bahnsteig, -e (2) **4A**
play spielen *v.* (1) **2A**
player Spieler, - / Spielerin, -nen *m./f.* (1) **2B**
pleasant angenehm *adj.* (1) **3B**
please bitte (1) **1A**; gefallen *v.* (2) **1A**
  Pleased to meet you. Freut mich. (1) **1A**
plumber Klempner, - / Klempnerin,
  -nen *m./f.* (3) **3B**
plus plus (1) **1B**
police officer Polizist, -en / Polizistin,
  -nen *m./f.* (2) **4A**
police station Polizeiwache, -n *f.* (3) **2A**
politician Politiker, - / Politikerin, -nen *m./f.* (3) **3B**
pollute verschmutzen *v.* (3) **4B**
pollution Verschmutzung *f.* (3) **4B**
poor arm *adj.* (1) **3B**
pork Schweinefleisch *n.* (1) **4A**
position Stelle, -n *f.* (3) **3A**

post office Post, *f.* (3) **2A**
  to go to the post office zur Post gehen *v.* (3) **2A**
postcard Postkarte, -n *f.* (3) **2A**
poster Poster, - *n.* (2) **2A**
pot Topf, -¨e *m.* (2) **2B**
potato Kartoffel, -n *f.* (1) **4A**
pound Pfund, -e *n.* (1) **4A**
  a pound of potatoes ein Pfund Kartoffeln (1) **4A**
practice üben *v.* (1) **2B**; Übung, -en *f.*
pregnant schwanger *adj.* (3) **1B**
preparation Vorbereitung, -en *f.*
prepare vorbereiten *v.* (1) **4A**; zubereiten *v.* (2) **3A**
  to prepare oneself (for) sich vorbereiten
    (auf) *v.* (3) **1A**
prescription Rezept, -e *n.* (3) **1B**
presentation Referat, -e *n.* (1) **2A**
preserve erhalten *v.* (3) **4B**
president Präsident, - / Präsidentin, -nen *m./f.* (2)
  4B
  federal president Bundespräsident, - /
    Bundespräsidentin, -nen *m./f.* (2) **4B**
pretty hübsch *adj.* (1) **3A**
  pretty well ziemlich gut *adv.* (1) **1A**
principal Schulleiter, - *m.* / Schulleiterin, -nen *f.* (1)
  1B
print drucken *v.* (2) **4B**
printer Drucker, - *m.* (2) **4B**
probably wohl *adv.* (3) **2A**; wahrscheinlich *adv.* (3)
  2A; sicher *adv.* (3) **2A**
problem Problem, -e *n.* (1) **1A**
profession Beruf, -e *m.* (1) **3B**
professional training Berufsausbildung, -en *f.* (3)
  3A
professor Professor, -en / Professorin,
  -nen *m./f.* (1) **1B**
program Programm, -e *n.* (2) **4B**
promotion Beförderung, -en *f.* (3) **3B**
pronunciation Aussprache *f.*
propose vorschlagen *v.* (3) **4B**
protect schützen *v.* (3) **4B**
proud stolz *adj.* (1) **3B**
psychologist Psychologe, -n / Psychologin,
  -nen *m./f.* (3) **3B**
psychology Psychologie *f.* (1) **2A**
public öffentlich *adj.* (2) **4A**
  public transportation öffentliche
    Verkehrsmittel *n.* (2) **4A**
pull ziehen *v.* (1) **3B**
purple lila *adj.* (2) **1B**
purse Handtasche, -n *f.* (2) **1B**
push drücken *v.* (1) **3B**
put stellen *v.* (2) **1B**; legen *v.* (3) **1A**; setzen *v.* (3)
  1A
  to put away wegräumen *v.* (2) **2B**
  to put on anziehen *v.* (2) **1B**

Q

quarter Viertel, - *n.* (1) **2A**
  quarter past/to Viertel nach/vor (1) **2A**
question Frage, -n *f.* (1) **1B**
quicksand Treibsand *m.* (3) **4A**

R

rabbit Kaninchen, - *n.* (3) **4A**
rain Regen *m.* (2) **3A**; regnen *v.* (1) **2A**
raincoat Regenmantel, -¨ *m.* (2) **3A**
raise Gehaltserhöhung, -en *f.* (3) **3B**
rarely selten *adv.* (1) **4A**
rather lieber *adj.* (2) **4A**
rating Bewertung, -en *f.* (2) **3B**
razor Rasierer, - *m.* (3) **1A**
read lesen *v.* (1) **2B**
ready fertig *adj.* (3) **3B**
real estate agent Immobilienmakler, - /
  Immobilienmaklerin, -nen *m./f.* (3) **3B**
realistic realistisch *adj.* (3) **2A**
really wirklich *adv.* (1) **4A**
receive bekommen *v.* (2) **1A**
receiver Hörer, - *m.* (3) **1A**
recess Pause, -n *f.* (1) **1B**
recognize erkennen *v.* (2) **3A**
recommend empfehlen *v.* (1) **2B**
record aufnehmen *v.* (2) **4B**
recycle recyceln *v.* (3) **4B**
red rot *adj.* (1) **3A**
  red-haired rothaarig *adj.* (1) **3A**
reference Referenz, -en *f.* (3) **3A**
refrigerator Kühlschrank, -¨e *m.* (2) **2B**
related verwandt *adj.* (3) **2A**
relative Verwandte, -n *m.* (1) **3A**
relax sich entspannen *v.* (3) **1A**
reliable zuverlässig *adj.* (3) **3B**
remember sich erinnern (an) *v.* (3) **1A**
remote control Fernbedienung, -en *f.* (2) **4B**
remove entfernen *v.* (2) **2B**
renewable energy erneuerbare Energie *f.* (3) **4B**
rent Miete, -n *f.* (2) **2A**; mieten *v.* (2) **2A**
repair reparieren *v.* (2) **4A**
repeat wiederholen *v.* (1) **2A**
repetition Wiederholung, -en *f.*
report berichten *v.* (3) **4B**
report card Zeugnis, -se *n.* (1) **1B**
**reservation: to make a (hotel)
  reservation** buchen *v.* (2) **3B**
resign kündigen *v.* (3) **3B**
rest sich ausruhen *v.* (3) **1A**
restaurant Restaurant, -s *n.* (1) **4B**
result Ergebnis, -se *n.* (1) **1B**
résumé Lebenslauf, -¨e *m.* (3) **3A**
retire in Rente gehen *v.* (2) **1A**
retiree Rentner, - / Rentnerin, -nen *m./f.* (3) **3B**
review Besprechung, -en *f.* (2) **4B**
rice Reis *m.* (1) **4A**
rich schwer *adj.* (1) **4B**
ride fahren *v.* (2) **2B**; reiten *v.* (1) **2B**
  to give (someone) a ride (jemanden)
    mitnehmen *v.* (3) **2B**
  to ride a bicycle Fahrrad fahren *v.* (1) **2B**
ring klingeln *v.* (2) **4B**
rinse spülen *v.* (2) **2B**
rise (sun) aufgehen *v.* (3) **4A**
river Fluss, -¨e *m.* (3) **3B**
rock Stein, -e *m.* (3) **4A**
roll Brötchen, - *n.* (1) **4A**

room Zimmer, - *n.* (1) **1A**
room service Zimmerservice *m.* (2) **3B**
roommate Mitbewohner, - / Mitbewohnerin,
  -nen *m./f.* (1) **2A**
rug Teppich, -e *m.* (2) **2A**
run laufen *v.* (1) **2B**; rennen *v.* (2) **1A**
Russia Russland *n.* (3) **2B**
Russian (person) Russe, -n / Russin, -nen *m./f.* (3)
  2B; **(language)** Russisch *n.* (3) **2B**

S

sad traurig *adj.* (1) **3B**
salad Salat, -e *m.* (1) **4A**
salary Gehalt, -¨er *n.* (3) **3A**
  high/low salary hohes/niedriges Gehalt,
    -¨er *n.* (3) **3A**
sale Verkauf, -¨e *m.*
  on sale im Angebot (2) **1B**
salesperson Verkäufer, - / Verkäuferin,
  -nen *m./f.* (2) **1B**
salt Salz, -e *n.* (1) **4B**
salty salzig *adj.* (1) **4B**
same gleich *adj.*
Saturday Samstag, -e *m.* (1) **2A**
  on Saturdays samstags *adv.* (1) **2A**
sausage Würstchen, - *n.* (1) **4A**
save speichern *v.* (2) **4B**; retten *v.* (3) **4B**
  to save the planet den Planeten retten *v.* (3) **4B**
say sagen *v.* (1) **2A**
scarf Schal, -s *m.* (2) **1B**
schedule Stundenplan, -¨e *m.* (1) **2A**; Fahrplan, -¨e
  m. (2) **4A**
scholarship Stipendium (*pl.* Stipendien) *n.* (1) **2A**
school Schule, -n *f.* (1) **1B**
science Naturwissenschaft, -en *f.* (1) **2A**
scientist Wissenschaftler, - / Wissenschaftlerin,
  -nen *m./f.* (3) **3B**
score Ergebnis, -se *n.* (1) **1B**
screen Bildschirm, -e *m.* (2) **4B**
screen name Benutzername, -n *m.* (2) **4B**
sea Meer, -e *n.* (3) **4A**
seafood Meeresfrüchte *f. pl.* (1) **4A**
season Jahreszeit, -en *f.* (3) **3A**
seatbelt Sicherheitsgurt, -e *m.* (2) **4A**
second zweite *adj.* (1) **2A**
  second-hand clothing Altkleider *pl.* (3) **4B**
see sehen *v.* (1) **2B**
  See you later. Bis später. (1) **1A**
  See you soon. Bis gleich. / Bis bald. (1) **1A**
  See you tomorrow. Bis morgen. (1) **1A**
selfish egoistisch *adj.* (1) **3B**
sell verkaufen *v.* (1) **4A**
seminar Seminar, -e *n.* (1) **2A**
seminar room Seminarraum (*pl.* Seminarräume)
  m. (1) **2A**
send schicken *v.* (3) **2A**; abschicken *v.* (3) **3B**
separate (sich) trennen *v.* (3) **1A**
separated getrennt *adj.* (3) **3A**
September September *m.* (1) **2A**
serious ernst *adj.* (1) **3B**; schwer *adj.* (3) **1B**
set setzen *v.* (3) **1A**; **(sun)** untergehen *v.* (3) **4A**
  to set the table den Tisch decken *v.* (2) **2B**
seven sieben (1) **2A**

shampoo Shampoo, -s *n.* (3) **1A**
shape Form, -en *f.* (3) **1B**
  in good shape fit *adj.* (1) **2B**
  to be in/out of shape in guter/schlechter Form
    sein *v.* (3) **1B**
shave sich rasieren *v.* (3) **1A**
shaving cream Rasierschaum, -¨e *m.* (3) **1A**
she sie *pron.* (1) **1A**
sheep Schaf, -e *n.* (3) **4A**
sheet Laken, - *n.* (2) **2B**
  sheet of paper Blatt Papier (*pl.* Blätter
    Papier) *n.* (1) **1B**
ship Schiff, -e *n.* (2) **4A**
shirt Hemd, -en *n.* (2) **1B**
shoe Schuh, -e *m.* (2) **1B**
shop einkaufen *v.* (1) **4A**
shopping Einkaufen *n.* (2) **1B**
shopping center Einkaufszentrum (*pl.*
  Einkaufszentren) *n.* (3) **2B**
short kurz *adj.* (1) **3A**; **(stature)** klein *adj.* (1) **3A**
  short film Kurzfilm, -e *m.* (3) **2A**
  short-sleeved kurzärmlig *adj.* (2) **1B**
shorts kurze Hose *f.* (2) **1B**
shot Spritze, -n *f.*
  to give a shot eine Spritze geben *v.* (3) **1B**
shoulder Schulter, -n *f.* (3) **1A**
show zeigen *v.* (2) **1A**
shower: to take a shower (sich) duschen *v.* (3) **1A**
shrimp Garnele, -n *f.* (1) **4A**
shy schüchtern *adj.* (1) **3B**
sibling Geschwister, - *n.* (1) **3A**
sick krank *adj.* (3) **1B**
  to get sick krank werden *v.* (3) **1B**
side dish Beilage, -n *f.* (1) **4B**
sidewalk Bürgersteig, -e *m.* (3) **2B**
sign unterschreiben *v.* (3) **2A**; Schild, -er *n.*
silk Seide, -n *f.* (2) **1B**
silverware Besteck *n.* (1) **4B**
since seit (1) **4B**
sincere aufrichtig *adj.* (1) **3B**
  Yours sincerely Gruß, -¨e (1) **3B**
sing singen *v.* (1) **2B**
single ledig *adj.* (1) **3A**
sink Spüle, -n *f.* (2) **2B**
sister Schwester, -n *f.* (1) **1A**
sister-in-law Schwägerin, -nen *f.* (1) **3A**
sit sitzen *v.* (2) **1B**
  to sit down sich (hin)setzen *v.* (3) **1A**
six sechs (1) **2A**
size Kleidergröße, -n *f.* (2) **1B**
ski Ski fahren *v.* (1) **2B**
skirt Rock, -¨e *m.* (2) **1B**
sky Himmel *m.* (3) **4A**
sleep schlafen *v.* (1) **2B**
  to go to sleep einschlafen *v.* (1) **4A**
slim schlank *adj.* (1) **3A**
slipper Hausschuh, -e *m.* (3) **1A**
slow langsam *adj.* (1) **3B**
  Please speak more slowly. Sprechen Sie bitte
    langsamer. (1) **3B**
  Slow down. Langsam fahren. (1) **3B**
small klein *adj.* (1) **3A**
smile lächeln *v.* (2) **1A**

smoke rauchen *v.*
  No smoking. Rauchen verboten. (1) **3B**
snack Snack, -s *m.* (1) **4B**
snake Schlange, -n *f.* (3) **4A**
sneakers Turnschuhe *m. pl.* (2) **1B**
sneeze niesen *v.* (3) **1B**
snow Schnee *m.* (2) **3A**; schneien *v.* (2) **3A**
so so *adv.* (1) **4A**
  so far, so good so weit, so gut (1) **1A**
  so that damit *conj.* (3) **2A**
soap Seife, -n *f.* (3) **1A**
soccer Fußball *m.* (1) **2B**
sock Socke, -n *f.* (2) **1B**
sofa Sofa, -s *n.* (2) **2A**
soil verschmutzen *v.* (2) **2B**
solar energy Sonnenenergie *f.* (3) **4B**
solid colored einfarbig *adj.* (2) **1B**
solution Lösung, -en *f.* (3) **4B**
some mancher/manche/manches *pron.* (2) **4B**
someone jemand *pron.* (2) **3B**
something etwas *pron.* (2) **3B**
  something else etwas anderes *n.* (3) **2A**
sometimes manchmal *adv.* (2) **3B**
somewhere else woanders *adv.* (1) **4A**
son Sohn, -¨e *m.* (1) **3A**
soon bald (1) **1A**
  See you soon. Bis bald.; Bis gleich. (1) **1A**
sorry: I'm sorry. Es tut mir leid. (1) **1A**
so-so so lala (1) **1A**
soup Suppe, -n *f.* (1) **4B**
soup spoon Esslöffel, - *m.* (1) **4B**
Spain Spanien *n.* (3) **2B**
Spanish (person) Spanier, - / Spanierin,
  -nen *m./f.* (3) **2B**; **(language)** Spanisch *n.* (3) **2B**
sparkling water Mineralwasser *n.* (1) **4B**
speak sprechen *v.* (1) **2B**
  to speak about sprechen über; reden
    über *v.* (3) **3A**
special besonderes *adj.* (3) **2A**
  nothing special nichts Besonderes *adj.* (3) **2A**
species Art, -en *f.* (3) **4B**
spelling Rechtschreibung *f.*
spend verbringen *v.* (2) **3A**
spicy scharf *adj.* (1) **4B**
split up sich trennen *v.* (3) **1A**
spoon Löffel, - *m.* (1) **4B**
sport Sport *m.* (1) **2B**; Sportart, -en *f.* (1) **2B**
sprain (one's wrist/ankle) sich (das Handgelenk /
  den Fuß) verstauchen *v.* (3) **1B**
spring Frühling, -e *m.* (1) **2B**
squirrel Eichhörnchen, - *n.* (3) **4A**
stadium Stadion (*pl.* Stadien) *n.* (1) **2B**
stairs Treppe, -n *f.* (2) **2A**
  to go up/down stairs die Treppe hochgehen/
    heruntergehen *v.* (3) **2B**
stamp Briefmarke, -n *f.* (3) **2A**
stand stehen *v.* (2) **1B**
  to stand in line Schlange stehen *v.* (2) **3B**
stapler Hefter, - *m.* (3) **3A**
star Stern -e *m.* (3) **4A**
start starten *v.* (2) **4B**; anfangen *v.* (1) **4A**;
  beginnen *v.* (2) **2A**
station wagon Kombi, -s *m.* (2) **4B**

statue Statue, -n *f.* (3) **2B**
stay bleiben *v.* (2) **1B**
steal stehlen *v.* (1) **2B**
steering wheel Lenkrad, -¨er *n.* (2) **4A**
stepbrother Halbbruder, -¨ *m.* (3) **3A**
stepdaughter Stieftochter, -¨ *f.* (1) **3A**
stepfather Stiefvater, -¨ *m.* (1) **3A**
stepmother Stiefmutter, -¨ *f.* (1) **3A**
stepsister Halbschwester, -n *f.* (1) **3A**
stepson Stiefsohn, -¨e *m.* (1) **3A**
stereo system Stereoanlage, -n *f.* (2) **4B**
still noch *adv.; still adj.*
  still water stilles Wasser *n.* (1) **4B**
stomachache Bauchschmerzen *m. pl.* (3) **1B**
stop sign Stoppschild, -er *n.* (2) **4A**
store Geschäft, -e *n.* (1) **4A**
storm Sturm, -¨e *m.* (2) **3A**
stove Herd, -e *m.* (2) **2B**
straight glatt *adj.* (1) **3A**
  straight hair glatte Haare *n. pl.* (1) **3A**
  straight ahead geradeaus *adv.* (2) **4A**
strawberry Erdbeere, -n *f.* (1) **4A**
stream Strom, -¨e *m.* (3) **4A**
street Straße, -n *f.* (2) **4A**
  to cross the street die Straße
    überqueren *v.* (3) **2B**
striped gestreift *adj.* (2) **1B**
strong stark *adj.* (1) **3B**
student Schüler, - / Schülerin, -nen *m./f.* (1) **1B**;
  (college/university) Student, -en / Studentin,
  -nen *m./f.* (1) **1A**
studies Studium (*pl.* Studien) *n.* (1) **2A**
study lernen *v.* (1) **2A**
stuffy nose verstopfte Nase *f.* (3) **1B**
style Stil, -e *m.* (2) **1B**
subject Fach, -¨er *n.* (1) **2A**
subway U-Bahn *f.* (2) **4A**
success Erfolg, -e *m.* (3) **3B**
such solcher/solche/solches *pron.* (2) **4B**
suit Anzug, -¨e *m.* (2) **1B**
suitcase Koffer, - *m.* (2) **3B**
summer Sommer, - *m.* (1) **2B**
sun Sonne, -n *f.* (3) **4A**
sunburn Sonnenbrand, -¨e *m.* (3) **1B**
Sunday Sonntag, -e *m.* (1) **2A**
  on Sundays sonntags *adv.* (1) **2A**
sunglasses Sonnenbrille, -n *f.* (2) **1B**
sunny sonnig *adj.* (3) **3A**
sunrise Sonnenaufgang, -¨e *m.* (3) **4A**
sunset Sonnenuntergang, -¨e *m.* (3) **4A**
supermarket Supermarkt, -¨e *m.* (1) **4A**
supposed: to be supposed to sollen *v.* (1) **3B**
surf surfen *v.* (2) **4B**
  to surf the Web im Internet surfen *v.* (2) **4B**
surprise überraschen *v.* (2) **1A**; Überraschung, -en
  f. (2) **1A**
sweater Pullover, - *m.* (2) **1B**
sweatshirt Sweatshirt, -s *n.* (2) **1B**
sweep fegen *v.* (2) **2B**
sweet süß *adj.* (1) **3B**
swim schwimmen *v.* (1) **2B**
swimming pool Schwimmbad, -¨er *n.* (1) **2B**
Switzerland die Schweiz *f.* (2) **3A**

Swiss schweizerisch, Schweizer *adj.* (3) **2B**;
(person) Schweizer, - / Schweizerin,
-nen *m./f.* (3) **2B**
symptom Symptom, -e *n.* (3) **1B**

T

table Tisch, -e *m.* (1) **1B**
  to set the table den Tisch decken (2) **2B**
tablecloth Tischdecke, -n *f.* (1) **4B**
take nehmen *v.* (1) **2B**
  to take (a class) belegen *v.* (1) **2A**
  to take out the trash den Müll rausbringen (2) **2B**
  to take a shower (sich) duschen *v.* (3) **1A**
  to take off abfliegen *v.* (2) **3B**
talk reden *v.* (2) **1A**
  to talk about erzählen von; sprechen/reden über *v.* (2) **3A**
tall groß *adj.* (1) **3A**
tank top Trägerhemd, -en *n.* (2) **1B**
taste schmecken *v.* (1) **4B**; Geschmack, -¨e *m.* (1) **4B**
taxi Taxi, -s *n.* (2) **4A**
taxi driver Taxifahrer, - / Taxifahrerin, -nen *m./f.* (3) **3B**
tea Tee, -s *m.* (1) **4B**
teacher Lehrer, - / Lehrerin, -nen *m./f.* (1) **1B**
team Mannschaft, -en *f.* (1) **2B**
teaspoon Teelöffel, - *m.* (1) **4B**
technology Technik *f.* (2) **4B**
  to use technology Technik bedienen *v.* (2) **4B**
telephone Telefon, -e *n.* (2) **4B**
  on the telephone am Telefon (3) **3A**
telephone number Telefonnummer, -n *f.* (3) **3A**
television Fernseher, - *m.* (2) **4B**
tell erzählen *v.* (2) **3A**
  to tell a story about erzählen von *v.* (2) **3A**
temperature Temperatur, -en *f.*
  What's the temperature? Wie warm/kalt ist es? (2) **3A**
tennis Tennis *n.* (1) **2B**
tent Zelt, -e *n.* (2) **3B**
ten zehn (1) **2A**
terrific großartig *adj.* (1) **3A**
test Prüfung, -en *f.* (1) **1B**
text message SMS, - *f.* (2) **4B**
textbook Lehrbuch, -¨er *n.;* Schulbuch, -¨er *n.* (1) **1B**
thank danken *v.* (1) **2A**
  Thank you. Danke. (1) **1A**
  Thank you very much. Vielen Dank. (1) **1A**
that das (1) **1A**; dass *conj.* (3) **2A**
the das/der/die
their ihr *poss. adj.* (1) **3A**
then dann *adv.* (2) **3B**
there da (1) **1A**
  Is/Are there...? Ist/Sind hier...? (1) **1B**; Gibt es...? (2) **2B**
  There is/are... Da ist/sind... (1) **1A**; Es gibt... (1) **2B**
  there and back hin und zurück (2) **3B**
  over there drüben *adv.* (1) **4A**
therefore also; deshalb *conj.* (3) **1B**

thermometer Thermometer, - *n.* (3) **1B**
these diese *pron.* (2) **4B**
  These are... Das sind... (1) **1A**
they sie *pron.* (1) **1A**
thin dünn *adj.* (1) **3A**
thing Sache, -n *f.* (1) **1B**; Ding, -e *n.*
think denken *v.* (2) **1A**
  to think about denken an *v.* (2) **3A**
  to think over überlegen *v.* (1) **4A**
third dritter/dritte/drittes *adj.* (1) **2A**
this das (1) **1A**; dieser/diese/dieses *pron.* (2) **4B**
  This is... Das ist... (1) **1A**
three drei (1) **2A**
through durch *prep.* (1) **3B**
throw werfen *v.* (1) **2B**
  to throw away wegwerfen *v.* (3) **4B**
thunder Donner, - *m.* (2) **3A**
Thursday Donnerstag, -e *m.* (1) **2A**
  on Thursdays donnerstags *adv.* (1) **2A**
ticket Flugticket, -s *n.* (2) **3B**; Fahrkarte, -n *f.* (2) **4A**
ticket collector Schaffner, - / Schaffnerin, -nen *m./f.* (2) **4A**
ticket office Fahrkartenschalter, - *m.* (2) **4A**
tidy ordentlich *adj.* (2) **2B**
tie Krawatte, -n *f.* (2) **1B**
tight eng *adj.* (2) **1B**
time Zeit, -en *f.;* Mal, -e *n.* (2) **3B**
  for the first/last time zum ersten/letzten Mal (2) **3B**
  the first/last time das erste/letzte Mal (2) **3B**
  this time diesmal *adv.* (2) **3B**
  What time is it? Wie spät ist es?; Wie viel Uhr ist es? (1) **2A**
times mal (1) **1B**
tip Trinkgeld, -er *n.* (1) **4B**
tired müde *adj.* (1) **3B**
tissue Taschentuch, -¨er *n.* (3) **1B**
to vor *prep.* (1) **2A**; nach; zu *prep.* (1) **4B**; auf, an *prep.* (2) **1B**
  in order to um...zu (2) **3B**
  to the right/left nach rechts/links (2) **2A**
toast anstoßen *v.* (2) **1A**
toaster Toaster, - *m.* (2) **2B**
today heute *adv.* (1) **2B**
  Today is ... Heute ist der ... (1) **2A**
  What day is it today? Welcher Tag ist heute? (2) **3A**
toe Zeh, -en *m.* (3) **1A**
together zusammen *adv.* (1) **4A**
toilet Toilette, -n *f.* (2) **2A**
tomato Tomate, -n *f.* (1) **4A**
tomorrow morgen *adv.* (1) **2B**
  the day after tomorrow übermorgen *adv.* (1) **2B**
  tomorrow morning morgen früh (1) **2B**
too zu *adv.* (1) **4A**; auch *adv.* (1) **1A**
tool kit Werkzeug, -e *n.*
tooth Zahn, -¨e *m.* (3) **1A**
toothache Zahnschmerzen *m. pl.* (3) **1B**
toothbrush Zahnbürste, -n *f.* (3) **1A**
toothpaste Zahnpasta (*pl.* Zahnpasten) *f.* (3) **1A**
tornado Tornado, -s *m.* (3) **4A**
toward in Richtung *f.* (3) **2B**
towel Handtuch, -¨er *n.* (3) **1A**

town Stadt, -¨e *f.* (3) **2B**
town hall Rathaus, -¨er *n.* (3) **2A**
toxic waste Giftmüll *m.* (3) **4B**
track Bahnsteig, -e *m.* (2) **4A**
track and field Leichtathletik *f.* (1) **2B**
traffic Verkehr *m.* (2) **4A**
traffic light Ampel, -n *f.* (3) **2B**
train Zug, -¨e *m.* (2) **4A**
transportation Verkehrsmittel *n.* (2) **4A**
  public transportation öffentliche Verkehrsmittel *n.* (2) **4A**
trash Müll *m.* (2) **2B**
  to take out the trash den Müll rausbringen (2) **2B**
travel reisen *v.* (1) **2A**
travel agency Reisebüro, -s *n.* (2) **3B**
traveler Reisende, -n *m./f.* (2) **3B**
tree Baum, -¨e *m.* (3) **4A**
trendy angesagt *adj.* (2) **1B**
trip Reise, -n *f.* (2) **3B**
truck LKW, -s *m.* (2) **4A**
truck driver LKW-Fahrer, - / LKW-Fahrerin, -nen *m./f.* (2) **4A**
trunk Kofferraum, -¨e *m.* (2) **4A**
try probieren *v.* (1) **3B**
  Give it a try! Probieren Sie mal! (1) **3B**
T-shirt T-Shirt, -s *n.* (2) **1B**
Tuesday Dienstag, -e *m.* (1) **2A**
  on Tuesdays dienstags *adv.* (1) **2A**
tuition fee Studiengebühr, -en *f.* (1) **2A**
tuna Thunfisch *m.* (1) **4A**
Turkey die Türkei *f.* (3) **2B**
Turkish (person) Türke, -n / Türkin, -nen *m./f.* (3) **2B**; **Turkish (language)** Türkisch *n.* (3) **2B**
turn abbiegen *v.* (3) **2B**
  to turn right/left rechts/links abbiegen *v.* (2) **4A**
  to turn off ausmachen *v.* (2) **4B**; einschalten *v.* (3) **4B**
  to turn on anmachen *v.* (2) **4B**; auschalten *v.* (3) **4B**
turning point Wende, -n *f.* (3) **4B**
twelve zwölf (1) **2A**
twenty zwanzig (1) **2A**
twin Zwilling, -e *m.* (1) **3A**
two zwei (1) **2A**

U

ugly hässlich *adj.* (1) **3A**
umbrella Regenschirm, -e *m.* (2) **3A**
under unter *prep.* (2) **1B**
understand verstehen *v.* (1) **2A**
underwear Unterwäsche *f.* (2) **1B**
undressed: to get undressed sich ausziehen *v.* (3) **1A**
unemployed arbeitslos *adj.* (3) **2A**
unfortunate arm *adj.* (1) **3B**
unfortunately leider *adv.* (1) **4A**
unfurnished unmöbliert *adj.* (2) **2A**
university Universität, -en *f.* (1) **1B**
unpleasant unangenehm *adj.* (1) **3B**
until bis *prep.* (3) **3B**; bis zu *prep.* (3) **2B**
up herauf *adv.* (2) **2A**
  to get up aufstehen *v.* (1) **4A**

to go up hochgehen *v.* (3) **2B**
U.S.A. die USA (die) *pl.*; die Vereinigten Staaten *pl.* (3) **2B**
use benutzen *v.* (2) **4A**; bedienen *v.* (2) **4B**
   to get used to sich gewöhnen an *v.* (3) **1A**
useful nützlich *adj.* (1) **2A**
useless nutzlos *adj.* (1) **2A**

V

vacancy Zimmer frei *f.* (2) **2A**
vacation Ferien; Urlaub, -e *m.* (3) **3B**
   to go on vacation Urlaub machen *v.* (2) **3B**
vacuum staubsaugen *v.* (2) **2B**
vacuum cleaner Staubsauger, - *m.* (2) **2B**
validate entwerten *v.* (2) **4A**
   to validate a ticket eine Fahrkarte entwerten *v.* (2) **4A**
valley Tal, -¨er *n.* (3) **4A**
vase Vase, -n *f.* (2) **2A**
vegetables Gemüse *n.* (1) **4A**
verb Verb, -en *n.* (3) **1A**
very sehr *adv.* (1) **4A**
   very well sehr gut (1) **1A**
veterinarian Tierarzt, -¨e / Tierärztin, -nen *m./f.* (3) **3B**
visa Visum (*pl.* Visa) *n.* (2) **3B**
visit besuchen *v.* (1) **4A**
vocabulary Wortschatz, -¨e *m.*
volcano Vulkan, -e *m.* (3) **4A**
volleyball Volleyball *m.* (1) **2B**

W

wait warten *v.* (1) **2A**
   to wait for warten auf *v.* (2) **3A**
waiter / waitress Kellner, - / Kellnerin, -nen *m./f.* (1) **3B**
   Waiter! Herr Ober! (1) **4B**
wake up aufwachen *v.* (3) **1A**
walk Spaziergang, -¨e *m.*
   to go for a walk spazieren gehen *v.* (1) **2B**
wall Wand, -¨e *f.* (2) **1B**
want wollen *v.* (1) **3B**
warm warm *adj.* (3) **2A**
wash waschen *v.* (1) **2B**
   to wash (oneself) sich waschen *v.* (3) **1A**
washing machine Waschmaschine, -n *f.* (2) **2B**
waste Müll *m.* (3) **4B**; Abfall, -¨e *m.* (3) **4B**
wastebasket Papierkorb, -¨e *m.* (1) **1B**
watch zuschauen *v.* (1) **4A**; anschauen *v.* (2) **3A**
   to watch television fernsehen *v.* (2) **4B**
   water Wasser *n.*
   sparkling water Mineralwasser *n.* (1) **4B**
   still water stilles Wasser *n.* (1) **4B**
water pitcher Wasserkrug, -¨e *m.* (1) **4B**
waterfall Wasserfall, -¨e *m.* (3) **4A**
we wir *pron.* (1) **1A**
weak schwach *adj.* (1) **3B**
wear tragen *v.* (1) **2B**
weather Wetter *n.* (2) **3A**
   What's the weather like? Wie ist das Wetter? (2) **3A**
Web Internet *n.* (2) **4B**

to surf the Web im Internet surfen *v.* (2) **4B**
Web site Website, -s *f.* (2) **4B**
wedding Hochzeit, -en *f.* (2) **1A**
Wednesday Mittwoch, -e *m.* (1) **2A**
   on Wednesdays mittwochs *adv.* (1) **2A**
week Woche, -n *f.* (1) **2A**
weekend Wochenende, -n *n.* (1) **2A**
weigh wiegen *v.* (2) **4B**
welcome (herzlich) willkommen (1) **1A**
   You're welcome. Gern geschehen. (1) **1A**
well gut *adv.*
   I am (very) well. Mir geht's (sehr) gut. (1) **1A**
   I am not (so) well. Mir geht's nicht (so) gut. (1) **1A**
   Get well! Gute Besserung! (2) **1A**
well-dressed gut gekleidet *adj.* (2) **1B**
well-known bekannt *adj.* (3) **2A**
wet nass *adj.* (3) **4A**
what was *interr.* (1) **2A**
   What is that? Was ist das? (1) **1B**
   What's up? Was geht ab? (1) **1A**
when wann *interr.* (1) **2A**
whenever wenn *conj.* (3) **2A**
where wo *interr.* (1) **2A**
   where from woher *interr.* (1) **2A**
   where to wohin *interr.* (1) **2A**
whether ob *conj.* (3) **2A**
which welcher/welche/welches *interr.* (1) **2A**
white weiß *adj.* (2) **1B**
who wer *interr.* (1) **2A**
   Who is it? Wer ist das? (1) **1B**
whom wen *acc. interr.* (1) **2A**; wem *dat. interr.* (1) **4B**
whose wessen *interr.* (2) **4B**
why warum *interr.* (1) **2A**
widow Witwe, -n *f.* (1) **3A**
widower Witwer, - *m.* (1) **3A**
wife Ehefrau, -en *f.* (1) **3A**
win gewinnen *v.* (1) **2B**
wind energy Windenergie *f.* (3) **4B**
window Fenster, - *n.* (1) **1A**
windshield Windschutzscheibe, -n *f.* (2) **4A**
windshield wiper Scheibenwischer, - *m.* (2) **4A**
windy windig *adj.* (2) **3A**
wine Wein, -e *m.* (1) **4B**
winter Winter, - *m.* (1) **2B**
wipe wischen *v.* (2) **2B**
wise weise *adj.* (1) **3B**
wish wünschen *v.* (3) **1A**
   to wish (for something) sich (etwas) wünschen *v.* (3) **1A**
with mit *(1)* **4B**
withdraw (money) (Geld) abheben *v.* (3) **2A**
within innerhalb *prep.* (2) **4B**
without ohne *prep.* (1) **3B**
woman Frau, -en *f.* (1) **1A**
wonder sich fragen *v.* (3) **1A**
wood Holz *n.* (2) **2B**
wool Wolle *f.* (2) **1B**
work Arbeit, -en *f.* (3) **3B**; arbeiten *v.* (1) **2A**; funktionieren *v.* (2) **4B**
   at work auf der Arbeit (3) **3B**
   to work on arbeiten an *v.* (2) **3A**

world Welt, -en *f.* (3) **4B**
worried besorgt *adj.* (1) **3B**
write schreiben *v.* (1) **2B**
   to write to schreiben an *v.* (2) **3A**
   to write to one another sich schreiben *v.* (3) **1A**

Y

year Jahr, -e *n.* (2) **3A**
yellow gelb *adj.* (2) **1B**
yes ja (1) **1B**; (contradicting) doch *adv.* (1) **2B**
yet schon (2) **1B**
yogurt Joghurt, -s *m.* (1) **4A**
you du/ihr/Sie *pron.* (1) **1A**
young jung *adj.* (1) **3A**; jugendlich *adj.* (3) **2A**
your euer/Ihr *poss. adj.* (1) **3A**
youth hostel Jugendherberge, -n *f.* (2) **3B**

Index

Understanding the Index references

The numbers following each entry can be understood as follows:

(2A) 51 = (Chapter, Lesson) page

So, the entry above would be found in Chapter 2, Lesson A, page 51.

About the Authors

Christine Anton, a native of Germany, is Associate Professor of German and Director of the Language Resource Center at Berry College. She received her B.A. in English and German from the Universität Erlangen and her graduate degrees in Germanic Languages and Literatures from the University of North Carolina at Chapel Hill. She has published two books on German realism and German cultural memory of National Socialism, and a number of articles on 19th and 20th century German and Austrian literature, as well as on second language acquisition. Dr. Anton has received several awards for excellence in teaching and was honored by the American Association of Teachers of German with the Duden Award for her "outstanding efforts and achievement in the teaching of German." Dr. Anton previously taught at the State University of New York and the University of North Carolina, Chapel Hill.

Tobias Barske, a native of Bavaria, is an Associate Professor of German and Applied Linguistics at the University of Wisconsin-Stevens Point. He has a Ph.D. in German Applied Linguistics from the University of Illinois at Urbana-Champaign with emphases on language and social interaction as well as language pedagogy. He has also studied at the Universität Regensburg in Germany. Tobias has over 10 years of experience teaching undergraduate and graduate courses at the university level and has earned numerous awards for excellence in teaching.

Jane Grabowski grew up in Germany and has an M.A. in German from Arizona State University. She is currently pursuing her Ph.D. and working on research relating to bilingualism, language contact, and the nature of linguistic evidence. Ms. Grabowski has spent a number of years teaching undergraduate German courses at the university level and enjoys volunteering her time to various translation projects.

Megan McKinstry has an M.A. in Germanics from the University of Washington. She is an Assistant Teaching Professor of German Studies and Co-Coordinator for Elementary German at the University of Missouri, where she received the University's "Purple Chalk" teaching award and an award for "Best Online Course." Ms. McKinstry has been teaching for over twelve years.

Television Credits

page 21 "Deutsche Bahn" By permission of Deutsche Bahn.

page 67 "TU Berlin" By permission of Technische Universität Berlin.

page 115 "Volkswagen" By permission of Volkswagen Group of America, Inc.

page 163 "Yello Strom" By permission of Yello Strom GmbH.

Photography and Art Credits

All images © Vista Higher Learning unless otherwise noted. All Fotoroman photos provided by Xavier Roy.

Cover: (tl, br) Xavier Roy; (tr) Gudrun Hommel; (bl) © Mihai-Bogdan Lazar/Shutterstock.com.

Front Matter (TAE): T1 (tl, br) Xavier Roy; (tr) Gudrun Hommel; (bl) © Mihai-Bogdan Lazar/Shutterstock.com; **T7** © Mike Flippo/Shutterstock.com; **T8** © rvlsoft/Shutterstock.com; **T24** © monkeybusinessimages/Big Stock Photo; **T25** © SimmiSimons/iStockphoto.

Front Matter (SE): i (tl, br) Xavier Roy; (tr) Gudrun Hommel; (bl) © Mihai-Bogdan Lazar/Shutterstock.com; **xi** © Petr Z/Shutterstock.com.

Chapter One: 1 Xavier Roy; **4** © 36clicks/iStockphoto; **8** © Laurence Mouton/Media Bakery; **9** (l) © Michaeljung/Dreamstime.com; (tr) © sashagala/Shutterstock.com; (br) © imac/Alamy; **13** (tl) Anne Loubet; (tm) © Igor Tarasov/Fotolia.com; (tr) © Jack Hollingsworth/Corbis; (ml) © gualtiero boffi/Shutterstock.com; (mml) © Tupungato/Shutterstock.com; (mmr) Nicole Winchell; (mr) © Tabitha Patrick/iStockphoto; (b) © Eugenio Marongiu/Shutterstock.com; **15** (tl) © Lazar Mihai-Bogdan/Shutterstock.com; (tm) Vanessa Bertozzi; (tr, bml, br) Nicole Winchell; (bl) Anne Loubet; (bmr) Gudrun Hommel; **16** © auremar/Fotolia.com; **20** © Richard Foreman/iStockphoto; **28** © Woodapple/Fotolia.com; **29** (l) © ChristArt #24461283/Fotolia.com; (tr) © ARND WIEGMANN/RTR/Newscom; (br) © Kyle Monk/Blend Images/Getty Images; **36** (all) Nicole Winchell; **38** © Sarah2/Shutterstock.com; **39** Martín Bernetti; **40** (t) © shishic/iStockphoto; (m) © PeterSVETphoto/Shutterstock.com; (b) © Hollandse Hoogte/Redux; **41** (tl) © Vaclav Volrab/Shutterstock.com; (tr) © Steve Raymer/Corbis; (m) © Knud Nielsen/Shutterstock.com; (b) © Horst Galuschka/dpa/Corbis; **44** © Chris Schmidt/iStockphoto; **45** © StockLite/Shutterstock.com.

Chapter Two: 47 Xavier Roy; **50** © Chris Schmidt/iStockphoto; **54** © Sabine Lubenow/Age Fotostock; **55** (l) © Hans Punz/ASSOCIATED PRESS; (tr) © Ingolf Pompe/Age Fotostock; (br) © laviana/Shutterstock.com; **56** (l) Nicole Winchell; (r) © Javier Larrea/Age Fotostock; **58** © Dan Barbalata/123RF; **66** (left col: t) © idp manchester airport collection/Alamy; (left col: ml) © Javier Larrea/Age Fotostock; (left col: mm) © Noam/Fotolia.com; (left col: mr) Martín Bernetti; (left col: bl) Ventus Pictures; (left col: bm) © Tetra Images/Alamy; (left col: br) © Jacob Wackerhausen/iStockphoto; (right col) © Martinap/Dreamstime.com; **74** © Roland Syba/Shutterstock.com; **75** (tl) © imagebroker.net/SuperStock; (tm) © Bongarts/Getty Images; (tr) © imago sportfotodienst/Newscom; (b) © Allan Grosskrueger/Dreamstime.com; **78** (t, br) Nicole Winchell; (ml) © Polka Dot Images/Jupiterimages; (mm, mr) Martín Bernetti; (bl) © Losevsky Photo and Video/Shutterstock.com; (bm) Gudrun Hommel; **83** © Janne Hämäläinen/Shutterstock.com; **84** © auremar/Shutterstock.com; **85** (tl) © Ilyashenko Oleksiy/Shutterstock.com; (tm) Martín Bernetti; (tr) Carlos Gaudier; (bl) © karens4/Big Stock Photo; (bml) © Val Thoermer/Big Stock Photo; (bmr) © Ben Blankenburg/Corbis; (br) © Danny Warren/iStockphoto; **86** (l) © Neustockimages/iStockphoto; (r) © 2009 Jupiterimages Corporation; **87** (tl) Martín Bernetti; (tm) Ventus Pictures; (tr) Katie Wade; (bl) © Brand X Pictures/Fotosearch; (bml) Ana Cabezas Martín; (bmr) Anne Loubet; (br) © Harry Neave/Fotolia.com; **88** (tl) Gudrun Hommel; (tr) © Steffen/Shutterstock.com; (ml) Nicole Winchell; (mr) © VVO/Shutterstock.com; (b) © Bettmann/CORBIS; **89** (tl) © Anne-Marie Palmer/Alamy; (tr) © Olgamakarova/Dreamstime.com; (m) © Fox Photos/Getty Images; (b) © Philip Lange/Shutterstock.com; **90–91** © Jorg Greuel/Getty Images; **92** © Sswartz/Dreamstime.com; **93** (t) © Yuri Arcurs/Shutterstock.com; (b) © Nadanka/Dreamstime.com.

Chapter Three: 95 Xavier Roy; **102** © Westend61/Getty Images; **103** (l) © John Dowland/Getty Images; (tr) © MICHAEL GOTTSCHALK/AFP/Getty Images; (br) © wrangler/Shutterstock.com; **105** © george olsson/Shutterstock.com; **106** (tl, tr, bl, bmr) Martín Bernetti; (tm) Ray Levesque; (bml) © david n madden/Shutterstock.com; (br) © prism68/Shutterstock.com; **114** (t) © Aspen Stock/Age Fotostock; (ml) Martín Bernetti; (mm) Carlos Gaudier; (mr) © Alexander Rochau/Fotolia.com; (bl) © Imag'In Pyrénées/Fotolia.com; (bm) © Pixtal/Age Fotostock; (br) © Raberry/Big Stock Photo; **118** (top row: tl) José Blanco; (top row: tm, top row: br) Martín Bernetti; (top row: tr) Anne Loubet; (top row: bl) © Rasmus Rasmussen/iStockphoto; (top row: bml) Ana Cabezas Martín; (top row: bmr) © Javier Larrea/Age Fotostock; (bottom row: l) © Vanessa Nel/Shutterstock.com; (bottom row: r) © Photoinjection/Shutterstock.com; **122** © Michelangelo Gratton/Getty Images; **123** (l) © Tatiana Lebedeva/Shutterstock.com; (tr) © andrewwheeler.com/Alamy; (br) © sonya etchison/Shutterstock.com; **125** Anne Loubet; **127** © Minerva Studio /Shutterstock.com; **133** Nicole Winchell; **134** (left col: tl) © Lichtmeister/Shutterstock.com; (left col: tr, left col: br) Gudrun Hommel; (left col: bl) © bikeriderlondon/Shutterstock.com; (right col) Anne Loubet; **136** (tl) © Andre Jenny/Alamy; (tr) © ShyMan/iStockphoto; (m) © Jeff Greenberg/Alamy; (b) © Frymire Archive/Alamy; **137** (tl) © aspen rock/Shutterstock.com; (tr) © Ruggles Susan/Age Fotostock; (m) © MWaits/Shutterstock.com; (b) © Sergey Peterman/Shutterstock.com; **138** © Aleksandar Mijatovic/Shutterstock.com; **139** © Serg64/Shutterstock.com; **140** Gudrun Hommel; **141** Gudrun Hommel.